Chocolate Sensations

FAYE LEVY

HPBooks

Chocolate Sensations

CONTENTS

Cover Photo: Chocolate Gâteau with Raspberries & Chocolate Leaves, pages 46-47.

CONTENTS

FAYE LEVY

Faye Levy is an internationally published cookbook author and one of this country's top culinary columnists. Faye's creative dishes have been featured on the covers of both *Bon Appétit* and *Gourmet*, America's most popular magazines of fine cooking. She has been writing *The Basics* column for *Bon Appétit* since 1982 and her work has been included in several books of recipe collections, such as *The Best of Gourmet* and *More of the Best of Bon Appétit*. Articles by Faye have also been published in *Chocolatier* magazine and *Cook's* magazine, as well as in the *Washington Post*, the *Chicago Tribune*, the *Boston Globe*, the *New York Post*, the *Los Angeles Herald Examiner* and in numerous other major newspapers throughout the country.

Born and brought up in Washington, D.C., Faye has lived in three continents and has written cookbooks in three languages. She is probably the first American ever to have written a cookbook for a prominent French publisher. A cookbook Faye coauthored with Master Chef Fernand Chambrette was published in Paris in 1984 by Flammarion, the most prestigious cookbook publisher in France, the original publisher of Escoffier, Bocuse and Lenotre. Three cookbooks she wrote in Hebrew were published by a leading Israeli publisher.

Faye holds the *Grand Diplôme* of the first graduating class of the famous Parisian cooking school *La Varenne*, where she spent over five years. She is the author of the school's first cookbook, *The La Varenne Tour Book*, a selection of favorite dishes that the chefs prepare while on demonstration tours. As La Varenne's editor, Faye developed and drafted the recipes for the school's other cookbooks and planned its curriculum.

A certified cooking teacher, Faye specializes in teaching the fundamentals of fine cuisine and dessert-making. Her students like her relaxed and practical approach, easy-to-follow recipes and emphasis on the pleasure of cooking. Faye lives in Santa Monica, California, with her husband/associate Yakir Levy. In their free time, they enjoy traveling around the world, tasting local specialties and discovering new chocolate desserts.

ACKNOWLEDGEMENTS

I want to express my deep gratitude to Veronica Durie, my editor, for originating the idea of this book. She is a special person and it has been a great pleasure working with her.

I would also like to thank the photography team not only for their superb work, but also for making the three weeks of photography most enjoyable. I was fortunate to have a first-class food professional, Mable Hoffman, as my food stylist, assisted by the talented Susan Brown Draudt. I truly appreciate the care they took in following my recipe directions and choosing the perfect accessories to make the desserts look even more sensational than they did in my own kitchen! I am thankful to the creative photographers of de-Gennaro Associates—Tommy Miyasaki, Dennis Skinner and David Wong—for making the photographs into works of art.

I have enjoyed learning from numerous cookbooks and I am grateful to their authors and to the great cooks I studied with. I would especially like to thank Anne Willan, president of La Varenne Cooking School in Paris, and Ruth Sirkis of R. Sirkis Publishing in Israel, who introduced me to the world of fine cuisine and taught me how to write cookbooks. For five years my beloved cooking teachers and associates at La Varenne, Master Chefs Fernand Chambrette, Albert Jorant and Claude Vauguet, and Denis Ruffel of the wonderful Parisian Pâtisserie Millet, shared with me their vast knowledge of the art of dessert-making and cooking in general. I wish to convey my heartfelt appreciation to them.

My sincere thanks to Jan Thiesen for coordinating the final stages of the book; Elaine Woodard and Retha Davis for their support and enthusiasm for the project; Don Burton for artistic direction; Kathleen Koopman for her design; and Leona Fitzgerald, Annie Horenn, Teri Appleton and Patsy Allen for their help in recipe testing.

Finally, a big thank-you to my husband and associate Yakir Levy for his important contribution to every stage of developing the desserts and writing the book.

We wish to thank Guittard Chocolate Co. for supplying chocolate for the photographs.

ANOTHER BEST-SELLING VOLUME FROM HPBooks®

Publisher: Rick Bailey; Executive Editor: Randy Summerlin
Editorial Director: Elaine R. Woodard; Editor: Veronica Durie
Art Director: Don Burton; Book Design: Kathleen Koopman
Production Coordinator: Cindy Coatsworth; Typography: Michelle Carter
Director of Manufacturing: Anthony B. Narducci
Food Stylist: Mable Hoffman; Assistant Stylist: Susan Brown Draudt
Photography: deGennaro Associates

Published by HPBooks
A Division of HPBooks, Inc.
P.O. Box 5367, Tucson AZ 85703 (602) 888-2150
ISBN 0-89586-411-8
Library of Congress Catalog Card Number 86-81503
©1986 HPBooks, Inc. Printed in the U.S.A.
1st Printing

INTRODUCTION

Chocolate's popularity is at an all-time high. For many people, dessert means "chocolate." Although chocolate desserts have long played a central part in the celebration of happy events, this role has been greatly expanded. Chocolate cakes star not only at children's parties but also as wedding cakes and on the dessert tables of the most elegant of restaurants.

Across the country cooking teachers are giving more and more classes on the preparation of exquisite chocolate desserts. Chocolate desserts are favorites among readers of national food-oriented magazines. Now a wider variety of brands and types of chocolate is available not only in specialty stores but also in progressive supermarkets. Chocolate exhibitions, chocolate shows, chocolate contests and other chocolate events take place on a regular basis in cities throughout the country. In a recent major story, "Chocolate, Food of the Gods," National Geographic pointed out that it has become a multibillion-dollar industry.

With the abundance of fine chocolates on the market, many of which are imported from Europe, we are developing a taste for top quality chocolate and an appreciation of refined chocolate desserts. We are getting away from frostings containing a large percentage of powdered sugar and favor those that give more emphasis to the flavor of pure chocolate.

A passionate fondness for chocolate has become so pervasive in America that a special word has been coined for chocolate aficionados—"chocoholics." Many people who would not go so far as to identify themselves as "addicted" to chocolate do pride themselves in being chocolate connoisseurs.

Moist brownies, chocolate layer cakes, and chocolate chip cookies have been favorite sweet treats in this country for years. Lately we have witnessed a renewed interest in these traditional American delicacies and in new creative versions of them, along with a growing popularity of all types of European chocolate desserts: delicious Italian gelatos and French parfaits, light cakes with luscious frostings, cream puffs, crisp cookies and buttery pastries, rich mousses and charlottes served with smooth custard sauces, Bavarian creams and airy soufflés. The large numbers of Americans who have traveled to Europe have contributed significantly to this phenomenon.

In spite of the general enthusiasm for chocolate, in many areas it is difficult to purchase fine chocolate cakes and desserts. Chocolate desserts designed for adults, such as truffles flavored with brandy or liqueur, cannot even be purchased in most states. The best way to enjoy the greatest variety of desserts of excellent quality is to make them at home. Preparing desserts provides pleasure and enables the cook to control their contents so they are fresh, natural and free of preservatives.

The emphasis of this book is practical. In developing the recipes, taste is my primary concern. Presentation of desserts is simple, quick and attractive.

What is Chocolate

Like coffee and wine, chocolate is complex. Its taste is affected by the quality of the cocoa beans, by how much they are roasted, and by the way in which the various steps in the production of chocolate are carried out. All these factors make possible a great variety of chocolates of different degrees of chocolate flavor and color.

Chocolate is made from beans that grow in pods on the cacao tree in Central and South America and in Africa. The beans are roasted and ground to a thick paste, which is essentially unsweetened chocolate. It contains chocolate solids and cocoa butter. Sugar is added in varying amounts to produce semisweet and bittersweet chocolate. Extra cocoa butter can be added to make extra-rich chocolate. To make cocoa, the chocolate is dried and a portion of the cocoa butter is removed.

Types of Chocolate

Bittersweet, extra-bittersweet and semisweet chocolates are quite similar for the purpose of dessert making and can usually be interchanged in recipes. Generally semisweet is the sweetest of the three, bittersweet is next and extra-bittersweet is the most bitter, as their names suggest. One manufacturer's bittersweet is sometimes sweeter than another's semisweet; while some manufacturers have several types of semisweet or bittersweet chocolates which differ from each other in their fluidity or in how much the cocoa bean is roasted. Fine chocolate is often sold in bars as "eating chocolate" and is good for cooking as well. Sometimes it is sold in the candy section of the supermarket instead of in the baking ingredients section. A great variety of brands of fine chocolate can be purchased at gourmet shops and by mail order. (For addresses see page 202.)

Unsweetened chocolate contains no sugar and is used in recipes in combination with sweet ingredients.

Milk chocolate is a sweet chocolate containing milk powder.

White chocolate also contains milk powder and sugar, like milk chocolate. It does not contain chocolate solids and is not officially considered "chocolate" in America (although it is in Europe) and here is labeled "coating." Be sure to use fine quality real white chocolate and not to confuse it with "fake" coatings. You can tell them apart by reading the ingredients on the label; "real" white chocolate should have cocoa butter, not palm oil or vegetable shortening, as an ingredient. Often the white chocolate sold in bulk is "real."

Couverture, sometimes called "coating chocolate," is the finest chocolate, with the highest cocoa butter content. Couverture is available by mail order and in specialty food shops as bittersweet, semisweet, white and milk chocolate. It is ideal for dipping because it is very fluid when melted and can be used to flavor desserts as well, whenever you would like to use the best quality chocolate. Some types of chocolate from Europe are labeled "fondant chocolate" and are good quality chocolates but are not as rich in cocoa butter as couverture. Do not confuse couverture with "confectionary coating," which has been treated so it melts easily and does not have the same good taste as true chocolate.

Chocolate pieces, or chocolate chips, are available as semisweet, bittersweet and milk, and as regular-sized, mini or maxi pieces. These started out as semisweet pieces for making chocolate chip cookies but now a greater variety is available. The mini chips are good for garnish because of their tiny size. The maxi are best for cookies. Chocolate pieces can be melted but they are designed to hold their shape and are not quite as rich in cocoa butter as plain chocolate. It is therefore best to reserve them for desserts in which you want them to be in pieces.

Unsweetened cocoa is the best type to use for making fine desserts, rather than sweetened cocoa.

Dutch-process cocoa, or cocoa processed with alkali, is a type of unsweetened cocoa. It is generally darker and a bit less bitter than regular cocoa and is preferred by many cooks. When it is important for a recipe, the ingredients specify "Dutch-process."

A sampler of chocolate types includes, clockwise from upper right: (1) chunks of white chocolate, (2) larger squares of semisweet and smaller squares of bittersweet chocolate in dish, (3) bars of bittersweet "couverture," (4) mini chocolate chips, (5) regular-size semisweet chocolate chips, (6) large milk chocolate chips and (7) large semisweet chocolate chips in bowl, (8) Dutch-process cocoa, (9) regular unsweetened cocoa, (10) chunks and curls of milk chocolate resting on (11) huge block of semisweet chocolate and (12) unsweetened chocolate on plate.

LIGHT CAKES, BUTTER CAKES & FUDGE CAKES

As a chocolate treat for brunch or teatime or for a finale to an elegant meal, one of these cakes would be perfect. Tall, tender Chocolate-Coconut Chiffon Cake or rich Self-Frosted Chocolate Cake is ideal for a party, while the light Chocolate Crown makes an enticing dessert after any dinner.

The chocolate cakes in this chapter are relatively easy and quick to make since they do not require filling or splitting into layers. Most of the cakes can stand unadorned; others require only a frosting or a simple glaze or sauce.

Whipped cream, whether plain, as sweetened Chantilly Cream, or flavored with liqueurs or chocolate, is the most wonderful accompaniment for both light cakes and fudge cakes. It plays a double role, adding richness and smoothness to complement light cakes and adding lightness to fudge cakes. The whipped cream can be used as a frosting or served on the side, or inside a ring-shaped cake as in the Chocolate Savarin.

Frosted cakes, especially those with whipped cream, are best served cold. If a cake is to be served plain, it tastes better at room temperature.

Light Cakes

Light cakes include cakes made without butter or enriched with a small amount of it, such as sponge cakes and chiffon cakes. A relatively high proportion of egg whites makes them light.

Many of these cakes, especially those made in the style of eastern Europe, are nut based. The rich nuts help prevent nut cakes from drying out. Only a small amount of flour, cornstarch or potato starch is added to give these cakes a little extra body so they won't collapse. A variety of nuts are used, from almonds in Chocolate Cake à l'Orientale to macadamias in Hawaiian Chocolate-Flecked Nut Cake.

Butter Cakes

Loaf cakes and coffeecakes enriched with a generous amount of butter have long been favorites throughout Europe and America. Often they are made from a white batter and are studded with bits of chocolate so the buttery taste of the cake is noticeable. In some cases the chocolate is melted and blended with the batter to give a rich result approaching a fudge cake.

This category includes many cakes that make good gifts because they keep well. What makes them stay moist and fresh-tasting so long is the relatively high proportion of nuts, butter, liqueur or some combination of these. Their richness makes frosting unnecessary and so they are easy to transport.

Fudge Cakes

Fudge cakes are becoming more American than apple pie. They contain generous amounts of chocolate and often of butter as well. This makes them the richest and usually the densest of cakes. They can contain ground nuts, as in the Queen of Sheba Cake and Chocolate-Hazelnut Cake with Fudge Frosting, or they can be flourless.

Shown on the preceding pages, an array of chocolate sensations, beginning with top row: Mocha Petits Pots de Crème, page 91; Bittersweet Belgian Truffles drizzled with melted white chocolate, page 172. Middle row: Triple-Chocolate Mousse Parfait, page 106; Chocolate Symphony, page 56; Chocolate-Coconut Chiffon Cake, page 18; Chocolate-Apricot Terrine, page 107. Front row: Chocolate-Dipped Orange Segments, pages 12-13; Sultan's Cream Puffs, page 73; Meringue Mushrooms, page 160; Rigo Jancsi, page 50; Chocolate-Marbled Chiffon Pie, page 71.

Hawaiian Chocolate-Flecked Nut Cake

Hawaii, the world's major supplier of macadamia nuts, inspired the name of this cake. The finely chopped chocolate in the batter harmonizes with the fine flavor of the nuts but does not overpower them. Macadamia nut liqueur, also a product of Hawaii, moistens the cake and flavors the light chocolate frosting.

Makes 10 to 12 servings

Macadamia Nut Cake:

2-1/3 cups macadamia nuts (about 10 oz.), preferably unsalted
10 whole macadamia nuts, preferably unsalted (for garnish)
5 oz. semisweet chocolate, coarsely chopped
3/4 cup sugar
1/4 cup all-purpose flour
1/2 teaspoon baking powder
5 eggs, separated, room temperature
1/4 teaspoon cream of tartar

Chocolate & Macadamia Liqueur Whipped Cream:

1-1/4 oz. semisweet chocolate, chopped
3/4 cup whipping cream, well-chilled
2-1/4 teaspoons sugar
1 tablespoon plus 1-1/2 teaspoons macadamia nut liqueur

2 tablespoons macadamia nut liqueur (for moistening)
Chocolate Leaves, page 196, or Chocolate Cutouts, page 195, if desired (for garnish)

1. Cake: If using salted nuts, preheat oven to 250F (120C). Put nuts for cake and 10 whole nuts for garnish in a large strainer. Rinse with warm water 10 seconds, tossing often. Drain 5 minutes in strainer, tossing occasionally. Transfer to a baking sheet. Bake 5 minutes, shaking baking sheet occasionally. Remove nuts to a shallow dish; cool completely. Set aside nuts for garnish.

2. Position rack in center of oven and preheat to 325F (165C). Lightly butter a 9" x 3" springform pan. Line base of pan with parchment paper or foil; butter paper or foil. Flour side of pan and lined base, tapping pan to remove excess.

3. Chop chocolate in a food processor until as fine as possible, scraping inward occasionally. Transfer chopped chocolate to a large bowl. Grind 1 cup of the nuts with 3 tablespoons sugar in processor until as fine as possible. Add to chocolate. Repeat with remaining 1-1/3 cups nuts and 3 more tablespoons sugar.

4. Sift flour and baking powder over nut mixture. Using a fork, stir gently until thoroughly blended. If mixture appears to be clumping together, separate by rubbing gently between your fingertips.

5. Beat egg yolks briefly in a large bowl. Beat in 1/4 cup sugar; continue beating at high speed about 5 minutes or until mixture is pale and very thick.

6. In a large dry bowl, beat egg whites with cream of tartar using dry beaters at medium speed until soft peaks form. Gradually beat in remaining 2 tablespoons sugar; continue beating at high speed until whites are stiff and shiny but not dry.

7. Sprinkle about 1/3 of nut mixture over egg-yolk mixture. Fold in gently until nearly incorporated. Gently fold in about 1/3 of whites. Repeat with remaining nut mixture and whites in 2 batches. Continue folding lightly but quickly, just until batter is blended.

8. Transfer batter to prepared pan; spread evenly. Bake about 55 minutes or until a cake tester inserted in center of cake comes out clean.

9. Cool in pan on a rack about 10 minutes. Run a thin-bladed flexible knife or metal spatula carefully around side of cake. Invert cake onto a rack. Release spring and remove side and base of pan. Carefully peel off paper or foil; cool cake completely. Turn cake onto another rack, then onto a platter so smooth side of cake faces up. *Cake can be prepared 2 days ahead and kept, wrapped, at room temperature.*

1. Chocolate & Macadamia Liqueur Whipped Cream: Chill a medium or large bowl and beaters for whipping cream.

2. Melt chocolate in a double boiler or small heatproof bowl over hot, not simmering, water over low heat, stirring occasionally. Stir until smooth. Remove from heat but leave chocolate above hot water.

3. Whip cream with sugar in chilled bowl until stiff. Add liqueur; beat until blended.

4. Remove chocolate from above water; cool 30 seconds. Quickly stir about 1/3 cup whipped cream into chocolate. Quickly fold mixture into remaining whipped cream until smooth. Fold quickly so chocolate does not harden upon contact with the cold whipped cream.

1. Assembly: Dip a pastry brush in macadamia nut liqueur. Holding brush flat, dab top and side of cake evenly with liqueur, dipping it again as necessary.

2. Using a long metal spatula, spread chocolate whipped cream evenly on side and top of cake; smooth side and top. Garnish with whole macadamia nuts and Chocolate Leaves or Cutouts. Refrigerate at least 1 hour before serving. *Frosted cake can be kept, covered with a cake cover or large bowl, up to 1 day in refrigerator.*

Chocolate Cake à l'Orientale

Candied ginger, oranges and almonds give this cake an Oriental touch, in keeping with today's fashion of incorporating the exciting tastes of the Orient into Western desserts. Orange segments dipped in chocolate set on a white background of whipped cream provide the elegant garnish. The cake is lighter than a butter cake, yet richer and moister than a sponge cake.

Makes 6 to 8 servings

Chocolate-Almond-Ginger Cake:
3 oz. semisweet chocolate, chopped
2 tablespoons strained fresh orange juice
1/4 cup unsalted butter, cut in 4 pieces
1/2 cup whole blanched almonds (about 2-1/4 oz.)
1/2 cup plus 1 tablespoon sugar
1/3 cup very finely chopped crystallized ginger (about 1-1/2 oz.)
2 tablespoons all-purpose flour
2 tablespoons cornstarch
3 eggs, separated, room temperature
1 tablespoon grated orange zest
1/4 teaspoon cream of tartar

Whipped Cream:
3/4 cup whipping cream, well-chilled
1-1/2 teaspoons sugar

Chocolate-Dipped Orange Segments:
1 small orange
2 oz. fine-quality bittersweet or semisweet chocolate, chopped

1. **Cake:** Position rack in center of oven and preheat to 350F (175C). Lightly butter a round 9-inch layer cake pan. Line base of pan with parchment paper or foil; lightly butter paper or foil.
2. Combine chocolate, orange juice and butter in a double boiler or heatproof medium bowl over hot, not simmering, water over low heat. Leave until chocolate and butter are melted, stirring occasionally. Stir until smooth. Remove from pan of water; cool mixture to body temperature.
3. Grind almonds with 3 tablespoons sugar in a food processor until as fine as possible, scraping inward occasionally. Transfer to a medium bowl; add chopped ginger. Sift flour and cornstarch over mixture; mix thoroughly.
4. Beat egg yolks briefly in a large bowl. Beat in 1/4 cup sugar; continue beating at high speed about 5 minutes or until mixture is pale and very thick. Gently stir in grated orange zest and chocolate mixture.
5. In a large dry bowl, beat egg whites with cream of tartar using dry beaters at medium speed until soft peaks form. Gradually beat in remaining 2 tablespoons sugar; continue beating at high speed until whites are stiff and shiny but not dry.
6. Gently fold about 1/3 of whites into chocolate mixture until nearly incorporated. Sprinkle about 1/2 of almond mixture over chocolate mixture; fold in gently. Fold in another 1/3 of whites, then remaining almond mixture, followed by remaining whites. Continue folding lightly but quickly, just until batter is blended.
7. Transfer batter to prepared pan. Bake about 28 minutes or until a cake tester inserted in center of cake comes out nearly clean.
8. Cool in pan on a rack 5 minutes. Run a thin-bladed flexible knife or metal spatula carefully around side of cake. Invert cake onto rack. Carefully peel off paper or foil; cool cake completely. Crust is crumbly; some may fall off. Carefully turn cake onto another rack, then onto a platter so crusty side faces down. Refrigerate cake at least 1 hour before frosting. *Cake can be kept, wrapped, up to 3 days in refrigerator.*

1. **Whipped cream:** Chill a medium or large bowl and beaters for whipping cream. Whip cream with sugar in chilled bowl until stiff.
2. Using a long metal spatula, spread whipped cream evenly on side and top of cake; smooth side and top. Refrigerate at least 1 hour before serving. *Frosted cake can be kept, covered with a cake cover or large bowl, up to 8 hours in refrigerator.*

1. **Chocolate orange segments:** Line rack with paper towels. Use a small sharp or serrated knife to remove zest and all bitter, white pith from orange. Hold orange over bowl to catch juice and cut down on each side of membranes to free one section. Cut to release section from orange. Fold back membrane. Continue with remaining sections. Put orange sections on lined rack. Let dry 1 hour, patting often with paper towels, turning fruit over occasionally and changing towels as needed. A small amount of moisture can make chocolate solidify suddenly.
2. Line a tray or plate with waxed paper. Melt chocolate in a small deep heatproof bowl set over hot, not simmering, water over low heat, stirring occasionally. Stir until smooth. Remove from heat; cool to slightly less than body temperature.
3. Dip 1/2 of one orange piece in chocolate. Let excess chocolate drip into bowl. Transfer orange section to waxed paper. Repeat with remaining sections, setting on waxed paper with chocolate half of all oranges pointing in same direction. Let stand at cool room temperature or refrigerate 30 minutes until chocolate sets. *Orange segments can be kept, uncovered, up to 4 hours in refrigerator.*
4. Garnish cake carefully with 6 to 8 chocolate-dipped orange segments, arranging them in a circle near edge of cake. Serve any remaining chocolate-dipped orange segments separately.

How to Garnish Chocolate Cake à l'Orientale

1/Separate orange sections. Place on a rack lined with paper towels. Let dry 1 hour, patting orange sections often with paper towels, turning orange sections over occasionally and changing towels as needed.

2/Dip 1/2 of each orange section in melted chocolate. Let excess chocolate drip into bowl. Transfer dipped orange section to waxed paper. Repeat with remaining orange sections; set on waxed paper with chocolate half of all oranges pointing in same direction.

Moist Mocha Squares

Like a soufflé, this dark cake is light-textured yet very moist. Although it is good on its own, the easy-to-make coffee sauce of creamy café-au-lait color dresses it up elegantly.

Makes 8 to 9 servings

Chocolate-Coffee Cake:
5 oz. semisweet chocolate, chopped
3 tablespoons water
1 teaspoon instant coffee powder or freeze-dried coffee granules
1/2 cup plus 2 tablespoons (5 oz.) unsalted butter, cut in pieces, room temperature
5 tablespoons all-purpose flour, sifted
4 eggs, separated, room temperature
1/2 cup plus 2 tablespoons sugar
1/4 teaspoon cream of tartar

Quick Coffee Sauce:
3/4 cup whipping cream, well-chilled
2 tablespoons sugar
1-1/2 teaspoons instant coffee powder or freeze-dried coffee granules

1. **Cake:** Position rack in center of oven and preheat to 325F (165C). Lightly butter an 8-inch-square baking pan. Line base of pan with parchment paper or waxed paper; butter paper. Flour sides of pan and lined base, tapping pan to remove excess.

2. Combine chocolate, water and coffee in a double boiler or small heatproof bowl over hot, not simmering, water over low heat. Leave until chocolate is melted, stirring occasionally. Stir until smooth. Add butter pieces; stir until blended. Remove from pan of water; cool mixture to body temperature.

3. Place flour in sifter.

4. Beat egg yolks lightly in a large bowl. Beat in 1/2 cup sugar; continue beating at high speed about 5 minutes or until mixture is pale and very thick.

5. In a large dry bowl, beat egg whites with cream of tartar using dry beaters at medium speed until soft peaks form. Gradually beat in remaining 2 tablespoons sugar; continue beating at high speed until whites are stiff and shiny but not dry.

6. Gently stir chocolate mixture into yolk mixture, using a wooden spoon. Sift flour over chocolate-yolk mixture; fold in gently using a spatula.

7. Gently fold whites into chocolate mixture in 3 batches.

8. Transfer batter to prepared pan. Bake about 40 minutes or until a cake tester inserted in center of cake comes out clean.

9. Cool cake in pan on a rack until lukewarm; cake will settle slightly in center. *Cake can be kept, wrapped, up to 3 days at room temperature.*

1. **Sauce:** Chill a medium or large bowl and beaters for whipping cream. Just before serving, combine cream, sugar and coffee powder in chilled bowl. Whip at medium-high speed until slightly thickened; cream should be sauce-like and not stiff enough to form peaks.

2. Cut cake in squares while in pan. Serve cake lukewarm or at room temperature. Spoon sauce over each piece of cake, covering it partially.

Chocolate-Pecan Gâteau

A variety of cuisines leave their mark on this impressive dessert: Native American pecans add richness to the light-textured, Austrian-style chocolate sponge cake. The cake is topped by a luscious French chocolate buttercream that gains its smoothness from Italian meringue.

Makes 10 to 12 servings

Chocolate-Pecan Butter Sponge Cake:

2 oz. semisweet chocolate, coarsely chopped
2/3 cup pecan halves (about 2 oz.)
3/4 cup plus 2 tablespoons sugar
3/4 cup plus 2 tablespoons cake flour
3 tablespoons unsweetened cocoa powder
1 teaspoon baking powder
6 eggs, separated, room temperature
1 tablespoon rum
1/2 teaspoon cream of tartar
1/2 cup (4 oz.) unsalted butter, melted and cooled

Chocolate Meringue Buttercream:

7 oz. fine-quality bittersweet or extra-bittersweet chocolate, chopped
2/3 cup sugar
1/3 cup water
2 egg whites, room temperature
3/4 cup (6 oz.) unsalted butter, cut in pieces, slightly softened but still cool
2 tablespoons rum

2 tablespoons rum (for moistening)
10 to 12 pecan halves (for garnish)

1. **Cake:** Position rack in center of oven and preheat to 350F (175C). Lightly butter a 9″ x 3″ springform pan. Line base of pan with parchment paper or foil; butter paper or foil. Flour side of pan and lined base, tapping pan to remove excess.
2. Grind chocolate in a food processor until as fine as possible, scraping inward occasionally. Transfer chocolate to a medium bowl. Grind 2/3 cup pecans with 2 tablespoons sugar in processor as finely as possible. Add to chocolate.
3. Sift flour, cocoa and baking powder over nut mixture; stir gently until thoroughly blended.
4. Beat egg yolks briefly in a large bowl. Beat in 1/2 cup sugar; continue beating at high speed about 5 minutes or until mixture is pale and very thick. Beat in rum.
5. In a large dry bowl, beat egg whites with cream of tartar using dry beaters at medium speed until soft peaks form. Gradually beat in remaining 1/4 cup sugar; continue beating at high speed until whites are stiff and shiny but not dry.
6. Sprinkle about 1/3 of nut mixture over egg-yolk mixture; fold gently until nearly incorporated. Gently fold in 1/3 of whites. Repeat with remaining nut mixture and whites in 2 batches. When batter is nearly blended, gradually pour in cool melted butter while folding. Continue folding lightly but quickly, just until batter is blended.
7. Transfer batter to prepared pan; spread evenly. Bake about 40 minutes or until a cake tester inserted in center of cake comes out clean.
8. Cool in pan on a rack about 5 minutes. Run a thin-bladed flexible knife or metal spatula carefully around side of cake. Invert cake onto rack. Release spring and remove side and base of pan. Carefully peel off paper or foil; cool cake completely. Turn cake onto another rack, then onto a platter so smooth side of cake faces up. *Cake can be kept, wrapped, up to 3 days in refrigerator.*
1. **Buttercream:** Melt chocolate in a double boiler or heatproof medium bowl over hot, not simmering, water over low heat, stirring occasionally. Stir until smooth. Remove from pan of water; cool to body temperature.
2. Combine sugar and water in a small heavy saucepan. Cook over low heat, stirring gently, until sugar dissolves. Increase heat to medium-high and bring to a boil. Boil without stirring 3 minutes. Meanwhile, beat egg whites in a large heatproof bowl until stiff but not dry. Continue boiling syrup until a candy thermometer registers 238F (115C) (soft-ball stage), about 4 minutes. (To test without thermometer see note at top of page 15.) Immediately remove from heat.
3. Using mixer at high speed, gradually pour hot syrup into center of whites; continue beating until meringue is cool and shiny.
4. Cream butter in a large bowl until very soft and smooth. Beat in chocolate in 3 batches. Beat in meringue in 3 batches. Gradually beat in rum, 1 teaspoon at a time.
1. **Assembly:** Dip a pastry brush in rum. Holding brush flat, dab top and side of cake evenly with rum, dipping it again as necessary.
2. Set aside 3/4 cup buttercream for garnishing. Using a long metal spatula, spread remaining buttercream evenly on side and top of cake; smooth side and top. Using a pastry bag and medium star tip, pipe a ruffle of reserved buttercream along top edge of cake. Arrange 10 to 12 pecan halves in circle on cake.
3. Refrigerate cake about 2 hours or until buttercream is firm. *Frosted cake can be kept, covered with a cake cover or large bowl, up to 2 days in refrigerator.* Serve at room temperature.

Variation

Instead of making frosting, serve slices of unfrosted cake with Vanilla Bean Custard Sauce, page 197.

Note: To test syrup for soft ball stage without a thermometer, remove pan from heat. Take a little hot syrup on a teaspoon and dip spoon into a cup of iced water, keeping spoon level. With your hands in water, remove syrup from spoon. CAUTION: Do not touch syrup unless your hands are in iced water. If syrup is ready, it will form a soft ball. If syrup dissolves into water, continue cooking and test again; if syrup was overcooked and forms firm ball, you can still use it. If syrup goes far beyond desired degree, quickly add 1/4 cup water and stir gently to combine it with syrup; temperature will decrease. Return to a boil and cook to correct temperature. Do not attempt to save syrup if it has begun to brown.

Chocolate Crown

A beautiful bittersweet ring-shaped cake of deep chocolate color and flavor. It has a dark shiny glaze, encircling a snowy white mound of Chantilly Cream.

Makes 8 to 10 servings

Chocolate Butter Sponge Cake:
5 oz. semisweet chocolate, chopped
3 tablespoons unsalted butter, cut in 3 pieces
5 tablespoons all-purpose flour
1/2 teaspoon baking powder
3 eggs, separated, room temperature
1/3 cup sugar
1 teaspoon pure vanilla extract
1/4 teaspoon cream of tartar

Chocolate Glaze:
5 oz. semisweet chocolate, chopped
2 tablespoons unsalted butter, cut in 2 pieces
2 tablespoons water
1 teaspoon pure vanilla extract

Chantilly Cream:
1/2 pint whipping cream (1 cup), well-chilled
1 tablespoon sugar
1 teaspoon pure vanilla extract

1. **Cake:** Position rack in center of oven and preheat to 350F (175C). Generously butter a 5-cup ring mold.
2. Combine chocolate and butter in a double boiler or small heatproof bowl over hot, not simmering, water over low heat. Leave until chocolate and butter are melted, stirring occasionally. Stir until smooth. Remove from pan of water; cool mixture to body temperature.
3. Sift flour and baking powder into a small bowl.
4. Beat egg yolks briefly in a large bowl. Beat in 3 tablespoons sugar; continue beating at high speed about 5 minutes or until mixture is pale and very thick. Beat in vanilla. Gently stir in chocolate mixture.
5. In a large dry bowl, beat egg whites with cream of tartar using dry beaters at medium speed until soft peaks form. Gradually beat in remaining 2-1/3 tablespoons sugar; continue beating at high speed until whites are stiff and shiny but not dry.
6. Gently fold about 1/3 of whites into chocolate mixture until nearly incorporated. Sprinkle about 1/2 of flour mixture over chocolate mixture; fold in gently. Fold in another 1/3 of whites, then remaining flour mixture, followed by remaining whites. Continue folding lightly but quickly, just until batter is blended.
7. Transfer batter to prepared mold; spread evenly. Bake about 17 minutes or until a cake tester inserted in cake comes out clean.
8. Cool cake in mold on a rack about 30 minutes; cake will settle slightly. Run a metal spatula carefully around outer edge of cake. Run a thin-bladed flexible knife around center. Invert cake onto a platter; cool completely. *Cake can be kept, covered with plastic wrap or foil, up to 1 day at room temperature.*
1. **Glaze:** Combine chocolate, butter and water in a double boiler or small heatproof bowl over hot, not simmering, water over low heat. Leave until chocolate and butter are melted, stirring occasionally. Stir until smooth. Remove from pan of water. Stir in vanilla.
2. Spoon glaze slowly over cooled cake, letting it trickle down inner and outer sides of cake. Wipe platter clean.
3. Serve cake within 30 minutes if soft glaze is desired; cool at room temperature 1-1/2 hours for firmer glaze. If weather is cool, keep cake at room temperature so glaze will be shiny. Refrigerate cake if weather is hot. *Glazed cake can be kept, covered with a cake cover or large bowl, up to 8 hours at cool room temperature or 1 day in refrigerator.*
1. **Chantilly Cream:** Chill a large bowl and beaters for cream.
2. Up to 30 minutes before serving, whip cream with sugar and vanilla in chilled bowl until stiff.
3. Using a pastry bag and medium star tip, pipe cream into center of glazed cake in a dome shape. Pipe decorative lines or swirls of whipped cream on top of dome. Serve as soon as possible.

How to Make Chocolate Savarin

1/Put cake on prepared rack, with firm crust-side facing down. Slowly and evenly ladle hot syrup over cake until it has absorbed as much syrup as possible. Let stand about 2 minutes. Reheat syrup that has dripped onto tray. Continue moistening cake and reheating syrup a few more times, until most of syrup is absorbed.

2/Close to serving time, brush 1/4 cup liqueur over entire surface of cake as evenly as possible. Pipe a mound of Chocolate Whipped Cream inside cake ring and a few rosettes at bottom edge. Garnish with a Chocolate Cutout.

Chocolate Savarin

A savarin is a light, ring-shaped cake made from a yeast batter and moistened with syrup. This one substitutes chocolate liqueur for the traditional rum and is served with chocolate whipped cream. When raspberries or strawberries are in season, use them to garnish each serving.

Makes 12 servings

Light Yeast Cake:
1/4 cup warm water (110F, 45C)
1 (1/4-oz.) pkg. active dry yeast
    (about 1 tablespoon)
1 tablespoon plus 1 teaspoon sugar
2 cups all-purpose flour
4 eggs
1 teaspoon salt
7 tablespoons unsalted butter, cut
    in 14 pieces, room temperature

Syrup:
1-1/4 cups sugar
2 cups water

1. **Cake:** Pour water into a small bowl; sprinkle yeast over water and add 1 teaspoon sugar. Let stand 10 minutes or until foamy. Stir to mix.
2. Sift flour into bowl of a heavy-duty mixer fitted with a dough hook. Add 2 eggs, salt and remaining 1 tablespoon sugar. Mix at low speed about 15 seconds or until a few tablespoons of flour are drawn into egg mixture. Add yeast mixture and remaining 2 eggs. Mix at low speed about 10 minutes or until dough is soft and smooth, occasionally scraping down dough from hook and side of bowl.
3. Continue to beat dough at medium speed, scraping down occasionally, about 12 minutes or until dough is very smooth and most of it comes away from side of bowl and wraps around hook. Dough will be soft and very sticky.
4. Lightly oil a medium bowl. Place dough in oiled bowl. Put butter pieces in single layer over top of dough. Cover with plastic wrap. Let dough rise in a warm draft-free place about 1 hour or until doubled in bulk.
5. Transfer dough to clean mixer bowl. Beat in butter with dough hook at low speed, scraping down often, about 3 minutes or until blended.
6. Generously butter a 5-cup ring mold. Transfer dough to prepared mold. Using a rubber spatula, smooth dough to an even layer. Cover with plastic wrap. Let rise in a warm draft-free place 25 minutes.
7. Position rack in center of oven and preheat to 400F (205C). Remove plastic wrap from dough. Let dough rise 15 to 30 minutes longer or until it reaches top of mold.
8. Bake about 23 minutes or until dough comes away from side of pan, top is browned and cake tester inserted into cake comes out clean. Invert cake onto a rack; cool completely. *Cake can be kept up to 3 days in an airtight container at room temperature.*

Chocolate Whipped Cream:

2-1/2 oz. semisweet chocolate, chopped

1-1/2 cups whipping cream, well-chilled

1 tablespoon plus 1-1/2 teaspoons sugar

3 tablespoons white crème de cacao

1/4 cup white crème de cacao (for moistening)

1 small Chocolate Cutout, page 195, if desired (for garnish)

1. Syrup: Heat sugar and water in a heavy medium saucepan over low heat, stirring gently until sugar is dissolved. Increase heat to high and bring to a boil. Remove from heat. *Syrup can be kept up to 2 days in refrigerator.* Before using, reheat just to a simmer.

2. Set a cake rack above a rimmed tray. Put cake on prepared rack, with firm crust-side facing down. Slowly and evenly ladle hot syrup over cake until it has absorbed as much syrup as possible. Let stand about 2 minutes. Return syrup that dripped onto tray to saucepan. Reheat to simmer over medium-high heat. Repeat moistening of cake. Continue moistening cake and reheating syrup a few more times, until most of syrup is absorbed; do not overheat syrup or it will caramelize. If sides of cake appear dry, gently brush syrup over them.

3. Let cake stand 30 minutes on rack to drain. Using two wide metal spatulas, carefully transfer cake to a platter.

1. Chocolate Whipped Cream: Chill a large bowl and beaters for whipping cream.

2. A short time before serving, melt chocolate in a double boiler or heatproof medium bowl over hot, not simmering, water over low heat, stirring occasionally. Stir until smooth. Remove from heat but leave chocolate above hot water.

3. Whip cream with sugar in chilled bowl until stiff. Add liqueur; beat just until blended.

4. Remove chocolate from water; cool 30 seconds. Quickly stir about 2/3 cup whipped cream into chocolate. Quickly fold mixture into remaining whipped cream until smooth. Fold quickly so chocolate does not harden upon contact with the cold whipped cream.

1. Assembly: As close as possible to serving time, brush 1/4 cup liqueur as evenly as possible over entire surface of cake.

2. Using a pastry bag and large star tip, pipe a mound of Chocolate Whipped Cream inside ring. If desired, pipe a few rosettes of cream at bottom edge of cake. Stick a Chocolate Cutout on center of mound, if desired, for garnish.

To make dough in a food processor: Instead of Cake Step 2, put yeast mixture, remaining 1 tablespoon sugar and eggs in food processor fitted with plastic or metal blade; process until blended, about 5 seconds. Sift in flour and salt; process 30 seconds without stopping machine. If dough is not entirely smooth, transfer to a medium bowl and slap dough a few times in bowl by hand. Follow Step 4. Instead of Step 5, stir in butter with cutting and folding motion using a wooden spoon. Gently slap dough a few times in bowl until butter is completely blended in. Continue as in recipe.

To make dough by hand: Instead of Step 2, sift flour into a large bowl and make a well in center. Add 2 eggs, salt and remaining 1 tablespoon sugar to well. Mix using a wooden spoon, gradually drawing in 2 or 3 tablespoons flour. Add remaining 2 eggs and yeast mixture to well. Stir to a soft dough. Dough will be very sticky. With cupped hand under dough, slap dough against bowl for about 1 minute. Follow Step 4. Instead of Step 5, stir in butter with cutting and folding motion using a wooden spoon. Gently slap dough a few times in bowl until butter is completely blended in. Continue as in recipe.

Chocolate-Coconut Chiffon Cake *Photo on pages 8-9.*

Incredibly tender, moist and rich, this tall, dark dramatic cake topped with generous swirls of creamy, chocolaty frosting is an ideal party dessert.

Makes 14 to 16 servings

Chocolate-Coconut Chiffon Cake:

3 oz. semisweet chocolate, chopped
2 oz. unsweetened chocolate, chopped
2 cups cake flour
1 teaspoon salt
1 tablespoon baking powder
1-1/2 cups sugar
6 egg yolks
1/2 cup vegetable oil
3/4 cup cold tap water
8 egg whites, room temperature
1/2 teaspoon cream of tartar
1 cup finely grated, dried, unsweetened coconut (about 3-1/4 oz.)

Chocolate Velvet Frosting:

6 oz. semisweet chocolate, chopped
3 tablespoons water
2 egg yolks
1-1/4 cups whipping cream, well-chilled
2 tablespoons sugar

1 tablespoon finely grated, dried, unsweetened coconut (for garnish)

1. Cake: Position rack in center of oven and preheat to 325F (165C). Have ready a 10'' x 4'' tube pan with removable tube; do not butter it. *Do not use a nonstick pan.*

2. Combine chocolates in a double boiler or heatproof medium bowl over hot, not simmering, water over low heat. Leave until melted, stirring occasionally. Stir until smooth. Remove from pan of water; cool to body temperature.

3. Sift flour, salt and baking powder into a large bowl. Add 1 cup sugar; stir until blended.

4. In another bowl combine egg yolks, oil and water; beat until smooth.

5. Make a large well in bowl of dry ingredients; pour in yolk mixture. Gently stir dry ingredients into yolk mixture using a wooden spoon. Gently stir in melted chocolate, stirring just until there are no lumps.

6. In a large dry bowl, beat egg whites with cream of tartar using dry beaters at medium speed until soft peaks form. Gradually beat in remaining 1/2 cup sugar; continue beating at high speed until whites are stiff and shiny but not dry.

7. Fold about 1/4 of whites into chocolate mixture until nearly incorporated. Gently fold chocolate mixture into remaining whites. When batter is nearly blended, sprinkle with coconut. Fold in lightly but quickly, just until batter is blended.

8. Transfer batter to prepared pan. Bake about 1 hour 10 minutes or until a cake tester inserted in cake comes out clean.

9. Invert pan on its "feet" or on heatproof funnel or bottle; let stand until completely cool, about 1-1/2 hours. Run a metal spatula gently around side of cake. Push up tube to remove side of pan. Run a thin-bladed flexible knife around tube. Run metal spatula carefully under cake to free it from base; turn out carefully onto a platter. *Cake can be kept, wrapped, up to 2 days at room temperature.*

1. Frosting: Chill a large bowl and beaters for whipping cream. Combine chocolate and water in a double boiler or heatproof medium bowl over hot, not simmering, water over low heat. Leave until chocolate is melted, stirring occasionally. Whisk until smooth. Remove from pan of water.

2. Whisk egg yolks, 1 at a time, into chocolate mixture. Set container of chocolate mixture above pan of hot water over low heat; whisk 1 minute. Remove from pan of water. Let stand about 15 minutes or until cool but not set; mixture will be very thick.

3. Whip cream with sugar in chilled bowl until soft peaks form. Stir about 1/2 cup whipped cream into chocolate mixture. Return mixture to bowl of cream; fold gently until blended.

4. Gently brush any crumbs off top of cake. Using a long metal spatula, spread frosting evenly and generously on side, top and inner surface of cake. Swirl top. Lightly sprinkle top outer edge of cake with 1 tablespoon coconut. Refrigerate at least 1 hour before serving. *Frosted cake can be kept, covered with a tall cake cover, up to 3 days in refrigerator.* Serve at room temperature.

Note: Unsweetened coconut can be purchased at specialty markets or at health-food stores. When finely grated it appears almost ground and is sometimes labeled *macaroon coconut*. Do not use the coarser shredded or flaked coconut.

Marbled Chocolate Coffeecake

Crowned by a shiny chocolate glaze, this Bundt cake is enriched with sour cream and swirled with chocolate.

Makes 8 to 10 servings

Marbled Chocolate-Sour Cream Coffeecake:
1-3/4 cups all-purpose flour
1 teaspoon baking powder
1/2 teaspoon baking soda
1/2 pint dairy sour cream (1 cup)
1 teaspoon pure vanilla extract
1 tablespoon unsweetened cocoa powder, sifted
3 oz. semisweet chocolate, finely grated
1/2 cup (4 oz.) unsalted butter, slightly softened
3/4 cup sugar
3 eggs

Chocolate Glaze:
4 oz. semisweet chocolate, chopped
2 tablespoons plus 1-1/4 teaspoons water
2 tablespoons plus 1 teaspoon unsalted butter, cut in 3 pieces, room temperature

1. **Coffeecake:** Position rack in center of oven and preheat to 350F (175C). Generously butter a 9-1/2" x 4" fluted tube pan or Bundt pan, taking care to butter tube and each fluted section.
2. Sift flour, baking powder and baking soda into a large bowl. In a medium bowl, mix sour cream and vanilla. In a small bowl, combine cocoa and chocolate; mix gently with a fork.
3. Cream butter in a medium or large bowl until light. Add sugar and beat until smooth and fluffy. Add eggs, 1 at a time, beating very thoroughly after each addition. Gently stir in about 1/2 of flour mixture. Stir in about 1/2 of sour-cream mixture. Gently stir in remaining flour, then remaining sour-cream mixture. Stir until no trace of flour remains. Do not beat.
4. Transfer 2 cups batter to medium bowl. Gently stir in chocolate mixture.
5. Pour 1 cup white batter into prepared pan; spread evenly. Pour chocolate batter into pan, then pour remaining white batter on top. Swirl a knife gently through batter to give a marbled effect.
6. Bake about 50 to 55 minutes or until a cake tester inserted in cake comes out clean.
7. Cool in pan on a rack 10 minutes. Run a thin-bladed flexible knife around tube but not around side of pan. Invert cake onto rack; cool completely. Transfer cake to a platter. *Cake can be kept, wrapped, up to 2 days at room temperature.*
1. **Glaze:** Combine chocolate and water in a double boiler or small heatproof bowl over hot, not simmering, water over low heat. Leave until chocolate is melted, stirring occasionally. Stir until smooth. Remove from pan of water. Add butter; stir until blended in.
2. Spoon glaze slowly over cake, letting it trickle down grooves on side of cake. Wipe platter clean.
3. Serve cake immediately if soft glaze is desired; cool at room temperature 1-1/2 hours for firmer glaze. Keep cake in refrigerator if weather is hot. If weather is cool, keep cake at room temperature so glaze will be shinier. *Glazed cake can be kept, covered with a cake cover or large bowl, up to 8 hours at cool room temperature or 1 day in refrigerator.* Serve at room temperature.

Variation
Omit glaze and sprinkle cake with powdered sugar before serving.

TIPS

○ *To ensure maximum lightness in light cakes, and even in some butter cakes and fudge cakes, the egg yolks and whites are whipped separately to incorporate air into both. They are then combined with the other ingredients gently and quickly, so the batter loses as little air as possible and rises properly.*

○ *Always allow about 20 minutes for oven to preheat. You might want to use an extra oven thermometer to be sure your oven temperature is accurate.*

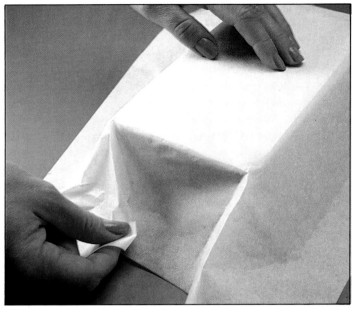

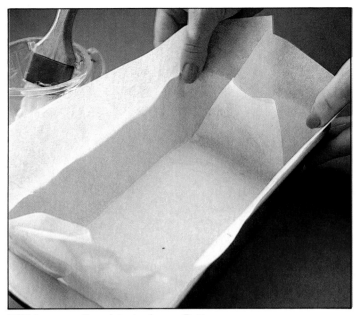

1/Shape a single piece of parchment paper or waxed paper neatly around outside of pan, folding it at the corners so it is smooth (like folding the ends when wrapping a present.)

2/Slide paper liner into loaf pan. Butter paper.

German Nut Loaf with Chocolate Chunks

Chunks of bittersweet chocolate and toasted hazelnuts in two forms—both ground and chopped—give interesting textures and sophisticated flavors to this golden-crusted, nutty, not-too-sweet cake. Serve it for afternoon tea or accompany it with whipped cream for dessert.

Makes about 12 servings

1-1/2 cups hazelnuts (about 7 oz.)
**4 oz. fine-quality bittersweet or
    extra-bittersweet chocolate, cut
    in approximately 3/8-inch cubes**
3/4 cup plus 1 tablespoon sugar
3/4 cup cake flour
3/4 teaspoon baking powder
Pinch of salt
**3/4 cup (6 oz.) unsalted butter,
    slightly softened**
**4 eggs, separated, room
    temperature**
1-1/2 teaspoons grated lemon zest
1/4 teaspoon cream of tartar

1. Position rack in center of oven and preheat to 350F (175C). Toast hazelnuts in a shallow baking pan in oven about 8 minutes or until skins begin to split. Transfer to a strainer. Rub hot nuts against strainer with a terrycloth towel to remove most of skins. Cool nuts completely.

2. Lightly butter a 9" x 5" loaf pan and line it entirely with parchment paper or waxed paper, letting paper extend about 1 inch above edge of pan. To line loaf pan, shape a single piece of paper neatly around outside of pan, folding it at the corners so it is smooth (like folding the ends when wrapping a present). Slide paper liner into pan. Butter paper.

3. Coarsely chop 1/2 cup nuts. Transfer to a medium bowl; add chocolate.

4. In a food processor, grind remaining 1 cup hazelnuts with 2 tablespoons sugar as finely as possible, scraping occasionally. Transfer to a large bowl.

5. Sift flour, baking powder and salt onto nut mixture; mix thoroughly.

6. Cream butter in a large bowl. Add 1/2 cup sugar; beat until smooth and fluffy. Add egg yolks, 1 at a time, beating very thoroughly after each addition. Beat in lemon zest. Stir in flour mixture until blended.

7. In a large dry bowl, beat egg whites with cream of tartar using dry beaters at medium speed until soft peaks form. Gradually beat in remaining 3 tablespoons sugar; continue beating at high speed until whites are stiff and shiny but not dry.

8. Gently fold about 1/3 of whites into egg-yolk mixture until nearly incorporated. Fold in remaining whites in 2 batches until batter is blended. Fold in chopped hazelnuts and chocolate pieces.

9. Transfer batter to prepared pan; spread evenly. Bake 60 to 65 minutes or until top is firm and a cake tester inserted in center of cake comes out clean of batter; a little chocolate may stick to tester because of chocolate pieces.

10. Cool in pan on a rack about 30 minutes. Invert cake onto rack. Carefully peel off paper; cool cake completely. *Cake can be kept, wrapped, up to 3 days at room temperature.*

Chocolate-Studded Kugelhopf

Travelers to Austria, Germany and Alsace will find the traditional kugelhopf everywhere. This extra-buttery version of the coffeecake has a new twist—milk chocolate chips are added to the customary raisins and almonds. The golden cake is made from an easy, yeast-leavened dough and is baked in a fluted tube pan. Kugelhopf is best served at teatime or for brunch.

Makes 12 to 16 servings

1/2 cup dark raisins
2 tablespoons kirsch
1 cup milk
2 (1/4-oz.) pkgs. active dry yeast
   (about 2 tablespoons)
2/3 cup sugar
3-1/2 cups all-purpose flour
1-1/2 teaspoons salt
3 eggs
1 cup (8 oz.) unsalted butter, cut in
   16 pieces, room temperature
16 to 18 whole blanched almonds
1 (12-oz.) pkg. milk chocolate
   pieces (2 cups)
Powdered sugar

1. Put raisins in a small jar or bowl. Pour kirsch over raisins. Cover tightly; shake to mix. Let soak at least 4 hours or overnight at cool room temperature or in refrigerator.
2. Heat milk to warm (110F, 45C) in a small saucepan. Pour 1/2 cup warm milk into a small bowl. Sprinkle yeast over milk; add 1/4 teaspoon sugar. Let stand 10 minutes or until foamy. Stir yeast mixture.
3. Put 1/2 cup flour in a medium bowl. Add yeast mixture and 1/4 cup milk; stir until combined. A few lumps may remain. Cover with plastic wrap; let stand about 15 minutes.
4. Meanwhile, spoon remaining 3 cups flour into mixer bowl; make a well in center of flour. Add salt, remaining sugar and remaining 1/4 cup milk. Using a wooden spoon mix ingredients in well briefly. Add eggs and 8 butter pieces to well. Using dough hook, mix at low speed, scraping bowl occasionally, until dough is smooth.
5. Gradually beat in remaining butter, 1 piece at a time. Beat in yeast mixture. Scrape down mixture.
6. Continue beating on medium speed with dough hook until mixture is very smooth, 10 to 12 minutes. Cover with plastic wrap. Set in a warm draft-free place 30 minutes or until it begins to rise but does not double in bulk.
7. Generously butter a 9-1/2" x 4" kugelhopf mold, fluted tube pan or Bundt pan, taking care to butter tube and each fluted section. Put 1 almond in base of each ridge in pan.
8. Stir chocolate, raisins and kirsch into risen batter. Carefully transfer batter to pan, taking care not to move almonds. Smooth top. Cover with plastic wrap. Let rise in a warm draft-free place 40 minutes.
9. Position rack in center of oven and preheat to 400F (205C). Remove plastic wrap from dough. Let dough rise about 20 minutes or until it nearly reaches top of pan.
10. Bake kugelhopf 10 minutes. Reduce oven temperature to 350F (175C); continue baking about 45 minutes longer or until a cake tester inserted in kugelhopf comes out clean. If kugelhopf begins to brown too much on top, cover it with foil.
11. Cool in pan on a rack about 10 minutes. Invert cake onto rack; cool completely. Transfer to a platter. *Cake can be kept, wrapped, up to 2 days at room temperature.* Sprinkle with powdered sugar just before serving.

Note: If a mixer with a dough hook is not available, dough can be made by hand. Follow recipe, using a wooden spoon to stir dough. With cupped hand under dough, slap dough against bowl for about 5 minutes or until dough is smooth.

Chocolate-Brazil Nut Cake

In this dark, exotic cake, the distinctive taste of Brazil nuts is complemented by the equally assertive flavor of chocolate. The crunchiness of the nuts contrasts with the smooth, honey-accented chocolate-ganache frosting.

Makes 12 servings

Chocolate-Brazil Nut Butter Cake:
1-1/2 cups Brazil nuts (about 7 oz.)
6 oz. semisweet chocolate, chopped
3/4 cup sugar
1/4 cup all-purpose flour
1/2 teaspoon baking powder
3/4 cup (6 oz.) unsalted butter, slightly softened
6 eggs, separated, room temperature
1/4 teaspoon cream of tartar

Chocolate-Honey Frosting:
1/2 cup whipping cream
6 oz. semisweet chocolate, very finely chopped
6 tablespoons (3 oz.) unsalted butter, slightly softened but still cool
3 tablespoons plus 1 teaspoon honey

Garnish:
About 1/4 cup Brazil nuts, chopped

1. Cake: Position rack in center of oven and preheat to 350F (175C). Toast nuts in a shallow baking pan in oven 10 minutes. Transfer 3/4 cup nuts to a large strainer. Turn off oven; leave in remaining 3/4 cup nuts. Rub nuts against strainer with a terrycloth towel to remove most of skins. Lift nuts from strainer and transfer to a large bowl. Tap strainer on surface to remove skins. Repeat procedure with remaining nuts. Cool nuts completely.

2. Melt chocolate in a double boiler or heatproof medium bowl over hot, not simmering, water over low heat, stirring occasionally. Stir until smooth. Remove from pan of water; cool to body temperature.

3. Lightly butter a 9″ x 3″ springform pan. Line base of pan with parchment paper or foil; butter paper or foil. Flour side of pan and lined base, tapping to remove excess.

4. Grind 3/4 cup nuts with 2 tablespoons sugar in a food processor until as fine as possible, scraping inward occasionally. Transfer to a large bowl. Repeat with remaining nuts and 2 more tablespoons sugar.

5. Sift flour and baking powder over nut mixture; mix thoroughly.

6. Cream butter in a large bowl. Add 6 tablespoons sugar and beat until smooth and fluffy. Add egg yolks, 1 at a time, beating thoroughly after each addition. Stir in melted chocolate.

7. In a large dry bowl, beat egg whites with cream of tartar using dry beaters at medium speed until soft peaks form. Gradually beat in remaining 2 tablespoons sugar; continue beating at high speed until whites are stiff and shiny but not dry.

8. Sprinkle about 1/3 of nut mixture over chocolate mixture; fold gently until nearly incorporated. Gently fold in about 1/3 of whites. Repeat with remaining nut mixture and whites in 2 batches. Continue folding lightly but quickly, just until batter is blended.

9. Transfer batter to prepared pan; spread evenly. Bake about 43 minutes or until a cake tester inserted in center of cake comes out clean.

10. Cool in pan on a rack 10 minutes; cake will settle slightly in center. Run a thin-bladed flexible knife or metal spatula carefully around side of cake. Invert cake onto rack. Release spring and remove side and base of pan. Carefully peel off paper or foil. Invert cake again onto another rack; cool completely. Turn cake onto a platter so smooth side of cake faces up. *Cake can be kept, wrapped, up to 2 days in refrigerator.*

1. Frosting: Bring cream to a full boil in a small heavy saucepan. Remove from heat; immediately add chopped chocolate. Using a small whisk, stir quickly until chocolate is completely melted and mixture is smooth. Transfer to a bowl. Cool to room temperature.

2. Whip mixture at high speed about 3 minutes or until it thickens and becomes paler.

3. Cream butter in a medium or large bowl until very soft and smooth. Add chocolate mixture in 3 batches, beating constantly until mixture is smooth. Gradually beat in honey.

1. Garnish: Set aside about 3 tablespoons frosting for garnishing. Using a long metal spatula, spread remaining frosting evenly on side and top of cake; smooth side and top. Swirl frosting at top, from edge inward, forming small curves.

2. Spoon reserved frosting into a pastry bag fitted with a small star tip. Pipe a ring of rosettes about halfway between edge and center of cake. Fill center of ring with chopped Brazil nuts. Press gently so they adhere to frosting. Refrigerate at least 1 hour before serving. *Frosted cake can be kept, covered, up to 3 days in refrigerator.* Serve at room temperature.

Chocolate-Wine Cake

When I took a course in marrying wine and food at the Academié du Vin in Paris, we discussed the difficulty of matching wine with chocolate. As ingredients in a dessert, however, they can go together well. Here, for example, red wine flavors both the moist, tender, dark chocolate cake and its shiny cocoa glaze. The tanginess of the wine complements the bittersweet taste of the chocolate and adds an intriguing flavor.

Makes 10 to 12 servings

Chocolate-Wine Butter Cake:
1 cup dry red wine (such as
   California Burgundy)
6 oz. semisweet chocolate, chopped
1-3/4 cups cake flour
1-1/4 teaspoons baking powder
1/2 teaspoon baking soda
1/2 cup plus 2 tablespoons (5 oz.)
   unsalted butter, slightly softened
1 cup sugar
3 eggs

Cocoa-Wine Glaze:
6 tablespoons sugar
3 tablespoons unsweetened cocoa
   powder, preferably
   Dutch-process, sifted
1/2 cup dry red wine
5 tablespoons unsalted butter,
   chilled, cut in 5 pieces

1. **Cake:** Position rack in center of oven and preheat to 350F (175C). Generously butter a 9-1/2" x 4" fluted tube pan or Bundt pan, taking care to butter tube and each fluted section.
2. Bring wine to a boil in a medium, non-aluminum saucepan. Boil about 2-1/2 minutes or until wine is reduced to 3/4 cup; if it reduces too far, add water to obtain 3/4 cup liquid. Pour 1/2 cup reduced wine into a bowl; cool to room temperature.
3. Combine chocolate and remaining 1/4 cup reduced wine in a double boiler or heatproof medium bowl over hot, not simmering, water over low heat. Leave until chocolate is melted, stirring occasionally. Stir until smooth. Remove from pan of water; cool mixture to body temperature.
4. Sift flour, baking powder and baking soda into a large bowl.
5. Cream butter in a large bowl. Add sugar; beat until smooth and fluffy. Add eggs, 1 at a time, beating very thoroughly after each addition. Gradually beat in chocolate mixture.
6. Stir in about 1/3 of flour mixture, followed by 1/2 of wine. When batter is nearly blended, stir in another 1/3 of flour mixture, followed by remaining wine, then remaining flour. Stir just until batter is blended.
7. Transfer batter to prepared pan; spread evenly. Bake about 55 minutes or until a cake tester inserted in cake comes out clean.
8. Cool in pan on a rack 15 minutes. Run a thin-bladed flexible knife around tube but not around side of pan. Invert cake carefully onto rack; cool completely. Transfer carefully to a platter. *Cake can be kept, wrapped, up to 3 days at room temperature.*
1. **Glaze:** Combine sugar, cocoa and wine in a small saucepan; whisk until blended. Bring to a boil over medium-high heat, whisking. Reduce heat to low; simmer 3 minutes, whisking occasionally. Remove from heat. Stir in butter, 1 piece at a time, until blended in.
2. Cool glaze 5 minutes. Refrigerate, stirring occasionally, about 40 minutes or until thick but still pourable.
3. Stir glaze until very smooth. Very slowly spoon glaze over cake, moving spoon back and forth to cover top ridges and letting glaze trickle down grooves on side of cake. If necessary, repeat spooning several times. Wipe platter clean.
4. Serve cake immediately if soft glaze is desired; cool at room temperature 1-1/2 hours for firmer glaze. Keep cake in refrigerator if weather is warm. If weather is cool, keep cake at room temperature so glaze will be shinier. *Glazed cake can be kept, covered with a cake cover or large bowl, up to 8 hours at cool room temperature or 1 day in refrigerator.* Serve at room temperature.

Queen of Sheba Cake

Imaginative French chefs named this sumptuous chocolate cake, made with generous amounts of butter and almonds, for the biblical Queen of Sheba. She is believed to have been a dark, rich beauty who reigned over the area that is now Yemen or Ethiopia. The cake is moist inside and therefore needs no filling. If you prefer, omit the frosting and serve the cake with whipped cream or with Vanilla Bean Custard Sauce, page 197.

Makes 8 servings

Chocolate-Almond Fudge Cake:
4 oz. semisweet chocolate, chopped
3/4 cup whole blanched almonds (about 3-1/2 oz.)
2/3 cup sugar
1/4 cup all-purpose flour
1/2 cup (4 oz.) unsalted butter, slightly softened
3 egg yolks
4 egg whites, room temperature
1/4 teaspoon cream of tartar

Ganache Butter Frosting:
1/3 cup whipping cream
4 oz. semisweet chocolate, very finely chopped
1/4 cup unsalted butter, slightly softened but still cool

1. **Cake:** Position rack in center of oven and preheat to 350F (175C). Butter a round 9-inch layer cake pan. Line base of pan with parchment paper or foil; butter paper or foil. Flour side of pan and lined base, tapping pan to remove excess.
2. Melt chocolate in a double boiler or heatproof medium bowl over hot, not simmering, water over low heat, stirring occasionally. Stir until smooth. Remove from pan of water; cool to body temperature.
3. Grind almonds with 2 tablespoons sugar in a food processor until as fine as possible, scraping inward occasionally. Transfer to a medium bowl. Sift flour over almonds; mix thoroughly.
4. Cream butter in a medium or large bowl until smooth and fluffy. Beat in cooled chocolate. Beat in egg yolks, 1 at a time, then 1/3 cup sugar. Continue to beat until mixture is smooth.
5. In a large dry bowl, beat egg whites with cream of tartar using dry beaters at medium speed until soft peaks form. Gradually beat in remaining 3-1/3 tablespoons sugar; continue beating at high speed until whites are stiff and shiny but not dry.
6. Fold about 1/4 of egg whites into chocolate mixture. Quickly spoon remaining whites on top and begin folding. Sprinkle almond mixture on top and fold lightly and quickly, just until batter is blended.
7. Transfer batter to prepared pan. Bake 25 to 30 minutes or until a cake tester inserted in cake about halfway between edge and center of pan comes out clean, but center of cake is still slightly soft.
8. Cool cake in pan on a rack 5 minutes. Run a thin-bladed flexible knife carefully around side of cake. Invert cake onto rack. Carefully peel off paper or foil; cool cake completely. Turn cake onto another rack, then onto a platter so smooth side of cake faces up. *Cake can be kept, wrapped, up to 2 days in refrigerator.*
1. **Frosting:** Bring cream to a full boil in a small heavy saucepan. Remove from heat; immediately add chopped chocolate. Using a small whisk, stir quickly until chocolate is completely melted and mixture is smooth. Transfer to a bowl. Cool to room temperature.
2. Whip mixture at high speed about 3 minutes or until it thickens and becomes paler.
3. Cream butter in a medium or large bowl until very soft and smooth. Add chocolate mixture in 3 batches, beating constantly until mixture is smooth.
4. Using a long metal spatula, spread frosting evenly on side and top of cake. If desired, swirl frosting on top. Refrigerate at least 2 hours before serving. *Frosted cake can be kept, covered, up to 2 days in refrigerator.* Serve at room temperature.

Chocolate-Hazelnut Cake with Fudge Frosting

The unusually moist interior of this very chocolaty cake is due to the generous quantities of chocolate, butter and nuts and the technique of melting the butter into the chocolate. The cake is coated with a not-too-sweet fudge frosting but is also delicious served on its own or accompanied by whipped cream or Spirited Custard Sauce, page 197, flavored with hazelnut liqueur.

Makes 8 to 10 servings

Chocolate-Hazelnut Cake:
1 cup hazelnuts (about 4-1/2 oz.)
1/2 cup sugar
5 oz. semisweet chocolate, chopped
2 tablespoons water
1/2 cup (4 oz.) unsalted butter, cut in 8 pieces, room temperature
4 eggs, separated, room temperature
1 teaspoon pure vanilla extract
2 tablespoons potato starch
1/4 teaspoon cream of tartar

Fudge Frosting:
1/2 cup whipping cream
1/4 cup sugar
2 oz. semisweet chocolate, very finely chopped
1 oz. unsweetened chocolate, very finely chopped
1/2 cup (4 oz.) unsalted butter, slightly softened but still cool
1/2 teaspoon pure vanilla extract

1. **Cake:** Position rack in center of oven and preheat to 350F (175C). Toast hazelnuts and remove skins, page 201; cool nuts completely.

2. Reduce oven temperature to 325F (165C). Lightly butter an 8-inch springform pan. Line base of pan with parchment paper or foil; butter paper or foil. Flour side of pan and lined base, tapping pan to remove excess.

3. Set aside 8 to 10 attractive hazelnuts for garnish. Grind remaining hazelnuts with 2 tablespoons sugar in a food processor until as fine as possible, scraping inward occasionally. Transfer to a medium bowl.

4. Combine chocolate and water in a double boiler or large heatproof bowl over hot, not simmering, water over low heat. Leave until chocolate is melted, stirring occasionally. Stir until smooth. Add butter; stir until blended in. Remove from pan of water.

5. Whisk egg yolks to blend. Gradually add yolks to chocolate mixture, whisking vigorously. Stir in 1/4 cup sugar, followed by vanilla, nuts and potato starch; mix well.

6. In a large dry bowl, beat egg whites with cream of tartar using dry beaters at medium speed until soft peaks form. Gradually beat in remaining 2 tablespoons sugar; continue beating at high speed until whites are stiff and shiny but not dry.

7. Gently fold about 1/3 of whites into chocolate mixture until nearly incorporated. Fold in remaining whites in 2 batches. Continue folding lightly but quickly, just until batter is blended.

8. Transfer batter to prepared pan; spread evenly. Bake about 1 hour or until a cake tester inserted in center of cake comes out clean.

9. Cool in pan on a rack about 10 minutes. Run a thin-bladed flexible knife or metal spatula carefully around side of cake. Invert cake onto rack. Gently release spring and remove side and base of pan. Carefully peel off paper or foil; cool cake completely. Invert cake onto another rack, then onto a platter so smoothest side of cake faces up. *Cake can be kept, wrapped, up to 2 days at room temperature or in refrigerator.*

1. **Frosting:** Combine cream and sugar in a heavy medium saucepan. Cook over low heat, stirring constantly, until sugar dissolves. Bring to a boil over medium-high heat, stirring constantly. Reduce heat and simmer 1 minute.

2. Remove from heat; cool 2 minutes. Immediately add semisweet chocolate. Using a small whisk, stir quickly until chocolate is completely melted and mixture is smooth. Add unsweetened chocolate; whisk until smooth. Chill chocolate mixture in refrigerator, stirring often, until cool but not set.

3. Cream butter in a medium or large bowl until very soft and smooth. Add chocolate mixture in 3 batches, beating constantly at low speed until mixture is smooth. Beat in vanilla.

4. Using a long metal spatula, spread frosting evenly on side and top of cake; smooth side and top. Garnish with reserved hazelnuts. Refrigerate at least 1 hour before serving. *Frosted cake can be kept, covered, up to 2 days in refrigerator.* Serve at room temperature.

Self-Frosted Chocolate Cake

This cake is simple and fun to make. Part of the rich, mousse-like mixture is used to make a glossy chocolate frosting which is softer than buttercream and spreads easily. With the addition of flour, the remaining mixture becomes a base for the tender, fudgy cake.

Makes 8 to 10 servings

**8-1/2 oz. fine-quality bittersweet
   chocolate, chopped
3/4 cup (6 oz.) unsalted butter, cut
   in pieces, room temperature
1/2 cup all-purpose flour
1/4 teaspoon baking powder
6 egg yolks
2/3 cup sugar
1 teaspoon pure vanilla extract
4 egg whites, room temperature**

1. Position rack in center of oven and preheat to 350F (175C). Butter an 8-inch springform pan. Line base of pan with parchment paper or foil; butter paper or foil. Flour side of pan and lined base, tapping to remove excess.
2. Melt chocolate in a double boiler or large heatproof bowl over hot, not simmering, water over low heat, stirring occasionally. Stir until smooth. Add butter; stir until blended in. Remove from pan of water; cool to body temperature.
3. Sift flour and baking powder into a small bowl.
4. Beat egg yolks lightly in a large bowl. Beat in 6 tablespoons sugar; continue beating at high speed about 5 minutes or until mixture is pale and very thick. Stir in melted chocolate mixture and vanilla.
5. In a large dry bowl, beat egg whites using dry beaters at medium speed until soft peaks form. Gradually beat in remaining 4-2/3 tablespoons sugar; continue beating at high speed until whites are stiff and shiny but not dry.
6. Gently fold about 1/3 of whites into chocolate mixture until nearly incorporated. Fold in remaining whites in 2 batches. Continue folding lightly but quickly, just until mixture is blended.
7. Gently spoon 2 cups mixture into a small bowl. Cover and refrigerate while making cake. This mixture will be used as frosting.
8. Sprinkle flour mixture over remaining chocolate mixture; fold in gently, just until batter is blended.
9. Transfer batter to prepared pan; spread evenly. Bake 30 to 35 minutes or until a cake tester inserted in center of cake comes out clean.
10. Cool in pan on a rack 10 minutes. Run a thin-bladed flexible knife around side of cake. Gently release spring and remove side of pan. Let cake cool until it is lukewarm; cake will settle slightly in center. Invert cake onto another rack; remove base of pan. Carefully peel off paper or foil; cool cake completely.
11. Let frosting mixture stand at room temperature about 1 hour or until it is easy to spread.
12. Turn cake onto another rack, then onto a platter so smooth side of cake faces up. Using a long metal spatula, spread frosting evenly on side and top of cake; swirl top. Refrigerate at least 2 hours before serving. *Cake can be kept, covered with a cake cover or large bowl, up to 4 days in refrigerator.* Serve at cool room temperature.

TIPS

○ *All leftover cakes can be frozen and will keep well for two or three months although they will not be as good as when fresh.*

○ *Do not chop chocolate with nuts in a food processor, because the chocolate can begin to melt and turn the nuts oily.*

○ *Vanilla beans can be reused. Rinse gently and leave to dry completely. Store in a closed jar at room temperature.*

○ *Instead of grating lemon or orange zest, it is often easier to remove it in thin strips with a zester and then chop in very fine pieces with a heavy knife.*

Flourless Fudge Cake with Raspberry-Brandy Sauce

The star of the dessert table in fine restaurants is often a flourless chocolate cake made from a soufflé-like mixture. In this version, raspberries and raspberry-brandy sauce add freshness, color and lightness to balance the richness and concentrated flavor of the dense bittersweet cake.

Makes 12 servings

Flourless Fudge Cake:
10 oz. semisweet chocolate, chopped
2 oz. unsweetened chocolate, chopped
1/3 cup water
1-1/2 cups (12 oz.) unsalted butter, cut in 12 pieces
1 cup sugar
6 eggs, separated, room temperature

Raspberry-Brandy Sauce:
2 cups milk
7 egg yolks, room temperature
1/3 cup sugar
3 tablespoons clear raspberry brandy

1-1/2 cups fresh raspberries (for garnish)

1. **Cake:** Position rack in center of oven and preheat to 300F (150C). Butter an 8-inch springform pan. Line base of pan with parchment paper or foil; butter paper or foil. Flour side of pan and lined base, tapping pan to remove excess.
2. Combine chocolates and water in a double boiler or large heatproof bowl over hot, not simmering, water over low heat. Leave until melted, stirring occasionally. Stir until smooth. With container of chocolate still in pan over hot water, add 1/3 of butter pieces. Let stand, stirring often, until blended. Gradually stir in 3/4 cup sugar until blended. Add remaining butter pieces. Continue stirring until mixture is smooth.
3. Remove chocolate mixture from pan of water; quickly whisk in egg yolks, 1 at a time.
4. In a large dry bowl, beat egg whites using dry beaters at medium speed until very foamy. Gradually beat in remaining 1/4 cup sugar; continue beating until soft peaks form.
5. Fold about 1/4 of whites into chocolate mixture. Return mixture to remaining whites; fold gently together. Chocolate mixture tends to sink but continue folding until batter is blended.
6. Transfer batter to prepared pan; pan will be quite full. Bake 1 hour. Reduce oven temperature to 250F (120C); bake 15 minutes longer or until a thick crust forms on top and center top does not shake when pan is moved gently. Cake should feel firm all over except in very center. Cake will crack on top; center will not rise quite as much as rest of cake.
7. Cool briefly in pan on a rack; cake will settle slightly in center. When side of pan is just warm, gently release spring but do not remove side of pan. Cool cake to room temperature. Gently remove side of pan. Carefully invert cake onto a plate. Slide a metal spatula gently under base of pan; remove base and paper or foil from cake. Cover and refrigerate at least 12 hours or overnight before serving. *Cake can be kept, wrapped, up to 1 week in refrigerator.*
1. **Sauce:** Bring milk to boil in a heavy medium saucepan. Remove from heat.
2. Whisk egg yolks lightly in a large heatproof bowl. Add sugar; whisk until thick and smooth. Gradually whisk in hot milk. Return mixture to pan, whisking constantly. Cook over medium-low heat, stirring mixture and scraping bottom of pan constantly with a wooden spoon, until mixture thickens slightly and reaches 170F to 175F (75C to 80C) on an instant-read thermometer. Begin checking after 5 minutes. To check thickness of sauce without a thermometer, remove sauce from heat. Dip a metal spoon in sauce and draw your finger across back of spoon. Your finger should leave a clear path in custard that clings to spoon. If it does not, continue cooking another 30 seconds and check again. Do not overcook sauce or it will curdle.
3. Pour immediately into a bowl. Stir about 30 seconds to cool, then let stand about 1/2 hour to cool completely. Cover and refrigerate. *Sauce can be kept, covered, up to 2 days in refrigerator.*
4. Stir in brandy a short time before serving.
1. **To serve:** Cut cake very carefully with a sharp knife to avoid crumbling. Serve chilled or at cool room temperature.
2. Set each slice of cake on an individual plate; spoon sauce around, not over it. Place 4 or 5 raspberries on sauce on each plate.

Flourless Fudge Cake with Raspberry-Brandy Sauce

How to Make White Chocolate Cheesecake

1/Using the back of a spoon, press cracker-crumb mixture in an even layer on base and about 1-1/4 inches up side of pan. Bake in preheated oven 10 minutes. Cool completely.

2/Just before serving, carefully run a metal spatula around cheesecake and remove side of pan. Garnish cheesecake with Quick Chocolate Curls. When serving, free each slice from underneath to remove crust from pan.

White Chocolate Cheesecake

White chocolate is my favorite type for flavoring cheesecake. Its delicate taste enhances the flavor of the cheese, instead of clashing with it as bittersweet chocolate often does. This cake, based on my mother's sour cream-topped cheesecake, has a creamy texture and a subtle flavor.

Makes 12 servings

Pecan-Cocoa Crumb Crust:
18 squares (about 5 oz.) graham crackers
1/4 cup pecan halves
3 tablespoons sugar
2 tablespoons unsweetened cocoa powder
7 tablespoons unsalted butter, melted and cooled

White Chocolate-Cheese Filling:
6 oz. fine-quality white chocolate, finely chopped
3/4 cup whipping cream
1 lb. cream cheese, cut in pieces, room temperature
3/4 cup plus 2 tablespoons sugar
4 eggs
1 teaspoon pure vanilla extract

Sour-Cream Topping:
1-1/2 cups dairy sour cream
1/4 cup sugar
1 teaspoon pure vanilla extract

1. Crust: Position rack in center of oven and preheat to 350F (175C). Lightly butter a round 9" x 3" springform pan.

2. Grind graham crackers in a food processor until as fine as possible; or put them in a plastic bag and crush them with a rolling pin. Measure 1-1/4 cups.

3. Coarsely chop pecan halves. Combine cracker crumbs with pecans and sugar in a large bowl; mix well. Sift in cocoa; stir until blended. Add melted butter; mix well with a fork.

4. Using the back of a spoon, press mixture in an even layer on base and about 1-1/4 inches up side of pan. Bake 10 minutes. Cool completely.

1. Filling: Combine chocolate and 1/2 cup whipping cream in a double boiler or heatproof medium bowl over hot, not simmering, water over low heat. Leave until melted, stirring often. Cool to room temperature. If necessary, whisk mixture until smooth.

2. Using flat (creaming) beater of mixer, if available, beat cream cheese with remaining 1/4 cup whipping cream at low speed until perfectly smooth. Gradually beat in sugar. Beat in eggs, 1 at a time, scraping bowl occasionally. Beat until perfectly smooth. Gradually add cooled chocolate and vanilla and stir until well blended.

3. Carefully pour filling into cooled crust. Bake about 1 hour 5 minutes or until center is barely firm and top begins to crack. Remove from oven; cool 15 minutes. Increase oven temperature to 425F (220C).

1. Topping: Combine sour cream, sugar and vanilla in a medium bowl; mix well. Carefully spread topping evenly on cheesecake without letting it drip over crust.

2. Return cheesecake to oven. Bake 7 minutes or until edge of topping sets. Remove from oven; cool to room temperature.

Quick Chocolate Curls, page 193

Garnish:

About 1/8 oz. semisweet chocolate *or* Quick Chocolate Curls, page 193, using white and bittersweet chocolate

1. Garnish: Grate semisweet chocolate over top of cheesecake, if desired. Cover pan with plastic wrap. Refrigerate at least 1 day before serving. *Cheesecake can be kept up to 4 days in refrigerator.*

2. Just before serving, carefully run a metal spatula around cheesecake and remove side of pan. Garnish with Quick Chocolate Curls, if desired. When serving, free each slice from underneath to remove crust from pan. For neat slices rinse knife after each cut.

Chef Chambrette's Chocolate Macaroon Cake

Master Chef Fernand Chambrette, my co-author in a cookbook we published in France, gave me the idea for this cake. It is a macaroon-lover's dream—a whole cake made from a chocolate macaroon-type mixture, topped with a white amaretto cream frosting and elegantly garnished with easy-to-make chocolate-dipped almonds. The small, flourless, deep-brown cake has a chewy crust and an incredibly moist center.

Makes 8 servings

Chocolate Macaroon Cake:

4 oz. semisweet chocolate, chopped
2 cups whole blanched almonds
    (about 9-1/2 oz.)
3/4 cup sugar
8 egg whites, room temperature

Amaretto Whipped Cream:

3/4 cup whipping cream,
    well-chilled
1 teaspoon sugar
2 tablespoons amaretto liqueur

Chocolate-Dipped Almonds:

1/2 oz. fine-quality bittersweet
    chocolate, chopped
6 to 8 whole blanched almonds

1. Cake: Position rack in center of oven and preheat to 325F (165C). Lightly butter an 8-inch springform pan. Line base and side of pan with parchment paper or waxed paper; generously butter paper.

2. Melt chocolate in a double boiler or heatproof medium bowl over hot, not simmering, water over low heat, stirring occasionally. Stir until smooth. Remove from pan of water; cool to body temperature.

3. Grind almonds with 2 tablespoons sugar in a food processor until as fine as possible. Add 2 egg whites (about 1/4 cup) and 1/4 cup sugar; process about 10 seconds or until smooth. Add 2 more whites (about 1/4 cup) and another 1/4 cup sugar; repeat processing. Transfer to a medium bowl.

4. In a large dry bowl, beat remaining 4 egg whites using dry beaters at medium speed until soft peaks form. Gradually beat in remaining 2 tablespoons sugar; continue beating at high speed until whites are stiff and shiny but not dry.

5. Gradually stir chocolate into almond mixture. Gently fold about 1/4 of whites into chocolate mixture until nearly incorporated. Fold in remaining whites in 3 batches. Chocolate mixture is dense and not easy to blend with whites but continue folding until batter is blended.

6. Transfer batter to prepared pan; spread evenly. Bake about 40 minutes or until cake springs back when pressed lightly.

7. Cool in pan on a rack 5 minutes. Invert cake onto rack. Gently release spring and remove side and base of pan. Carefully peel off paper or foil; cool cake completely. Turn cake onto another rack, then onto a platter so smooth side of cake faces up. *Cake can be kept, wrapped, up to 3 days at room temperature.*

1. Whipped cream: Chill a medium or large bowl and beaters for whipping cream. Whip cream with sugar in chilled bowl until soft peaks form. Gradually beat in amaretto; whip until stiff.

2. Using a long metal spatula, spread cream evenly on side and top of cake; smooth side and top. Refrigerate about 1 hour before serving. *Frosted cake can be kept, covered with a cake cover or a large bowl, up to 4 hours in refrigerator.*

1. Almonds: Melt chocolate in a very small heatproof bowl over hot, not simmering, water over low heat, stirring occasionally. Stir until smooth. Remove from pan of water; cool to body temperature.

2. Line plate with waxed paper. Dip pointed end of each almond in chocolate; let excess drip into bowl. Gently set on paper-lined plate. Refrigerate to set chocolate. Just before serving, arrange on cake with chocolate ends pointing inward.

LAYER CAKES, TORTES & MOUSSE CAKES

A wide selection of cakes, fillings and frostings in exciting combinations make the creations in this chapter the most festive of desserts.

The most frequently used cake bases for layer cakes, tortes and mousse cakes are sponge cakes of two types—those made with separated eggs and those, called *genoises*, in which whole eggs are whipped until very light. For crunchy layers, *dacquoises*, or light nutty meringues, are used. Butter cakes are best for especially rich layers.

Chocolate Layer Cakes

The cake layers of classic French chocolate gâteaux generally are flavored with cocoa so they remain light, while Austrian layer cakes can contain either cocoa or chocolate. In these types of European cakes, chocolate appears in the rich fillings and frostings. Traditional American cakes follow the Austrian custom in flavoring the cake layers with either cocoa or chocolate, but the fillings and frostings are often sweeter and less buttery than the European ones.

Chocolate Tortes

Many elegant layer cakes are referred to as *tortes*, a term which comes from the German word for cake. Often these are nut cakes with lavish fillings and frostings. The famous Sachertorte, however, is not a nut cake and not necessarily a layer cake.

Nuts give many chocolate tortes a distinct flavor and a pleasant crunchiness, making them delicious even when served plain. In many tortes the same nut appears in both the cake and the filling. Austrian and Hungarian tortes in particular often contain generous amounts of walnuts, hazelnuts or almonds. The French prefer to stick chopped toasted nuts on the side of the cake as in Classic Chocolate Gâteau, or to use them in the filling in the form of praline, or caramelized toasted nuts.

Fillings & Frostings for Layer Cakes & Tortes

For chocolate layer cakes and tortes there are four basic fillings and frostings: chocolate ganache, buttercream, flavored whipped cream and powdered sugar icing.

Ganache is the most chocolaty filling of all. It tastes like the inside of a truffle and for good reason—it is the same mixture! Ganache is basically made of only two ingredients, chocolate and cream, although it can be further enriched with butter or can be mixed with extra flavorings.

Buttercream is used in the greatest array of cakes because it is the most versatile filling and frosting. It can be made in an endless variety of flavors and is very smooth and easy to spread and pipe.

Whipped cream, whether plain, chocolate-flavored or spiked with liqueur, makes a delicious filling and frosting, but it does not keep long.

Powdered sugar icing, long a favorite for topping American cakes, is very sweet and less popular today. However, when enough butter is added it turns into a cousin of buttercream, as in Chocolate-Pecan Torte, and it can be delicious.

Cakes in good-quality pastry shops always impressed me when they were elegantly frosted in one color and decorated with another; I thought that this could be done only in a professional kitchen because there must be so many frostings and fillings around. The chefs at La Varenne in Paris showed me that there is actually a very easy technique for doing this. Simply make buttercream, divide it in two, and add a flavoring of a different color to each. I use this technique often now to easily obtain beautiful cakes with two or three buttercreams. Look for these frostings in Marjolaine, Biarritz Pistachio-Chocolate Cake and Two-Tone Chocolate-Raspberry cake.

Chocolate Mousse Cakes

Mousse cakes are a new category of desserts made of cake with mousse filling. In recent years they have become great favorites, partly because of their lavish appearance. The layers of mousse filling are strikingly thick which makes a mousse cake exceptionally attractive when cut. The fillings are lighter because most of them are based on cream instead of butter or are lightened by Italian meringue. These cakes are the most important modern development in the art of dessert-making and have come into being as a result of the revolution in French cooking known as "nouvelle cuisine."

The filling of these cakes is much softer than most standard recipes. Instead of being spread, it is usually layered with the cake in a mold.

Chocolate Dream

This impressive, not-too-sweet chocolate layer cake is surprisingly easy to make. Layers of moist chocolate genoise are sandwiched with a generous amount of chocolate cream filling. More cream filling coats the sides, while the top is crowned with a dark chocolate glaze.

Makes 8 to 10 servings

Rich Chocolate Genoise:
1 oz. unsweetened chocolate, chopped
3 oz. semisweet chocolate, chopped
2 tablespoons unsalted butter
3/4 cup cake flour
1/2 teaspoon baking powder
4 eggs, room temperature
3/4 cup sugar

Chocolate Whipped Cream:
3 oz. semisweet chocolate, chopped
1-1/4 cups whipping cream, well-chilled

Chocolate Glaze:
3 oz. semisweet chocolate, finely chopped
1/4 cup whipping cream

1. **Genoise:** Position rack in center of oven and preheat to 350F (175C). Lightly butter an 8-inch springform pan. Line base of pan with parchment paper or foil and butter paper or foil. Flour side of pan and lined base, tapping pan to remove excess.
2. Combine chocolates and butter in a double boiler or heatproof medium bowl over hot, not simmering, water over low heat. Leave until melted, stirring occasionally. Stir until smooth. Remove from pan of water; cool mixture to body temperature.
3. Sift flour and baking powder into a medium bowl.
4. Beat eggs lightly in a large bowl. Whisk in sugar. Set bowl in a pan of hot water over very low heat. Whisk about 3 minutes or until mixture is barely lukewarm to the touch. Remove from pan of water. Beat mixture at high speed about 5 minutes or until completely cool and very thick.
5. Sift about 1/3 of flour mixture over egg mixture; fold in as gently as possible. Repeat with remaining flour mixture in 2 batches. When batter is nearly blended, add 1/2 cup batter to chocolate mixture; fold until blended. Add chocolate batter to remaining batter; fold gently until blended.
6. Carefully pour batter into prepared pan; spread evenly. Bake about 35 minutes or until cake shrinks slightly from side of pan and top springs back when lightly pressed.
7. Cool in pan on a rack about 5 minutes. Run a metal spatula or thin-bladed knife carefully around edge of cake. Invert cake onto a rack. Carefully peel off paper or foil; cool cake completely.
8. Using a long serrated knife, cut cake in 2 layers.
1. **Whipped cream:** Chill a large bowl and beaters for whipping cream. Melt chocolate in a double boiler or small heatproof bowl over hot, not simmering water, over low heat. Stir until smooth. Remove from heat but leave bowl of chocolate over hot water.
2. Whip cream in chilled bowl until stiff.
3. Remove chocolate from pan of water; cool 30 seconds. Quickly stir about 1/2 cup whipped cream into chocolate. Quickly fold mixture into remaining whipped cream until smooth. Work quickly so chocolate does not harden upon contact with the cold whipped cream.
4. Set bottom layer of cake on a platter. Spoon all but about 3/4 cup chocolate cream filling over it. Spread in a smooth layer. Refrigerate 30 minutes, leaving remaining cream at room temperature. Top with second cake layer. Spread remaining cream around side of cake; smooth with spatula. Refrigerate 1 hour.
1. **Glaze:** Put chocolate in a small heatproof bowl. Bring cream to a full boil in a small heavy saucepan. Pour over chocolate all at once. Stir with a whisk until chocolate is completely melted and mixture is smooth. Cool to approximately body temperature or until thickened.
2. Spoon glaze over top of cake. Spread in a smooth layer just to edge. Do not let glaze mix with frosting on side. Swirl glaze slightly in center. If desired, make lines on side of cake with large side of cake decorating comb. Refrigerate 1 hour or until glaze sets. *Frosted cake can be kept, covered, up to 2 days in refrigerator.*

1/Beginning at outside edge of 1 pan, pipe a white circle, following markings on parchment paper. Pipe a chocolate circle inside it, then a white circle, and fill center circle with chocolate batter. Repeat with a second pan. With third pan, reverse order and begin with a chocolate circle.

2/Spread frosting on assembled cake as desired. Decorate side or top with a few Chocolate Cutouts. Refrigerate cake at least 1 hour before serving.

Checkerboard Conversation Cake

Guests always try to guess how this "puzzle" was put together. The special technique is easy—you pipe the white and chocolate batters in circles and the cake comes out looking like it is made of squares! Raspberry preserves delicately flavor the chocolate frosting and are spread as a filling between the cake layers.

Makes about 12 servings

Checkerboard Cake:

3 cups plus 3 tablespoons cake flour
2-1/2 teaspoons baking powder
1/2 cup plus 1 tablespoon milk
1/2 cup plus 1 tablespoon unsweetened Dutch-process cocoa
1 cup plus 6 tablespoons (11 oz.) unsalted butter, slightly softened
1-1/4 cups plus 2 tablespoons sugar
6 eggs
2 teaspoons pure vanilla extract

1. **Cake:** Preheat oven to 350F (175C). Cut 3 8-inch rounds of parchment paper. With the aid of cutters or small pan lids, trace 3 circles on each parchment round: a 2-inch, a 4-inch and a 6-inch. Line base of 3 round 8-inch layer pans with parchment rounds, tracing side down. Butter paper and sides of pans. Prepare 2 large pastry bags fitted with large plain tips.
2. Sift flour and baking powder into a large bowl. In another bowl whisk 1/2 cup milk into cocoa until blended.
3. Cream butter in a large bowl. Add sugar; beat until smooth. Add eggs, 1 at a time, beating very thoroughly after each addition; batter may appear separated. Beat in 3/4 cup flour mixture. Beat in vanilla. Using a wooden spoon, stir in remaining flour mixture. Continue stirring until no trace of flour remains; do not beat.
4. Transfer 2-3/4 cups batter to a medium bowl. Add cocoa mixture; stir just until blended.
5. Stir remaining 1 tablespoon milk into white batter.
6. Spoon white batter into 1 pastry bag and chocolate batter into second pastry bag.
7. Beginning at outside of 1 pan, pipe a white circle, following markings on parchment paper. Pipe a chocolate circle inside it, then a white circle, and fill center circle with chocolate. Repeat with a second pan. When piping batter into third pan, reverse order and begin with a chocolate circle.
8. Fill any spaces with any remaining batter of appropriate color and smooth them gently without mixing batters.
9. Bake about 16 to 18 minutes or until a cake tester inserted in center of cakes comes out clean.
10. Invert cakes onto racks. Carefully peel off paper; cool cakes completely.

Raspberry Ganache Frosting:

6 oz. semisweet chocolate, finely chopped

1/3 cup whipping cream

6 tablespoons (3 oz.) unsalted butter, slightly softened but still cool

1/2 cup red raspberry preserves, strained

1/2 cup red raspberry preserves (for filling)

White or dark Chocolate Cutouts, page 195, if desired

1. **Frosting:** Put chocolate in a small heatproof bowl. Bring cream to a full boil in a small heavy saucepan. Pour cream over chocolate all at once. Stir with a whisk until chocolate is completely melted and mixture is smooth. Cover and refrigerate 10 minutes.

2. Cream butter in a large bowl until very soft and smooth. Add chocolate mixture in 3 batches, beating constantly until mixture is smooth. Gradually beat in strained preserves.

1. **Assembly:** Use layer that began with a chocolate outer circle for center. Spread preserves on bottom layer. Set center layer on top and spread preserves over it. Top with third cake layer.

2. Using a long metal spatula, spread frosting on side and top of cake. Swirl frosting at top, forming small curves. Or smooth top and decorate with a zig-zag motion using cake decorating comb. If desired, spoon any remaining frosting into a pastry bag fitted with small star tip. Pipe a ring of small rosettes around edge of cake. Decorate side or top with a few Chocolate Cutouts. Refrigerate at least 1 hour before serving. *Frosted cake can be kept, covered, up to 4 days in refrigerator.* Serve at room temperature.

Note: One pastry bag can be used instead of two to make this cake. Pipe white batter first, skipping places for chocolate batter. Fill pastry bag with chocolate batter and pipe it into spaces.

Chocolate Cake with White Chocolate Ganache

This light, delicate cake is frosted with buttery white ganache. For a perfect summer dessert, serve it with fresh strawberries, blueberries or sliced peaches.

Makes 8 servings

Cocoa Genoise, page 46

Creme de Cacao Syrup:

1/4 cup sugar

1/4 cup water

2 tablespoons white creme de cacao

Buttery White Chocolate Ganache:

10 ounces fine-quality white chocolate, very finely chopped

3/4 cup whipping cream

1/2 cup (4 ounces) unsalted butter, cut in pieces

Grated semisweet chocolate, page 191, or Quick Chocolate Curls, page 193 (for garnish)

• Prepare Cocoa Genoise, page 46, Steps 1-7.

1. **Syrup:** Heat sugar and water in a small heavy saucepan over low heat, stirring, until sugar dissolves. Increase heat to medium-high and, without stirring, bring to a boil.

2. Pour into a heatproof bowl; cool completely. Stir in creme de cacao; cover.

1. **Buttery White Chocolate Ganache:** Put chocolate in a heatproof medium bowl. Heat cream in a small heavy saucepan over medium-high heat, stirring with a whisk, until cream comes to a full boil. Pour over chocolate all at once. Stir with whisk until chocolate is completely melted and mixture is smooth. If chocolate does not melt completely, set bowl of mixture above a pan of hot water over low heat and stir gently with whisk until chocolate is completely melted and mixture is smooth.

2. Cool to room temperature, occasionally stirring gently. Refrigerate, stirring occasionally, about 45 minutes, or until cold and beginning to thicken.

3. Whisk mixture briefly until smooth. Cream butter in large bowl, using flat (creaming) beater if available, until very soft and smooth. Add white chocolate mixture in 3 batches, beating constantly at low speed until smooth.

1. **Assembly:** Using a long serrated knife, cut cake in 2 layers.

2. Using a brush, dab bottom layer with creme de cacao syrup. Spread with about 1/3 of ganache.

3. Dab syrup on spongy side of top layer. Turn over and set on bottom layer, crust side up.

4. Using a long metal spatula, spread remaining ganache evenly on side and top of cake; smooth side and top. If desired, swirl frosting on top. Garnish with grated chocolate or Quick Chocolate Curls. Refrigerate at least 1 hour before serving. *Cake can be kept, covered, up to 3 days in refrigerator.* Serve at cool room temperature.

Biarritz Pistachio-Chocolate Cake *Photo on page 38.*

Named for one of France's most popular resort towns, this colorful classic cake features three buttercreams—pistachio, vanilla and chocolate—all made from one basic mixture. The buttercream is relatively easy to make and does not require a sugar thermometer.

Makes about 12 servings

Chocolate-Pistachio Genoise:
3 oz. fine-quality bittersweet chocolate
3 tablespoons unsalted butter
1/2 cup shelled, unsalted, green pistachios (about 2 oz.)
1 cup sugar
3/4 cup plus 2 tablespoons cake flour
1/2 teaspoon baking powder
5 eggs, room temperature

Kirsch Syrup:
3 tablespoons sugar
3 tablespoons water
1 tablespoon plus 2 teaspoons kirsch

Pistachio, Chocolate & Vanilla Buttercreams:
4 eggs, room temperature
1 cup sugar
1-1/2 cups (12 oz.) unsalted butter, slightly softened but still cool
2 teaspoons pure vanilla extract
4 oz. fine-quality bittersweet chocolate
1/2 cup shelled, unsalted, green pistachios (about 2 oz.)

3/4 cup shelled, unsalted, green pistachios (about 3 oz.), finely chopped (for garnish)

1. **Genoise:** Position rack in center of oven and preheat to 350F (175C). Lightly butter a 9-inch springform pan. Line base of pan with parchment or foil; butter paper or foil. Flour side of pan and base, tapping pan to remove excess.
2. Combine chocolate and butter in a double boiler or heatproof medium bowl over hot, not simmering, water over low heat. Leave until melted, stirring occasionally. Stir until smooth. Remove from pan of water; cool mixture to body temperature.
3. Grind 1/2 cup pistachios with 2 tablespoons sugar in a food processor until as fine as possible, scraping occasionally. Transfer to a medium bowl.
4. Sift flour and baking powder over ground pistachios; mix well.
5. Beat eggs briefly in a large bowl. Whisk in remaining 3/4 cup plus 2 tablespoons sugar. Set bowl in a pan of hot water over very low heat. Whisk about 3 minutes or until it is barely lukewarm to touch. Remove from water. Beat mixture at high speed 5 minutes or until completely cool and very thick.
6. Sprinkle about 1/3 of nut mixture over batter; fold in as gently as possible. Repeat with remaining nut mixture in 2 batches. When batter is nearly blended, add 1 cup batter to chocolate mixture; fold until blended. Add chocolate batter to remaining batter; fold gently until blended.
7. Transfer batter to prepared pan; spread evenly. Bake about 40 minutes or until cake shrinks slightly from side of pan and until a cake tester inserted in center of cake comes out clean.
8. Cool in pan on a rack about 10 minutes. Run a metal spatula up and down or a thin-bladed flexible knife carefully around edge of cake. Invert cake onto a rack. If cake remains in pan, release spring to make unmolding easier. Carefully peel off paper or foil; cool cake completely. Crust is crumbly and a little of it will come off.
1. **Syrup:** Heat sugar and water in a small heavy saucepan over low heat, stirring until sugar dissolves. Increase heat to medium-high and, without stirring, bring to a boil. Pour into a heatproof bowl; cool completely.
2. Stir in kirsch; cover.
1. **Buttercreams:** Whisk eggs lightly in a large bowl. Beat in sugar. Set bowl in a pan of hot water over low heat. Using a whisk, beat 6 minutes or until just warm to touch. Remove from pan of water. Using a mixer, beat at high speed about 7 minutes or until completely cool.
2. Cream butter in a large bowl until very soft and smooth. Beat in 1/2 cup egg mixture. Beat in remaining egg mixture in about 7 batches, beating constantly and stopping occasionally to scrape down bowl. Beat in vanilla.
3. Set aside 2/3 cup buttercream in a medium bowl. Melt chocolate in a double boiler or small heatproof bowl over hot, not simmering, water over low heat, stirring occasionally. Stir until smooth. Remove from pan of water; cool to body temperature. Whisk into reserved 2/3 cup buttercream; set aside for decoration.
4. Grind 1/4 cup pistachios in a food processor until fine. Transfer 1 cup Vanilla Buttercream to a medium bowl; stir in ground pistachios. Leave remaining Vanilla Buttercream plain. Chop another 1/4 cup pistachios; set aside for filling.
1. **Assembly:** Using a long serrated knife, cut cake in 2 layers. Set bottom layer on a cardboard round the same diameter as cake or on base of springform pan.
2. Using a brush, dab bottom cake layer with about 2/3 of Kirsch Syrup. Spoon all of Pistachio Buttercream onto layer; spread very carefully with a long metal spatula. Evenly sprinkle with chopped pistachios. Press lightly to stick them to buttercream.
3. Dab syrup very lightly on soft side of top cake layer. Turn over and set on cake, crust-side up. Remove any loose crust from side of cake. Spread Vanilla Buttercream on side and top of cake; smooth side and top.

4. Using a pastry bag and small or medium star tip, pipe Chocolate Buttercream in a ruffle or in rosettes near top edge of cake. Lift cake on base and stick finely chopped pistachios onto its side in a thin border near base. Sprinkle remaining finely chopped pistachios over Vanilla Buttercream on top of cake. Refrigerate 2 hours before serving. *Frosted cake can be kept, covered, up to 3 days in refrigerator.* Serve at room temperature.

Gingered Chocolate-Brazil Nut Layer Cake

Ginger syrup and candied ginger give this moist nutty cake a pleasant zip and complement both the flavor of the Brazil nuts and the creamy chocolate frosting. Instead of the Brazil nut garnish, you can use slices of chocolate-dipped candied ginger, page 182.

Makes 10 to 12 servings

Brazil Nut-Cocoa Genoise:
1/2 cup Brazil nuts (about 2-1/4 oz.)
3/4 cup sugar
1/2 cup cake flour
1/4 cup unsweetened Dutch-process
    cocoa powder
1/2 teaspoon baking powder
4 eggs, room temperature
3 tablespoons unsalted butter,
    melted and cooled

Ginger Syrup:
1/4 cup minced gingerroot
About 1/2 cup water
1/4 cup sugar

Chocolate-Ginger Frosting:
7 oz. semisweet chocolate, chopped
1 tablespoon Ginger Syrup (above)
2 tablespoons water
2 egg yolks, room temperature
1-1/4 cups whipping cream,
    well-chilled

1/4 cup finely chopped crystallized
    ginger
5 lengthwise-cut Brazil nut halves,
    if desired (for garnish)

1. Genoise: Position rack in center of oven and preheat to 350F (175C). Lightly butter an 8-inch springform pan. Line base of pan with parchment paper or foil; butter paper or foil. Flour side of pan and lined base, tapping pan to remove excess.
2. Grind Brazil nuts with 2 tablespoons sugar in a food processor until as fine as possible, scraping inward occasionally. Transfer to a medium bowl.
3. Sift flour, cocoa and baking powder over nut mixture; stir until blended.
4. Beat eggs lightly in a large bowl. Whisk in remaining sugar. Set bowl in a pan of hot water over very low heat. Whisk about 3 minutes or until mixture is barely lukewarm to the touch. Remove from pan of water. Beat mixture at high speed about 5 minutes or until completely cool and very thick.
5. Sprinkle about 1/3 of nut mixture over batter; fold in as gently as possible. Repeat with remaining nut mixture in 2 batches. When batter is nearly blended, gradually pour in cool melted butter while folding. Continue folding lightly but quickly, just until batter is blended.
6. Transfer batter to prepared pan; spread evenly. Bake about 40 to 45 minutes, or until cake shrinks slightly from side of pan and top springs back when lightly pressed.
7. Cool in pan on a rack 5 minutes. Run a thin-bladed flexible knife carefully around edge of cake. Invert cake onto a rack. Carefully peel off paper or foil; cool cake completely. Cake will settle as it cools.
1. Syrup: Combine gingerroot and 1/2 cup water in a small saucepan; bring to a boil. Cover and reduce heat to low. Cook 15 minutes. Strain into a bowl, pressing on gingerroot. Cool completely.
2. Measure gingerroot cooking liquid and add enough water to obtain 1/4 cup. Transfer to a small heavy saucepan; add sugar. Warm over low heat, stirring, until sugar dissolves. Increase heat to medium-high and bring to a boil. Pour into a bowl; cool completely.
1. Frosting: Chill a large bowl and beaters for whipping cream. Combine chocolate, 1 tablespoon Ginger Syrup and 2 tablespoons water in a double boiler or heatproof medium bowl over hot, not simmering, water over low heat. Leave until chocolate is melted, stirring occasionally. Whisk until smooth. Remove from pan of water.
2. Whisk egg yolks, 1 at a time, into chocolate mixture. Set mixture above hot water over low heat; whisk 1 minute. Remove from pan of water. Let stand 15 minutes or until cool but not set; mixture will be very thick.
3. Whip cream in chilled bowl until soft peaks form. Stir about 1/2 cup cream into chocolate mixture. Return mixture to bowl of cream; fold gently until blended.
1. Assembly: Using a long serrated knife, cut cake very carefully in 2 layers. Set one layer on cake plate.
2. Using a brush, dab cake with about 1/2 of syrup. Spread with 1-1/3 cups frosting. Sprinkle evenly with all of crystallized ginger.
3. Dab syrup on spongy side of top layer. Turn over and set on cake, crust-side up. Using a long metal spatula, spread remaining frosting on side and top of cake, spreading it generously on side. Smooth side and top. Set 5 Brazil nut halves in flower shape on center of cake. Refrigerate at least 1 hour before serving. *Frosted cake can be kept, covered, up to 3 days in refrigerator.* Serve at room temperature.

Chocolate Yule Log

The chocolate-flecked Cointreau filling and the rich chocolate frosting of this easy-to-roll genoise cake are made from the same buttercream, which is divided in half. Instead of decorating the log with the traditional Meringue Mushrooms, page 160, you can use white and dark chocolate leaves, page 196, or leave it plain.

Makes 12 servings

Sponge Cake:
6 tablespoons all-purpose flour
1/4 cup cornstarch
4 eggs
3 egg yolks
7 tablespoons sugar
1 teaspoon grated orange zest

Cointreau Syrup:
1/4 cup sugar
1/4 cup water
2 tablespoons Cointreau

Cointreau & Chocolate Buttercreams:
4 egg yolks, room temperature
1/2 cup sugar
1/3 cup water
5 oz. bittersweet or semisweet
   chocolate, chopped
1 cup (8 oz.) unsalted butter,
   slightly softened but still cool
2 tablespoons Cointreau
1 oz. bittersweet or semisweet
   chocolate, finely grated (about
   1/3 cup)

Meringue Mushrooms, page 160, if
   desired

1. Cake: Position rack in center of oven and preheat to 400F (205C). Lightly butter corners of a 17″ x 11″ rimmed baking sheet. Line with foil or parchment paper; butter foil or paper.
2. Sift flour and cornstarch into a medium bowl.
3. Beat eggs and egg yolks briefly in a large bowl. Beat in sugar; continue beating at high speed about 5 minutes or until mixture is very thick. Fold in grated orange zest.
4. Sift about 1/3 of flour mixture over batter; fold in as gently as possible. Repeat with remaining flour mixture in 2 batches.
5. Transfer batter to prepared baking sheet; spread evenly but lightly. Bake about 7 minutes or until cake is just firm and springy to touch and beginning to brown.
6. Transfer cake with foil or paper to a rack. Cool to room temperature. Cover with a towel if not using immediately.
1. Syrup: Heat sugar and water in a small heavy saucepan over low heat, stirring, until sugar dissolves. Increase heat to medium-high and, without stirring, bring to a boil.
2. Pour into a heatproof bowl; cool completely. Stir in Cointreau; cover.
1. Buttercreams: Beat egg yolks in bowl of mixer until blended.
2. Combine sugar and water in a small heavy saucepan. Cook over low heat, stirring gently, until sugar dissolves. Increase heat to medium-high and bring to a boil. Boil without stirring until a candy thermometer registers 238F (115C) or soft-ball stage, about 4 minutes. See page 15 for soft-ball test. Immediately remove from heat.
3. Using a whisk, gradually beat hot syrup in a very thin stream into egg yolks. Immediately beat at high speed of mixer, until completely cool and thick.
4. Melt chopped chocolate in a double boiler or heatproof medium bowl over hot, not simmering, water over low heat, stirring occasionally. Stir until smooth. Remove from pan of water; cool to body temperature. Meanwhile continue with next step.
5. Cream butter in a large bowl until smooth and fluffy. Add egg yolk mixture in 4 batches, beating thoroughly after each addition.
6. Transfer 1 cup buttercream to a medium bowl. Whisk in Cointreau. Gently stir in grated chocolate.
7. Gradually stir melted chocolate into remaining buttercream.
1. Assembly: Using brush, dab Cointreau Syrup generously on cake.
2. Spread Cointreau Buttercream on cake. Roll it up, beginning with a long end, like a jelly roll. Roll carefully but tightly; if not rolled tightly enough, slices will have holes.
3. Frost with Chocolate Buttercream. Make lengthwise lines in frosting with a spatula or fork to resemble bark. Refrigerate at least 1 hour before serving so frosting sets. *Frosted cake can be kept, covered, up to 4 days in refrigerator.*
4. Serve at room temperature. Garnish if desired with a few Meringue Mushrooms. Serve more Meringue Mushrooms separately.

From top: Chocolate-Cashew-Maple Cake, page 47; Biarritz Pistachio-Chocolate Cake, page 36; Two-Tone Chocolate-Raspberry Cake, page 48.

Gâteau Diable (French Devil's Food Cake)

French Devil's Food Cake is "devilishly" rich, with a flourless chocolate-almond cake, a filling and frosting of rum buttercream, and a crisp coating of bittersweet chocolate and almonds.

Makes 10 servings

Flourless Chocolate-Almond Cake:

3 oz. semisweet chocolate, chopped
1/4 cup unsalted butter
3/4 cup whole blanched almonds
   (about 3-1/2 oz.)
1/2 cup sugar
1 egg
8 egg yolks
5 egg whites, room temperature
1/4 teaspoon cream of tartar

Rum Buttercream:

3 egg yolks, room temperature
6 tablespoons sugar
1/4 cup water
3/4 cup (6 oz.) unsalted butter,
   slightly softened but still cool
2 tablespoons plus 2 teaspoons rum

Chocolate-Almond Coating:

1/3 cup chopped slivered almonds
6 oz. fine-quality bittersweet
   chocolate, preferably *couverture*,
   chopped

1. Cake: Position rack in center of oven and preheat to 325F (165C). Lightly butter an 8-inch springform pan. Line base of pan with parchment paper or foil; butter paper or foil. Flour side of pan and lined base, tapping pan to remove excess.

2. Combine chocolate and butter in a double boiler or heatproof medium bowl over hot, not simmering, water over low heat. Leave until melted, stirring occasionally. Stir until smooth. Remove from pan of water. Cool slightly.

3. Grind almonds with 1/4 cup sugar in a food processor until as fine as possible, scraping inward occasionally.

4. Using flat (creaming) beater of mixer, if available, beat 1 egg very lightly in a large bowl. Add the ground almond mixture and 2 tablespoons of the sugar; beat until well-blended and pale. Add egg yolks in 2 batches, beating until blended after each addition. Switch to regular beaters and beat at high speed 5 minutes, or until mixture is pale and very thick. Fold in chocolate mixture.

5. In a large dry bowl, whip egg whites with cream of tartar using dry beaters at medium speed until soft peaks form. Gradually beat in remaining 2 tablespoons sugar; continue whipping at high speed until whites are stiff and shiny but not dry.

6. Gently fold about 1/3 of whites into chocolate mixture until nearly incorporated. Fold in remaining whites in 2 batches. Continue folding lightly but quickly, just until batter is blended.

7. Transfer batter to prepared pan. Bake about 40 to 45 minutes or until a cake tester inserted in center of cake comes out clean.

8. Cool in pan on a rack 5 minutes. Invert cake onto a rack. Carefully peel off paper or foil; cool cake completely.

1. Buttercream: Beat egg yolks in bowl of mixer until blended.

2. Combine sugar and water in a small heavy saucepan. Cook over low heat, stirring gently, until sugar dissolves. Increase heat to medium-high and bring to a boil. Boil without stirring until mixture reaches soft-ball stage, about 4 minutes. To test, remove pan from heat. Take a little of hot syrup on a teaspoon and dip spoon into a cup of iced water, keeping spoon level. With your hands in water, remove syrup from spoon. CAUTION: Do not touch syrup unless your hands are in iced water. If syrup is ready, it will form a soft ball. If syrup dissolves into water, continue cooking briefly and test again; if syrup is overcooked and forms firm ball, you can still use it.

3. Using a whisk, gradually beat hot syrup into egg yolks in a very thin stream. Immediately beat at high speed of mixer until completely cool and thick.

4. Cream butter in a large bowl until smooth and fluffy. Add egg yolk mixture in 4 batches, beating thoroughly after each addition. Gradually beat in rum.

5. Using a long serrated knife, cut cake in 2 layers. Set bottom layer on a cardboard round the same diameter as cake, if available, then on a plate. Spread about 3/4 cup buttercream over layer.

6. Set second layer on top. Using a long metal spatula, spread remaining buttercream on side and top; smooth side and top. Buttercream will make a very thin frosting. Refrigerate at least 2 hours before continuing. *Frosted cake can be kept, covered with an overturned bowl, up to 3 days in refrigerator.*

1. Coating: Preheat oven to 350F (175C). Toast almonds in a shallow baking pan, stirring a few times, 4 minutes or until lightly browned. Transfer to a plate; cool completely.

2. Use metal spatula to help remove cake from plate. Set cake on a rack resting on a rimmed tray.

3. Melt chocolate in a double boiler or heatproof medium bowl over hot, not simmering, water over low heat, stirring very often with a rubber spatula. Stir until smooth. Remove from pan of water.

4. Cool chocolate, stirring often, until it reaches 88F (30C) on an instant-read thermometer, or slightly cooler than body temperature. If it is too hot, it melts buttercream.

5. Stir toasted almonds into chocolate. Pour about 1/2 of coating over top center of cake and spread gently to sides. Spread remaining coating gently over sides and, if necessary, use it to touch up top. Spread very gently so coating does not mix with buttercream; it sets quickly in contact with cold buttercream.

6. Transfer cake carefully to a platter using 2 wide utensils such as pancake turners. Refrigerate about 10 minutes to set coating. *Frosted cake can be kept, covered with an overturned bowl, up to 1 day in refrigerator.* Serve at cool room temperature.

TIPS

○ *Chocolate can be added to cakes in different forms. The manner in which it is added affects not only the flavor, but also the color and texture of the cake. Unsweetened cocoa gives the lightest texture and is often the best choice for sponge cakes. Unsweetened cocoa and melted chocolate give a uniform chocolate color to cakes but melted chocolate makes cakes richer because of its higher fat content. This makes it the favorite for fudge cakes and many butter cakes.*

○ *Chopped or grated chocolate enables sponge cakes to keep a relatively light texture and gives them a different appearance. The chocolate color does not spread throughout the cake, but rather the cake is dotted with chocolate. Chocolate chips or chunks are good additions to butter cakes, which have a dense batter that prevents the chunks from sinking.*

1/Leaving waxed paper attached, wrap chocolate band around cake so chocolate adheres to buttercream. Chocolate band should meet at both ends but not overlap. Refrigerate until chocolate sets.

2/Gently peel off waxed paper from chocolate band. Garnish cake with candied violets.

Chocolate Angel Layer Cake

Filled and frosted with pure white chocolate meringue buttercream, the moist, dark chocolate angel food cake is then wrapped in a ribbon of crisp bittersweet chocolate around its side for a dramatic presentation.

Makes about 10 servings

Chocolate Angel Food Cake:
2/3 cup powdered sugar, sifted
3 tablespoons unsweetened Dutch-process cocoa powder
1/2 cup cake flour
6 egg whites
1/2 teaspoon cream of tartar
1/2 cup granulated sugar

White Chocolate Meringue Buttercream:
3 oz. fine-quality white chocolate, chopped
2/3 cup sugar
1/3 cup water
2 egg whites
3/4 cup (6 oz.) unsalted butter, cut in pieces, slightly softened but still cool

1. **Cake:** Position rack in center of oven and preheat to 350F (175C). Have ready an 8-inch springform cake pan; do not butter it.
2. Sift powdered sugar, cocoa and flour into a medium bowl.
3. In a large dry bowl, beat egg whites with cream of tartar using dry beaters at medium speed until soft peaks form. Gradually beat in 1/4 cup granulated sugar; continue beating at high speed until whites are stiff and shiny but not dry.
4. Sprinkle remaining 1/4 cup granulated sugar over egg white mixture; fold in gently but quickly. Sift about 1/4 of cocoa mixture over egg white mixture; fold in. Repeat with remaining cocoa mixture in 3 batches.
5. Transfer batter to pan; spread evenly. Bake about 30 minutes or until a cake tester inserted in center of cake comes out clean.
6. Cool in pan on a rack 5 minutes or until cake settles to level of pan. Turn over on rack but leave in pan. Leave upside down until completely cooled; cake will come away from pan. If necessary, free cake with the aid of a metal spatula. Remove pan.
1. **Buttercream:** Melt white chocolate in a double boiler or heatproof medium bowl over hot, not simmering, water over low heat. Whisk until smooth. Remove from pan of water. Cool to body temperature.
2. Combine sugar and water in a small heavy saucepan. Cook over low heat, stirring gently, until sugar dissolves. Increase heat to medium-high and bring to a boil. Boil without stirring 3 minutes. Meanwhile, beat whites in a large heatproof bowl until stiff but not dry. Continue boiling syrup until a candy thermometer registers 238F (115C) or soft-ball stage, about 4 minutes. See page 15 for a soft-ball test. Immediately remove from heat.
3. With mixer at high speed gradually beat hot syrup into center of whites. Continue beating until meringue is cool and shiny.

Garnish:
4 oz. fine-quality bittersweet
    chocolate, chopped, if desired
    (for wrapping)
Candied violets

4. Cream butter in a large bowl until very soft and smooth. Beat in white chocolate in 2 batches, beating well after each addition. Beat in meringue in 3 batches.

5. Using a long serrated knife, cut cake gently, slowly and carefully in 2 layers. Set bottom layer on a flat tray; cake will seem very moist inside.

6. Spread about 1 cup buttercream on bottom cake layer. Set second layer on top. Using a long metal spatula, spread remaining buttercream evenly on side and top of cake; smooth side and top. Refrigerate 30 minutes. *Frosted cake can be kept, covered, up to 3 days in refrigerator.*

1. Garnish: Cut a 28″ x 6″ piece of waxed paper; fold in half lengthwise. Set it on a tray. Melt chocolate in a double boiler or heatproof medium bowl over hot, not simmering, water over low heat, stirring occasionally. Stir until smooth. Remove from pan of water; cool slightly.

2. Spread a very even layer of chocolate on waxed paper, covering paper entirely except for 1 inch on each short end. Be certain not to leave any holes. Let stand until chocolate is slightly firm, about 10 minutes. On a hot day, refrigerate briefly. Do not let chocolate set or it will be brittle. Leaving waxed paper attached, wrap chocolate band around cake so chocolate adheres to buttercream. Chocolate band should meet at both ends but not overlap. Chocolate band will come a bit higher than top of cake. Refrigerate until chocolate sets. Carefully peel off waxed paper from chocolate.

3. Set candied violets on cake for garnish.

TIPS

○ For those cakes that call for a springform pan you can also use a cake pan of the same size with a removable, push-up base. In a pan of this type, the side of the pan is easy to remove and the base slides down when the cake is turned over onto a rack. Use a metal spatula to release the cake from the base of this type of pan or from a springform pan.

○ Unfrosted cakes should always be wrapped well for keeping; they keep a few days at cool room temperature or they can be frozen. Once frosted, they should be refrigerated.

○ Most chocolate cakes keep quite well because the chocolate helps to keep them moist. Those with nuts keep even better because the nuts fulfill the same function.

Marjolaine

This elegant multi-layered cake, a classic from France, is now a favorite dessert in fine American restaurants as well. The small rich cake is composed of layers of hazelnut-almond cake with three fillings: chocolate, praline and vanilla, all of which are made from one basic buttercream mixture.

Makes 8 to 10 servings

Hazelnut-Almond Cake:
1 cup hazelnuts (about 4-1/4 oz.)
3/4 cup whole blanched almonds (about 3-1/2 oz.)
3/4 cup sugar
2 tablespoons all-purpose flour
5 egg whites, room temperature
1/4 teaspoon cream of tartar

Praline, Chocolate & Vanilla Buttercreams:
Hazelnut Praline, page 86
4 egg yolks, room temperature
1/2 cup sugar
1/3 cup water
4 oz. bittersweet chocolate, chopped
1 cup (8 oz.) unsalted butter, slightly softened but still cool
1 teaspoon pure vanilla extract

Powdered sugar (for garnish)

1. Cake: Position rack in center of oven and preheat to 350F (175C). Put hazelnuts in 1 shallow baking pan and almonds in another. Toast hazelnuts and remove skins, page 201; cool nuts completely. Toast almonds 10 minutes. Transfer to a plate; cool nuts completely.

2. Increase oven temperature to 375F (190C). Lightly butter corners of a 17" x 11" rimmed baking sheet. Line base with foil or parchment paper; butter foil or paper.

3. Combine hazelnuts, almonds and 1/2 cup sugar in a food processor. Grind until mixture is as fine as possible, scraping inward occasionally. Transfer to a medium bowl. Sift flour over nuts; stir until blended.

4. In a large dry bowl, beat egg whites with cream of tartar using dry beaters at medium speed until soft peaks form. Gradually beat in remaining 1/4 cup sugar; continue beating at high speed until whites are stiff and shiny but not dry.

5. As quickly as possible, gently fold in nut mixture in 3 batches until thoroughly blended.

6. Transfer batter to prepared baking sheet; spread evenly but lightly. Bake about 10 minutes or until very light brown on top, golden brown on edges and pulling away from edges.

7. Transfer cake with its paper or foil to a rack. Cool to room temperature.

1. Buttercreams: Prepare Hazelnut Praline.

2. Beat egg yolks in bowl of mixer until blended.

3. Combine sugar and water in a small heavy saucepan. Cook over low heat, stirring gently, until sugar dissolves. Increase heat to medium-high and bring to a boil. Boil without stirring until a candy thermometer registers 238F (115C) or soft-ball stage, about 4 minutes. See page 15 for soft-ball test. Immediately remove from heat.

4. Using a whisk, gradually beat hot syrup in a very thin stream into egg yolks. Immediately beat at high speed of mixer until completely cool and thick.

5. Melt chocolate in a double boiler or heatproof medium bowl over hot, not simmering, water over low heat, stirring occasionally. Stir until smooth. Remove from pan of water; cool to body temperature. Meanwhile, continue with next step.

6. Cream butter in a large bowl until smooth and fluffy. Add egg yolk mixture in 4 batches, beating thoroughly after each addition. Beat in vanilla.

7. Transfer 1/2 cup buttercream to a small bowl. Whisk in chocolate.

8. Transfer another 1/2 cup buttercream to a second small bowl. Whisk in praline.

1. Assembly: Turn out cake onto a cutting board. Cut in 4 equal pieces crosswise; they will be about 4 inches wide.

2. Put 1 cake layer on a long platter. Spread all of Vanilla Buttercream evenly over it. Set another layer on top; spread with all of Chocolate Buttercream. Set another layer on top; spread with all of Praline Buttercream. Set remaining layer on top. Smooth sides very gently with a metal spatula so each buttercream forms a smooth distinct layer. Refrigerate 30 minutes. *Filled cake can be kept, covered, up to 3 days in refrigerator.*

3. Cut 6 strips of waxed paper 1/2-inch wide. A short time before serving, set paper strips diagonally on top of cake so they are parallel to each other and spaced at equal distances. Shake or sift powdered sugar generously over cake. Carefully lift paper strips straight up, leaving a design on cake. Wipe platter with damp paper towels to remove excess powdered sugar. When serving, rinse knife after each cut.

Hazelnut-Truffle Cake

This light hazelnut sponge cake, layered with rich chocolate frosting, is inspired by a gâteau I learned during a course in cake- and dessert-making at Le Nôtre's school for professional chefs, located near Paris. The frosting of buttery ganache tastes like the inside of a truffle.

Makes 8 to 10 servings

Hazelnut Cake:
1-1/2 cups hazelnuts (about 6-1/2 oz.)
3/4 cup plus 3 tablespoons sugar
3 tablespoons plus 2 teaspoons all-purpose flour
5 eggs, separated, room temperature
1/4 teaspoon cream of tartar
3 tablespoons unsalted butter, melted and cooled

Chocolate-Truffle Frosting:
8 oz. semisweet chocolate, finely chopped
2/3 cup whipping cream
1/2 cup (4 oz.) unsalted butter, slightly softened but still cool

6 to 8 hazelnuts (for garnish)

1. Cake: Position rack in center of oven and preheat to 350F (175C). Toast hazelnuts and remove skins, page 201; cool nuts completely.

2. Lightly butter 2 round 9-inch layer pans. Line base of each pan with a round of parchment paper or foil; butter paper or foil. Flour sides of pans and lined bases, tapping pan to remove excess.

3. Grind nuts with 1/4 cup sugar in a food processor until as fine as possible, scraping inward occasionally. Transfer to a medium bowl.

4. Sift flour onto nuts; mix well.

5. Beat egg yolks lightly in a large bowl. Beat in 1/2 cup sugar; continue beating at high speed about 5 minutes or until mixture is pale and very thick.

6. In a large dry bowl, beat egg whites with cream of tartar using dry beaters at medium speed until soft peaks form. Gradually beat in remaining 3 tablespoons sugar; continue beating at high speed until whites are stiff and shiny but not dry.

7. Sprinkle about 1/3 of hazelnut mixture over egg yolk mixture; fold gently until nearly incorporated. Gently fold in 1/3 of whites. Repeat with remaining hazelnut mixture and whites in 2 batches. When batter is nearly blended, gradually pour in cool melted butter while folding. Continue folding lightly but quickly, just until batter is blended.

8. Divide batter between prepared pans; spread evenly. Bake about 16 to 18 minutes or until a cake tester inserted in center of cakes comes out clean. Run a thin-bladed flexible knife around side of each cake. Invert cakes onto racks. Carefully peel off paper or foil; cool cakes completely.

1. Frosting: Put chocolate in a heatproof medium bowl. Bring cream to a full boil in a small heavy saucepan. Pour cream over chocolate all at once. Stir with a whisk until chocolate is completely melted and mixture is smooth. Cool to room temperature.

2. Whip mixture at high speed for about 3 minutes or until it thickens and becomes paler in color.

3. Cream butter in a large bowl until very soft and smooth. Add chocolate mixture in 3 batches, beating constantly until mixture is smooth.

4. Spread about 1/3 of frosting on 1 cake layer. Set second layer on top. Using a long metal spatula, spread remaining frosting on top and side of cake. If desired, swirl frosting on top. Garnish with 6 to 8 hazelnuts. Refrigerate 2 hours before serving. *Frosted cake can be kept, covered, up to 2 days in refrigerator.* Serve at room temperature.

Classic Chocolate Gâteau

Photo of variation on cover.

The cocoa genoise used here is the basis for many fine European chocolate cakes. It is moistened with rum syrup, filled and frosted with a smooth, luscious chocolate buttercream and garnished with toasted almonds—a classic combination that remains one of the most popular.

Makes 8 servings

Cocoa Genoise:
3/4 cup cake flour
1/4 cup unsweetened cocoa powder, preferably Dutch-process
1/2 teaspoon baking powder
4 eggs, room temperature
3/4 cup sugar
1/4 cup unsalted butter, melted and cooled

1-1/4 cups slivered almonds, chopped with a knife into small cubes (for coating)

Rum Syrup:
1/4 cup sugar
1/4 cup water
2 tablespoons rum

Classic Chocolate Buttercream:
4 egg yolks, room temperature
1/2 cup sugar
1/3 cup water
8 oz. fine-quality bittersweet or semisweet chocolate, chopped
1 cup (8 oz.) unsalted butter, slightly softened but still cool

1. Genoise: Position rack in center of oven and preheat to 350F (175C). Lightly butter an 8-inch springform pan. Line base of pan with parchment paper or foil; butter paper or foil. Flour side of pan and lined base, tapping pan to remove excess.

2. Sift flour cocoa and baking powder into a medium bowl.

3. Beat eggs briefly in a large heatproof bowl. Whisk in sugar. Set bowl in a pan of hot water over very low heat. Whisk about 3 minutes or until mixture is barely lukewarm to touch. Remove from pan of water. Beat mixture at high speed about 5 minutes or until completely cool and very thick.

4. Sift about 1/3 of flour mixture over batter; fold in as gently as possible. Repeat with remaining flour mixture in 2 batches. When batter is nearly blended, gradually pour in cool melted butter while folding. Continue folding lightly but quickly, just until batter is blended.

5. Transfer batter to prepared pan; spread evenly. Bake about 40 minutes or until cake shrinks slightly from side of pan and top springs back when lightly pressed. Cool in pan on a rack about 10 minutes.

6. Toast almonds in a shallow baking pan in oven, stirring often, about 5 minutes or until lightly browned. Transfer to a bowl; cool completely.

7. Run a thin-bladed flexible knife carefully around top edge of cake. Then run a metal spatula around side. Invert cake onto rack. Carefully peel off paper or foil; cool cake completely.

1. Syrup: Heat sugar and water in a small heavy saucepan over low heat, stirring, until sugar dissolves. Increase heat to medium-high and, without stirring, bring to a boil.

2. Pour into a heatproof bowl; cool completely. Stir in rum; cover.

1. Buttercream: Beat egg yolks in bowl of mixer until blended.

2. Combine sugar and water in a small heavy saucepan. Cook over low heat, stirring gently, until sugar dissolves. Increase heat to medium-high and bring to a boil. Boil without stirring until a candy thermometer registers 238F (115C) or soft-ball stage, about 4 minutes. See page 15 for soft-ball test. Immediately remove from heat.

3. Using a whisk, gradually beat hot syrup in a very thin stream into egg yolks. Immediately beat at high speed of mixer until completely cool and thick.

4. Melt chocolate in a double boiler or heatproof medium bowl over hot, not simmering, water over low heat, stirring occasionally. Stir until smooth. Remove from pan of water; cool to body temperature. Meanwhile, continue with next step.

5. Cream butter in a large bowl until smooth and fluffy. Add egg yolk mixture in 4 batches, beating thoroughly after each addition. Whisk in cool chocolate.

1. Assembly: Set aside 1/3 cup buttercream for garnish. Using a long serrated knife, cut cake in 3 layers. Set bottom layer on a cardboard round the same diameter as cake, or on base of springform pan.

2. Using a brush, dab layer with about 1/3 of Rum Syrup. Spread with a thin layer of buttercream, using a generous 1/2 cup buttercream.

3. Set second layer on top. Dab with syrup. Spread another thin layer of buttercream.

4. Dab syrup on spongy side of top layer. Turn over and set on cake, crust-side up.

5. Using a long metal spatula, spread remaining buttercream evenly on side and top of cake; smooth side and top. If desired, swirl buttercream on top. Lift cake on base and stick toasted almonds by handfuls onto its side.

6. Using a pastry bag and medium star tip, pipe small rosettes of reserved buttercream at top edge of cake.

7. Refrigerate 2 hours before serving. *Frosted cake can be kept, covered, up to 3 days in refrigerator.* Serve at room temperature.

Variation
Chocolate Gâteau with Raspberries & Chocolate Leaves: In syrup substitute clear raspberry brandy for rum, if desired. Omit almonds. Prepare about 10 Dark Chocolate Leaves and 10 Milk Chocolate Leaves, page 196. Garnish cake and platter with leaves and about 1 to 2 cups fresh raspberries.

Chocolate-Cashew-Maple Cake   *Photo on page 38.*

Decorated with a feathery chocolate design, this cake is composed of moist thin layers of dark chocolate cake, subtly flavored with cashews and topped with golden maple frosting.

Makes 10 to 12 servings

Chocolate-Cashew Cake:
5 oz. semisweet chocolate, chopped
1-1/4 cups unsalted cashew nuts
   (about 6 oz.)
2/3 cup sugar
1/4 cup all-purpose flour
1/2 teaspoon baking powder
2/3 cup unsalted butter, slightly
   softened
5 eggs, separated, room
   temperature
1/4 teaspoon cream of tartar

Maple Frosting:
1/2 cup pure maple syrup
3 egg yolks, room temperature
3/4 cup (6 oz.) unsalted butter,
   slightly softened but still cool

Garnish:
1 oz. semisweet chocolate, chopped

1. Cake: Preheat oven to 350F (175C). Lightly butter 2 round 9-inch layer pans. Line base of each pan with a round of parchment paper or foil; butter paper or foil. Flour sides of pans and lined bases, tapping pan to remove excess.
2. Melt 5 ounces chocolate in a double boiler or heatproof medium bowl over hot, not simmering, water over low heat, stirring occasionally. Stir until smooth. Remove from pan of water; cool to body temperature.
3. Grind nuts with 3 tablespoons sugar in a food processor until as fine as possible, scraping inward occasionally. Transfer to a medium bowl.
4. Sift flour and baking powder onto nut mixture; stir until blended.
5. Cream butter in a large bowl. Add 5 tablespoons sugar; beat until smooth and fluffy. Beat in egg yolks, 1 at a time.
6. In a large dry bowl, beat egg whites with cream of tartar using dry beaters at medium speed until soft peaks form. Gradually beat in remaining 2-2/3 tablespoons sugar; continue beating at high speed until whites are stiff and shiny but not dry.
7. Stir melted chocolate into egg yolk mixture.
8. Gently fold about 1/4 of whites into chocolate mixture until nearly incorporated. Sprinkle about 1/4 of nut mixture over chocolate mixture; fold in gently. Repeat with remaining whites and nut mixture, each in 3 batches. Continue folding lightly but quickly, just until batter is blended.
9. Divide batter between prepared pans; spread evenly. Bake about 16 to 20 minutes or until a cake tester inserted in center of cakes comes out clean.
10. Cool in pans on racks 5 minutes; cakes will settle during cooling. Run a thin-bladed flexible knife around sides of cakes several times. Invert cakes onto racks. Carefully peel off paper or foil; cool cakes completely. *Cake can be prepared 2 days ahead and kept wrapped in refrigerator.*
1. Frosting: Prepare a parchment piping cone, page 192, or have ready a small pastry bag with very fine plain tip.
2. Bring maple syrup to a boil in a small saucepan.
3. Using a hand whisk, beat egg yolks in a large bowl until blended. Gradually pour syrup onto yolks, whisking constantly. Whip at high speed of mixer until completely cool and very thick.
4. Cream butter in a large bowl until smooth and fluffy. Beat in maple mixture in 5 batches, beating thoroughly after each addition.
5. Set bottom cake layer on a platter. Spread a very thin layer of frosting over it. Set second layer on top. Set aside 2 tablespoons frosting for garnish in a small bowl. Using a long metal spatula, spread remaining frosting on side and top; smooth side and top.
1. Garnish: Melt 1 ounce chocolate in a very small heatproof bowl over hot, not simmering, water over low heat, stirring occasionally. Stir until smooth. Remove from water; cool slightly. Whisk into reserved 2 tablespoons frosting.
2. Spoon chocolate mixture into parchment piping cone or pastry bag. Beginning in center of cake, pipe chocolate mixture in a spiral design. Using dull side of a thin-bladed knife, draw knife in a line from center of cake to edge. Then draw knife in a line inward from edge to center. Draw knife 8 or 10 times in this way, so that lines formed on chocolate design are spaced equally apart; they will make a feathery design on cake. *Frosted cake can be kept, covered, up to 2 days in refrigerator.* Serve at room temperature.

Two-Tone Chocolate-Raspberry Cake *Photo on page 38.*

Raspberry-topped pink rosettes of buttercream on a background of chocolate make a dramatic, beautiful garnish on this cake. It is made from light, bittersweet chocolate sponge cake layers sandwiched with raspberry filling and topped with chocolate-raspberry frosting. Both filling and frosting are made from the same basic buttercream mixture.

Makes 10 to 12 servings

Bittersweet Chocolate Sponge Cake:
3/4 cup cake flour
1/3 cup unsweetened Dutch-process cocoa powder
6 eggs, separated, room temperature
3/4 cup plus 1 tablespoon sugar
1/2 teaspoon cream of tartar
1 oz. bittersweet chocolate, coarsely grated (about 1/2 cup)

Raspberry-Brandy Syrup:
3 tablespoons sugar
3 tablespoons water
2 tablespoons clear raspberry brandy

Raspberry & Chocolate-Raspberry Buttercreams:
1-2/3 cups fresh raspberries (about 8 oz.)
4 egg yolks, room temperature
1/2 cup plus 2 tablespoons sugar
1/3 cup water
1 cup (8 oz.) unsalted butter, slightly softened but still cool
4 oz. bittersweet chocolate, chopped

Fresh raspberries (10 to 20)
Raspberry Sauce, page 131, if desired

1. Cake: Position rack in center of oven and preheat to 350F (175C). Lightly butter a 9-inch springform pan. Line base of pan with parchment or foil; butter lightly. Flour side of pan and base, tapping pan to remove excess.

2. Sift flour and cocoa into a medium bowl.

3. Beat egg yolks lightly in a large bowl. Beat in 1/2 cup sugar; continue beating at high speed about 5 minutes or until mixture is pale and very thick.

4. In a large dry bowl, beat egg whites with cream of tartar using dry beaters at medium speed until soft peaks form. Gradually beat in remaining 5 tablespoons sugar and continue beating at high speed until whites are stiff and shiny but not dry.

5. Gently fold about 1/4 of whites into egg yolk mixture until nearly incorporated. Sprinkle grated chocolate over mixture; fold in. Sprinkle about 1/3 of cocoa mixture over egg yolk mixture; fold in gently. Fold in another 1/4 of whites. Continue folding in alternate batches of cocoa mixture and whites, folding lightly but quickly, just until batter is blended.

6. Transfer batter to prepared pan; spread evenly. Bake about 35 minutes or until a cake tester inserted in center of cake comes out clean.

7. Cool in pan on a rack 3 minutes. Run a thin-bladed flexible knife around side of pan. Invert cake onto rack. Carefully peel off paper or foil; cool cake completely.

1. Syrup: Heat sugar and water in a very small heavy saucepan over low heat, stirring, until sugar dissolves. Increase heat to medium-high and, without stirring, bring to a boil.

2. Pour into a heatproof bowl; cool completely. Stir in raspberry brandy; cover.

1. Buttercreams: Puree 1-2/3 cups raspberries in a food processor or blender until very smooth. Strain puree into a medium bowl, pressing on pulp in strainer. Use a rubber spatula to scrape mixture from underside of strainer. Measure 1/2 cup puree.

2. Beat egg yolks in bowl of mixer until combined.

3. Combine sugar and water in a small heavy saucepan. Cook over low heat, stirring gently, until sugar dissolves. Increase heat to medium-high and bring to a boil. Boil without stirring until a candy thermometer registers 238F (115C) or soft-ball stage, about 4 minutes. See page 15 for a soft-ball test. Immediately remove from heat.

4. Using a whisk, gradually beat hot syrup in a very thin stream into egg yolks. Immediately beat at high speed of mixer until completely cool and thick.

5. Cream butter in a large bowl until smooth and fluffy. Add egg yolk mixture in 4 batches, beating thoroughly after each addition. Gradually beat in reserved 1/2 cup raspberry puree.

6. Set aside 1 cup Raspberry Buttercream for pink filling and 1/3 cup buttercream for garnish. Put buttercream for garnish into pastry bag fitted with medium star tip.

7. Melt chocolate in a double boiler or heatproof medium bowl over hot, not simmering, water over low heat, stirring occasionally. Stir until smooth. Remove from pan of water; cool to body temperature. Whisk into remaining buttercream.

1. **Assembly:** Using a serrated knife, cut cake in 2 layers. Set one layer on cake plate.
2. Using brush, dab cake with Raspberry-Brandy Syrup. Spread with reserved Raspberry Buttercream. Dab syrup on soft side of top layer. Turn over and set on cake, crust-side up.
3. Using a long metal spatula, spread Chocolate Buttercream evenly over side and top of cake; smooth side and top. Pipe 8 to 10 rosettes of reserved Raspberry Buttercream for garnish. If desired, pipe a small ring of rosettes near center of cake. Refrigerate at least 1 hour. *Frosted cake can be kept, covered, up to 3 days in refrigerator.*
4. For serving, bring cake to room temperature. Just before serving, top each rosette at edge of cake with a raspberry. Fill inner ring of rosettes with a few raspberries. Serve with Raspberry Sauce, if desired.

Chocolate-Pecan Torte

This is one of the easiest tortes to make. The cocoa-flavored cake layers contain a generous amount of ground pecans, which provide moistness and texture. The chocolate and cinnamon frosting combines the best features of buttercream and powdered sugar icing and is rich yet quick to prepare.

Makes 12 servings

Pecan-Cocoa Cake:
3-1/2 cups pecans (12 oz.)
1-1/2 cups sugar
3 tablespoons all-purpose flour
2 tablespoons unsweetened cocoa powder
1 teaspoon ground cinnamon
1 teaspoon baking powder
6 eggs, separated, room temperature
1/4 teaspoon cream of tartar

Chocolate-Cinnamon Frosting:
5 oz. semisweet chocolate, chopped
1 cup (8 oz.) unsalted butter, slightly softened but still cool
1 cup powdered sugar
1 tablespoon unsweetened cocoa powder
1/2 teaspoon ground cinnamon
2 eggs, room temperature

12 pecan halves (for garnish)

1. **Cake:** Position rack in center of oven and preheat to 350F (175C). Lightly butter 2 round 9-inch layer pans. Line base of each pan with a round of parchment paper or foil; butter paper or foil. Flour sides of pans and lined bases, tapping pan to remove excess.
2. Grind 1-3/4 cups pecans with 1/4 cup sugar in a food processor until as fine as possible, scraping inward occasionally. Transfer to a medium bowl. Repeat with remaining 1-3/4 cups pecans and another 1/4 cup sugar.
3. Sift flour, cocoa, cinnamon and baking powder onto pecan mixture; stir until thoroughly blended.
4. Beat egg yolks briefly in a large bowl. Beat in 1/2 cup sugar; continue beating at high speed about 5 minutes or until mixture is pale and very thick.
5. In a large dry bowl, beat egg whites with cream of tartar using dry beaters at medium speed until soft peaks form. Gradually beat in remaining 1/2 cup sugar; continue beating at high speed until whites are stiff but not dry.
6. Sprinkle about 1/3 of pecan mixture over egg yolk mixture; fold gently until nearly incorporated. Gently fold in 1/3 of whites. Repeat with remaining pecan mixture and whites in 2 batches. Continue folding lightly but quickly, just until batter is blended.
7. Transfer to prepared pans; spread evenly. Bake about 30 minutes or until a cake tester inserted in center of cakes comes out clean.
8. Without removing cakes, set rack on each pan. Turn over and leave cakes upside down 10 minutes with pans still on cakes. Turn back over. Run a thin-bladed flexible knife around side of each cake. Invert cakes onto racks. Carefully peel off paper or foil; cool cakes completely. *Cakes can be kept, covered, up to 2 days in refrigerator.*
1. **Frosting:** Melt chocolate in a double boiler or heatproof medium bowl over hot, not simmering, water over low heat, stirring occasionally. Stir until smooth. Remove from pan of water; cool to body temperature.
2. Cream butter in a large bowl until very soft and smooth. Sift powdered sugar, cocoa and cinnamon into a medium bowl. Add to butter mixture; beat until soft and smooth. Beat in eggs, 1 at a time, at high speed. Beat in melted chocolate.
3. Spread about 1/3 of frosting on 1 cake layer. Set second layer on top. Carefully trim top layer if necessary, using a serrated knife, so cake is even. Using a long metal spatula, spread remaining frosting evenly on side and top of cake; smooth side and top. Garnish top with a circle of 12 pecans near edge of cake. Refrigerate at least 1 hour before serving. *Frosted cake can be kept, covered, up to 2 days in refrigerator.* Serve at room temperature.

1/Using a sharp knife, cut cake crosswise in 2 equal pieces, about 8 inches wide.

2/With the aid of a metal spatula, set chocolate-glazed squares side by side on top of cake, touching each other. Refrigerate cake at least 30 minutes.

Rigo Jancsi *Photo on pages 8-9.*

During a recent European chocolate research trip, my husband and I revisited some of our favorite dessert cities in Italy, Austria, Germany, Switzerland and France. One of the highlights was a Hungarian cake that we had in Salzburg, Austria. It was a chocolaty, light-textured cake, with thick layers of two fillings and a dark chocolate glaze. This is a recreation of that cake.

Makes 20 small servings

Rich Chocolate Sponge Cake:
3 oz. bittersweet chocolate, chopped
2 tablespoons unsalted butter
1 tablespoon water
4 eggs, separated, room temperature
1/2 cup sugar
1/4 teaspoon cream of tartar
6 tablespoons all-purpose flour, sifted

1/3 cup apricot preserves (for spreading)

Shiny Chocolate Glaze:
2 oz. bittersweet chocolate, chopped
3 tablespoons unsweetened Dutch-process cocoa powder
5 tablespoons sugar
1/4 cup water

1. **Cake:** Position rack in center of oven and preheat to 375F (190C). Lightly butter corners of a 17″ x 11″ rimmed baking sheet. Line base with foil or parchment paper; butter foil or paper.
2. Combine chocolate, butter and water in a double boiler or heatproof medium bowl over hot, not simmering, water over low heat. Leave until melted, stirring occasionally. Stir until smooth. Remove from pan of water; cool mixture to body temperature.
3. Beat egg yolks lightly in a large bowl. Beat in 6 tablespoons sugar; continue beating at high speed about 5 minutes or until mixture is pale and very thick. Quickly stir chocolate mixture into egg yolk mixture.
4. In a large dry bowl, beat egg whites with cream of tartar using dry beaters at medium speed until soft peaks form. Gradually beat in remaining 2 tablespoons sugar; continue beating at high speed until whites are stiff and shiny but not dry.
5. Gently fold about 1/3 of whites into chocolate mixture until nearly incorporated. Sprinkle about 1/2 of flour over chocolate mixture; fold in gently. Fold in another 1/3 of whites, then remaining flour, followed by remaining whites. Continue folding lightly but quickly, just until batter is blended.
6. Transfer batter to prepared baking sheet; spread evenly. Layer will be very thin. Bake about 10 minutes or just until firm.
7. Carefully transfer cake with paper or foil to a rack. Cool to room temperature. Slide a cutting board under cake with cake still on paper or foil. Using a sharp knife, cut cake crosswise in 2 equal pieces, about 8 inches wide. Carefully lift 1 piece from paper or foil onto rack. Set second layer on platter.
8. Heat apricot preserves in a small saucepan over low heat until hot but not boiling. Strain into a small bowl, pressing on pieces.

Chocolate & Vanilla Cream Fillings:

4 oz. bittersweet chocolate, chopped

1 pint whipping cream (2 cups), well-chilled

3 tablespoons sugar

2 teaspoons pure vanilla extract

9. Using a pastry brush, brush preserves lightly over layer of cake on platter. Let stand 30 minutes to dry slightly.

10. Set rack with second cake piece above a tray.

1. Glaze: Melt chocolate in a double boiler or heatproof medium bowl over hot, not simmering, water over low heat, stirring occasionally. Stir until smooth. Remove from pan of water.

2. Mix cocoa, sugar and water in a bowl. Add to melted chocolate; mix well. Set above hot water. Heat about 5 minutes or until sugar dissolves. Cool to 94F to 98F (34C to 35C) on an instant-read thermometer or approximately body temperature.

3. Pour chocolate glaze over cake layer on rack. Spread very lightly until smooth and evenly covered; touch it as little as possible so glaze will be smooth. Refrigerate about 30 minutes or until set.

1. Fillings: Chill a large bowl and beaters for whipping cream. Melt chocolate in a small heatproof bowl set over a pan of hot water over low heat. Stir until smooth. Turn off heat but leave chocolate above water.

2. Whip cream in chilled bowl with sugar and vanilla until stiff. Remove 1 cup whipped cream and set aside for top of cake.

3. Remove chocolate from above water; cool 30 seconds. Quickly stir about 2/3 cup whipped cream into chocolate. Quickly fold mixture into remaining whipped cream in bowl until smooth. Fold quickly so chocolate does not harden upon contact with cold whipped cream.

1. Assembly: Spread chocolate whipped cream smoothly in an even layer over apricot-glazed cake layer.

2. Spoon reserved whipped cream in small dabs over top. Using a small spatula, smooth top lightly. Refrigerate about 30 minutes to firm cream.

3. Cut chocolate-glazed cake layer into about 2-inch squares by cutting it in 4ths lengthwise and in 5ths crosswise; use a large knife and cut with heel of knife. With the aid of a metal spatula, set squares side by side on top of cake, touching each other. Refrigerate cake at least 30 minutes. *Filled cake can be kept, covered with a cake cover or large bowl, up to 3 days in refrigerator.*

4. To serve, follow edges of top squares of cake and cut carefully through filling and bottom layer. Use a large knife to cut each row and a smaller knife to cut into individual squares. Rinse knife between each cut.

Black Forest Cherry Torte

A classic favorite throughout Europe, this version of the cake is more in the Austrian and French style than in the original German tradition. It combines a dark chocolate-colored, light-textured cake, kirsch and plenty of whipped cream. Tart cherries are customary but sweet ones are used here because they are easier to find. If fresh cherries are not in season, use frozen or canned.

Makes 10 servings

Poached Cherries:
14 oz. fresh sweet cherries
Zest of 1 lemon
1/2 cup sugar
1 vanilla bean, if desired
2 cups water
2 teaspoons fresh strained lemon
   juice

Rich Cocoa Sponge Cake:
2/3 cup all-purpose flour
1/3 cup unsweetened Dutch-process
   cocoa powder
1/2 teaspoon baking powder
5 eggs, separated, room
   temperature
3/4 cup plus 2 tablespoons sugar
1/4 teaspoon cream of tartar
5 tablespoons butter, melted and
   cooled

3 tablespoons kirsch (for
   moistening)

Kirsch Whipped Cream:
1 pint whipping cream (2 cups),
   well-chilled
2 tablespoons plus 1 teaspoon sugar
4-1/2 teaspoons kirsch

Garnish:
Quick Chocolate Curls, page 193
12 long Chocolate Scrolls, page 195,
   if desired

1. **Cherries:** Remove cherry stems. Pit cherries with cherry pitter or point of vegetable peeler, reserving any juice.
2. Using a vegetable peeler, peel wide strips of yellow part only of lemon peel, without white pith. Combine sugar, vanilla bean, if desired, lemon strips and water in a medium saucepan. Heat over low heat, stirring, until sugar dissolves. Increase heat to high and bring to a boil without stirring. Add lemon juice and cherries with their juice. Cover and cook over low heat about 8 minutes or until tender.
3. Cool to room temperature. Cover and refrigerate at least 2 hours or overnight.
1. **Cake:** Preheat oven to 350F (175C). Butter an 8-inch springform pan. Line base of pan with parchment paper or foil; butter paper or foil. Flour side of pan and lined base, tapping pan to remove excess.
2. Sift flour, cocoa and baking powder into a medium bowl.
3. Beat egg yolks lightly in large bowl. Beat in 3/4 cup sugar; continue beating at high speed about 5 minutes or until mixture is pale and very thick.
4. In a large dry bowl, beat egg whites with cream of tartar using dry beaters at medium speed until soft peaks form. Gradually beat in remaining 2 tablespoons sugar; continue beating at high speed until whites are stiff and shiny but not dry.
5. Gently fold about 1/3 of whites into egg yolk mixture until nearly incorporated. Sprinkle about 1/2 of cocoa mixture over egg yolk mixture; fold in gently. Fold in another 1/3 of whites, then remaining cocoa mixture, followed by remaining whites. When batter is nearly blended, gradually pour in cool melted butter while folding. Continue folding lightly but quickly, just until batter is blended.
6. Transfer batter to prepared pan; spread evenly. Bake about 35 minutes or until a cake tester inserted in center of cake comes out clean.
7. Cool in pan on a rack 5 minutes. Run a thin-bladed flexible knife carefully around side of pan. Invert cake onto rack. Carefully remove base of pan and peel off foil or parchment. Cool cake completely. *Cake can be kept, wrapped, up to 1 day in refrigerator.*
8. Remove vanilla bean, if used, from cherry poaching syrup. Measure 1/3 cup syrup. Add 3 tablespoons kirsch; cover. Thoroughly drain 1-3/4 cups cherries on paper towels. Set aside 10 attractive cherries for top of cake.
9. Using a long serrated knife, cut cake in 3 layers.
1. **Whipped cream:** Chill a large bowl and beaters for whipping cream. Whip cream with sugar in chilled bowl until stiff.
2. Add kirsch; beat at low speed until just blended.
1. **Assembly:** Set bottom cake layer on a serving plate. Brush with kirsch syrup. Spread with about 1 cup whipped cream. Set about 3/4 cup cherries on top, arranging them evenly over cream. Press them gently into cream. Set second cake layer on top. Brush with kirsch syrup. Spread with 1 cup whipped cream. Scatter another 3/4 cup cherries over cream. Brush spongy side of third layer with syrup. Turn over and set on cake crust-side up.
2. Reserve about 1/3 cup whipped cream for garnish. Spread remaining cream on side and top of cake.
1. **Garnish:** Use a long metal spatula or pie server to stick Quick Chocolate Curls on side of cake a few at a time. Set Chocolate Scrolls in center of cake.
2. Using a pastry bag and large star tip, pipe reserved whipped cream in 10 rosettes on top edge of cake. Refrigerate until ready to serve. *Frosted cake can be kept, covered, up to 6 hours in refrigerator.*
3. Up to 2 hours before serving, thoroughly drain reserved cherries on paper towels. Change paper towels; drain again. Set each cherry on a rosette of whipped cream.

Viennese Chocolate-Nut Torte

The Viennese love chocolate tortes with nuts, especially hazelnuts and almonds. This one is made of two cakes—hazelnut and chocolate—made from one batter. The filling and frosting is known in Vienna as Parisian cream, and is a creamy version of French chocolate ganache.

Makes about 10 servings

Chocolate & Hazelnut Cake Layers:
1 cup hazelnuts (about 4-1/4 oz.)
2 oz. semisweet chocolate, chopped
2 tablespoons water
6 eggs, room temperature
2 egg yolks, room temperature
1 cup sugar
3/4 cup cake flour, sifted
6 tablespoons unsalted butter, melted and cooled

Cognac Syrup:
3 tablespoons sugar
3 tablespoons water
2 tablespoons cognac

Parisian Cream:
8 oz. fine-quality semisweet chocolate, chopped
1/2 pint whipping cream (1 cup)

Garnish:
4 Chocolate Scrolls, page 195, if desired
1 whole hazelnut
1 tablespoon chopped hazelnuts

1. **Cake:** Position rack in center of oven and preheat to 350F (175C). Toast hazelnuts and remove skins, page 201; cool nuts completely.
2. Lightly butter 3 round 8-inch layer pans. Line base of each pan with a round of parchment paper or foil; butter paper or foil. Flour sides of pans and lined bases, tapping pans to remove excess.
3. Combine chocolate and water in a small heatproof bowl over hot, not simmering, water over low heat. Leave until melted, stirring occasionally. Stir until smooth. Remove from pan of water. Cool slightly.
4. Grind nuts as fine as possible, in food processor, scraping occasionally.
5. Whisk eggs and egg yolks in a large heatproof bowl. Whisk in sugar. Set bowl in a pan of hot water over very low heat. Whisk about 5 minutes or until mixture is barely lukewarm. Remove from pan of water. Beat mixture at high speed about 5 minutes or until completely cool and very thick.
6. Sift about 1/3 of flour over egg mixture; gently fold in. Repeat with remaining flour in 2 batches. When batter is nearly blended, gradually pour in cool melted butter while folding. Continue folding lightly but quickly, just until batter is blended.
7. In a medium bowl, set aside 3 cups batter for flavoring with chocolate. Mix about 1/2 cup of this batter into chocolate. Add chocolate mixture to bowl and fold until blended. Transfer to 1 of layer pans; spread evenly.
8. Fold ground hazelnuts into remaining batter. Divide between 2 remaining layer pans and spread evenly.
9. If possible, bake all cakes in center of oven. Bake cakes about 18 to 20 minutes or until a cake tester inserted in center of cakes comes out clean. If baking on 2 racks, switch positions after 12 minutes.
10. Run a knife around each cake. Invert cakes onto racks. Carefully peel off paper or foil; cool cakes completely.
1. **Syrup:** Heat sugar and water in a very small pan over low heat, stirring until sugar dissolves. Increase heat to medium-high and bring to a boil.
2. Pour into bowl and cool completely. Stir in cognac; cover.
1. **Cream:** Put chocolate in a heatproof medium bowl. Bring cream to a full boil in a heavy medium saucepan. Pour over chocolate all at once. Stir with a whisk until chocolate is completely melted and mixture is smooth. Refrigerate 1 hour or until cold.
2. Whip mixture at high speed 3 minutes or until it forms soft peaks.
1. **Assembly:** Set 1 hazelnut cake layer on a platter. Brush syrup on cake. Spread about 2/3 cup Parisian Cream on layer. Set chocolate layer on top; brush with syrup. Spread about 2/3 cup Parisian Cream on chocolate layer. Brush syrup on remaining cake layer. Turn over and set on cake, moistened side down. Using a long metal spatula, spread remaining frosting evenly on side and top of cake. If Parisian Cream begins to stiffen while you are assembling cake, beat a few seconds before spreading on cake.
2. Garnish with 4 Chocolate Scrolls in an **X.** Set 1 hazelnut in center. Put chopped hazelnuts in 2 corners formed by **X,** across from each other. *Frosted cake can be kept, covered, up to 4 days in refrigerator.* Serve at room temperature.

How to Make Sachertorte

1/Pour glaze over center of cake. Spread with 1 motion of spatula so glaze flows down side. Do not touch top any more. Quickly spread glaze smooth on side.

2/If desired, pipe a generous amount of whipped cream alongside each cake slice.

Sachertorte

After my husband and I visited Vienna and tasted this cake for the first time ten years went by before we managed to visit again. During that period we ate desserts in many of Europe's best restaurants and pastry shops and we wondered whether Vienna's desserts would taste as good the second time around. They certainly did! Sachertorte, the most famous culinary creation of Austria, was made prominent during a lengthy trial in which two Viennese institutions, the Sacher Hotel and the celebrated pastry shop Demel's, claimed to own the original, authentic recipe. It is a not-too-sweet chocolate cake with apricot glaze and a sweet chocolate icing and is served with generous amounts of whipped cream. In Austria the cake can now be seen in the windows of most of the konditorei, or pastry shops, and is made into large and small round cakes, and even into rectangular petits fours.

Makes 8 servings

Bittersweet Chocolate Cake:
4-1/2 oz. fine quality bittersweet
   chocolate, chopped
1/2 cup (4 oz.) unsalted butter,
   slightly softened
2/3 cup sugar
5 eggs, separated, room
   temperature
1 teaspoon pure vanilla extract
2/3 cup cake flour, sifted

1/3 cup plus 1 tablespoon apricot
   preserves (for brushing)

1. Cake: Position rack in center of oven and preheat to 350F (175C). Lightly butter a 9-inch springform pan. Line base of pan with parchment paper or foil and butter paper or foil. Flour side of pan and lined base, tapping pan to remove excess.

2. Melt chocolate in a double boiler or heatproof medium bowl over hot, not simmering, water over low heat, stirring occasionally. Stir until smooth. Remove from pan of water; cool to body temperature.

3. Cream butter in a large bowl. Add 1/2 cup of sugar; beat until smooth and fluffy. Beat in egg yolks, 1 at a time. Beat 3 minutes until fluffy. Stir in chocolate and vanilla. Transfer to another large bowl.

4. In a large dry bowl, beat egg whites using dry beaters at medium speed until soft peaks form. Gradually beat in remaining 2-2/3 tablespoons sugar; continue beating at high speed until whites are stiff and shiny but not dry.

5. Gently fold about 1/3 of whites into chocolate mixture until nearly incorporated. Sprinkle about 1/3 of flour over chocolate mixture; fold in gently. Repeat with remaining whites and flour, each in 2 batches. Continue folding lightly but quickly, just until batter is blended.

6. Transfer batter to prepared pan and spread evenly. Bake about 35 to 40 minutes or until a cake tester inserted in center of cake comes out clean.

Sweet Chocolate Glaze:
1-1/4 cups sugar
1/2 cup water
6 oz. fine-quality bittersweet
chocolate, chopped
1/2 teaspoon vegetable oil

1-1/2 cups whipping cream,
well-chilled (for accompaniment)

7. Cool in pan on a rack 5 minutes. Run a thin-bladed flexible knife around edge of cake. Invert cake onto a rack. Carefully peel off paper or foil; cool cake completely.

8. Turn cake smoothest side up. Set on a cardboard round or base of spring-form pan the same diameter as cake, then on a rack.

9. Heat apricot preserves in a small saucepan over low heat until hot but not boiling. Strain into a small bowl, pressing on apricot pieces.

10. Using a pastry brush, brush preserves over side and top of cake. Let stand 2 hours to dry.

1. Glaze: Combine sugar and water in a heavy medium saucepan. Heat over low heat, stirring, until sugar dissolves. Bring to a boil. Pour into a heatproof bowl; cool syrup to body temperature.

2. When syrup is cool, melt chocolate in a double boiler or heatproof medium bowl over hot, not simmering, water over low heat, stirring occasionally. Stir until smooth. Remove from pan of water; cool slightly. Using a whisk, gently stir chocolate into syrup in 3 batches.

3. Set container of chocolate-syrup mixture above hot water over low heat. Heat, stirring, 5 minutes. Stir in oil. Remove from pan of water and cool, stirring gently with spatula, until it is just warm (105 to 110F, 40 to 45C).

4. Pour glaze over center of cake. Spread with 1 motion of spatula so glaze flows down side. Do not touch top any more. Quickly spread glaze smooth on side.

5. Transfer cake carefully with wide spatulas to platter. Cake can be served immediately. *Frosted cake can be kept, covered with a cake cover or large bowl, 1 day at room temperature.*

6. Chill a bowl and beaters for whipping cream. Whip cream in chilled bowl to soft peaks. Serve a generous spoonful of whipped cream alongside each cake slice; *or* whip cream until stiff and pipe next to each cake slice using a pastry bag and medium star tip.

TIPS

○ *Organization is very important: Before beating the yolks or whites, preheat the oven, prepare the cake pan and get out spatulas and any specified tools so there will be no need to look for anything after the batter is ready.*

○ *Melt butter in a small saucepan over very low heat. Butter burns easily.*

○ *If possible, beat egg yolks in one bowl and egg whites in another, so the yolks do not lose air because of the need to transfer them to another bowl.*

○ *Beating egg whites should always be the last step in the preparation of cake batter. Beaten egg whites cannot wait. Fold them into the other ingredients as soon as they are beaten, and put the cake in the oven immediately.*

Chocolate Symphony

Photo on pages 8-9.

Fine pâtisseries in France proudly display cakes of this type, made of a soft creamy mousse layered with delicately crisp chocolate-nut meringues. I learned how to make them from my friend Denis Ruffel, one of the most talented pastry chefs in France and head pastry chef of the excellent Parisian pâtisserie Millet. Three chocolate preparations make this harmonious dessert: a chocolate dacquoise cake, a chocolate Grand Marnier Bavarian cream and a garnish of chocolate-ganache rosettes.

Makes 10 to 12 servings

Chocolate Dacquoise:

Scant 1 cup whole blanched
   almonds (about 5 oz.)
3/4 cup plus 3 tablespoons sugar
1/4 cup unsweetened Dutch-process
   cocoa powder
2 tablespoons plus 1-1/2 teaspoons
   all-purpose flour
5 egg whites, room temperature
1/4 teaspoon cream of tartar

Chocolate Bavarian Cream:

5 oz. fine-quality bittersweet
   chocolate, coarsely chopped
1 (1/4-oz.) envelope plus 3/4
   teaspoon unflavored gelatin
5 tablespoons water
1-1/4 cups milk
5 egg yolks, room temperature
7 tablespoons sugar
5 tablespoons Grand Marnier
1-1/2 cups whipping cream,
   well-chilled

Ganache:

7-1/2 oz. semisweet chocolate,
   finely chopped
3/4 cup whipping cream

1. Dacquoise: Preheat oven to 300F (150C). Butter corners of 2 baking sheets and line bases with parchment or foil. Butter and lightly flour paper or foil, tapping baking sheet to remove excess flour. Using inside of an 8-inch springform pan rim as guide, trace a circle onto each baking sheet.

2. Have ready a rubber spatula for folding and a pastry bag fitted with a 1/2-inch plain tip.

3. Grind almonds with 1/2 cup sugar in a food processor until as fine as possible, scraping inward occasionally. Transfer to a medium bowl.

4. Sift cocoa and flour into a small bowl.

5. In a large dry bowl, beat egg whites with cream of tartar using dry beaters at medium speed until soft peaks form. Increase speed to high. Gradually beat in remaining 7 tablespoons sugar; continue beating at high speed until whites are stiff and shiny. Gently fold in cocoa mixture in 2 batches as quickly as possible until thoroughly blended. Gently fold in nut mixture in 2 batches.

6. Immediately spoon mixture into pastry bag. Beginning at center of a circle marked on baking sheet, pipe mixture in a tight spiral until circle is completely covered. Repeat with second circle. If any mixture remains, pipe it in small mounds onto same baking sheets used for circles.

7. Bake in center of oven 45 minutes or until dacquoise rounds are firm to touch. If baking on 2 shelves in oven, switch their positions halfway through baking time.

8. Gently release layers from paper or foil, using a large metal spatula. Gently peel off any remaining paper or foil if necessary. Transfer layers to a rack; cool completely. *Layers can be kept up to 5 days in an airtight container in dry weather.* Save small mounds for accompanying ice cream.

1. Bavarian: Melt chocolate in a double boiler or heatproof medium bowl over hot, not simmering, water over low heat, stirring occasionally. Meanwhile, follow next 4 steps.

2. Sprinkle gelatin over 5 tablespoons water in a small cup. Let stand while preparing custard.

3. Bring milk to a boil in a small heavy saucepan.

4. Whisk egg yolks lightly in a large heatproof bowl. Add sugar; whisk until thick and smooth. Gradually whisk in hot milk. Return mixture to saucepan, whisking. Cook over medium-low heat, stirring mixture and scraping bottom of pan constantly with a wooden spoon, until mixture thickens slightly and reaches 165F to 170F (75C) on an instant-read thermometer; begin checking after 5 minutes. To check whether it is thick enough without a thermometer, remove mixture from heat. Dip a metal spoon in mixture and draw your finger across back of spoon. Your finger should leave a clear path in mixture that clings to spoon. If it does not, continue cooking another 30 seconds and check again. Do not overcook mixture or it will curdle.

5. Remove from heat and immediately add softened gelatin, whisking until it is completely dissolved. Pour into a large bowl; stir about 30 seconds to cool.

6. Remove chocolate from pan of water. Stir until smooth. Using a whisk, stir custard mixture, about 1/2 cup at a time, into melted chocolate.

7. Return mixture to large bowl. Cool to room temperature, stirring occasionally. Gradually stir in Grand Marnier.

8. Refrigerate chocolate mixture about 20 minutes, stirring often, or chill mixture by setting bowl in a larger bowl of iced water about 10 minutes, stirring very often, or until mixture is cold and beginning to thicken but is not set. Meanwhile, chill a large bowl and beaters for whipping cream.

9. Whip cream in chilled bowl until nearly stiff. Gently fold cream into chocolate mixture, blending thoroughly.

10. Put bottom cake layer in a 9-inch springform pan. Pour 3 cups Bavarian cream over cake. Tap pan on work surface to remove bubbles. Freeze 10 minutes, leaving remaining mixture at room temperature.

11. Set top cake layer in place. Pour remaining Bavarian cream over it; spread evenly. Refrigerate 12 hours or overnight; cover when top sets. Run spatula around cake. Carefully release spring and remove side of pan. *Cake can be kept, covered, up to 2 days in refrigerator.*

1. Ganache: Put chocolate in a heatproof medium bowl. Bring cream to a full boil in a small heavy saucepan. Pour over chocolate all at once. Stir with a whisk until chocolate is completely melted and mixture is smooth.

2. Cool to room temperature. Refrigerate about 15 minutes, stirring often, or until thick enough to pipe but not set. If ganache becomes too stiff to pipe, set bowl of mixture above a saucepan of hot water over low heat. Let ganache soften, stirring occasionally, until smooth and soft enough to be piped.

3. Using a pastry bag and medium star tip, pipe rosettes of ganache on top of cake in lines radiating out from center like the spokes of a wheel. Pipe a ruffle of ganache around base of cake. Chill 30 minutes or until set. When serving, use a heavy knife and be sure to cut through bottom cake layer.

TIPS

○ *Use a heavy knife to chop crystallized ginger; it is too sticky to be chopped in a food processor.*

○ *A Bundt pan is sometimes called a German cake pan.*

○ *On very warm days, keep milk chocolate pieces in the refrigerator.*

○ *Use a sharp heavy knife to cut chocolate in pieces. Do not worry if some of chocolate breaks in smaller pieces; use them also.*

○ *To avoid sticking, butter fluted pans generously, especially the ridges and tube, because you cannot run a knife around the edge of the cake to help turn it out.*

○ *Hazelnuts are sometimes labeled filberts.*

○ *Do not cover chocolate-dipped nuts or fruits in the refrigerator because moisture condenses on the chocolate.*

Striped Chocolate Mousse Cake

A soft, rich, chocolate-bourbon mousse is encased here in a frame of vanilla sponge cake and strawberry jam stripes. The result is a pretty cake with a certain resemblance to a charlotte.

Makes 8 to 10 servings

Sponge Cake:
5 egg yolks
3/4 cup sugar
1 teaspoon pure vanilla extract
4 egg whites, room temperature
1/4 teaspoon cream of tartar
2/3 cup cake flour, sifted

Bourbon Syrup:
3 tablespoons sugar
3 tablespoons water
1 tablespoon plus 2 teaspoons
  bourbon

1/2 cup strawberry preserves (for
  spreading)

Chocolate-Bourbon Mousse:
8 oz. semisweet chocolate, coarsely
  chopped
1/4 cup unsalted butter, cut in 4
  pieces, room temperature
3 tablespoons bourbon
4 eggs, separated, room
  temperature
1 tablespoon sugar
1/3 cup whipping cream,
  well-chilled

2/3 cup whipping cream,
  well-chilled (for garnish)

1. **Cake:** Position rack in center of oven and preheat to 400F (205C). Lightly butter corners of a 17" x 11" rimmed baking sheet. Line base with foil or parchment paper; butter foil or paper. Butter a round 8-inch layer pan.
2. Beat egg yolks lightly in a large bowl. Beat in 1/2 cup sugar and beat at high speed about 5 minutes or until mixture is pale and very thick. Beat in vanilla.
3. In a large dry bowl, beat egg whites with cream of tartar using dry beaters at medium speed until soft peaks form. Gradually beat in remaining 1/4 cup sugar; beat at high speed until whites are stiff and shiny but not dry.
4. Gently fold about 1/3 of whites into egg yolk mixture until nearly incorporated. Sprinkle about 1/2 of flour over egg yolk mixture; fold in gently. Fold in another 1/3 of whites, then remaining flour, followed by remaining whites. Continue folding lightly but quickly, just until batter is blended.
5. Add enough batter to layer pan to fill it 1/3 full. Transfer remaining batter to prepared baking sheet; spread evenly but lightly. Layer will be very thin. Transfer both cakes to oven, if possible in center; if there is no room, put round cake on lower rack. Bake about 7 minutes or until cake on baking sheet is just firm, springy to the touch and beginning to brown. Remove it from oven. Transfer layer pan to center oven rack. Bake about 2 minutes longer or just until it springs back when lightly pressed.
6. Lift cake from baking sheet with paper or foil. Carefully transfer to a rack. Cool to room temperature. Cover with a towel if not using immediately. Invert round cake onto a rack.
1. **Syrup:** Heat sugar and water in a small saucepan over low heat, stirring until sugar dissolves. Increase heat to medium-high and bring to a boil.
2. Pour into a heatproof bowl; cool completely. Stir in bourbon; cover.
1. **Assembly:** Put cake, still on paper or foil, on a board. Carefully peel paper or foil from sides of cake. Using a sharp knife, cut cake crosswise in 6 strips, each about 2-1/2 inches wide. After each cut, sprinkle knife with powdered sugar to prevent it from sticking to cake. Reserve scraps.
2. Carefully remove cake strips from paper or foil. Spread 5 cake strips with a thin layer of preserves. Stack strips on top of each other. Set remaining cake strip on top. Refrigerate 1 hour. Carefully cut pile of cake crosswise in slices, about 1/2 inch thick.
3. Trim round cake layer until its diameter is 6 inches. Reserve scraps.
4. Lightly oil side of an 8-inch springform pan. Put round cake layer in base of springform. Brush it thoroughly with Bourbon Syrup.
5. Arrange cake slices standing up against side of springform pan with cake and jam forming striped pattern against side of springform. Add small pieces of cake scraps to fill in any holes between cake center and side.
1. **Mousse:** Chill a small bowl and beaters for whipping cream. Melt chocolate in a double boiler over hot, not simmering, water, stirring occasionally. Remove from pan of water; stir until smooth.
2. Add butter pieces and 2 tablespoons bourbon; whisk until smooth. Whisk in remaining bourbon. Add egg yolks, 1 at a time, whisking vigorously after each addition.
3. In a dry medium bowl, beat egg whites using dry beaters at medium speed until soft peaks form. Gradually beat in sugar; continue beating at high speed until whites are stiff and shiny but not dry.
4. Using a whisk, quickly fold 1/4 of whites into chocolate mixture. Gently fold in remaining whites.

5. Whip 1/3 cup cream in chilled bowl until nearly stiff. Fold into chocolate mixture. Refrigerate 10 minutes.

6. Spoon 1-3/4 cups mousse into cake-lined pan. Add a layer of cake scraps; there is no need to make it a tight layer. Brush cake layer lightly with Bourbon Syrup, without letting much syrup drip on mousse. Spoon remaining mousse on top.

7. Refrigerate about 8 hours or until set. *Cake can be kept, covered, up to 2 days in refrigerator.*

1. To serve: Gently release spring and remove side of springform pan to unmold.

2. Chill a medium bowl and beaters for whipping cream. Whip cream in chilled bowl until stiff.

3. Using a pastry bag and large star tip, pipe a ruffle of whipped cream at top edge of dessert, resting partly on top of cake strips to cover any uneven edges.

Chocolate Swiss Roll with Berries & Cream

This festive cake is ideal for summer—it is rich but light, chocolaty, quick to prepare and full of berries. Do not worry if it cracks a little during rolling; the raspberry-brandy whipped cream and fruit garnish will cover the entire cake.

Makes 8 to 10 servings

Chocolate Sponge Cake:
3 oz. semisweet chocolate, chopped
2 tablespoons unsalted butter
1 tablespoon water
6 tablespoons all-purpose flour
3 tablespoons cornstarch
6 egg yolks
1/2 cup sugar
4 egg whites, room temperature
1/4 teaspoon cream of tartar

Berry & Cream Filling:
1-1/4 cups crosswise slices of
  strawberries
2-1/2 cups whipping cream,
  well-chilled
3 tablespoons plus 1 teaspoon sugar
4-1/2 teaspoons clear raspberry
  brandy
3/4 cup raspberries
3/4 cup blackberries

Garnish:
A few small whole strawberries
A few blackberries
A few raspberries
A few small Chocolate Cutouts,
  such as crescents, page 195, if
  desired

1. Cake: Position rack in center of oven and preheat to 375F (190C). Lightly butter corners of a 17" x 11" rimmed baking sheet. Line base and sides with foil or parchment paper. If necessary, use 2 overlapping pieces of foil so sides are lined completely. Butter foil or paper.

2. Combine chocolate, butter and water in a double boiler or heatproof medium bowl over hot, not simmering, water over low heat. Leave until melted, stirring occasionally. Stir until smooth. Remove from pan of water; cool mixture to body temperature.

3. Sift flour and cornstarch into a medium bowl.

4. Beat egg yolks lightly in large bowl. Beat in 6 tablespoons sugar; continue beating at high speed about 5 minutes or until mixture is pale and very thick. Fold chocolate mixture quickly into yolk mixture.

5. In a large dry bowl, beat egg whites with cream of tartar using dry beaters at medium speed until soft peaks form. Beat in remaining 2 tablespoons sugar; beat at high speed until whites are stiff but not dry.

6. Gently fold about 1/3 of whites into chocolate mixture until nearly incorporated. Sprinkle about 1/2 of flour mixture over chocolate mixture; fold in gently. Fold in another 1/3 of whites, then remaining flour mixture, followed by remaining whites. Continue folding lightly but quickly, just until blended.

7. Transfer batter to prepared baking sheet; spread evenly but lightly. Bake about 6 minutes or until cake is just firm and springs slightly back from edges. Cake will be very thin.

8. Transfer cake with foil or paper to rack. Cool to room temperature.

1. Filling: Chill a large bowl and beaters for whipping cream. Halve any large slices of strawberries.

2. Whip cream with sugar in chilled bowl until stiff. Add raspberry brandy; beat at low speed until just blended. Reserve 3 cups cream for filling in a medium bowl; fold in berries.

1. Assembly: Move cake, still on its foil or paper, to a large board or tray. Spread gently with filling, using a metal spatula. Avoid squashing berries.

2. With the aid of the foil or paper, gently roll up cake, beginning at long side. With the aid of the foil or paper, turn cake over onto platter. Gently turn over again so seam side is down. Spread cake with remaining cream. Refrigerate at least 30 minutes before serving. *Completed cake can be kept up to 8 hours in refrigerator.*

• **Garnish:** Decorate with a row of berries alternating with small Chocolate Cutouts. Cut with a serrated knife.

Zuccotto

This hemispherical-shaped dessert is made by lining a bowl with sponge cake, then adding layers of chocolate cream and chocolate chip whipped cream with candied fruit. In Italy Zuccotto is decorated with powdered sugar and cocoa but here whipped cream and cocoa are used.

Makes 10 servings

Sponge Cake:
6 tablespoons all-purpose flour
7 tablespoons potato starch
4 eggs, separated, room
   temperature
1/2 cup sugar
1/2 teaspoon pure vanilla extract
1/4 teaspoon cream of tartar

Double Chocolate Cream Filling:
1/2 cup hazelnuts
1 pint whipping cream (2 cups),
   well-chilled
1/4 cup sugar
1/4 cup diced candied fruit, finely
   chopped
1/3 cup mini, semisweet, real
   chocolate pieces
3 oz. semisweet chocolate, chopped

3 tablespoons brandy (for
   moistening)
4 teaspoons water (for moistening)

3/4 cup whipping cream,
   well-chilled (for frosting)
About 2 teaspoons unsweetened
   cocoa powder, preferably
   Dutch-process (for sprinkling)

1. **Cake:** Position rack in center of oven and preheat to 400F (205C). Lightly butter corners of a 17″ x 11″ rimmed baking sheet. Line base with foil or parchment paper; butter foil or paper.
2. Sift flour and potato starch into a medium bowl.
3. Beat egg yolks briefly in a large bowl. Beat in 1/4 cup sugar; continue beating at high speed 5 minutes or until mixture is pale and very thick. Beat in vanilla.
4. In a large dry bowl, beat egg whites with cream of tartar using dry beaters at medium speed until soft peaks form. Gradually beat in remaining 1/4 cup sugar; continue beating at high speed until whites are stiff but not dry.
5. Sprinkle about 1/3 of flour mixture over egg yolk mixture; fold gently until nearly incorporated. Gently fold in about 1/3 of whites. Repeat with remaining flour and whites, each in 2 batches, adding each batch when previous one is nearly blended in. Continue folding lightly but quickly, just until blended.
6. Transfer batter to prepared baking sheet and spread evenly but lightly. Bake about 6 minutes or until cake is just firm and springy to touch; its color will remain pale.
7. Transfer cake with foil or paper to a rack. Cool to room temperature. Cover with towel if not using immediately.

1. **Filling and Assembly:** Reduce oven temperature to 350F (175C). Toast hazelnuts and remove skins, page 201; cool nuts completely. Chop in small pieces.
2. Chill a large bowl and beaters for whipping cream. Cut an 18″ x 12″ sheet of waxed paper. Cut it in half lengthwise. Fold each piece in half lengthwise. Line a 6-cup smooth glass bowl with the 2 folded strips of waxed paper so that they meet in an **X** on bottom of bowl.
3. Turn cake over onto another rack or tray. Carefully peel off paper or foil. Turn over again onto a board or tray.
4. Cut 3 crosswise strips of cake, about 3-1/4 inches wide. Use 1 strip to line center of bowl. Using other 2 strips, line bowl completely with 1 layer of cake, cutting them as necessary. Fill in any holes with small pieces of cake. Be sure cake reaches all the way to rim of bowl. Reserve remaining cake.
5. Whip cream in chilled bowl until soft peaks form. Beat in sugar; whip until stiff. Fold in hazelnuts, candied fruit and mini chocolate pieces. Set aside 2-1/2 cups cream mixture for flavoring with chocolate.
6. Melt chocolate in a double boiler or small heatproof bowl over hot, not simmering, water over low heat, stirring occasionally. Stir until smooth. Remove chocolate from pan of water; cool 30 seconds.
7. Quickly stir about 1/2 cup reserved cream mixture into chocolate until blended. Return to reserved 2 cups cream mixture; fold quickly until blended.
8. Mix brandy with water in a small bowl. Brush brandy on cake layer lining large bowl.
9. Pour chocolate mixture into cake-lined bowl. Top gently with white mixture. Cut remaining cake to fit top of bowl. Set it in place; brush with remaining brandy mixture. Cover and refrigerate at least 10 hours. *Cake can be kept, covered, up to 2 days in refrigerator.*

1. **To serve:** Chill a medium or large bowl and beaters for whipping cream. Cut 4 strips of waxed paper 1-1/2 inches wide and about 12 inches long. Fold each in half lengthwise. Lightly butter 1 side of each strip.
2. Whip cream in chilled bowl until it is very stiff.
3. Unmold cake onto a platter; remove paper. Spread whipped cream over cake. Set strips of paper on cake, buttered-side up, so each is draped across cake and all cross in center.
4. Using a small sieve, sift cocoa onto cake to cover areas of cake without strips of paper. Lifting top strip first, lift each strip straight up; it will leave a design. Carefully smooth cream with metal spatula if necessary. *Cake can be kept, covered with a large overturned bowl, up to 4 hours in refrigerator.* Serve cold.

White Chocolate Mousse Cake With Dark Chocolate Chips

Layers of a tender chocolate cake are filled with a white chocolate mousse dotted with dark chocolate chips. A chocolate glaze on top and a ruffle of whipped cream complete this delight.

Makes about 12 servings

Moist Chocolate Cake:
4 oz. semisweet chocolate
1-1/2 cups cake flour
1-1/2 teaspoons baking powder
1/2 cup plus 2 tablespoons (5 oz.) unsalted butter, slightly softened
1/2 cup firmly packed light-brown sugar
2/3 cup granulated sugar
2 eggs
3/4 cup milk

White Chocolate Mousse:
1-1/4 cups whipping cream
1-1/2 teaspoons unflavored gelatin
3 tablespoons water
4 oz. fine-quality white chocolate, chopped
3 tablespoons unsalted butter, room temperature
2 eggs, separated, room temperature
2 tablespoons sugar
1/4 cup mini, semisweet, real chocolate pieces

Chocolate Glaze:
4 oz. semisweet chocolate, chopped
2 tablespoons unsalted butter
2 tablespoons water

Garnish:
1-1/2 cups whipping cream, well-chilled
1 tablespoon mini, semisweet, real chocolate pieces

1. **Cake:** Position rack in center of oven and preheat to 350F (175C). Lightly butter 2 round 9-inch layer pans. Line base of each pan with parchment or foil; butter paper or foil. Flour pans and lined bases; tap pan to remove excess.
2. Melt chocolate in a double boiler or heatproof medium bowl over hot, not simmering, water over low heat, stirring occasionally. Stir until smooth. Remove from pan of water; cool to body temperature.
3. Sift flour and baking powder into a medium bowl. Cream butter in a large bowl. Add sugars; beat until smooth and fluffy. Add eggs, 1 at a time, beating very thoroughly after each addition. Beat in melted chocolate at low speed.
4. Using mixer at lowest speed, blend in about 1/4 of flour mixture. Blend in about 1/3 of milk. Repeat with remaining flour mixture in 3 batches, alternating with remaining milk in 2 batches. Continue mixing just until batter is blended. Transfer batter to prepared pans; spread evenly.
5. Bake about 25 minutes or until a cake tester inserted in centers of cakes comes out clean.
6. Cool in pans on racks 5 minutes. Invert cakes onto racks. Carefully peel off paper or foil; cool cakes completely.
1. **Mousse:** Oil inner side of a 9″ x 3″ springform pan. Put 1 cake layer in pan.
2. Chill a large bowl and beaters for whipping cream. Refrigerate 1 cup cream. Sprinkle gelatin over water in a small cup. Let stand 5 minutes while preparing chocolate mixture.
3. Combine white chocolate and remaining 1/4 cup cream in a double boiler or small heatproof bowl over hot, not simmering, water over low heat. Leave until partially melted, stirring occasionally. Remove from pan of water. Whisk until smooth. Whisk in butter.
4. Set cup with gelatin in a shallow pan of hot water over low heat. Melt gelatin, stirring often, about 3 minutes. Stir into chocolate mixture.
5. Add egg yolks, 1 at a time, stirring vigorously after each addition.
6. In a dry medium bowl, beat egg whites using dry beaters at medium speed until soft peaks form. Gradually beat in sugar and continue beating at high speed until whites are stiff and shiny but not dry.
7. Fold about 1/4 of whites into chocolate mixture. Return mixture to remaining whites; fold gently until blended.
8. Whip cream in chilled bowl until nearly stiff. Gently fold cream into chocolate mixture, blending thoroughly. Fold in chocolate pieces.
9. Pour 2 cups mousse over cake in pan. Spread so mousse flows between cake and pan. Freeze 15 minutes, keeping remaining mousse at room temperature.
10. Put second cake layer on top. Pour remaining mousse over it. Spread so mousse flows between side of cake and side of pan. Smooth top. Refrigerate about 4 hours or until set.
1. **Glaze:** Combine chocolate, butter and water in a double boiler or heatproof medium bowl over hot, not simmering, water over low heat. Leave until melted, stirring occasionally. Stir until smooth. Remove from pan of water; cool to body temperature or until thickened.
2. Pour glaze over center of chilled cake. Using a long metal spatula, slowly spread glaze towards edge, turning cake. Spread nearly to edge but leave about 1/4 inch border unglazed. Refrigerate at least 30 minutes or until set. *Cake can be kept, covered, up to 2 days in refrigerator.*
3. Put damp towel around sides of pan. Run a thin-bladed flexible knife or metal spatula carefully around edge of dessert. Release spring and remove side of pan carefully. If necessary, use spatula to smooth mousse on side.
• **Garnish:** Chill a large bowl and beaters for whipping cream. Whip cream in chilled bowl until stiff. Using a pastry bag and large star tip, pipe a ruffle of whipped cream at top outer edge of cake. Set chocolate pieces on cream. Pipe ruffle of cream around base of cake.

PIES & PASTRIES

Pies and pastries play the role of crisp containers to contrast with soft chocolate fillings such as chocolate mousse, Bavarian cream and pastry cream. Even the pastry itself is sometimes flavored with chocolate, like the chocolate dough used in Chocolate-Mint Cream Puffs.

Chocolate Pies & Tarts

Both American flaky pie pastry and French sweet pie pastry are excellent with chocolate fillings. Instead of pastry, quick crusts made from chocolate wafers, amaretti cookies or other packaged cookies can make delicious cases for creamy chocolate mousses and other soft mixtures. Crusts can also be made entirely of chocolate and nuts, as in Chocolate-Marbled Chiffon Pie.

Traditional American treats, like pecan pie and custard pie, become even better when enriched with chocolate. Nuts are a wonderful addition to many chocolate pies and tarts, such as Chocolate-Almond Fudge Tart with its topping of whipped cream and toasted sliced almonds, or fudgy Double-Chocolate Peach Pie.

Other Chocolate Pastries

Cream puffs made of choux pastry are the easiest pastries to make and are well-loved companions for chocolate. Profiteroles topped with hot chocolate sauce are one of the most popular desserts in fine restaurants but are simple to prepare. Chocolate Gâteau Paris Brest is a spectacular ring-shaped cake made of choux pastry topped with toasted almonds and filled with a creamy chocolate-praline cream.

Although puff pastry is time-consuming to make at home, now it can be purchased not only from bakeries but also at fine supermarkets. It is layered with a creamy chocolate filling and frosted with quick glaze to make Chocolate Napoleon.

Yeast-risen doughs can also be matched with chocolate fillings and toppings. Chocolate-Pear Pizza, for example, has a base of yeast dough covered with chocolate sauce and sliced pears. To make a rich type of cinnamon rolls, easy brioche dough is used. It is spread with a cinnamon-flavored pastry-cream filling and is liberally studded with dark chocolate chips and white raisins.

Strawberry-White Chocolate Tart

Photo on page 70.

This dessert looks like a classic strawberry tart but holds a surprise—a white-chocolate filling, which provides a sweet, creamy complement to the berries.

Makes 8 servings

Sweet Pie Pastry:
6 tablespoons sugar
1/4 teaspoon salt
1-1/2 cups all-purpose flour
1/2 cup (4 oz.) unsalted butter,
   well-chilled, cut in 16 pieces
3 egg yolks, beaten
1 to 2 teaspoons iced water, if
   needed

White Chocolate Pastry Cream:
3 egg yolks, room temperature
3 tablespoons sugar
1 tablespoon cornstarch
1/2 cup whipping cream
1/2 cup milk
4 oz. fine-quality white chocolate,
   chopped

Strawberry Topping:
5 cups small strawberries (about
   1-1/4 lbs.)
1/2 cup strawberry preserves

1. Pastry: Combine sugar, salt and flour in a food processor fitted with a metal blade. Process briefly to blend. Scatter butter pieces over mixture. Process using quick on/off pulses until mixture resembles coarse meal. Pour egg yolks evenly over mixture in processor. Process using quick on/off pulses, scraping down occasionally, until dough forms sticky crumbs that can easily be pressed together but does not come together in a ball. If crumbs are dry, sprinkle with 1/2 teaspoon water and process using quick on/off pulses until dough forms sticky crumbs. Add more water in same way, 1/2 teaspoon at a time, if crumbs are still dry.

2. Transfer dough to a work surface. Blend dough further by pushing about 1/4 of it away from you and smearing it with the heel of your hand against work surface. Repeat with remaining dough in 3 batches. Repeat with each batch if dough is not yet well-blended.

3. Using a rubber spatula, transfer dough to a sheet of plastic wrap. Wrap dough and push together. Shape dough in a flat disc. Refrigerate at least 6 hours. *Dough can be kept up to 2 days in refrigerator.*

4. Butter a 9- to 9-1/2-inch tart pan with removable base. Let dough soften 1 minute at room temperature. Set dough on a cold lightly floured surface. Knock dough firmly with a heavy rolling pin several times to flatten it. Roll out dough, flouring often and working as quickly as possible, to a round about 1/4 inch thick and about 11-1/2 inches in diameter. Roll up dough loosely around rolling pin; unroll over pan. Gently ease dough into pan. If dough tears, use a piece of dough hanging over rim of pan to patch it up.

5. Using your thumb, gently push down dough slightly at top edge of pan, making top edge of dough thicker than remaining dough. Roll rolling pin across pan to cut off dough at edges. With your finger and thumb, press to push up top edge of dough all around pan so it is about 1/4 inch higher than rim of pan. Refrigerate about 10 minutes. Prick dough all over with a fork. Cover with plastic wrap; refrigerate 1 hour. *Tart shell can be kept, covered, up to 1 day in refrigerator.*

6. Position rack in lower third of oven and preheat to 425F (220C). Line tart shell with parchment paper or foil; fill with dried beans or pie weights. Set tart shell on a baking sheet. Bake 10 minutes or until side is firm and beginning to brown. Reduce oven temperature to 375F (190C). Carefully remove paper or foil with beans. Bake tart shell 14 minutes or until base is firm and just beginning to brown.

7. Set tart shell on a flat-bottomed upside-down bowl. Remove side of pan. Transfer shell to a rack; cool to lukewarm. Gently pull out base of pan. Cool shell completely. Transfer to a platter. *Tart shell can be kept, covered, up to 1 day at room temperature.*

1. Pastry cream: Whisk egg yolks lightly in a heatproof medium bowl. Add sugar and whisk until blended. Lightly whisk in cornstarch.

2. Bring cream and milk to a boil in a heavy medium saucepan over medium-high heat. Gradually whisk hot cream mixture into egg-yolk mixture. Return to saucepan. Cook over medium heat, whisking constantly, until mixture is very thick and nearly comes to a boil. Remove from heat. Transfer to a shallow bowl; dab with a small piece of butter to prevent a skin from forming. Cool to room temperature.

3. Melt white chocolate in a double boiler or heatproof medium bowl over hot, not simmering, water over low heat, stirring occasionally. Stir until smooth. Remove from pan of water; cool to body temperature.

4. Whisk white chocolate into pastry cream. Cover and refrigerate at least 2 hours. *Pastry cream can be kept, covered, up to 2 days in refrigerator.*

1. **Topping:** Up to a few hours before serving, spread pastry cream in baked tart shell. Top with strawberries, pointing upward, arranged close together.
2. Heat preserves in a small saucepan over low heat until hot but not boiling. Strain into a small bowl, pressing on strawberry pieces.
3. Using a pastry brush, gently brush preserves on strawberries, brushing each berry individually. Refrigerate until ready to serve. If possible, serve tart within 4 hours so pastry remains crisp.

To make pastry by hand: Sift flour onto a work surface; make a well in center. Put egg yolks, salt and sugar in well; mix briefly, using your fingers. Pound butter pieces with rolling pin or your fist to soften them slightly. Separate butter again in pieces; add to well. Using your fingers, mix and crush ingredients in center of well until mixed but still not smooth. Draw in flour and crumble ingredients through your fingers, raising them in the air, until dough begins to come together. Add a little water, 1/2 teaspoon at a time, if dough is too dry.

Chocolate Bavarian Pie

Bavarian cream is one of the most luscious of desserts on its own but it is even more interesting as a pie because of the contrast with the texture of the crust. In this pie, the creamy chocolate filling is served in an easy-to-make crisp dark chocolate crust.

Makes 8 servings

Chocolate-Wafer Crust:
6-1/2 oz. chocolate wafers (about 29 wafers)
6 tablespoons unsalted butter, melted and cooled

Chocolate Bavarian Cream:
3 oz. fine-quality semisweet chocolate, chopped
1-3/4 teaspoons unflavored gelatin
3 tablespoons water
3/4 cup milk
3 egg yolks, room temperature
1/4 cup sugar
1/2 pint whipping cream (1 cup), well-chilled

Garnish:
Quick Chocolate Curls, page 193, or Chocolate Leaves, page 196, if desired

1. **Crust:** Preheat oven to 350F (175C). Grind cookies in a food processor to fairly fine crumbs; measure 1-1/2 cups. Transfer measured crumbs to a medium bowl. Add melted butter; mix lightly with a fork.
2. Lightly pat crumb mixture in even layer in a 9-inch pie pan, using a fork. Be sure to pat crumbs all the way up to rim of pan. Bake about 10 minutes or until crisp. Cool completely.
1. **Bavarian Cream:** Melt chocolate in a double boiler or heatproof medium bowl over hot, not simmering, water over low heat, stirring occasionally. Meanwhile, follow next 4 steps.
2. Sprinkle gelatin over 3 tablespoons water in a small cup. Let stand while preparing custard.
3. Bring milk to a boil in a very small heavy saucepan.
4. Whisk egg yolks lightly in a large heatproof bowl. Add sugar; whisk until well-blended. Gradually whisk in hot milk. Return mixture to saucepan, whisking constantly. Cook over medium-low heat, stirring mixture and scraping bottom of pan constantly with a wooden spoon, until mixture thickens slightly and reaches 165F to 170F (75C) on an instant-read thermometer; begin checking after 5 minutes. To check whether it is thick enough without a thermometer, remove custard from heat. Dip a metal spoon in custard and draw your finger across back of spoon. Your finger should leave a clear path in mixture that clings to spoon. If it does not, continue cooking another 30 seconds and check again. Do not overcook or it will curdle.
5. Remove from heat. Immediately add softened gelatin, whisking until it is completely dissolved. Pour into a large bowl; stir about 30 seconds to cool.
6. Remove chocolate from pan of water; stir until smooth. Using a whisk, stir custard mixture into melted chocolate, about 1/2 cup at a time.
7. Return mixture to large bowl; cool to room temperature, stirring occasionally.
8. Refrigerate chocolate mixture about 20 minutes, stirring often. Or, chill mixture by setting bowl in a larger bowl of iced water about 10 minutes, stirring very often, or until mixture is cold and beginning to thicken but is not set. Meanwhile, chill a large bowl and beaters for whipping cream.
9. Whip cream in chilled bowl until nearly stiff. Gently fold cream into chocolate mixture, blending thoroughly. Pour mixture into pie crust. Refrigerate about 2 hours or until set. *Pie can be kept, covered, up to 2 days in refrigerator.*
• **Garnish:** Top with Quick Chocolate Curls or Chocolate Leaves, if desired, just before serving.

Berries, Chocolate & Cream Tart

The German technique of brushing the pastry base with melted chocolate provides flavor and helps keep the pastry crisp in this light, summery tart. It is filled with a generous mound of fluffy whipped cream, dotted with colorful berries and chocolate chips.

Makes 6 to 8 servings

Sweet Pie Pastry:
5 tablespoons sugar
Pinch of salt
1-1/4 cups all-purpose flour
6 tablespoons unsalted butter,
    well-chilled, cut in 12 pieces
2 egg yolks, beaten
1 to 2 teaspoons iced water, if
    needed

*Berry & Chocolate Cream
Filling:*
2 oz. semisweet chocolate, chopped
1/2 pint whipping cream (1 cup),
    well-chilled
2 tablespoons sugar
1/2 cup blueberries
1/2 cup raspberries
1/4 cup mini, semisweet, real
    chocolate pieces

1. **Pastry:** Make dough for Sweet Pie Pastry following directions on page 64, steps 1 through 7; dough should be rolled out 1/4 inch thick and 9-1/2 inches in diameter to fit into a buttered 8-inch tart pan with removable base.
2. Bake and cool as directed.
1. **Filling:** Melt chopped chocolate in a double boiler or small heatproof bowl over hot, not simmering, water over low heat, stirring occasionally. Stir until smooth. Remove from pan of water; cool to body temperature.
2. Brush chocolate on base and side of baked tart shell. Refrigerate about 30 minutes or until set. Chill a large bowl and beaters for whipping cream.
3. Whip cream with sugar in chilled bowl until stiff. Set aside 3 or 4 of each type of berry for garnish. Fold chocolate pieces and remaining blueberries and raspberries into cream.
4. Spoon cream mixture into tart. Spread evenly, mounding in center. Refrigerate about 30 minutes. *Tart can be kept up to 1 day in refrigerator.*
5. Up to 30 minutes before serving, garnish tart with reserved berries. To serve, cut with a sharp heavy knife. Use a little extra pressure to cut pastry base with its hard chocolate coating.

Double-Chocolate Pecan Pie

A fudgy version of America's traditional favorite. If desired, accompany each wedge of pie by whipped cream or a scoop of vanilla ice cream.

Makes 8 to 10 servings

1 (9-inch) unbaked pie shell, page
    69
3/4 cup light corn syrup
1/2 cup granulated sugar
1 tablespoon unsweetened cocoa
    powder
1/4 cup unsalted butter, cut in 4
    pieces
3 eggs
1 teaspoon pure vanilla extract
1 cup pecans, coarsely chopped
    (about 3-1/2 oz.)
1 cup semisweet real chocolate
    pieces (6 oz.)
1/2 cup pecan halves

1. Make dough and line a 9-inch pie pan following directions in Chocolate-Cashew Custard Pie, page 69, Steps 1 through 4. Position rack in lower third of oven and preheat to 425F (220C).
2. Mix corn syrup, sugar, cocoa and butter in a heavy medium saucepan. Bring to a boil over medium heat, stirring constantly. Reduce heat to low; cook without stirring 5 minutes. Remove from heat; cool 10 minutes.
3. Lightly beat eggs in a large bowl. Stirring constantly with a whisk, slowly but steadily pour syrup mixture into eggs. Whisk until well-blended; mixtures will not blend at first but will do so after continued whisking. Cool 5 minutes.
4. Stir in vanilla, chopped pecans and chocolate pieces. Pour into pie shell. Arrange pecan halves on top in an attractive pattern.
5. Bake 15 minutes. Reduce oven temperature to 350F (175C). Bake 20 minutes or until a thin-bladed knife inserted halfway between center and edge of filling comes out nearly clean, with only a bit of batter sticking to it; if it comes out chocolaty because it hit a chocolate piece, test again. Cool on a rack. Serve pie slightly warm or at room temperature.

How to Make Berries, Chocolate & Cream Tart

1/Transfer dough to a work surface. Blend dough further by pushing about 1/4 of it away from you and smearing it with the heel of your hand against work surface. Repeat with remaining dough in 3 batches.

2/Quickly roll out dough to a round, about 1/4 inch thick and about 9-1/2 inches in diameter. Roll up dough loosely around rolling pin; unroll over pan. Gently ease dough into pan.

3/Gently push down dough slightly at top edge of pan, making top edge of dough thicker than remaining dough. Roll rolling pin across pan to cut off dough at edges. With your finger and thumb, press to push up top edge of dough all around pan so it is about 1/4 inch higher than rim of pan.

4/Brush chocolate on base and side of baked tart shell. Refrigerate about 30 minutes or until set.

Chocolate-Almond Fudge Tart

The dark fudgy filling of this tart is baked in sweet almond pastry, then topped with whipped cream and sprinkled with a generous amount of toasted sliced almonds.

Makes 8 servings

Almond Pastry:
1/2 cup whole blanched almonds
　　(about 2-1/2 oz.)
1/4 cup sugar
1/4 teaspoon salt
1-1/2 cups all-purpose flour
7 tablespoons unsalted butter,
　　well-chilled, cut in 14 pieces
1 egg, beaten
1/2 to 1 teaspoon iced water, if
　　needed

Chocolate-Almond Filling:
4 oz. bittersweet chocolate,
　　chopped
7 tablespoons unsalted butter
1/2 cup whole blanched almonds
　　(about 2-1/2 oz.)
1/2 cup sugar
2 eggs
1 tablespoon all-purpose flour

Almond & Cream Topping:
1/4 cup sliced almonds
1/2 pint whipping cream (1 cup),
　　well-chilled
1-1/4 teaspoons sugar
3/4 teaspoon pure vanilla extract

1. Pastry: Grind almonds with 2 tablespoons sugar in a food processor fitted with a metal blade until as fine as possible, scraping inward occasionally. Add salt, flour and remaining 2 tablespoons sugar to processor. Process briefly to blend.

2. Scatter butter pieces over mixture. Process using quick on/off pulses until mixture resembles coarse meal. Pour egg evenly over mixture in processor. Process using quick on/off pulses, scraping down occasionally, until dough forms sticky crumbs that can easily be pressed together but dough does not come together in a ball. If crumbs are dry, sprinkle with 1/2 teaspoon water and process using quick on/off pulses until dough forms sticky crumbs. Add more water in same way, 1/2 teaspoon at a time, if crumbs are still dry.

3. Transfer dough to a work surface. Blend dough further by pushing about 1/4 of it away from you and smearing it with the heel of your hand against work surface. Repeat with remaining dough in 3 batches. Repeat with each batch if dough is not yet well-blended.

4. Using a rubber spatula, transfer dough to a sheet of plastic wrap. Wrap dough and push together. Shape dough in a flat disc. Refrigerate 6 hours. *Dough can be kept up to 2 days in refrigerator.*

5. Butter a 9- to 9-1/2-inch tart pan with removable base. Let dough soften 1 minute at room temperature. Set dough on a cold lightly floured surface. Knock dough firmly with a heavy rolling pin several times to flatten it. Roll out dough, flouring often and working as quickly as possible, to a round about 1/4 inch thick and about 11-1/2 inches in diameter. Roll up dough loosely around rolling pin; unroll over pan. Gently ease dough into pan. Dough is crumbly; if it tears, use a piece of dough hanging over rim of pan to patch it up.

6. Using your thumb, gently push down dough slightly at top edge of pan, making top edge of dough thicker than remaining dough. Roll rolling pin across pan to cut off dough at edges. With your finger and thumb, press to push up top edge of dough all around pan so it is about 1/4 inch higher than rim of pan. Refrigerate about 10 minutes. Prick dough all over with a fork. Cover with plastic wrap; refrigerate 1 hour. *Tart shell can be kept, covered, up to 1 day in refrigerator; or it can be frozen.*

7. Position rack in lower third of oven and preheat to 425F (220C). Line tart shell with parchment paper or foil; fill with dried beans or pie weights. Set tart shell on a baking sheet. Bake 10 minutes or until side is firm and beginning to brown. Reduce oven temperature to 375F (190C). Carefully remove paper or foil with beans. Bake shell 10 minutes or until base is firm.

8. Transfer tart pan to a rack; cool while preparing filling. Reduce oven temperature to 350F (175C).

1. Filling: Combine chocolate and butter in a double boiler or heatproof medium bowl over hot, not simmering, water over low heat. Leave until melted, stirring occasionally. Stir until smooth. Remove from pan of water; cool mixture slightly.

2. Grind almonds with 2 tablespoons sugar in a food processor until as fine as possible, scraping inward occasionally.

3. Whisk eggs lightly in a medium bowl. Whisk in remaining 6 tablespoons sugar; whisk until blended. Still using whisk, stir in chocolate mixture, almonds and flour.

4. Pour into partially baked tart shell. Bake about 25 minutes or until a cake tester inserted in center of filling comes out clean.

5. Set tart on a flat-bottomed upside-down bowl; remove side of pan. Transfer tart to a rack.

1. **Topping:** Toast sliced almonds in a shallow baking pan in oven, stirring often, about 6 minutes or until lightly browned. Transfer to a plate.

2. When tart has cooled to lukewarm, gently pull out base of pan. Cool completely. Transfer to a platter. Refrigerate 30 minutes. *Tart can be kept, covered, up to 2 days in refrigerator.*

3. Chill a large bowl and beaters for whipping cream. Whip cream with sugar and vanilla in chilled bowl until stiff.

4. Spread cream over top of tart, covering it completely. Swirl top. Sprinkle toasted sliced almonds over top.

Chocolate-Cashew Custard Pie

The contrast of three textures—flaky pie crust, crunchy cashews and creamy dark chocolate filling—makes this a delightful treat. This pie is much richer than traditional custard pies.

Makes about 10 servings

Pie Shell:
1-1/4 cups unsifted all-purpose
    flour
1/4 teaspoon salt
5 tablespoons unsalted butter,
    well-chilled, cut in 10 pieces
2 tablespoons vegetable shortening,
    well-chilled, cut in 4 pieces
About 1 tablespoon plus 2-1/2
    teaspoons iced water

Chocolate-Cashew Filling:
10 oz. semisweet chocolate,
    chopped
6 egg yolks, room temperature
1-1/2 cups whipping cream
1/2 cup unsalted cashews (about
    2-1/4 oz.)

1. **Pie shell:** Combine flour and salt in a food processor fitted with a metal blade. Process briefly to blend. Scatter butter and shortening pieces over mixture. Process using quick on/off pulses until mixture resembles coarse meal. Sprinkle 1 tablespoon water evenly over mixture in processor. Process using quick on/off pulses until water is absorbed. Sprinkle 1 teaspoon water over mixture. Process using quick on/off pulses, scraping down occasionally, until dough forms sticky crumbs that can easily be pressed together but dough does not come together in a ball. If crumbs are dry, sprinkle with more water as needed, 1/2 teaspoon at a time. Process using quick on/off pulses until dough forms sticky crumbs.

2. Using a rubber spatula, transfer dough to a sheet of plastic wrap. Wrap dough and push together. Shape dough in a flat disc. Refrigerate at least 2 hours. *Dough can be kept up to 2 days in refrigerator.*

3. Let dough soften 1 minute at room temperature. Set dough on a cold lightly floured surface. Knock it firmly with a heavy rolling pin several times to flatten it. Roll out dough, flouring often and working as quickly as possible, to a round about 1/8 inch thick and about 11-1/2 inches in diameter. Roll up dough loosely around rolling pin; unroll over a 9-inch pie pan. Gently ease dough into pan, letting excess dough hang over edge of pan.

4. Trim dough about 1/2 inch from edge of pan with scissors. Fold edge of dough under so it comes just to rim of pan but covers rim. Crimp edge of dough, forming a high border. Prick dough lightly with a fork. Cover with plastic wrap; refrigerate 1 hour. *Pie shell can be kept, covered, up to 1 day in refrigerator.*

5. Position rack in center of oven and preheat to 425F (220C). Line pie shell with buttered parchment paper or foil, buttered-side down. Fill with dried beans or pie weights. Bake 10 minutes or until side is firm. Carefully remove paper or foil with beans. Bake pie shell 7 minutes or until base is firm. Transfer to a rack; cool. Reduce oven temperature to 325F (165C).

1. **Filling:** Melt chocolate in a double boiler or heatproof medium bowl over hot, not simmering, water over low heat, stirring occasionally. Stir until smooth. Remove from pan of water; cool to body temperature.

2. Whisk egg yolks with cream in a large bowl until blended. Gradually stir in chocolate, using a whisk. Pour into partially baked pie shell.

3. Arrange cashews on top in 3 circles, with all of cashews facing in same direction and lined up so baked pie can be cut in pieces between rows of cashews and not through them. Leave center of pie uncovered by cashews.

4. Return pie to center of oven. Bake about 30 minutes or until top looks just set and does not move or stick to your finger when lightly touched (touch it quickly because it is hot).

5. Cool to room temperature. Refrigerate at least 1 hour before serving. *Pie can be kept, covered, up to 2 days in refrigerator.* Serve at room temperature.

To make dough by hand: Sift flour and salt into a bowl. Cut butter and shortening into flour with a pastry blender or 2 knives until mixture resembles coarse meal. Gradually sprinkle water over mixture, mixing and tossing lightly with a fork, until dough holds together.

Chocolate-Marbled Chiffon Pie

Photo on pages 8-9.

Creamy white and dark chocolate fillings are swirled together inside a rich chocolate-nut crust.

Makes 8 servings

Chocolate-Walnut Crust:
1-1/2 cups walnuts (about 5 oz.)
3 oz. bittersweet chocolate, chopped
3 tablespoons unsalted butter
3 tablespoons sugar

White & Dark Chocolate Chiffon Filling:
1 (1/4-oz.) envelope unflavored gelatin (scant 1 tablespoon)
1/4 cup cold water
3 oz. fine-quality white chocolate, chopped
3/4 cup milk
3 eggs, separated
5 tablespoons sugar
4 oz. bittersweet chocolate, chopped
1/2 pint whipping cream (1 cup), well-chilled

1. Crust: Preheat oven to 350F (175C). Toast walnuts in a shallow baking dish in oven 5 minutes. Transfer to a plate; cool completely.

2. Combine chocolate and butter in a double boiler or heatproof medium bowl over hot, not simmering, water over low heat. Leave until melted, stirring occasionally. Stir until smooth. Remove from pan of water; cool slightly.

3. Grind nuts with sugar in a food processor until as fine as possible, scraping inward occasionally. Transfer to a medium bowl.

4. Add chocolate mixture to nut mixture; mix well with a fork. Spread evenly in a 9-inch pie pan, using the back of a spoon. Push mixture evenly up side of pan so it forms a border about 1/4 inch above rim of pan. Refrigerate 30 minutes or until firm.

1. Filling: Sprinkle gelatin over 1/4 cup water in a small cup. Let stand while preparing custard.

2. Melt white chocolate in a double boiler or small heatproof bowl over hot, not simmering, water over low heat, stirring occasionally. Whisk until smooth. Remove from pan of water; cool to body temperature.

3. Bring milk to a boil in a very small heavy saucepan.

4. Whisk egg yolks lightly in a large heatproof bowl. Add 3 tablespoons sugar; whisk until well-blended. Gradually whisk in hot milk. Return mixture to saucepan, whisking constantly. Cook over medium-low heat, stirring mixture and scraping bottom of pan constantly with a wooden spoon, until mixture thickens slightly and reaches 165F to 170F (75C) on an instant-read thermometer; begin checking after 4 minutes. To check whether it is thick enough without a thermometer, remove custard from heat. Dip a metal spoon in custard and draw your finger across back of spoon. Your finger should leave a clear path in mixture that clings to spoon. If it does not, continue cooking another 30 seconds and check again. Do not overcook custard or it will curdle.

5. Remove from heat. Immediately add softened gelatin, whisking until it is completely dissolved. Pour into a large bowl; stir about 30 seconds to cool. Whisk in white chocolate until blended.

6. Chill mixture by setting bowl in a larger bowl of iced water about 10 minutes, stirring very often, or until mixture is cold and barely beginning to thicken but is not set. If mixture becomes too firm, it will be difficult to marble. Meanwhile, chill a large bowl and beaters for whipping cream.

7. Melt bittersweet chocolate in a double boiler or small heatproof bowl over hot, not simmering, water over low heat, stirring occasionally. Remove from heat but leave chocolate above water.

8. Whip cream in chilled bowl until nearly stiff. Refrigerate cream if custard mixture is not yet ready.

9. When custard is thickened, remove from bowl of iced water. In a small dry bowl, whip egg whites using dry beaters at medium speed until soft peaks form. Gradually beat in remaining 2 tablespoons sugar; continue whipping at high speed until whites are stiff and shiny but not dry.

10. Gently fold cream into custard mixture. Gently fold in egg whites, blending thoroughly.

11. Transfer 2 cups custard to a bowl. Remove dark chocolate from above water. Whisk 3/4 cup custard from bowl into chocolate. Return chocolate mixture to remaining custard in bowl; fold quickly until blended.

12. Spoon about half of dark chocolate mixture into pie shell. Spoon white chocolate mixture over it. Quickly spoon remaining dark chocolate in 4 large spoonfuls on top of white mixture, spacing them evenly apart. Gently swirl a thin knife through mixtures to marble them. Refrigerate about 2 hours or until set. *Pie can be kept, covered, up to 2 days in refrigerator.*

Strawberry-White Chocolate Tart, page 64.

Chocolate-Mint Cream Puffs

Light puffs of chocolate dough coated with a dark chocolate glaze hold a refreshing mint filling.

Makes about 16 puffs

Chocolate Choux Pastry:
1/2 cup all-purpose flour
1 tablespoon unsweetened
    Dutch-process cocoa powder
1/2 cup water
1/4 teaspoon salt
2 teaspoons sugar
1/4 cup unsalted butter, cut in
    pieces
3 eggs

Mint Pastry Cream:
1 large bunch fresh mint (about
    4-3/4 oz.)
2 cups milk
5 egg yolks, room temperature
7 tablespoons sugar
3 tablespoons cornstarch
1/4 cup butter, room temperature

Chocolate Glaze:
4 oz. semisweet chocolate, chopped
2 tablespoons unsalted butter
2 tablespoons water

Fresh mint sprigs, if desired (for
    garnish)

1. Pastry: Position rack in lower third of oven and preheat to 400F (205C). Lightly butter 2 baking sheets. Sift flour and cocoa onto a piece of waxed paper.
2. Combine water, salt, sugar and butter in a small heavy saucepan. Cook over low heat, stirring constantly, until butter melts. Bring to a boil; remove from heat. Immediately add flour mixture all at once; stir quickly with a wooden spoon until mixture is smooth. Set pan over low heat; beat mixture about 30 seconds.
3. Remove from heat; cool about 3 minutes. Add 1 egg; beat thoroughly into mixture. Add second egg; beat mixture until smooth. Beat third egg in a small bowl. Gradually beat 1 or 2 tablespoons of this egg into dough, adding enough so dough becomes very shiny and is soft enough just to fall from spoon. To check, scoop up about 1/3 of dough on wooden spoon, hold spoon sideways and wait for dough to fall; if it falls into pan in 10 to 15 seconds, it is ready; if it takes longer or does not fall, add a little more egg.
4. Add a pinch of salt to remaining egg; beat until blended. Reserve as glaze.
5. Using a pastry bag and 1/2-inch plain tip, shape mounds of dough about 1-1/2 inches in diameter, spacing them about 2 inches apart on buttered baking sheets. Brush with egg glaze, gently pushing down any points.
6. Bake about 30 minutes or until dough is puffed and firm. Using a serrated knife, carefully cut off top third of each puff; set aside as a "hat." Transfer puffs to a rack to cool. *Puffs can be kept up to 1 day in an airtight container but taste best on day they are baked.*
1. Pastry Cream: Remove mint leaves from stems; you should have about 4 cups leaves. Coarsely chop leaves.
2. Bring milk to a boil in a heavy medium saucepan. Add mint; remove from heat and stir. Cover and let stand 1 hour. Strain milk into a heavy medium saucepan, pressing on mint in strainer.
3. Whisk egg yolks lightly in a heatproof medium bowl. Add sugar; whisk until blended. Lightly stir in cornstarch, using whisk.
4. Bring mint-flavored milk to a boil in a heavy medium saucepan. Gradually whisk hot milk into egg-yolk mixture. Return to saucepan. Cook over medium-low heat, whisking constantly, until mixture is very thick and barely comes to a boil. Do not overcook or yolks will curdle. Remove from heat. Whisk in butter.
5. Transfer to a bowl; dab with a small piece of butter to prevent a skin from forming. Refrigerate until completely cool.
6. When pastry cream is cool, whisk until smooth. Using a pastry bag and medium star tip, pipe pastry cream generously into cream puffs. Set reserved "hats" on top. Refrigerate 1 hour. *Filled puffs can be kept up to 1 day in refrigerator.*
1. Glaze: Combine chocolate, butter and water in a double boiler or heatproof medium bowl over hot, not simmering, water over low heat, stirring occasionally. Stir until smooth. Remove from pan of water.
2. Cool mixture about 5 minutes or until thickened and cooled to just slightly above body temperature.
3. Using a teaspoon, spoon glaze over each filled puff, covering top third and letting glaze run down side. Cool about 15 minutes; on a hot day, refrigerate. To serve, garnish each plate with a fresh mint sprig.

Sultan's Cream Puffs

Photo on pages 8-9.

In classic cuisine, desserts containing almonds, citrus fruits or other ingredients that were associated with the Near East were sometimes called *à la sultane.* These almond-topped cream puffs filled with a creamy chocolate-orange mixture are rich enough to please any sultan!

Makes about 15 puffs

Choux Pastry:
1/2 cup plus 1 tablespoon
   all-purpose flour
1/2 cup water
1/4 teaspoon salt
1/4 cup unsalted butter, cut in
   pieces
3 eggs

2 tablespoons sliced almonds

Chocolate-Orange Mousseline Filling:
2 large navel oranges
1 cup milk
3 oz. semisweet chocolate, chopped
3 egg yolks, room temperature
1/4 cup sugar
1 tablespoon plus 2 teaspoons
   cornstarch
1/2 cup whipping cream,
   well-chilled

Powdered sugar (for sprinkling)

1. Pastry: Position rack in lower third of oven and preheat to 400F (205C). Lightly butter 2 baking sheets. Sift flour onto a piece of waxed paper.

2. Combine water, salt and butter in a small heavy saucepan. Cook over low heat, stirring constantly, until butter melts. Bring to a boil; remove from heat. Immediately add flour all at once; stir quickly with a wooden spoon until mixture is smooth. Set pan over low heat; beat mixture about 30 seconds.

3. Remove from heat; cool about 3 minutes. Add 1 egg; beat thoroughly into mixture. Add second egg; beat mixture until smooth. Beat third egg in a small bowl. Gradually beat 1 or 2 tablespoons of this egg into dough, adding enough so dough becomes very shiny and is soft enough just to fall from spoon. To check, scoop up about 1/3 of dough on wooden spoon, hold spoon sideways and wait for dough to fall; if it falls into pan in 10 to 15 seconds, it is ready; if it takes longer or does not fall, add a little more egg.

4. Add a pinch of salt to remaining egg; beat until blended. Reserve as glaze.

5. Using a pastry bag and 1/2-inch plain tip, shape mounds of dough about 1-1/2 inches in diameter, spacing them about 2 inches apart on buttered baking sheets. Brush them with egg glaze, gently pushing down any points. Sprinkle a few almond slices on each.

6. Bake 20 minutes. Reduce oven temperature to 350F (175C). Continue baking about 15 minutes or until dough is puffed and browned; cracks that form during baking should also be brown. Using a serrated knife, carefully cut off top half of each puff; set aside as a "hat." Transfer puffs to a rack to cool. *Puffs can be kept up to 1 day in an airtight container but taste best on day they are baked.*

1. Filling: Using a vegetable peeler, pare colored part of orange peel in long strips, without including white pith.

2. Scald milk and strips of orange zest in a heavy medium saucepan over medium heat by heating until bubbles form around edge of pan. Remove from heat. Cover and let stand 20 minutes. Strain milk into another heavy medium saucepan.

3. Melt chocolate in a double boiler or small heatproof bowl over hot, not simmering, water over low heat, stirring occasionally. Stir until smooth. Remove from pan of water.

4. Whisk egg yolks lightly in a heatproof medium bowl. Add sugar; whisk until blended. Lightly stir in cornstarch, using whisk.

5. Bring orange-flavored milk to a boil. Gradually whisk hot milk into egg-yolk mixture. Return to saucepan; whisk thoroughly. Cook over medium-low heat, whisking constantly, until mixture is very thick and just begins to bubble. Do not overcook or yolks will curdle. Remove from heat.

6. Stir chocolate until smooth. Whisk into milk mixture. Transfer to a bowl; dab with a small piece of butter to prevent a skin from forming. Refrigerate until completely cool. Chill a medium bowl and beaters for whipping cream.

7. When chocolate mixture is cool, whisk it until smooth. Whip cream in chilled bowl until stiff. Fold it into chocolate mixture.

8. A short time before serving, fill cream puffs with Chocolate-Orange Mousseline Filling using a pastry bag and medium star tip. Set reserved "hats" on top at an angle to show filling. Shake or sift powdered sugar over cream puffs. *Filled puffs can be kept up to 1 day in refrigerator.*

How to Decorate Chocolate Napoleon

1/Pipe crosswise parallel lines of chocolate 1/2 inch apart on iced pastry strip.

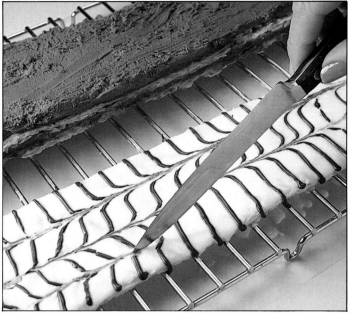

2/Beginning at 1 short end of pastry strip about 1/2 inch from long edge, draw dull side of a thin-bladed knife across chocolate lines, pulling it lengthwise along strip. Alternating end of cake from which you begin, draw knife across lines 2 or 3 more times at equal distances.

Chocolate Napoleon

Napoleon is a classic that remains popular because of the contrast between the generous amount of creamy filling and the thin layers of crisp flaky puff pastry. Now it is easy to make with purchased puff pastry.

Makes 8 to 10 servings

1/2 (1-lb.) pkg. frozen puff pastry sheets or 14 oz. fresh puff pastry

Chocolate Mousseline Filling:
2 egg yolks, room temperature
3 tablespoons sugar
1 tablespoon plus 2 teaspoons cornstarch
3/4 cup milk
6 oz. semisweet chocolate, chopped
3/4 cup whipping cream, well-chilled

Powdered Sugar Glaze:
1 oz. semisweet chocolate, chopped (for garnish)
2 tablespoons plus 2 teaspoons whipping cream
3/4 cup powdered sugar, sifted

1. **Pastry:** If using a sheet of frozen dough, defrost dough 20 minutes and unfold sheet.
2. Sprinkle water lightly on a 17″ x 11″ baking sheet.
3. On a cold lightly floured surface, quickly roll fresh pastry to a 17″ x 11″ rectangle; if using a packaged sheet, roll it to enlarge mainly in lengthwise direction. Keep dough as straight as possible and flour often. Roll dough around rolling pin; unroll onto prepared baking sheet. Trim edges if necessary. Prick dough all over with fork at close intervals. Refrigerate 30 minutes. Meanwhile, position rack in center of oven and preheat to 400F (205C).
4. Bake dough 12 minutes or until it begins to brown. Reduce oven temperature to 350F (175C); bake 5 minutes or until golden brown and crisp. Set a large rack over baking sheet; turn pastry over onto rack. Sheet will be very thin. Cool on rack.
5. Slide pastry sheet onto a large cutting board. Using a small sharp knife and cutting with its point, trim edges of pastry straight. Cut it lengthwise in 3 equal strips; each will be about 3-1/8 inches wide.
1. **Filling:** Whisk egg yolks lightly in a small heatproof bowl. Add sugar and whisk until blended. Lightly stir in cornstarch, using whisk.
2. Bring milk to a boil in a small heavy saucepan. Gradually whisk hot milk into egg-yolk mixture. Return to saucepan; whisk thoroughly. Cook over medium-low heat, whisking constantly, until mixture is very thick and comes just to a boil. Do not overcook or yolks will curdle. Remove from heat.
3. Melt chocolate in a double boiler or heatproof medium bowl over hot, not simmering, water over low heat, stirring occasionally. Stir until smooth. Remove from pan of water; cool slightly.

4. Whisk chocolate into filling mixture. Transfer to a bowl; dab with a small piece of butter to prevent a skin from forming. Cool to room temperature. Cover and refrigerate 20 minutes. Chill a medium or large bowl and beaters for whipping cream.

5. Whip cream in chilled bowl until stiff. Whisk chocolate mixture until smooth. Fold cream into chocolate mixture. Refrigerate about 10 minutes.

1. Assembly: Spread 1-1/2 cups Chocolate Mousseline Filling on each of 2 pastry strips. Set 1 filling-topped strip on a platter. Top with second filling-topped strip. Refrigerate while making frosting.

2. Prepare a parchment paper piping cone, page 192, or have ready a small pastry bag with very fine plain tip.

3. Melt chocolate in a small bowl over hot, not simmering, water over low heat, stirring occasionally. Stir until smooth. Remove from pan of water; cool slightly. Spoon into paper piping cone or pastry bag.

4. Stir cream into powdered sugar in a small bowl. Beat with a wooden spoon until smooth. Spread on third pastry strip. Quickly smooth icing with a metal spatula.

5. Using paper cone or pastry bag, pipe crosswise parallel lines of chocolate on icing, 1/2 inch apart. Beginning at 1 short end of cake about 1/2 inch from long edge, draw dull side of a thin-bladed knife across chocolate lines, pulling it lengthwise over cake. Alternating end of cake from which you begin, draw knife across lines 2 or 3 more times at equal distances,

6. Set frosted pastry strip on top of cake; press lightly. Refrigerate 30 minutes. *Napoleon can be kept, covered, up to 1 day in refrigerator but tastes best on day it was baked.*

7. To serve, cut carefully into approximately 1-1/2 inch slices using a serrated knife.

TIPS

○ *The best surface to use for rolling dough is a marble slab that can be chilled in refrigerator or freezer. However, any other smooth surface can be used. To chill a surface that cannot be refrigerated, set a thin tray with ice cubes on surface and leave for about 20 minutes. Wipe surface completely dry before using.*

○ *When rolling dough, slide a rubber spatula or base of a tart pan under dough to free it occasionally from surface so it will not stick.*

○ *Use metal pie pans for baking pie pastry and decorative glass dishes for baking crumb crusts.*

○ *If a pastry bag is not available, cream puffs can be shaped with 2 tablespoons and filled using a teaspoon.*

○ *If tops of profiteroles or cream puffs do not brown enough, transfer them to top third of oven for last 3 minutes of baking.*

Chocolate Gâteau Paris Brest

Praline cream is the traditional filling for this elegant, ring-shaped cream puff cake, but here it has a new chocolate twist. This elegant, light dessert is a perfect finale for a dinner party.

Makes 6 to 8 servings

Choux Pastry:
1/2 cup plus 1 tablespoon all-purpose flour
1/2 cup water
1/4 teaspoon salt
1/4 cup unsalted butter, cut in pieces
3 eggs

2 tablespoons sliced almonds (for sprinkling)

Praline Chocolate Whipped Cream:
1/3 cup whole blanched almonds
1/4 cup sugar
3 tablespoons water
3 oz. semisweet chocolate, coarsely chopped
1-1/2 cups whipping cream, well chilled

Powdered sugar (for sprinkling)

1. Pastry: Position rack in lower third of oven and preheat to 400F (205C). Lightly butter a baking sheet. Using an 8-inch cake pan, draw an 8-inch circle on baking sheet; it will be only barely visible. Sift flour onto waxed paper.
2. Combine water, salt and butter in a small heavy saucepan. Cook over low heat, stirring constantly, until butter melts. Bring to a boil; remove from heat. Immediately add flour all at once; stir quickly with a wooden spoon until mixture is smooth. Set pan over low heat; beat mixture about 30 seconds.
3. Remove from heat; cool about 3 minutes. Add 1 egg; beat thoroughly into mixture. Add second egg; beat mixture until smooth. Beat third egg in a small bowl. Gradually beat 1 or 2 tablespoons of this egg into dough, adding enough so dough becomes very shiny and is soft enough just to fall from spoon. To check, scoop up about 1/3 of dough on wooden spoon, hold spoon sideways and wait for dough to fall; if it falls into pan in 10 to 15 seconds, it is ready; if it takes longer or does not fall, add a little more egg.
4. Add a pinch of salt to remaining egg; beat until blended. Reserve as glaze.
5. Using a pastry bag and large plain tip about 5/8-inch in diameter, evenly pipe choux pastry in an 8-inch ring onto baking sheet, following marked circle. Pipe another ring inside first, touching it. Pipe a third ring on top of crack joining first 2 rings. Brush dough with egg glaze. Gently mark lines on dough by pressing with bottom of a fork dipped in water. Sprinkle almonds on top.
6. Bake 20 minutes. Reduce oven temperature to 350F (175C). Continue baking about 20 minutes or until dough is puffed and browned; cracks that form during baking should also brown. Leave oven on to toast almonds.
7. Using a serrated knife, carefully split cake in half horizontally. Cool both halves separately on a rack. *Cake can be kept, covered, up to 1 day at room temperature but tastes best on day it is baked.*
1. Praline Chocolate Whipped Cream: Toast almonds in a shallow baking pan about 8 minutes. Remove from oven; leave in baking pan to keep warm.
2. Lightly oil a baking sheet.
3. Combine sugar and water in a heavy, very small saucepan that does not have a black interior. Heat mixture over low heat until sugar dissolves, gently stirring occasionally. Increase heat to high and boil, brushing down any sugar crystals from side of pan with a brush dipped in water, until mixture begins to brown. Reduce heat to medium low. Continue cooking, swirling pan gently, until mixture is a rich brown color and a trace of smoke begins to rise from pan. Do not let caramel get too dark or it will burn and praline will be bitter; if caramel is too light, praline will be too sweet.
4. Immediately remove caramel from heat; stir in warm nuts, being careful not to splash, until they are well-coated with caramel. Stir over low heat 1-1/2 minutes. Immediately transfer to oiled baking sheet.
5. Cool completely. Break praline into small chunks.
6. Grind praline in food processor, scraping mixture occasionally, until as fine as possible. Immediately transfer praline to an airtight container. *Praline can be kept several months in an airtight container at room temperature or in freezer.*
7. Chill a large bowl and beaters for whipping cream. Melt chocolate in a small heatproof bowl set over hot, not simmering, water over low heat. Stir until smooth. Remove from heat but leave chocolate above hot water.
8. Whip cream in chilled bowl until stiff.
9. Remove chocolate from above water; cool 30 seconds. Quickly stir about 1/2 cup whipped cream into chocolate. Quickly fold mixture into remaining whipped cream until smooth. Fold quickly so that chocolate does not harden upon contact with cold whipped cream. Fold in praline.
10. Using a pastry bag and large star tip, pipe all of Praline-Chocolate Whipped Cream onto lower half of cake in a ruffle so it shows at edge. Cover with top half of cake. Refrigerate 30 minutes. *Filled cake can be kept, covered, up to 8 hours in refrigerator.* Sprinkle with powdered sugar before serving.

Chocolate-Cinnamon Raisin Rolls

Photo on page 189.

These rolls are made of a rich brioche-like dough spread with cinnamon cream and sprinkled with chocolate pieces and raisins. They are perfect for brunch or teatime.

Makes 15 sweet rolls

Easy Brioche Dough:
2 tablespoons warm water (110F, 45C)
1 (1/4-oz.) pkg. active dry yeast (about 1 tablespoon)
1 tablespoon sugar
2 cups all-purpose flour
1-1/4 teaspoons salt
3 eggs
1 egg yolk
1/2 cup (4 oz.) unsalted butter, cut in 16 pieces, room temperature

Cinnamon Pastry Cream:
5 egg yolks, room temperature
6 tablespoons sugar
3/4 teaspoon ground cinnamon
2 tablespoons plus 2 teaspoons cornstarch
1-1/2 cups milk

3/4 cup semisweet real chocolate pieces
1/2 cup light raisins
1 egg, beaten with a pinch of salt (for glaze)

1. **Dough:** Pour water into a small deep bowl or cup. Sprinkle yeast over water; add 1/4 teaspoon sugar. Let stand 10 minutes or until foamy. Stir yeast mixture.

2. Put flour into bowl of mixer; make a well in center. Add salt, remaining 2-3/4 teaspoons sugar and whole eggs. Mix central ingredients briefly with dough hook of mixer. Add yeast mixture. Using dough hook, mix at low speed until mixture comes together to a dough, pushing in flour occasionally. Scrape down mixture. Add egg yolk; beat with dough hook until blended. Continue beating with dough hook on medium speed about 12 minutes or until mixture is very smooth.

3. Add butter pieces. Beat on low speed, scraping down dough often, just until butter is blended in. Dough will be soft.

4. Lightly oil a medium bowl. Place dough in oiled bowl; turn dough over to oil surface. Cover with plastic wrap; let dough rise in a warm draft-free place about 1-1/2 hours or until nearly doubled in bulk.

5. Gently turn dough over several times to knock out air. Return to bowl. Cover and refrigerate at least 4 hours or overnight.

1. **Pastry cream:** Whisk egg yolks lightly in a heatproof medium bowl. Add sugar and cinnamon; whisk until blended. Lightly whisk in cornstarch.

2. Bring milk to a boil in a heavy medium saucepan. Gradually whisk hot milk into egg-yolk mixture. Return to saucepan. Cook over medium-low heat, whisking constantly, until mixture is very thick and barely comes to a boil; it will be too thick to bubble. Reduce heat to low. Cook, whisking constantly, 1 minute. Do not overcook or yolks will curdle. Remove from heat. Transfer to a bowl; dab with a small piece of butter to prevent a skin from forming. Refrigerate until completely cool, at least 1-1/2 hours or overnight.

3. Lightly butter 2 baking sheets. On a cool floured surface, roll out dough to a 15" x 10" rectangle, flouring often.

4. Whisk pastry cream. Spread over dough, leaving a 1-inch border on 1 long side. Sprinkle pastry cream evenly with chocolate pieces and raisins. Brush plain border with egg glaze. Roll up dough from opposite long side like a jelly roll. Press roll of dough along egg-brushed border to seal.

5. Trim ends. Cut a 1-inch slice of rolled dough. Using rubber spatula, set slice on buttered baking sheet, with its more narrow side (side that was pressed with knife) facing down. Continue slicing dough and transferring slices to baking sheet, spacing them about 2 inches apart. Work quickly so dough will not become too soft. If desired, press any uneven slices to an even round shape. Let rise, uncovered, in a draft-free area about 30 minutes. Meanwhile, position rack in center of oven and preheat to 400F (205C).

6. Bake rolls 12 minutes. If there is room for only 1 baking sheet on center rack, bake in 2 batches. Reduce oven temperature to 350F (175C). Bake 10 to 12 minutes or until rolls are golden brown.

7. Transfer to a rack; cool slightly. *Pastries can be kept up to 1 day in an airtight container but are best freshly baked.* Serve warm or at room temperature.

Profiteroles with Hazelnut Cream

Profiteroles are small cream puffs served with a shiny hot chocolate sauce. As an alternative to whipped cream, the puffs can be filled with ice cream. Good choices would be: vanilla, coffee, French-Italian Chocolate, page 126, Chocolate-Almond, page 127, or Chocolate-Mint, page 129.

Makes about 20 profiteroles

Choux Pastry:
1/2 cup plus 1 tablespoon
   all-purpose flour
1/2 cup water
1/4 teaspoon salt
1/4 cup unsalted butter, cut in
   pieces
3 eggs

Hazelnut Whipped Cream:
1 cup hazelnuts
2 tablespoons plus 1 teaspoon sugar
1/2 pint whipping cream (1 cup),
   well-chilled
1/4 cup hazelnut liqueur
   (Frangelico)

Rich Chocolate Sauce:
5 oz. semisweet chocolate, chopped
4 egg yolks, room temperature
1/4 cup whipping cream
1/4 cup milk

1. Pastry: Position rack in lower third of oven and preheat to 400F (205C). Lightly butter 2 baking sheets. Sift flour onto a piece of waxed paper.
2. Combine water, salt and butter in a small heavy saucepan. Cook over low heat, stirring constantly, until butter melts. Bring to a boil; remove from heat. Immediately add flour all at once; stir quickly with a wooden spoon until mixture is smooth. Set pan over low heat; beat mixture about 30 seconds.
3. Remove from heat; cool about 3 minutes. Add 1 egg; beat thoroughly into mixture. Add second egg; beat mixture until smooth. Beat third egg in a small bowl. Gradually beat 1 or 2 tablespoons of this egg into dough, adding enough so dough becomes very shiny and is soft enough just to fall from spoon. To check, scoop up about 1/3 of dough on wooden spoon, hold spoon sideways and wait for dough to fall; if it falls into pan in 10 to 15 seconds, it is ready; if it takes longer or does not fall, add a little more egg.
4. Add a pinch of salt to remaining egg; beat until blended. Reserve as glaze.
5. Using a pastry bag and medium-sized plain tip, shape mounds of dough about 1-1/4 inches in diameter, spacing them about 2 inches apart on buttered baking sheets. Brush them with egg glaze, gently pushing down any points.
6. Bake about 28 minutes or until dough is puffed and browned; cracks that form during baking should also be brown. Using a serrated knife, carefully cut off top third of each puff; set aside as a "hat." Transfer puffs to a rack to cool. *Puffs can be kept up to 1 day in an airtight container but taste best on day they are baked.*
1. Whipped cream: Preheat oven to 350F (175C). Toast hazelnuts and remove skins, page 201; cool nuts completely. Chill a large bowl and beaters for whipping cream.
2. Grind nuts with 1 tablespoon sugar in a food processor until as fine as possible, scraping inward occasionally. Transfer to a medium bowl.
3. Whip cream with remaining 4 teaspoons sugar in chilled bowl until stiff. Fold in ground nuts in 2 batches. Gradually fold in liqueur. Spoon into cream puffs. Set reserved "hats" on top.
1. Sauce: Melt chocolate in a double boiler or heatproof medium bowl over hot, not simmering, water over low heat, stirring occasionally. Stir until smooth. Remove from pan of water.
2. Whisk egg yolks and cream in a heatproof medium bowl. Whisk in chocolate until blended. Set mixture above hot water over low heat. Heat, whisking, about 2 minutes or until lukewarm. Remove from pan of water.
3. Scald milk in a small saucepan by heating until bubbles form around edge of pan. Gradually whisk into chocolate mixture. *Sauce can be kept, covered, up to 1 week in refrigerator; reheat in pan above hot water before serving.*
4. Spoon warm sauce over profiteroles when serving.

Variation
Profiteroles with Ice Cream: Fill each cream puff generously with ice cream. Set reserved "hat" on top. Freeze while preparing sauce.

Profiteroles with Chocolate Ice Cream

Chocolate-Pear Pizza

Do not worry—there is no tomato sauce or cheese here; this pastry is related to pizza only in its form. Its base is made of a rich, sweet, yeast dough, which is spread with chocolate sauce and topped with pear slices.

Makes 2 pizzas, each 6 servings

Sweet Yeast Dough:
3/4 cup warm water (110F, 45C)
1 (1/4-oz.) pkg. active dry yeast (about 1 tablespoon)
1 tablespoon sugar
3 cups all-purpose flour
1 teaspoon salt
2 eggs
6 tablespoons unsalted butter, cut in 6 pieces, room temperature

Chocolate-Pear Topping:
5 tablespoons unsalted butter, chilled
4 oz. semisweet chocolate, finely chopped
2 ripe medium pears (about 14 oz.)
2 teaspoons grated lemon zest
1/3 cup sugar

1. Dough: Pour 1/4 cup warm water into a small bowl. Sprinkle yeast over water; add 1 teaspoon sugar. Let stand 10 minutes or until foamy.
2. Combine flour, salt and remaining 2 teaspoons sugar in a food processor fitted with a dough blade or metal blade. Process briefly to blend. Add eggs. With blades of processor turning, quickly pour in yeast mixture and remaining water. Process 1 minute to knead dough. Add butter; process just until absorbed. Dough will be soft and sticky.
3. Lightly oil a medium bowl. Place dough in oiled bowl; turn dough over to oil surface. Cover with plastic wrap. Let dough rise in a warm draft-free place about 1 hour or until doubled in bulk.
4. Lightly butter 2 baking sheets. Divide dough in 2 equal parts. Place each on a baking sheet. Pat with lightly floured hands to a 10-inch circle.
1. Topping: Refrigerate 3 tablespoons butter. Combine chocolate and remaining 2 tablespoons butter in a double boiler or heatproof medium bowl over hot, not simmering, water over low heat. Leave until melted, stirring occasionally. Stir until smooth. Remove from pan of water.
2. Peel pears; halve and core. Cut in lengthwise slices, about 1/8 inch thick.
3. Using a rubber spatula, spread warm chocolate mixture evenly over each round of dough, leaving a 3/4-inch border.
4. Arrange pear slices in a ring on chocolate mixture with slices pointing inward, leaving center of chocolate uncovered.
5. Sprinkle grated lemon zest evenly over pears. Cut chilled butter into very thin slices, about 1/8 inch thick. Halve butter slices and scatter over pears. Sprinkle pears with sugar. Let rise 15 minutes. Meanwhile, position rack in center of oven and preheat to 425F (220C).
6. Bake 20 minutes or until dough browns and pears are tender. Serve pizza warm or at room temperature. Serve pizza on day it was baked; or freeze and reheat before serving.

To make dough by hand: Instead of Step 2, sift flour into a bowl; make a well in center. Add yeast mixture, remaining water, eggs, remaining sugar and salt to well. Mix ingredients in middle of well. Stir in flour; mix well. Knead dough vigorously, slapping it on a work surface, until it is smooth and elastic. Pound butter with your fist to soften thoroughly. Set butter on top of dough; knead until blended in. If dough is very sticky, flour it occasionally while kneading.

TIPS

○ Use a small whisk for stirring when making pastry cream. This makes it easier to reach all parts of the saucepan.

○ Fresh puff pastry can often be purchased at pastry shops. Frozen puff pastry sheets can be purchased at many supermarkets.

○ Do not worry if there is a tear in a sheet of filo dough because when it is folded into a triangle, the many folds will keep the filling in.

How to Make Chocolate-Pear Pizza

1/Arrange pear slices in a ring on chocolate mixture with slices pointing inward, leaving center of chocolate uncovered. Sprinkle with grated lemon zest, butter slices and sugar. Let rise 15 minutes before baking.

2/Bake 20 minutes or until dough browns and pears are tender. Serve pizza warm or at room temperature.

Chocolate Marzipan Filo Triangles

These crisp flaky pastries encase a rich chocolate-almond filling and are easy to prepare using packaged sheets of filo dough.

Makes about 36 pastries

1 lb. filo sheets (about 20 sheets)

Chocolate-Marzipan Filling:
1 oz. semisweet chocolate, chopped
1 oz. unsweetened chocolate, chopped
1 cup whole blanched almonds (about 5 oz.)
1/2 cup sugar
1 egg, beaten to mix
2 tablespoons plus 2 teaspoons brandy

1-1/2 cups (12 oz.) unsalted butter, melted and cooled (for brushing)
About 2 teaspoons sesame seeds (for sprinkling)

• If filo sheets are frozen, defrost them in refrigerator 8 hours or overnight.
1. Filling: Combine chocolates in a double boiler or heatproof medium bowl over hot, not simmering, water over low heat. Leave until melted, stirring occasionally. Stir until smooth. Remove from pan of water; cool to body temperature.
2. Grind almonds with 2 tablespoons sugar in a food processor until as fine as possible, scraping inward occasionally. Add remaining 6 tablespoons sugar; process until blended. Add egg; process until blended. Add chocolate; process again until blended. Add brandy; process until blended.
3. Position rack in center of oven and preheat to 350F (175C). Butter 2 baking sheets. Remove filo sheets from their package; spread out on a dry towel. Using a sharp knife, cut stack in half lengthwise to form 2 stacks of sheets, about 16'' x 7''. Immediately cover filo with a piece of waxed paper, then with a damp towel. Work with only 1 sheet at a time and always keep remaining sheets covered with paper and towel so they do not dry out.
4. Carefully remove 1 filo sheet from pile. Brush with melted butter; fold in half lengthwise so dimensions are about 16'' x 3-1/2''. Place about 1-1/2 teaspoons Chocolate-Marzipan Filling at 1 end of strip. Fold end of strip diagonally over filling to form a triangle. Continue folding it over and over, keeping it in a triangular shape after each fold, until end of strip is reached. Brush sheet with butter before last fold to stick triangle together.
5. Set triangular pastry on a buttered baking sheet. Brush with melted butter. Cover baking sheet with plastic wrap. Continue making triangular pastries with remaining filo sheets and filling, covering each. *Pastries can be kept, covered tightly, up to 1 day in refrigerator.*
6. Brush pastries again with melted butter; sprinkle with sesame seeds. Bake about 25 minutes or until golden brown. If baking on 2 racks, switch their positions halfway through baking time. Serve warm, or at room temperature.

Soufflés, Baked Custards, Puddings & Crepes

Hot desserts like soufflés, puddings and crepes are preferred by many people as winter treats. Baked custards and some puddings, however, are served cold and are loved all year round.

These groups include several simple everyday sweet dishes, but also some of the most spectacular of desserts, from Dark Chocolate-Bourbon Soufflé to Chocolate-Orange Boule de Neige to Chocolate Crepe Gâteau with Brazil Nuts.

Chocolate Soufflés

The most impressive and airy of hot chocolate desserts, soufflés, are favorite desserts for ordering at restaurants and are the pride of good home cooks. In spite of their sophisticated appearance and the mystique surrounding them, they are actually easy to prepare. They are often made from a thick base of chocolate pastry cream, similar to the pastry cream used to fill cream puffs, lightened with whipped egg whites. Much of the preparation can be done ahead; only the whipping of the whites, the final blending of the mixture and the brief baking must be done at the last minute. The soufflés in this section are among the richest of dessert soufflés because of the addition of chocolate.

To the French taste, a soufflé should be very soft in the center and therefore does not usually need a sauce. Many Americans prefer their soufflés firmer and like to accompany them with a sauce, such as the hazelnut liqueur sauce served with Hazelnut-Praline-Chocolate Soufflé.

Chocolate Puddings

The category *chocolate pudding* actually covers a wide variety of desserts. The simplest puddings, the most homey of desserts, are based on bread or rice and bring back memories of family suppers. Some puddings are served hot, others cold, others at room temperature.

Most puddings are baked. Steamed Chocolate-Macadamia Nut Pudding, however, cooks on top of the stove in a water bath and is amazingly light for such a rich mixture. Although it is called *pudding*, it is surely one of the most elegant of desserts

and various versions can be found in Austria and Germany.

Chocolate Baked Custards

Baked custards are among the most exquisite finales to any meal. Yet these smooth, creamy desserts are quick and easy to prepare at home. An added bonus is that the required ingredients— milk, eggs, sugar and chocolate—are usually at hand.

The creamiest type of baked custards, known as "petits pots de crème," are baked and served in individual containers. This type of custard is the richest because it contains a large proportion of egg yolks and no egg whites.

It is no coincidence that the French call silky smooth custards "crèmes." Smoothness is their main characteristic and everything possible is done to ensure this quality. For this reason, many of these desserts are baked in a water bath: the dishes of custard mixture are set in a large shallow pan in the oven, and the pan is filled with hot water. The water provides moisture and moderates the oven temperature so the custards bake slowly and evenly and do not dry or separate as a result of direct oven heat.

Chocolate Crepes

Golden crepes with a rich chocolate filling are an easy and convenient dessert because they can be prepared ahead and reheated. A favorite French snack is a crepe, lightly heated in butter and filled with melted chocolate. Parisians have the choice of having it served to them at a crêperie or by a street vendor, who folds the filled crepe in four and wraps it in paper so it can be eaten during a stroll along the avenues.

Chocolate fillings for crepes are as easy as melting chocolate in cream and stirring in sliced fruit, as in Chocolate-Banana Crepes. Even the crepes themselves can be chocolate-flavored, with the addition of cocoa to the batter. In Crêpes Belle Hélène, these chocolate crepes are filled with sautéed sweetened pears and coated with dark chocolate sauce.

Dark Chocolate-Bourbon Soufflé

Make the bourbon sauce to accompany this rich, chocolaty soufflé if you like your soufflé relatively firm. If you like a soft soufflé in the French tradition, serve it with or without sauce.

Makes 4 servings

Bourbon Sauce:
1 cup milk
3 egg yolks, room temperature
3 tablespoons sugar
1 tablespoon bourbon whiskey

Chocolate-Bourbon Soufflé:
1/2 cup whipping cream
1/2 cup milk
3 egg yolks, room temperature
5 tablespoons sugar
1/4 cup all-purpose flour
4 oz. semisweet chocolate, finely
  chopped
2 tablespoons bourbon whiskey
5 egg whites, room temperature
Pinch of cream of tartar

1. Bourbon Sauce: Bring milk to a boil in a small heavy saucepan.
2. Whisk egg yolks lightly in a heatproof medium bowl. Add sugar; whisk until well-blended. Gradually whisk in hot milk. Return mixture to saucepan, whisking constantly. Cook over medium-low heat, stirring mixture and scraping bottom of pan constantly with a wooden spoon, until mixture thickens slightly and reaches 170F to 175F (75C to 80C) on an instant-read thermometer; begin checking after 5 minutes. To check whether it is thick enough without a thermometer, remove sauce from heat. Dip a metal spoon in sauce and draw your finger across back of spoon. Your finger should leave a clear path in mixture that clings to spoon. If it does not, continue cooking another 30 seconds and check again. Do not overcook sauce or it will curdle.
3. Immediately pour into a bowl. Stir about 30 seconds to cool. Cool completely. Stir in bourbon. *Sauce can be kept, covered, up to 2 days in refrigerator.*
1. Chocolate-Bourbon Soufflé: Bring cream and milk to a boil in a small heavy saucepan over medium-high heat.
2. Whisk egg yolks with 4 tablespoons sugar in a heatproof medium bowl until blended. Lightly stir in flour, using a whisk. Gradually whisk hot cream mixture into egg yolk mixture. Return to saucepan. Cook over medium heat, whisking constantly, until mixture is very thick and comes nearly to a boil. Remove from heat.
3. Add chocolate; whisk until melted. If not using immediately, dab this soufflé base with a small piece of butter to prevent a skin from forming. *Mixture can be kept, covered, up to 1 day in refrigerator.*
4. When ready to bake soufflé, position rack in lower third of oven and preheat to 400F (205C). Generously butter a 5-cup soufflé dish, making sure rim is well-buttered. Have a round heatproof platter ready near oven. If sauce was cold, let it come to room temperature.
5. If chocolate mixture was cold, heat in a small saucepan over low heat, whisking, until just warm. Remove from heat. Stir in bourbon.
6. In a large dry bowl, whip egg whites with cream of tartar using dry beaters at medium speed until soft peaks form. Gradually beat in remaining 1 tablespoon sugar; continue whipping at high speed until whites are stiff and shiny but not dry.
7. Quickly fold about 1/4 of whites into chocolate mixture. Spoon this mixture over remaining whites; fold in lightly but quickly, just until mixture is blended.
8. Transfer mixture to prepared soufflé dish; smooth top. For a soft soufflé with a very moist center, bake about 22 minutes or until puffed and browned; when you gently move oven rack, soufflé should shake very slightly in center. For a firmer soufflé, reduce oven temperature to 375F (190C) and continue baking about 5 minutes longer; when you carefully move dish, soufflé should not shake. Do not overbake or soufflé may burn on top and may shrink. Set soufflé dish on platter and serve immediately. Serve sauce separately.

TIP

○ *In some custard recipes, the center is not yet set when the dessert is done but the chocolate solidifies as it cools and causes the dessert to become firmer. The deeper and larger the dish used, the longer the time required for the custard mixture to set.*

Individual Chocolate-Grand Marnier Soufflés in Orange Cups

A dark chocolate soufflé baked and served in an orange makes an exquisite dessert. The moist, light soufflé is made with fresh orange juice and is delicately flavored with Grand Marnier.

Makes 4 generous or 8 light servings

8 large oranges, preferably navel oranges
3 egg yolks, room temperature
1/4 cup granulated sugar
3 tablespoons all-purpose flour
4 oz. semisweet chocolate, finely chopped
2 tablespoons plus 1 teaspoon Grand Marnier
4 egg whites, room temperature
Pinch of cream of tartar

Powdered sugar, if desired (for sprinkling)

1. Cut a very thin slice from 1 end of each orange so it stands up without rolling; be careful to leave some pith on bottom of orange or soufflé mixture will leak out. Cut top third off other end of orange. Using a sharp knife or serrated knife, cut from center to edge of orange several times. Cut around pulp of orange, as if prepare grapefruit. Using a grapefruit knife or serrated knife, scoop out flesh and juice into a strainer set over a bowl. Be careful not to pierce rind; rind should be clean of pulp. Press on flesh and strain juice. Set aside 1 cup juice for soufflé. Reserve remaining juice for other uses.
2. Heat 1 cup juice in a small heavy saucepan until lukewarm.
3. Whisk egg yolks with 3 tablespoons granulated sugar in a medium bowl until blended. Lightly stir in flour, using whisk. Gradually whisk juice into egg-yolk mixture. Return to saucepan. Cook over medium-low heat, whisking constantly, about 5 minutes or until mixture is very thick and comes nearly to a boil. Remove from heat.
4. Add chocolate; whisk until melted. If not using immediately, dab this soufflé base with a small piece of butter to prevent a skin from forming. *Mixture can be kept, covered, up to 1 day in refrigerator.*
5. When ready to bake soufflés, position rack in lower third of oven and preheat to 425F (220C). Butter a large gratin dish or other shallow baking dish and set oranges in it. Butter 2 (2/3-cup) ramekins.
6. If chocolate mixture was cold, heat in a small saucepan over low heat, whisking, just until warm. Remove from heat. Stir in Grand Marnier.
7. In a large dry bowl, whip egg whites with cream of tartar using dry beaters at medium speed until soft peaks form. Gradually beat in remaining 1 tablespoon granulated sugar; continue whipping at high speed until whites are stiff and shiny but not dry.
8. Quickly fold about 1/4 of whites into chocolate mixture. Spoon this mixture over remaining whites; fold in lightly but quickly, just until mixture is blended.
9. Spoon mixture into orange shells, filling them about 3/4 full. Spoon any remaining mixture into buttered ramekins, filling them nearly to the top. Bake ramekins about 10 minutes and oranges about 17 minutes or until soufflés are puffed and tops are firm and do not shake when shelf of oven is gently moved. Sprinkle with powdered sugar, if desired, and serve immediately. Serve 1 or 2 oranges per person.

Note: All of soufflé mixture can be baked in ramekins.

TIPS

○ *In order for custards to cook properly, the water in the water bath should remain hot but not boiling. If the water begins to boil, the texture of the dessert becomes marred by small holes.*

○ *If much of the water evaporates from the water bath during baking, especially with large desserts, add a little more hot water to maintain a level halfway up the dishes.*

How to Make Individual Chocolate-Grand Marnier Soufflés in Orange Cups

1/Cut from center to edge of orange several times. Cut around pulp of orange; scoop out flesh and juice. Rind should be clean of pulp.

2/Bake filled oranges about 17 minutes or until soufflés are puffed and tops are firm. Sprinkle with powdered sugar, if desired, and serve immediately.

Milk Chocolate Soufflés

Lovers of milk chocolate will count these easy-to-make soufflés among their favorite desserts.

Makes 4 servings·

1 cup milk
3 egg yolks, room temperature
2 tablespoons plus 2 teaspoons
  granulated sugar
1/4 cup all-purpose flour
5 oz. fine-quality milk chocolate,
  finely chopped
5 egg whites, room temperature
Pinch of cream of tartar

Powdered sugar, if desired (for
  sprinkling)

1. Bring milk to a boil in a small heavy saucepan over medium-high heat.
2. Whisk egg yolks with 2 tablespoons granulated sugar in a heatproof medium bowl until blended. Lightly stir in flour, using whisk. Gradually whisk hot milk into egg yolk mixture. Return to saucepan. Cook over medium heat, whisking constantly, until mixture is very thick and comes nearly to a boil. Remove from heat.
3. Add chocolate; whisk until melted. If not using immediately, dab this soufflé base with a small piece of butter to prevent a skin from forming. *Mixture can be kept, covered, up to 1 day in refrigerator.*
4. When ready to bake soufflés, position rack in lower third of oven and preheat to 425F (220C). Generously butter 4 (1-1/4-cup) soufflé dishes; set on a baking sheet. Have ready 4 heatproof plates near oven.
5. If chocolate mixture was cold, heat in a small saucepan over low heat, whisking, until just warm. Remove from heat.
6. In a large dry bowl, whip egg whites with cream of tartar using dry beaters at medium speed until soft peaks form. Gradually beat in remaining 2 teaspoons granulated sugar; continue whipping at high speed until whites are stiff and shiny but not dry.
7. Quickly fold about 1/4 of whites into chocolate mixture. Spoon over remaining whites; fold in lightly but quickly, just until mixture is blended.
8. Transfer to prepared soufflé dishes; smooth top. Bake about 12 minutes or until soufflés are well-puffed and lightly browned; when you gently move oven rack, soufflés should shake only slightly. Set soufflés on plates. Sprinkle with powdered sugar, if desired, and serve immediately.

Hazelnut Praline-Chocolate Soufflé

Praline made from toasted hazelnuts and caramel is a wonderful partner for chocolate. Although there are several steps involved in making the praline, this moist, high soufflé is worth it! Besides, the praline can be made ahead.

Makes 4 servings

Hazelnut Praline:
1/3 cup hazelnuts (about 1-1/2 oz.)
3 tablespoons sugar
2 tablespoons water

Hazelnut Liqueur Sauce:
1/2 cup whipping cream,
   well-chilled
1 teaspoon sugar
2 tablespoons plus 1 teaspoon
   hazelnut liqueur (Frangelico)

Chocolate Soufflé:
1 cup milk
3 egg yolks, room temperature
1/4 cup granulated sugar
1/4 cup all-purpose flour
2 oz. semisweet chocolate, finely
   chopped
5 egg whites, room temperature
Pinch of cream of tartar

Powdered sugar, if desired (for
   sprinkling)

1. Hazelnut Praline: Preheat oven to 350F (175C). Toast hazelnuts and remove skins, page 201. Remove from oven; leave in baking pan to keep warm.
2. Lightly oil a baking sheet.
3. Combine sugar and water in a heavy, very small saucepan that does not have a black interior. Heat mixture over low heat until sugar dissolves, gently stirring occasionally. Increase heat to high and boil, without stirring, but occasionally brushing down any sugar crystals from side of pan with a brush dipped in water, until mixture begins to brown. Reduce heat to medium-low. Continue cooking, swirling pan gently, until mixture is a rich brown color and a trace of smoke begins to rise from pan. Do not let caramel get too dark or it will burn and praline will be bitter; if caramel is too light, praline will be too sweet.
4. Immediately remove caramel from heat; stir in warm nuts, being careful not to splash, until they are well-coated with caramel. Stir over low heat 1-1/2 minutes. Immediately transfer to oiled baking sheet.
5. Cool completely. Break praline into small chunks. Grind praline in food processor, scraping mixture inwards occasionally, until as fine as possible.
6. Immediately transfer praline to an airtight container. *Praline can be kept several months in an airtight container at room temperature or in freezer.*
1. Hazelnut Liqueur Sauce: Chill a medium bowl and beaters for whipping cream. Whip cream with sugar in chilled bowl at medium-high speed until mixture is slightly thickened and pours rather slowly; cream should be sauce-like and not stiff enough to form peaks.
2. Stir in liqueur. Cover and refrigerate until ready to serve.
1. Chocolate Soufflé: Bring milk to a boil in a heavy small saucepan.
2. Whisk egg yolks with 2 tablespoons granulated sugar in a heatproof medium bowl until blended. Lightly stir in flour, using a whisk. Gradually whisk in hot milk. Return mixture to saucepan. Cook over low heat, whisking constantly, about 2 minutes or until mixture is very thick and comes nearly to a boil. Remove from heat.
3. Add chocolate; whisk until melted. If not using immediately, dab this soufflé base with a small piece of butter to prevent a skin from forming. *Soufflé base can be kept, covered, up to 1 day in refrigerator.*
4. When ready to bake soufflé, position rack in lower third of oven and preheat to 400F (205C). Generously butter a 5-cup soufflé dish, making sure rim is well-buttered. Have a round heatproof platter ready near oven.
5. If soufflé base was cold, heat in a small saucepan over low heat, whisking, until just warm. Remove from heat. Stir in praline powder.
6. In a large dry bowl, whip egg whites with cream of tartar using dry beaters at medium speed until soft peaks form. Gradually beat in remaining 2 tablespoons granulated sugar; continue whipping at high speed until whites are stiff and shiny but not dry.
7. Quickly fold about 1/4 of whites into chocolate mixture. Spoon this mixture over remaining whites; fold in lightly but quickly, just until mixture is blended. Be careful not to deflate mixture; a few streaks of white may remain.
8. Transfer mixture to prepared soufflé dish; smooth top. For a soft soufflé with a very moist center, bake about 22 minutes or until puffed and browned; when you gently move rack, soufflé should shake very slightly in center. For a firmer soufflé, reduce oven temperature to 375F (190C) and continue baking about 5 minutes longer; when you carefully move dish, soufflé should not shake. Do not overbake or soufflé may burn on top and may shrink. Set soufflé dish on prepared platter. Sprinkle with powdered sugar, if desired, and serve immediately. Serve sauce separately.

Chocolate-Orange Boule de Neige

This elegant chocolate dessert is an orange-flavored version of an all-time favorite at La Varenne Cooking School in Paris, where I studied and worked for over five years. It consists of a very rich baked custard covered completely with rosettes of whipped cream. Fitting this dessert into a menu plan is easy because it keeps very well. In fact, the custard should be baked ahead so it sets completely and the flavors meld.

Makes 8 to 10 servings

Dense Chocolate-Orange Custard:
8 oz. semisweet chocolate, chopped
1/2 cup strained fresh orange juice
3/4 cup sugar
1 cup (8 oz.) unsalted butter, cut in 8 pieces
4 eggs, beaten, room temperature
1 tablespoon plus 2 teaspoons grated orange zest

Candied Orange Zest:
1 large orange
1/4 cup sugar
1 cup water

Grand Marnier Whipped Cream:
1-1/2 cups whipping cream, well-chilled
2 tablespoons sugar
2 tablespoons Grand Marnier

1. Custard: Position rack in center of oven and preheat to 350F (175C). Line a 1-quart charlotte mold with 2 layers of foil so they fit tightly.
2. Combine chocolate and orange juice in a heavy, medium saucepan set in a shallow pan of hot water over low heat. Leave until melted, stirring occasionally. Stir until smooth. Stir in sugar and butter. Leave saucepan in water over low heat until sugar dissolves and butter melts, stirring often.
3. Remove saucepan from water; set over low heat. Cook mixture, stirring constantly, until hot (about 150F, 65C on an instant-read or candy thermometer); do not boil.
4. Remove from heat; very gradually whisk in eggs. Strain into a large bowl.
5. Stir in grated zest. Pour into lined mold. Bake 40 to 45 minutes or until a thick crust forms on top and center still moves when mold is moved gently.
6. Cool in mold on a rack. Mixture will sink in center as it cools. To counteract this tendency, press on edges of dessert to flatten them slightly. Cool to room temperature, pressing again on edges a few times. Cover and refrigerate 6 hours. *Dessert can be kept up to 2 weeks in refrigerator.*
1. Candied orange zest: Using a vegetable peeler, pare colored part of orange peel in long strips, without including white pith. Cut zest in very thin strips, about 1/8 inch wide, with a large sharp knife.
2. Put strips of zest in a small saucepan; cover with water. Bring to a boil; boil 3 minutes. Drain, rinse with cold water; drain well.
3. Combine sugar and 1 cup water in a small heavy saucepan. Heat mixture over low heat until sugar dissolves, gently stirring occasionally. Increase heat to high and bring to a boil.
4. Add strips of zest to syrup; shake pan gently so zest is submerged. Poach zest, uncovered, over medium heat 20 minutes or until it is very tender and syrup thickens.
5. Cool zest completely in syrup. *Candied zest can be kept in its syrup up to 1 week in refrigerator.*
6. A short time before serving, run a thin-bladed knife around outer layer of foil in charlotte mold; turn out dessert onto a round platter. Carefully peel off foil. Dessert will be quite soft. Return to refrigerator.
7. Drain Candied Orange Zest on paper towels.
1. Whipped cream: Chill a large bowl and beaters for whipping cream. Whip cream with sugar in chilled bowl until soft peaks form. Add Grand Marnier; continue beating until cream is very stiff.
2. Using a pastry bag and medium star tip, pipe rosettes of whipped cream over dessert, beginning in center and piping circles of rosettes until chocolate is completely covered.
3. Garnish with about 20 strands of candied zest, carefully placing them on cream 1 strand at a time and arranging them randomly on top and side of dessert. Refrigerate until ready to serve.

Gingered Chocolate Custards

A powerful punch of fresh ginger essence imparts a refreshing zip to these exceptionally creamy custards, which are favorites in my chocolate cooking classes. The chopped ginger is strained out of the custard so only the exotic flavor remains.

Makes 4 servings

3/4 cup plus 2 tablespoons minced peeled gingerroot (about 6 oz. gingerroot)
1/2 cup water
3/4 cup sugar
1/2 pint whipping cream (1 cup)
3-1/2 oz. semisweet chocolate, chopped
1/2 cup milk
4 egg yolks, room temperature

1/2 cup whipping cream, well-chilled, if desired (for garnish)
About 2 teaspoons chopped crystallized ginger, if desired (for garnish)

1. Position rack in center of oven and preheat to 350F (175C).
2. Combine gingerroot, water and 1/2 cup sugar in a small heavy saucepan. Cook over low heat, stirring constantly, until sugar dissolves. Increase heat to high and bring to a boil. Reduce heat to low. Cover and simmer about 10 minutes or until ginger is tender. Uncover and increase heat to medium. Cook, stirring constantly, about 5 minutes or until liquid is absorbed.
3. Stir in cream; bring nearly to a simmer. Cook over low heat 4 minutes. Cool 3 minutes.
4. Combine chocolate and milk in a double boiler or heatproof medium bowl over hot, not simmering, water over low heat. Leave until nearly melted, stirring occasionally. Remove from pan of water; stir gently until smooth with a whisk.
5. Using whisk, gradually stir hot ginger-cream mixture into chocolate mixture. Be sure to stir in any chocolate adhering to side of pan.
6. Whisk egg yolks lightly in a large bowl. Add remaining 1/4 cup sugar; whisk just until blended. Gradually pour in about 3/4 cup chocolate mixture in a thin stream, stirring constantly with whisk. Using a wooden spoon, gradually stir in remaining chocolate mixture. Strain mixture into a large measuring cup, pressing on ginger. Skim foam from surface of mixture.
7. Set 4 (2/3-cup) ramekins in a roasting pan or large shallow baking dish. Pour custard mixture into ramekins, dividing it evenly among them. Skim any remaining foam from mixture in ramekins.
8. Place pan with ramekins in oven. Add enough nearly boiling water to pan to come halfway up sides of ramekins. Set a sheet of foil gently on top to cover ramekins loosely, without folding foil around edges of pan. Bake about 35 minutes or until top is nearly set and moves only very slightly when pan is moved gently. During baking, if water in pan comes close to a boil, add a few tablespoons cold water to pan.
9. Carefully remove ramekins from pan of water; cool on a rack to room temperature. Cover and refrigerate 3 hours. *Custards can be kept up to 2 days in refrigerator.*
10. If desired, chill a medium bowl and beaters for whipping cream. Whip cream in chilled bowl until very stiff. Using a pastry bag and large star tip, pipe a rosette of whipped cream on center of each dessert. Sprinkle each rosette with crystallized ginger, if desired. Serve dessert cold in ramekins.

TIPS

○ When baking custards in several ramekins, check each one to see if it is done because the temperature may not be uniform in the front and back of the oven.

○ A metal pancake turner or a kitchen towel is easier to use than potholders for removing small ramekins from the water bath.

○ Custard recipes can easily be doubled and baked in a larger number of ramekins. If using larger-size ramekins, cooking time will vary according to depth of the mixture.

How to Make Gingered Chocolate Custards

1/Cover and simmer gingerroot in syrup until tender. Uncover and increase heat to medium. Cook, stirring constantly, about 5 minutes or until liquid is absorbed.

2/Place pan with filled ramekins in preheated oven. Add enough nearly boiling water to pan to come halfway up sides of ramekins. Set a sheet of foil gently on top to cover ramekins loosely, without folding foil around edges of pan. Bake about 35 minutes or until top is nearly set.

Bittersweet Chocolate-Chestnut Soufflé

Chestnut and chocolate appear in many Austrian, French and Swiss desserts. In this soufflé, the sweet chestnut puree complements the bittersweet chocolate. The soufflé can be prepared quickly because the puree binds the mixture and there is no need to make a flour-thickened soufflé base.

Makes 4 servings

4 oz. bittersweet chocolate, chopped
1/3 cup whipping cream
1 (8-3/4-oz.) can sweetened chestnut puree (3/4 cup)
3 egg yolks, room temperature
6 egg whites, room temperature
Pinch of cream of tartar
Powdered sugar, if desired (for sprinkling)

1. Combine chocolate and cream in a double boiler or small heatproof bowl over hot, not simmering, water over low heat. Leave until melted, stirring occasionally. Stir until smooth. Remove from pan of water.
2. Stir chestnut puree into chocolate mixture. Beat in egg yolks, 1 at a time. *Mixture can be kept, covered, up to 1 day in refrigerator.*
3. When ready to bake soufflé, position rack in lower third of oven and preheat to 400F (205C). Generously butter a 5-cup soufflé dish, making sure rim of dish is well-buttered. Have ready a round heatproof platter near oven.
4. If chocolate mixture was cold, heat in a small saucepan over low heat, whisking, until just warm. Remove from heat.
5. In a large dry bowl, whip egg whites with cream of tartar using dry beaters at medium speed until soft peaks form. Continue whipping at high speed until whites are stiff and shiny but not dry.
6. Quickly fold about 1/4 of whites into chocolate mixture. Spoon this mixture over remaining whites; fold in quickly, just until mixture is blended.
7. Transfer mixture to prepared soufflé dish; smooth top. For a soft soufflé with a very moist center, bake about 25 minutes or until puffed; when you gently move rack, soufflé should shake very slightly in center. For a firmer soufflé, reduce oven temperature to 375F (190C) and continue baking about 5 minutes longer; when you carefully move dish, soufflé should not shake. Do not overbake or soufflé may burn on top and may shrink. Set soufflé dish on platter. Sprinkle with powdered sugar, if desired, and serve immediately.

Chocolate Crème Brûlée with Raspberries

A crunchy crust of caramelized sugar and a satiny chocolate custard hide a surprise of fresh raspberries. This modern version makes use of a cooked custard, which is creamier than a baked custard, as a base for the crème brûlée. In restaurants, the top is caramelized with a blow-torch, but this home version is done in the broiler and works easily with brown sugar. The brief broiling does not cook the berries because they are protected by the thoroughly chilled custard.

Makes 6 servings

Rich Cooked Chocolate Custard:

6 oz. fine-quality bittersweet
  chocolate, chopped
1-1/3 cups whipping cream
5 egg yolks, room temperature
3 tablespoons sugar

Fruit & Topping:

1-1/2 cups raspberries, well-chilled
1/2 cup plus 1 tablespoon packed
  dark-brown sugar
1/2 cup whipping cream,
  well-chilled

18 raspberries (for garnish)

1. **Custard:** Melt chocolate in a double boiler or heatproof medium bowl over hot, not simmering, water over low heat, stirring occasionally. Stir until smooth. Remove from pan of water; cool to body temperature.
2. Scald cream in a small heavy saucepan by heating until bubbles form around edge of pan.
3. Whisk egg yolks lightly in a heatproof medium bowl. Add sugar; whisk until well-blended. Gradually whisk in hot cream. Return mixture to saucepan, whisking constantly. Cook over low heat, stirring mixture and scraping bottom of pan constantly with a wooden spoon, until mixture thickens slightly and reaches 160F (70C) on an instant-read thermometer; begin checking after 5 minutes. To check whether it is thick enough without a thermometer, remove mixture from heat. Dip a metal spoon in it and draw your finger across back of spoon. Your finger should leave a clear path in mixture that clings to spoon. If it does not, continue cooking another 30 seconds and check again. Do not overcook mixture or it will curdle.
4. Immediately pour into a bowl; stir about 30 seconds to cool. Cool 5 minutes.
5. Pour 1 cup custard over melted chocolate; whisk until blended. Using a whisk, gradually stir remaining custard into chocolate.
6. Pour chocolate custard into a large bowl; cool to room temperature, stirring occasionally. Cover and refrigerate at least 4 or up to 6 hours.
1. **Fruit & Topping:** Put 1/4 cup berries in 1 layer in each of 6 (2/3-cup) ramekins. Stir custard. Carefully spoon about 1/3 cup custard over berries in each ramekin. Spread with a rubber spatula to cover berries.
2. Set broiler rack about 4-1/2 inches from heat source. Preheat broiler. Sift 1-1/2 tablespoons brown sugar evenly over each custard, covering it completely. Brush any sugar off rim of dish.
3. Position 2 ramekins so broiler element can heat them evenly. Broil custards, 2 at a time, keeping door open, about 1 minute or until brown sugar turns a slightly darker shade and forms a slightly firm crust. Check crust by tapping very gently with a spoon, not with your fingers. Watch carefully; sugar burns easily. Repeat with remaining ramekins.
4. Refrigerate custards 1 hour. *Custards can be kept, uncovered, up to 1 day in refrigerator.*
5. Chill a medium bowl and beaters for whipping cream. Whip cream in chilled bowl until very stiff. Using a pastry bag and medium star tip, pipe a few rosettes of whipped cream onto each custard. Garnish with raspberries.

TIPS

○ *When using a tester to check baked custards, try to insert it straight down so it will not make a large hole.*

○ *When preparing custard mixtures, do not whisk hard. Whisking the eggs vigorously creates foam that solidifies in the oven and mars the smooth surface of the dessert.*

○ *Fine-quality chocolate blends more thoroughly into custard mixtures than does ordinary chocolate.*

1/Cook yolk and cream over low heat until mixture thickens slightly and reaches 160F (70C) on thermometer. Or, dip a metal spoon in mixture and draw your finger across back of spoon. Your finger should leave a clear path in mixture on spoon.

2/Put 1/4 cup berries in 1 layer in each of 6 (2/3-cup) ramekins. Stir chocolate custard. Carefully spoon about 1/3 cup custard over berries in each ramekin. Spread with a rubber spatula to cover berries.

Mocha Petits Pots de Crème
Photo on pages 8-9.

During baking, the chocolate forms a dark, glossy topping on these coffee-accented custards. The garnish of whipped cream is not traditional but it adds color and a pleasant lightness.

Makes 4 servings

Baked Mocha Custards:
4 oz. bittersweet chocolate, chopped
1-1/2 cups milk
2 tablespoons instant coffee granules
4 egg yolks, room temperature
5 tablespoons sugar

Kahlúa Whipped Cream:
1/3 cup whipping cream, well-chilled
1/2 teaspoon sugar
2 teaspoons coffee liqueur, such as Kahlúa

4 chocolate coffee beans, if desired (for garnish)

1. **Custards:** Position rack in center of oven and preheat to 350F (175C).
2. Combine chocolate and 1/2 cup milk in a double boiler or heatproof medium bowl over hot, not simmering, water over low heat, stirring occasionally. When nearly melted, remove from water and stir gently with a whisk until smooth.
3. Bring remaining 1 cup milk to a boil in a small saucepan. Remove from heat; whisk in coffee. Cool 3 minutes. Using a whisk, gradually stir milk into chocolate mixture.
4. Whisk egg yolks lightly in a large bowl. Add sugar; whisk just until blended. Gradually pour in about 3/4 cup chocolate mixture in a thin stream, stirring constantly with whisk. Using a wooden spoon, gradually stir in remaining chocolate mixture. Strain into a large measuring cup. Skim foam from surface.
5. Set 4 (2/3-cup) ramekins in a roasting pan or large shallow baking dish. Pour custard mixture into ramekins, dividing it evenly among them. Skim any remaining foam from mixture in ramekins.
6. Place pan with ramekins in oven. Add enough nearly boiling water to pan to come halfway up sides of ramekins. Set a sheet of foil gently on top to cover ramekins loosely, without folding foil around edges of pan. Bake about 25 minutes or until top is nearly set and moves only very slightly when pan is moved gently, or until a cake tester inserted very gently in mixture about 1/2 inch from edge of each ramekin comes out clean. During baking, if water in pan comes close to a boil, add a few tablespoons cold water to pan.
7. Carefully remove ramekins from pan of water; cool on a rack to room temperature. Cover and refrigerate 3 hours. *Custards can be kept up to 1 day in refrigerator.*
1. **Whipped cream:** Chill a small bowl and beaters for whipping cream. Whip cream with sugar in chilled bowl until soft peaks form. Add liqueur; continue whipping until cream is very stiff.
2. Using a pastry bag and large star tip, pipe a rosette of Kahlúa Whipped Cream on each serving. If desired, top each rosette with a chocolate coffee bean. Serve dessert cold in ramekins.

Steamed Chocolate-Macadamia Nut Pudding

Steaming makes this superb, unusual pudding incredibly light, yet very moist. The hemispherical, elegant dessert of Austrian-German inspiration has an intense chocolate flavor. Macadamia Cream is a delicious accompaniment, but plain whipped cream can be substituted.

Makes 6 to 8 servings

Chocolate-Macadamia Pudding:

1 cup macadamia nuts (about 4-1/4 oz.), unsalted or desalted, page 201

4 oz. fine-quality semisweet chocolate, chopped

2/3 cup sugar

1/2 cup (4 oz.) unsalted butter, slightly softened

5 eggs, separated, room temperature

Macadamia Cream:

1/2 pint whipping cream, well-chilled (1 cup)

2 tablespoons macadamia nut liqueur or hazelnut liqueur

1. Chocolate-Macadamia Pudding: Preheat oven to 350F (175C). Generously butter a 6-cup heatproof bowl; sprinkle with sugar. Choose a heavy pot or stew pan large enough to hold bowl with about 1-1/2 inches of space on all sides.
2. Toast nuts in a shallow baking pan in oven 3 minutes. Transfer to a plate; cool completely.
3. Melt chocolate in a double boiler or heatproof medium bowl over hot, not simmering, water over low heat, stirring occasionally. Stir until smooth. Remove from pan of water; cool to body temperature.
4. Grind nuts with 2 tablespoons sugar in a food processor until as fine as possible, scraping inward occasionally. Transfer to a medium bowl. Set aside additional 2 tablespoons sugar for beating into egg whites.
5. Cream butter in a medium bowl. Add remaining sugar; beat until fluffy. Beat in egg yolks, 1 at a time. Stir in melted chocolate and macadamia nuts. Prepare a kettle of boiling water for use in Step 8.
6. In a large dry bowl, whip egg whites using dry beaters at medium speed until soft peaks form. Gradually beat in reserved 2 tablespoons sugar; continue whipping at high speed until whites are stiff and shiny but not dry.
7. Fold about 1/4 of whites into chocolate mixture. Spoon this mixture over remaining whites; fold in lightly but quickly, just until mixture is blended.
8. Transfer mixture to prepared bowl. Cover tightly with 2 layers of foil. Tie string around side of bowl so foil is tightly secured. Set in pot. Pour in enough boiling water to come halfway up side of bowl. Cover pot. Set pot over low heat so water just simmers; cook 1 hour and 45 minutes. Check water occasionally; it should simmer but not boil hard. If it boils, add a few tablespoons cold water. If much of water evaporates, add more water. To check if pudding is done, uncover and insert a cake tester; it should come out dry. Otherwise cover again and steam a few minutes longer. *Pudding can be kept warm, covered, up to 1 hour in its pot of water off heat.*
1. Macadamia Cream: Chill a medium bowl and beaters for whipping cream. Just before serving, whip cream in chilled bowl at medium-high speed until soft peaks form. Add liqueur; beat until blended.
2. Remove pudding from water; discard foil. Set platter on top. Holding firmly together, quickly flip so pudding is right-side up and slips from mold onto platter.
3. Serve hot. Cut into wedges to serve. Spoon some Macadamia Cream over each piece. *Pudding can be kept, covered, up to 4 days in refrigerator.* Serve any leftovers cold.

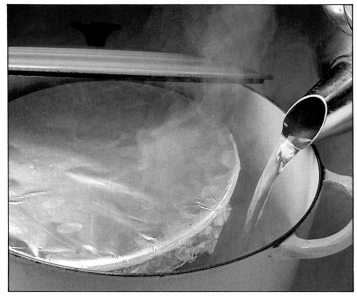

1/Cover pudding tightly with 2 layers of foil. Tie string around side of bowl. Set in pot. Pour in enough boiling water to come halfway up side of bowl. Cover pot. Set pot over low heat so water just simmers; cook 1 hour and 45 minutes.

2/Serve pudding hot, cut into wedges. Spoon some Macadamia Cream over each serving.

Chocolate Bread Pudding

For informal family gatherings, especially in the winter, this moist, light bread pudding is an ideal dessert. It is easy to prepare yet smoother and more elegant than most bread puddings. Serve it on its own or accompanied by Vanilla Bean or Coffee Custard Sauce, page 197.

Makes 4 to 6 servings

5 (3-1/2" x 5" x 1/2") slices French
    bread (4 oz.)
3 oz. semisweet chocolate, chopped
1/2 cup (4 oz.) unsalted butter,
    slightly softened
1/4 cup sugar
4 eggs, separated, room
    temperature
Pinch of cream of tartar

1. Position rack in center of oven and preheat to 250F (120C). Bake bread on baking sheet 10 minutes. Turn slices over; bake 5 minutes or until dry. Cool completely. Break into pieces.
2. Grind bread in food processor until it becomes fine crumbs.
3. Increase oven temperature to 350F (175C). Butter a 1-quart charlotte mold or soufflé dish. Coat side and bottom with sugar, tapping to remove excess.
4. Melt chocolate in a double boiler or small heatproof bowl over hot, not simmering, water over low heat, stirring occasionally. Stir until smooth. Remove from pan of water; cool to room temperature.
5. Cream butter in a large bowl. Add 3 tablespoons sugar; beat until smooth and fluffy. Add egg yolks, 1 at a time, and beat very thoroughly after each addition. Stir in bread crumbs and melted chocolate.
6. In a large dry bowl, whip egg whites with cream of tartar using dry beaters at medium speed until soft peaks form. Gradually beat in remaining tablespoon sugar; continue whipping at high speed until whites are stiff but not dry.
7. Stir 1/4 of whites into chocolate mixture until blended. Fold in remaining whites in 3 batches; mixture will be thick and seem difficult to blend but continue folding until blended.
8. Transfer mixture to prepared mold. Set mold in a roasting pan or large baking dish; put in oven. Add enough nearly boiling water to larger pan to come halfway up side of mold. Cover gently with foil without folding foil around edges of mold. Bake about 55 minutes or until a cake tester inserted in center of pudding comes out clean.
9. Remove from pan of water; cool on rack. Pudding settles as it cools.
10. Run a thin-bladed flexible knife or metal spatula around pudding and invert onto a platter. Serve lukewarm or cold. *Pudding can be kept covered up to 2 days in refrigerator.*

Black Forest Trifle

The English originated the famous trifle, a pudding made of pieces of cake layered with custard, whipped cream and fruit. The lovely combination of chocolate and cherries was popularized by the German Black Forest cake. Here is a marriage of both. Traditionally leftover sponge cake is used for trifle but you can use other light-textured cakes and cut them in strips. This version utilizes ladyfingers which are a great substitute if you do not happen to have any leftover cake in the house. If possible, use a wide-bottomed glass bowl or a glass soufflé dish so the attractive layers are visible.

Makes 8 servings

Cooked Chocolate Custard:
8 oz. semisweet chocolate, chopped
1 cup milk
1 tablespoon cornstarch
1-1/2 cups whipping cream
2 eggs, room temperature
2 egg yolks, room temperature
3 tablespoons sugar

Ladyfinger & Fruit Layers:
About 3-1/2 oz. ladyfingers (about 3 inches long)
1/4 cup kirsch
1/2 cup red-cherry preserves
2 cups fresh, dark, sweet cherries, (8 oz.), halved and pitted

Kirsch Whipped Cream:
1/2 pint whipping cream (1 cup), well-chilled
1 tablespoon sugar
2 tablespoons kirsch

Semisweet chocolate (for garnish)
6 whole, dark, sweet cherries, stems trimmed to about 1 inch (for garnish)

1. Cooked Chocolate Custard: Combine 8 ounces chocolate and 1/2 cup milk in a double boiler or heatproof medium bowl over hot, not simmering, water over low heat. Leave until melted, stirring occasionally. Stir until smooth. Remove from pan of water; cool to body temperature.

2. Mix cornstarch with 1 tablespoon of milk in a small cup until dissolved.

3. Scald cream with remaining 7 tablespoons milk in a heavy medium saucepan by heating until bubbles form around edge of pan.

4. Whisk eggs and egg yolks lightly in a heatproof medium bowl. Add sugar; whisk until blended. Whisk in dissolved cornstarch. Gradually whisk in hot cream mixture. Return mixture to saucepan, whisking constantly. Cook over low heat, whisking constantly, about 5 minutes or until mixture thickens slightly and reaches 150F (65C) on an instant-read thermometer. Do not boil. Remove from heat; cool to room temperature, stirring occasionally. Whisk in cool chocolate mixture. Cover and refrigerate 4 hours.

1. Ladyfinger & Fruit Layers: If using packaged ladyfingers, which are usually split in half horizontally and are joined in a row, there is no need to separate them into individual ones. Put enough ladyfinger halves in a 1-1/2-quart glass bowl or deep baking dish to make 1 layer. If using homemade ladyfingers, leave them whole. Brush 2 tablespoons kirsch evenly over them. Stir custard; pour 1-3/4 cups custard over ladyfingers in bowl. Cover with plastic wrap. Refrigerate 1 to 2 hours to firm custard slightly.

2. Heat preserves until melted in a small saucepan over low heat, stirring occasionally and mashing cherries that are in preserves.

3. Arrange remaining ladyfinger halves in 1 layer on custard in bowl. Brush with remaining kirsch. Spoon preserves evenly over them. Scatter fresh cherries on top. Carefully spoon remaining custard over cherries. Cover and refrigerate 8 hours or overnight. *Dessert can be kept, covered, up to 2 days in refrigerator.*

1. Kirsch Whipped Cream: Chill a medium bowl and beaters for whipping cream. Up to a few hours before serving, whip cream with sugar in chilled bowl until soft peaks form. Add kirsch; whip until stiff.

2. Carefully spoon whipped cream on top of dessert; spread in an even layer. Grate chocolate onto center of dessert. Set whole cherries around edge.

Chocolate-Banana Crepes

Chocolate cream and bananas make a rich, very easy-to-prepare filling for these lacy crepes.

Makes 8 small or 4 generous
   servings

Crepes:
3/4 cup plus 1 tablespoon milk
2 eggs
2 tablespoons unsalted butter,
   melted and cooled
1/2 cup all-purpose flour
1/4 teaspoon salt
1 to 2 tablespoons vegetable oil (for
   brushing pan)

Chocolate-Banana Filling:
4 oz. fine-quality semisweet
   chocolate, chopped
1/4 cup whipping cream
2 large bananas (about 14 oz.)
2 tablespoons rum

1 tablespoon butter, melted (for
   brushing crepes)
1/2 cup whipping cream,
   well-chilled, if desired (for
   garnish)
1 banana, if desired (for garnish)

1. Crepes: Combine milk, eggs and melted butter in a food processor fitted with metal blade or in a blender. Sift in flour and salt; process 5 seconds. Scrape down batter. Process batter 20 seconds. Transfer to a bowl. Cover and refrigerate 1 hour.

2. Heat an 8-inch crepe pan or skillet over medium-high heat. Brush pan lightly with oil. Heat until hot enough so a drop of batter added to pan sizzles immediately. Remove drop of batter; remove pan from heat. Stir batter. Fill a 1/4-cup measure about 3/4 full with batter; pour into hot pan. Tilt and rotate pan quickly so batter covers bottom in a thin layer. Return any excess batter to bowl. Return pan to medium-high heat. Loosen edge of crepe from pan with a pancake turner or metal spatula. Cook crepe until underside browns lightly. Turn over and briefly brown other side. Transfer crepe to a plate.

3. Continue making crepes with remaining batter, stirring batter before preparing each crepe. Brush pan lightly with oil as necessary; if using a nonstick crepe pan, no further oil will be needed. Stack crepes on plate. *Crepes can be kept, covered, up to 2 days in refrigerator. Bring to room temperature before continuing.*

4. Position rack in center of oven and preheat to 400F (205C). Butter a large shallow baking dish. Chill a medium bowl and beaters for whipping cream for garnish.

1. Chocolate-Banana Filling: Combine chocolate and 1/4 cup cream in a double boiler or small heatproof bowl over hot, not simmering, water over low heat. Leave until melted, stirring occasionally.

2. Meanwhile, cut bananas in small dice; you will have 2 cups.

3. Stir chocolate mixture until smooth. Remove from pan of water. Gradually stir in rum. Gently stir in bananas.

1. Assembly: Spoon 3 tablespoons filling onto less-attractive side of each crepe; spread gently to within about 1/2 inch of side. Roll up crepes tightly like cigars. Arrange, seam-side down, in buttered baking dish in 1 layer. Brush crepes with melted butter.

2. Bake crepes 5 to 7 minutes or until hot. Meanwhile, whip 1/2 cup cream in chilled bowl until soft peaks form. Slice banana.

3. Serve crepes hot, allowing 1 or 2 per serving. Spoon a little whipped cream onto or next to each crepe; top cream with a few banana slices.

TIPS

○ *Unfilled crepes can be frozen for several weeks.*

○ *Nonstick crepe pans are the easiest to use.*

○ *Canned, sweetened, chestnut puree is often labeled chestnut spread or crème de marrons.*

○ *To mince gingerroot in a food processor, drop pieces of gingerroot through top of processor with blade of processor turning.*

○ *To halve cherries, cut around pit like for avocado. Twist slightly to separate halves and pry out pit with the point of a knife. If you have a cherry pitter, pit cherries and cut in half.*

Chocolate Crepe Gâteau with Brazil Nuts

An impressive "cake" made of layers of crepes baked with Brazil-nut-chocolate filling, then topped with a shiny chocolate sauce.

Makes 6 to 8 servings

Crepes:
2/3 cup milk
1/2 cup water
3 eggs
3 tablespoons unsalted butter, melted and cooled
3/4 cup all-purpose flour, sifted
1/2 teaspoon salt
1 to 2 tablespoons vegetable oil (for brushing pan)

Crepe Gâteau:
3 oz. semisweet chocolate, chopped
1 cup Brazil nuts (about 5 1/4 oz.)
1/2 cup sugar
5 tablespoons unsalted butter, slightly softened
2 eggs, beaten
2 tablespoons all-purpose flour
10 crepes (see above), room temperature
1 tablespoon unsalted butter, melted

Chocolate Sauce:
4 oz. semisweet chocolate, chopped
1/2 cup whipping cream

2 tablespoons coarsely chopped Brazil nuts (for sprinkling)

1. Crepes: Combine milk, water, eggs and melted butter in a food processor fitted with metal blade or in a blender. Sift in flour and salt; process 5 seconds. Scrape down batter. Process batter 20 seconds. Transfer to a bowl. Cover and refrigerate 1 hour.

2. Heat an 8-inch crepe pan or skillet over medium-high heat. Brush pan lightly with oil. Heat until hot enough so a drop of batter added to pan sizzles immediately. Remove drop of batter; remove pan from heat. Stir batter. Fill a 1/4-cup measure about 3/4 full with batter; pour into hot pan. Tilt and rotate pan quickly so batter covers bottom in a thin layer. Return any excess batter to bowl. Return pan to medium-high heat. Loosen edge of crepe from pan with a pancake turner or metal spatula. Cook crepe until underside browns lightly. Turn over and briefly brown other side. Transfer crepe to a plate.

3. Continue making crepes with remaining batter, stirring batter before preparing each crepe. Brush pan lightly with oil as necessary; if using a nonstick crepe pan, no further oil will be needed. Stack crepes on plate. *Crepes can be kept, covered, up to 2 days in refrigerator. Bring to room temperature before continuing.*

1. Crepe Gâteau: Position rack in center of oven and preheat to 350F (175C).

2. Melt chocolate in a double boiler or small heatproof bowl over hot, not simmering, water over low heat, stirring occasionally. Stir until smooth. Remove from pan of water; cool to body temperature.

3. Grind nuts with 2 tablespoons sugar in a food processor until as fine as possible, scraping inward occasionally. Transfer to a medium bowl.

4. Cream butter in a medium bowl. Add remaining 6 tablespoons sugar; beat until fluffy. Beat in chocolate. Gradually beat in eggs. Using a wooden spoon, stir in nut mixture and flour.

5. Lightly butter an 8-inch springform pan. Put 1 crepe flat on base. Spread with 1/4 cup chocolate mixture. Set second crepe on top, smoothing it over filling. Spread with another 1/4 cup chocolate mixture. Continue with remaining crepes and chocolate mixture until only 3 crepes are left. If crepes are slightly larger than pan, fold their edges upward slightly or trim them to fit. Spread eighth crepe and ninth crepe with only 3 tablespoons filling each. Set last crepe on top; brush with melted butter.

6. Set pan on a baking sheet. Bake about 40 minutes or until filling is firm and heated through. Meanwhile, prepare sauce.

1. Chocolate Sauce: Combine chocolate and cream in a double boiler or heatproof medium bowl over hot, not simmering, water over low heat. Leave until nearly melted, stirring occasionally. Stir until sauce is smooth. *Sauce can be made 1 week ahead and kept, covered, in refrigerator. Reheat in a pan of hot water before serving.*

2. When gâteau is completed, let stand 5 minutes to settle. Release spring of pan and unmold dessert. Spoon a little Chocolate Sauce on top of gâteau; spread over top, letting it run down side. Sprinkle chopped Brazil nuts on center of sauce. To serve, cut in wedges. Serve remaining sauce separately.

Crêpes Belle Hélène

These chocolate crepes made from a cocoa batter are filled with sautéed fresh pears and served with dark chocolate sauce. Like the classic pears Belle Hélène, combining poached pears and chocolate sauce, they are accompanied by vanilla ice cream.

Makes 4 servings

Chocolate Crepes:
3/4 cup milk
2 eggs
2 tablespoons unsalted butter, melted and cooled
1 teaspoon sugar
Pinch of salt
7 tablespoons all-purpose flour
1 tablespoon unsweetened Dutch-process cocoa powder
1 to 2 tablespoons vegetable oil (for brushing pan)

Pear Filling:
1-1/2 lbs. ripe pears
1 lemon, halved
3 tablespoons unsalted butter
5 to 6 tablespoons sugar

1 tablespoon unsalted butter, melted (for brushing crepes)
Dark Chocolate Sauce, page 197
2 tablespoons coarsely chopped walnuts, pecans, pistachios or blanched almonds, if desired (for garnish)
Vanilla ice cream (for accompaniment)

1. Chocolate Crepes: Combine milk, eggs, melted butter, sugar and salt in a food processor fitted with metal blade or in a blender. Sift in flour and cocoa; process 5 seconds. Scrape down batter. Process batter 20 seconds. Transfer to a bowl. Cover and refrigerate 1 hour.

2. Heat an 8-inch crepe pan or skillet over medium-high heat. Brush pan lightly with oil. Heat until hot enough so a drop of batter added to pan sizzles immediately. Remove drop of batter; remove pan from heat. Stir batter. Fill a 1/4-cup measure about 3/4 full with batter; pour into hot pan. Tilt and rotate pan quickly so batter covers bottom in a thin layer. Return any excess batter to bowl. Return pan to medium-high heat. Loosen edge of crepe from pan with a pancake turner or metal spatula. Cook crepe until underside browns very lightly. Turn over and briefly cook other side until set. Transfer crepe to a plate.

3. Continue making crepes with remaining batter, stirring batter before preparing each crepe. Brush pan lightly with oil as necessary; if using a nonstick crepe pan, no further oil will be needed. Stack crepes on plate. *Crepes can be kept, covered, up to 2 days in refrigerator. Bring to room temperature before continuing.*

1. Pear Filling: Peel pears; rub with cut side of halved lemon. Halve, core and thinly slice pears.

2. Melt butter in a large skillet. Add pears; turn slices over so both sides are coated with butter. Cook, uncovered, over medium-low heat, stirring often, about 20 minutes or until very tender. Continue cooking over medium heat about 5 minutes to evaporate some of liquid. Add 5 tablespoons sugar. Cook over medium-high heat, stirring, until mixture is thickened and pears are coated. Remove from heat. Taste and add more sugar if desired. *Filling can be kept, covered, up to 1 day in refrigerator; reheat before filling crepes.*

1. Assembly: Preheat oven to 400F (205C). Butter a shallow baking dish. Spoon about 2 tablespoons filling onto less-attractive side of each crepe near 1 edge; roll up like cigars. Arrange, seam-side down, in buttered baking dish in 1 layer. Brush crepes with melted butter. Bake about 7 minutes or until very hot.

2. Reheat Chocolate Sauce above hot water if necessary.

3. To serve, spoon 2 hot crepes onto each plate. Spoon sauce over each crepe; sprinkle with chopped nuts. Serve with vanilla ice cream.

TIPS

○ *Melt butter in a small saucepan over low heat. Cool it completely before adding to batter.*

○ *If possible, buy already shelled peeled pistachios without brown skins. They are available at fine nut shops.*

MOUSSES, BAVARIAN CREAMS & CHARLOTTES

Chocolate mousses, Bavarian creams and charlottes are the dessert-lover's dream. Many of these fabulous cold chocolate desserts are light and creamy and are the perfect finale for a sumptuous dinner. Others are dense in texture and very rich in chocolate taste and color, making them favorites with dedicated chocolate fans. Mousses, Bavarians creams and most charlottes do not require baking and can easily fit into meal- or party-planning because they can be made ahead and served at leisure.

Chocolate Mousses

Chocolate mousse is perhaps the most popular of all elegant desserts. It has the advantage of being one of the quickest and easiest to make as well. It can vary in texture from soft and creamy to firm and dense with chocolate. Light mousses have an airy texture from the addition of whipped cream, beaten egg whites, or both. Usually the chocolate is combined with butter and eggs; a small amount of sugar may also be added. A mousse's flavor can be pure chocolate or can be accented by liqueurs or nuts.

The softer types of chocolate mousse are served in individual cups, ramekins or meringue baskets, while the firmer ones can be unmolded and even cut into slices. Besides being wonderful on their own, chocolate mousses make luscious fillings for cakes and pies.

Chocolate Bavarian Creams

Bavarian creams are extremely delicate and are among the creamiest of all chocolate desserts, whether they are flavored with dark or white chocolate. They are made from custard sauce, *crème anglaise*, bound with a little gelatin and light-ened by whipped cream. Bavarian creams can be molded in a variety of attractive shapes, as in ring-shaped Caramel Mocha Bavarian Cream, or can be simply prepared in a serving dish and cut into pieces, as in White Chocolate Bavarian Squares. Layered Bavarian creams, like Ribboned Chocolate-Banana Bavarian, seem especially glamorous.

Chocolate Charlottes

The chocolate charlotte, another light dessert, is one of the most festive endings to a meal. Charlottes are made of a frame of ladyfingers, either plain or chocolate ladyfingers as in Double-Chocolate Charlotte, holding one or more fillings of mousse or Bavarian cream.

Most of the charlottes in this book are of the modern type. They are simpler to prepare than traditional versions because they are assembled in a springform pan rather than in a charlotte mold. There is no need to spend a long time cutting ladyfingers to make a pattern; they just stand against the sides of the mold. Instead of turning the charlotte out, the charlotte is unmolded simply by removing the sides of the pan.

By contrast to these light charlottes, there are dense chocolate desserts combining ladyfingers and mousse-like fillings that have a high proportion of chocolate. Perhaps the most lavish of these is Chocolate-Cognac Marquise, a rectangular loaf which resembles an extraordinary chocolate bar. The richness of Chocolate-Apricot Terrine, another dense chocolate dessert, is balanced by the tartness of the fruit. Whipped cream or custard sauce are the ideal accompaniments for these super-rich desserts because they provide a light contrast and refresh the palate so the chocolate can be enjoyed to its fullest!

Chocolate Mousse Supreme

Cream is not used in classic recipes for chocolate mousse, but it contributes richness and a velvety texture to this one. If you like, accompany it with crunchy cookies, such as Crisp Chocolate Chip-Macadamia Nut Cookies, page 154.

Makes 6 servings

8 oz. fine-quality bittersweet
   chocolate, chopped
2 tablespoons brandy
1/4 cup water
2 tablespoons unsalted butter, room
   temperature, cut in 4 pieces
3 eggs, separated, room
   temperature
1 tablespoon sugar
1/2 cup whipping cream,
   well-chilled

1. Chill a small bowl and beaters for whipping cream.
2. Combine chocolate, brandy and water in a double boiler or heatproof medium bowl over hot, not simmering, water over low heat. Leave until melted, stirring occasionally. Stir until smooth.
3. Remove from pan of water; whisk in butter. Beat egg yolks in a small bowl. Add to chocolate mixture; whisk vigorously.
4. In a dry medium bowl, whip egg whites using dry beaters at medium speed until soft peaks form. Gradually beat in sugar; continue whipping at high speed until whites are stiff and shiny but not dry.
5. Fold about 1/4 of whites into chocolate mixture. Spoon this mixture over remaining whites; fold gently until blended.
6. Whip cream in chilled bowl until nearly stiff. Fold into chocolate mixture.
7. Divide mousse among 6 small ramekins or dessert glasses. Refrigerate at least 3 hours before serving. *Mousse can be kept, covered, up to 2 days in refrigerator.*

Chocolate-Pecan Mousse Loaf

The soft, mousse-like mixture is just firm enough to unmold but still very light in texture. The dessert gains an intriguing flavor from a combination of semisweet and milk chocolates and coffee, with a slight crunch of pecans.

Makes 8 servings

Chocolate-Pecan Mousse:
2 teaspoons instant coffee granules
1 tablespoon very hot water
6 oz. semisweet chocolate, chopped
8 oz. fine-quality milk chocolate,
   chopped
3/4 cup (6 oz.) unsalted butter, cut
   in pieces
4 egg yolks, room temperature
1/2 cup pecans, chopped
5 egg whites, room temperature
2 tablespoons sugar

Garnish:
3/4 cup whipping cream,
   well-chilled
2 teaspoons sugar
8 pecan halves
Candied violets or candied rose
   petals, if desired

1. **Chocolate Pecan Mousse:** Lightly oil an 8" x 4" loaf pan. Line base of pan with waxed paper; lightly oil paper.
2. Dissolve coffee in hot water in a small cup; cool.
3. Combine chocolates, butter and dissolved coffee in a double boiler or heatproof medium bowl over hot, not simmering, water over low heat. Leave until melted, stirring occasionally. Stir until smooth. Remove from pan of water.
4. Whisk in egg yolks, 1 at a time. Stir in chopped pecans.
5. In a large dry bowl, whip egg whites using dry beaters at medium speed until soft peaks form. Gradually beat in sugar; continue whipping at high speed until whites are stiff and shiny but not dry.
6. Fold about 1/4 of whites into chocolate mixture until blended. Return mixture to remaining whites; fold gently just until blended.
7. Carefully pour mixture into prepared loaf pan. Refrigerate 8 hours or until set. *Dessert can be kept, covered, up to 3 days in refrigerator.*
8. To unmold dessert, dip pan, nearly to depth of contents, in warm, not hot, water about 10 seconds. Run a thin-bladed flexible knife around its edge. Dry base of pan. Set an oval or oblong platter on top of mold. Holding firmly together, quickly flip so dessert is right-side up. Remove paper. Return dessert to refrigerator.
1. **Garnish:** Chill a medium bowl and beaters for whipping cream. Whip cream with sugar in chilled bowl until very stiff.
2. Using a pastry bag and medium star tip, pipe a ruffle of whipped cream around base of dessert. Top it with a few pecan halves and candied violets or candied rose petals, if desired. Spoon any remaining cream into a serving dish.
• **To serve:** Cut dessert very carefully and rinse and dry knife after each cut. Slices are soft; use a pancake turner or pie server to help remove them.

White Chocolate Mousse with Strawberry Sauce

Photo on page 105.

Strawberry Sauce provides a contrast of a bright-red color to show off the white mousse, as well as tartness and freshness to balance its sweetness.

Makes 4 servings

White Chocolate Mousse:
4 oz. fine-quality white chocolate, very finely chopped
1/4 cup whipping cream
3 tablespoons unsalted butter, room temperature, cut in 6 pieces
3 eggs, separated, room temperature
1-1/4 teaspoons finely grated or chopped lemon zest
1 teaspoon pure vanilla extract
2 teaspoons sugar

Strawberry Sauce:
3 cups strawberries (about 12 oz.)
About 1/2 cup powdered sugar, sifted
1 teaspoon fresh strained lemon juice

4 small strawberries or 8 thin, round, strawberry slices (for garnish)

1. Mousse: Put white chocolate in a small heatproof bowl. Bring cream to a full boil in a small heavy saucepan. Pour cream over chocolate all at once. Whisk until chocolate is completely melted and mixture is smooth.

2. Whisk in butter. Whisk in egg yolks, 1 at a time. Stir in zest and vanilla.

3. In a dry medium bowl, whip egg whites using dry beaters at medium speed until soft peaks form. Gradually beat in sugar; continue whipping at high speed until whites are stiff and shiny but not dry.

4. Stir about 1/4 of whites into chocolate mixture. Spoon this mixture over remaining whites; fold gently until blended.

5. Pour into a shallow bowl. Cover and refrigerate 4 hours or until firm enough to spoon into ovals. *Mousse can be kept, covered, up to 1 day in refrigerator.*

1. Sauce: Puree strawberries in a food processor or blender. Add 1/2 cup powdered sugar. Process until pureed. Transfer to a bowl.

2. Whisk in lemon juice. Taste and whisk in 1 tablespoon powdered sugar, if needed. Cover and refrigerate 30 minutes. *Sauce can be kept, covered, up to 1 day in refrigerator.*

1. To serve: Carefully spoon 2 oval-shaped tablespoons of mousse onto each serving plate. Stir Strawberry Sauce. Spoon sauce around, not over, mousse.

2. Set a strawberry on each plate or a strawberry slice on each oval.

Chocolate Mascarpone Mousse

Mascarpone, an Italian cheese that resembles soft cream cheese, gives a wonderful light creamy texture to this quick, easy-to-make mousse. The cheese is available at Italian markets and fine cheese stores. It should be soft, delicate in flavor and as fresh as possible. If you like, garnish each serving with a raspberry or a small strawberry.

Makes 4 servings

3 oz. semisweet chocolate, chopped
6 oz. mascarpone cheese, room temperature
3 tablespoons sugar
2 eggs, separated, room temperature
1 tablespoon rum

1. Melt chocolate in a double boiler or small heatproof bowl over hot, not simmering, water over low heat, stirring occasionally. Stir until smooth. Remove from pan of water; cool to body temperature.

2. Stir cheese gently with a wooden spoon until smooth; do not beat. Stir in 2 tablespoons sugar. Add egg yolks, 1 at a time, stirring after each addition. Gradually stir in chocolate in 3 batches. Gradually stir in rum.

3. In a small dry bowl, whip egg whites using dry beaters at medium speed until soft peaks form. Gradually beat in remaining 1 tablespoon sugar; continue whipping at high speed until whites are stiff and shiny but not dry.

4. Gently fold egg whites, in 3 batches, into chocolate mixture.

5. Divide among 4 small dessert dishes. Refrigerate about 1-1/2 hours or until set. *Mousse can be kept, covered, up to 1 day in refrigerator.*

Dark Chocolate Mousse in Meringue Cups

These elegant, pure white, mini-vacherins are filled with a traditional bittersweet mousse, which complements the crunchy sweet meringue. The mousse is quick and easy to prepare and can also be served alone. The cooked meringue from which the cases are shaped is a pleasure to use; it pipes easily and beautifully and keeps well.

Makes 8 servings

Meringue Cups:
4 egg whites, room temperature
1-1/4 cups sugar

Dark Chocolate Mousse:
6 oz. fine-quality bittersweet
   chocolate, chopped
2 tablespoons unsalted butter
4 eggs, separated, room
   temperature
1 tablespoon rum
1 tablespoon sugar

1. Meringue Cups: Position rack in center of oven and preheat to 200F (95C). Lightly butter corners of 2 baking sheets; line with foil. Butter and flour foil, tapping to remove excess flour. Using a 3-inch cookie cutter as a guide, mark 8 circles 1-1/2 inches apart onto baking sheets.

2. Combine egg whites and sugar in a large heatproof bowl. Set bowl in a pan of hot water over low heat. Beat with a hand mixer at low speed 4 minutes, then at medium speed about 3 minutes or until mixture is warm to touch.

3. Remove from pan of water. Continue beating at high speed until completely cooled. Meringue will be very shiny and sticky.

4. Spoon meringue into a pastry bag fitted with small or medium star tip.

5. Pipe meringue in a tight spiral, beginning in center of 1 marked circle on baking sheet, until marked circle is completely covered with meringue. Without stopping, continue piping a second layer of meringue on rim of circle, then a third layer so rim is higher than base and forms a case. Pipe 7 more Meringue Cups.

6. Bake about 1 hour or until meringue feels firm and dry to touch and is not sticky at bottom. Carefully transfer meringues to a rack, using a slotted metal spatula; cool. *Meringues can be kept in an airtight container up to 1 week in dry weather.*

1. Dark Chocolate Mousse: Melt chocolate in a double boiler or heatproof medium bowl over hot, not simmering, water over low heat, stirring occasionally. Stir until smooth. Remove from pan of water.

2. Stir in butter. Whisk egg yolks to blend. Add all at once to chocolate; whisk vigorously. Whisk in rum.

3. In a dry medium bowl, whip egg whites using dry beaters at medium speed until soft peaks form. Gradually beat in sugar; continue whipping at high speed until whites are stiff and shiny but not dry.

4. Quickly stir about 1/4 of whites into chocolate mixture, using whisk. Gently fold in remaining whites.

5. Spoon mousse into a shallow bowl. Refrigerate 1 hour.

1. Assembly: Spoon enough mousse into each Meringue Cup to fill it to the top, using about 2 tablespoons mousse for each cup. Spoon remaining mousse into a serving dish. Refrigerate filled Meringue Cups, uncovered, 1-1/2 hours or until mousse sets. *Dessert can be kept, covered, up to 1 day in refrigerator.*

2. Serve cold; serve mousse in bowl separately.

How to Make Chocolate Mousse in Meringue Cups

1/Pipe meringue in a tight circle, beginning in center of 1 marked circle on baking sheet, until circle is completely covered with meringue. Without stopping, continue piping a second layer of meringue on rim of circle, then a third layer so rim is higher than base and forms a case.

2/Spoon enough mousse into each Meringue Cup to fill it to the top, using about 2 tablespoons mousse for each cup. Refrigerate filled Meringue Cups, uncovered, 1-1/2 hours or until mousse sets.

Creamy Chocolate Mousse with Grand Marnier

For a light texture, only the whites of the eggs are used in this soft, creamy, easy-to-make mousse. Orange zest adds freshness and Grand Marnier adds spirit to complement the richness of the chocolate.

Makes 4 servings

7 oz. fine-quality semisweet
   chocolate, chopped
1/2 cup whipping cream
5 egg whites
2 tablespoons sugar
1 tablespoon Grand Marnier
2 teaspoons grated orange zest

1/3 cup whipping cream,
   well-chilled, if desired (for
   garnish)
4 small squares of candied orange
   peel, 4 pieces of candied violet
   or 4 small Chocolate Leaves,
   page 196, if desired (for garnish)

1. Combine chocolate and 1/2 cup cream in a double boiler or heatproof medium bowl over hot, not simmering, water over low heat. Leave until melted, stirring occasionally. Stir until smooth. Remove from pan of water; cool 3 minutes.

2. In a large dry bowl, whip egg whites using dry beaters at medium speed until soft peaks form. Gradually beat in sugar; continue whipping at high speed until whites are stiff and shiny but not dry.

3. Stir Grand Marnier and orange zest into chocolate. Fold in about 1/4 of whites until blended. Spoon this mixture over remaining whites; fold gently just until blended.

4. Divide among 4 (2/3-cup) ramekins. Refrigerate 3 hours. *Mousse can be kept, covered, up to 1 day in refrigerator.*

5. Chill a small bowl and beaters for whipping cream. Whip 1/3 cup cream in chilled bowl until very stiff.

6. Using a pastry bag and medium star tip, pipe a large rosette of whipped cream on center of each portion. Garnish each rosette with a piece of candied orange peel, violet or a Chocolate Leaf.

Molded Chocolate Mousse

The raisin-studded mousse is prepared in paper baking cups and is extremely easy to unmold—just peel off the paper. It is surrounded by creamy Brandy Custard Sauce and garnished with raisins.

Makes 8 servings

1/2 cup dark raisins
1/4 cup brandy

Chocolate Mousse:
8 oz. fine-quality semisweet
    chocolate, chopped
1/2 cup (4 oz.) unsalted butter,
    slightly softened
3 tablespoons powdered sugar
3 eggs, separated, room
    temperature

Brandy Custard Sauce:
1-1/2 cups milk
5 egg yolks, room temperature
1/4 cup plus 2 teaspoons sugar
1 tablespoon plus 1-1/2 teaspoons
    brandy (from raisins above)

● Put raisins in a small jar or bowl; pour brandy over them. Cover tightly; shake to mix. Cover and leave to macerate at least 30 minutes or up to 2 hours at room temperature.

1. Mousse: Melt chocolate in a double boiler or heatproof medium bowl over hot, not simmering, water over low heat, stirring occasionally. Stir until smooth. Remove from pan of water; cool to body temperature. Set 8 paper baking cups in muffin pans.

2. Cream butter in a medium or large bowl until smooth. Add 2 tablespoons powdered sugar; beat until blended. Beat in egg yolks, 1 at a time. Beat in chocolate in 2 batches.

3. Drain raisins, reserving brandy. Gradually beat 2 tablespoons brandy into chocolate mixture. Stir in 1/4 cup raisins. Combine remaining raisins and remaining brandy; cover and set aside.

4. In a dry medium bowl, whip egg whites using dry beaters at medium speed until soft peaks form. Gradually beat in remaining 1 tablespoon powdered sugar; continue whipping at high speed until whites are stiff and shiny but not dry.

5. Fold whites, in 3 batches, into chocolate mixture. Spoon into paper baking cups, using about 6 tablespoons mousse for each cup. Tap down molds to even top surface. Refrigerate about 5 hours or until firm. *Mousse can be kept, covered, up to 1 week in refrigerator.*

1. Custard sauce: Bring milk to a boil in a heavy medium saucepan.

2. Whisk egg yolks lightly in a large heatproof bowl. Add sugar and whisk until well-blended. Gradually whisk in hot milk. Return mixture to saucepan, whisking constantly. Cook over medium-low heat, stirring mixture and scraping bottom of pan constantly with a wooden spoon, until mixture thickens slightly and reaches 170 to 175F (75 to 80C) on an instant-read thermometer; begin checking after 5 minutes. To check whether it is thick enough without a thermometer, remove sauce from heat. Dip a metal spoon in sauce and draw your finger across back of spoon. Your finger should leave a clear path in mixture that clings to spoon. If it does not, continue cooking another 30 seconds and check again. Do not overcook sauce or it will curdle.

3. Immediately strain into a bowl. Stir about 30 seconds to cool. Cool completely. Refrigerate at least 30 minutes before serving. *Sauce can be kept, covered, up to 2 days in refrigerator.*

4. Gradually stir in brandy.

5. To unmold, turn "cupcakes" over onto small plates; gently peel off papers. Spoon Brandy Custard Sauce around each molded mousse and a little on top. Set a few raisins on sauce on each plate.

Triple-Chocolate Mousse Parfait, page 106; White Chocolate Mousse with Strawberry Sauce, page 101; Molded Chocolate Mousse, above.

Triple-Chocolate Mousse Parfait

Photo on page 105.

In this stunning new dessert, three chocolate mousses are layered, parfait-style, in stemmed glasses to show off the different hues of chocolate. The three delicious mousses of white chocolate, milk chocolate and dark chocolate are made by the same simple method; only the butter and sugar quantities vary.

Makes 5 servings

White Chocolate Mousse:

4 oz. fine-quality white chocolate, chopped
1/4 cup whipping cream
3 tablespoons unsalted butter, room temperature
2 eggs, separated, room temperature
1/2 teaspoon sugar

Milk Chocolate Mousse:

4 oz. fine-quality milk chocolate, chopped
1/4 cup whipping cream
2 tablespoons unsalted butter, room temperature
2 eggs, separated, room temperature
1 teaspoon sugar

Dark Chocolate Mousse:

4 oz. fine-quality bittersweet chocolate, chopped
1/4 cup whipping cream
1 tablespoon unsalted butter, room temperature
2 eggs, separated, room temperature
1 teaspoon sugar

White Quick Chocolate Curls, page 193, White Chocolate Leaves, page 196, or candied violets, if desired (for garnish)

1. White Chocolate Mousse: Combine chocolate and cream in a double boiler or small heatproof bowl over hot, not simmering, water over low heat. Leave until partially melted, stirring occasionally. Remove from pan of water. Whisk until smooth.

2. Whisk in butter. Add egg yolks, 1 at a time, whisking vigorously after each addition.

3. In a small dry bowl, whip egg whites using dry beaters at medium speed until soft peaks form. Add sugar; continue whipping at high speed until whites are stiff and shiny but not dry.

4. Quickly fold about 1/4 of whites into chocolate mixture. Spoon this mixture over remaining whites; fold gently until blended.

5. Divide mixture among 5 wine glasses or other 1-cup glasses, using about 1/3 cup mousse for each glass. If mousse drips on side of glass, wipe it clean. Refrigerate about 1-1/2 hours or until top is partially set.

1. Milk Chocolate Mousse: Prepare mousse following same method as for White Chocolate Mousse, steps 1 through 4.

2. Gently spoon Milk Chocolate Mousse over top of white mousse in glasses in an even layer. Refrigerate 45 minutes or until top is partially set.

1. Dark Chocolate Mousse: Prepare mousse following same method as for White Chocolate Mousse, steps 1 through 4.

2. Gently spoon Dark Chocolate Mousse over top of Milk Chocolate Mousse in glasses in an even layer. Refrigerate about 2 hours or until set. Cover with plastic wrap when set. *Dessert can be kept up to 2 days in refrigerator.*

3. If desired, garnish with White Chocolate Curls, White Chocolate Leaves or candied violets, or any combination.

Chocolate-Apricot Terrine

Photo on pages 8-9.

A terrine is a loaf-shaped dish and the food served in it. This chocolate terrine is composed of a very rich, creamy mousse-like mixture. Like the classic Sachertorte, this dessert combines chocolate and apricots, but here the apricot flavor is stronger because instead of the apricot glaze in the torte, we use dried apricots and apricot brandy.

Makes 8 servings

1/3 cup dried apricots, very finely chopped with a knife (about 1-1/2 oz.)
5 tablespoons apricot-flavored brandy
4 oz. semisweet chocolate, chopped
4 egg yolks, room temperature
3/4 cup sugar
3/4 cup (6 oz.) unsalted butter, slightly softened
3/4 cup unsweetened Dutch-process cocoa powder, sifted
1/2 pint whipping cream (1 cup), well-chilled
1 (3-oz.) pkg. ladyfingers (about 3 inches long) or about 6 oz. White Ladyfingers, page 168
About 9 dried apricot halves
Spirited Custard Sauce, page 197, flavored with apricot brandy

1. Put chopped dried apricots in a small jar or bowl. Pour 2 tablespoons brandy over apricots. Cover tightly; shake to mix. Cover and leave to macerate at least 2 hours or up to overnight at room temperature.
2. Oil an 8'' x 4'' loaf pan. Cut a 12'' x 8'' piece and an 18'' x 12'' piece of waxed paper. Fold 18-inch piece in 3 lengthwise; set lengthwise in loaf pan. Set second piece of waxed paper crosswise on top so pan is completely lined. Oil paper.
3. Melt chocolate in a double boiler or small heatproof bowl over hot, not simmering, water over low heat, stirring occasionally. Stir until smooth. Remove from pan of water; cool to body temperature. Chill a large bowl and beaters for whipping cream.
4. Beat egg yolks in a large bowl until blended. Add sugar; beat at high speed, scraping often, 5 minutes or until mixture lightens and becomes pale. Using a wooden spoon, gently stir in melted chocolate in 2 batches.
5. Cream butter in a medium bowl until smooth and fluffy. Beat in 1/2 cup cocoa, 1 tablespoon at a time, until smooth. Beat in chocolate mixture at low speed in 4 batches.
6. Whip cream in chilled bowl until soft peaks form. Lightly stir in 1 tablespoon cocoa. Beat it at low speed until blended, scraping down occasionally. Repeat with remaining 3 tablespoons cocoa.
7. Gradually fold cocoa cream into chocolate mixture in 3 batches. Fold in chopped apricots with their brandy.
8. Set 4 packaged ladyfinger halves or homemade White Ladyfingers lengthwise in base of mold, 1 at each corner. Arrange enough apricot halves, rounded-side down, on remaining surface of base of mold to make 1 layer. Brush ladyfingers with apricot brandy.
9. Pour 2 cups chocolate mixture into lined mold; spread smooth. Top with 1 layer of ladyfinger halves or whole homemade ladyfingers placed lengthwise, trimming them, if necessary, to fit. Brush with apricot brandy. Pour in remaining chocolate mixture. Top with another layer of ladyfinger halves, spongy-side up, or whole homemade ladyfingers, placed lengthwise. Brush with remaining brandy.
10. Cover and refrigerate overnight. *Terrine can be kept up to 1 week in refrigerator.*
11. Prepare Spirited Custard Sauce.
12. To serve, unmold terrine onto a platter. Gently peel off paper. Serve in slices and spoon sauce around each slice.

Variation
Omit apricots and their soaking brandy. Arrange a complete layer of ladyfingers on base of pan.

1/Cut a 25-inch-long sheet of waxed paper; fold in half. Wrap paper around soufflé dish containing raspberry mousse so paper extends about 3 inches above rim to make a collar. Fasten tightly with tape.

2/To serve, carefully peel off paper collar. Pipe rosettes of whipped cream at top edge of dessert. Top rosettes with whole raspberries. Set a Chocolate Cutout in center.

Black & White Floating Islands

This new specialty of one of my favorite Parisian restaurants is a combination of two traditional desserts: snow eggs and chocolate mousse, set on creamy Vanilla Bean Custard Sauce.

Makes 6 servings

Vanilla Bean Custard Sauce,
  page 197

Chocolate Mousse:
3 oz. fine-quality semisweet
  chocolate, chopped
2 tablespoons water, rum, cognac
  or Grand Marnier
1 tablespoon unsalted butter, room
  temperature
2 eggs, separated, room
  temperature
1-1/2 teaspoons sugar

Poached Meringues:
2 egg whites, room temperature
1/3 cup sugar

● Prepare Vanilla Bean Custard Sauce and refrigerate.
1. Chocolate Mousse: Combine chocolate and water in a double boiler or small heatproof bowl over hot, not simmering, water over low heat. Leave until melted, stirring occasionally. Stir until smooth. Remove from pan of water.
2. Stir in butter. Add egg yolks, 1 at a time, stirring vigorously after each addition.
3. In a dry medium bowl, whip egg whites using dry beaters at medium speed until soft peaks form. Beat in sugar; continue whipping at high speed until whites are stiff and shiny but not dry.
4. Fold about 1/4 of whites into chocolate mixture. Spoon this mixture over remaining whites; fold gently until blended.
5. Pour mousse into a shallow bowl. Cover and refrigerate at least 2 hours or until set. *Mousse can be kept, covered, up to 1 day in refrigerator.*
1. Poached Meringues: Bring 1 quart water to a boil in a small sauté pan or a shallow medium saucepan. Reduce heat to medium-low so water just simmers.
2. In a small dry bowl, whip egg whites using dry beaters at medium speed until stiff. Switch speed to high. Gradually beat in sugar; continue whipping at high speed until whites are shiny but not dry.
3. Dip a tablespoon into simmering water, then use it to take an oval spoonful of meringue. Tap handle of spoon sharply against side of pan to detach meringue so it falls into water. Add about 4 more spoonfuls of meringue. Poach about 30 seconds on each side or until firm, turning them once. Lift out with a slotted spoon; drain on paper towels. Poach remaining meringue. Leave plenty of space between meringues so they will be easy to turn over.
4. Divide Vanilla Bean Custard Sauce among 6 individual gratin dishes or shallow dessert dishes. Trim meringues if necessary so they have an even oval shape. Add 1 meringue to each dish. Next to meringue, carefully spoon 1 oval-shaped tablespoon of Chocolate Mousse, about same size as meringue. Serve immediately. Serve any remaining mousse separately.

Cold Chocolate-Raspberry Soufflé

Chocolate and raspberries are a favorite American combination. In this cold soufflé, the vivid pink of the fresh-raspberry-mousse layers provides an exciting color and flavor contrast to the ribbon of dark chocolate mousse in the center. To show off the beauty of the colors to their greatest advantage, assemble and present this dessert in a glass soufflé dish and include all three layers in each portion when serving.

Makes 8 to 10 servings

Raspberry Mousse:
3 cups raspberries (about 12 oz.)
1 (1/4-oz.) envelope unflavored gelatin (scant 1 tablespoon)
1/2 cup water
2/3 cup sugar
1/2 pint whipping cream (1 cup), well-chilled

Chocolate Mousse:
1-1/4 teaspoons unflavored gelatin
2 tablespoons plus 1 teaspoon water
7 oz. semisweet chocolate, chopped
5 tablespoons unsalted butter, room temperature, cut in 5 pieces
4 eggs, separated, room temperature
2 tablespoons plus 2 teaspoons clear raspberry brandy
1 tablespoon plus 1 teaspoon sugar

Garnish:
1/3 cup whipping cream, well-chilled
6 to 8 raspberries
1 heart-shaped, fluted or round Chocolate Cutout, page 195, about 1-1/2 to 2 inches across or a little grated chocolate

1. **Raspberry Mousse:** Puree raspberries in a food processor or blender until very smooth. Strain puree into a large bowl, pressing on pulp in strainer. Use a rubber spatula to scrape mixture from underside of strainer.
2. Sprinkle gelatin over 1/4 cup water in a small cup. Let stand while preparing mousse.
3. Combine sugar and remaining 1/4 cup water in a small saucepan. Stir until thoroughly mixed. Heat over low heat, stirring, until sugar dissolves completely. Increase heat to medium and bring to a boil. Simmer 30 seconds without stirring.
4. Remove syrup from heat; immediately whisk in softened gelatin. Cool 3 minutes, stirring often. Gradually pour gelatin mixture into raspberry puree, whisking constantly.
5. Refrigerate mixture about 30 minutes, stirring often, or chill mixture by setting bowl in a larger bowl of iced water about 15 minutes, stirring very often, or until mixture is cold and thickened to the consistency of unbeaten egg whites but is not set. Meanwhile, chill a large bowl and beaters for whipping cream.
6. Whip cream in chilled bowl until nearly stiff. Gently fold cream into berry mixture.
7. Pour 2 cups mousse into a 1-quart soufflé dish. Cover and freeze 30 minutes. Keep remaining mousse at room temperature.
1. **Chocolate Mousse:** Sprinkle gelatin over water in a small cup. Let stand 5 minutes.
2. Combine chocolate and butter in a double boiler or heatproof medium bowl over hot, not simmering, water over low heat. Leave until melted, stirring occasionally. Stir until smooth. Remove from pan of water.
3. Set gelatin bowl in a shallow pan of hot water over low heat. Melt gelatin, stirring often, about 3 minutes. Stir into chocolate mixture.
4. Add egg yolks, 1 at a time, stirring vigorously after each addition. Add brandy; stir until blended.
5. In a dry medium bowl, whip egg whites using dry beaters at medium speed until soft peaks form. Gradually beat in sugar; continue whipping at high speed until whites are stiff and shiny but not dry.
6. Fold about 1/4 of whites into chocolate mixture. Spoon this mixture over remaining whites; fold gently until blended.
7. Cut a 25-inch-long sheet of waxed paper; fold in half. Wrap paper around soufflé dish containing raspberry mousse so it extends about 3 inches above rim to make a collar. Fasten tightly with tape.
8. Pour Chocolate Mousse into soufflé dish; gently spread smooth. Freeze 10 minutes.
9. Gently ladle remaining Raspberry Mousse over Chocolate Mousse. Refrigerate 5 hours or until completely set. *Dessert can be kept, covered, up to 3 days in refrigerator.*
1. **Garnish:** Chill a small bowl and beaters for whipping cream. Whip cream in chilled bowl until very stiff.
2. To serve, carefully peel off and discard paper collar. Using a pastry bag and large star tip, pipe rosettes of whipped cream at top edge of dessert. Top rosettes with whole raspberries. Set Chocolate Cutout in center or sprinkle with grated chocolate.

Chocolate-Rum Bavarian Cream

In this incredibly creamy chocolate dessert, a favorite in my chocolate-dessert classes, the rum provides a lively contrast to the richness of the mixture.

Makes 8 servings

Bavarian Cream:

4 oz. semisweet chocolate, chopped
1 (1/4-oz.) envelope unflavored
    gelatin (scant 1 tablespoon)
1/4 cup water
1 cup milk
4 egg yolks, room temperature
6 tablespoons sugar
1/4 cup golden rum
1-1/4 cups whipping cream,
    well-chilled

Garnish:

1/2 cup whipping cream,
    well-chilled
1 teaspoon sugar
8 chocolate coffee beans or a little
    grated semisweet chocolate

1. **Bavarian Cream:** Melt chocolate in a double boiler or heatproof medium bowl over hot, not simmering, water over low heat, stirring occasionally. Meanwhile, follow next 4 steps.
2. Sprinkle gelatin over 1/4 cup water in a small cup. Let stand while preparing custard.
3. Bring milk to a boil in a small heavy saucepan.
4. Whisk egg yolks lightly in a large heatproof bowl. Add sugar; whisk until well-blended. Gradually whisk in hot milk. Return mixture to saucepan, whisking constantly. Cook over medium-low heat, stirring and scraping bottom of pan constantly with a wooden spoon, until mixture thickens slightly and reaches 165F to 170F (75C) on an instant-read thermometer; begin checking after 5 minutes. To check whether it is thick enough without a thermometer, remove custard from heat. Dip a metal spoon in custard and draw your finger across back of spoon. Your finger should leave a clear path in mixture that clings to spoon. If it does not, continue cooking another 30 seconds and check again. Do not overcook custard or it will curdle.
5. Remove from heat. Immediately add softened gelatin, whisking until it is completely dissolved. Pour into a large bowl. Stir about 30 seconds to cool.
6. Remove chocolate from pan of water; stir until smooth. Using a whisk, stir custard mixture, about 1/2 cup at a time, into melted chocolate.
7. Return mixture to large bowl; cool to room temperature, stirring occasionally. Gradually stir in rum.
8. Refrigerate chocolate mixture about 20 minutes, stirring often, or chill mixture by setting bowl in a larger bowl of iced water about 10 minutes, stirring very often, or until mixture is cold and beginning to thicken but is not set. Meanwhile, lightly oil a 5-cup ring mold. Chill a large bowl and beaters for whipping cream.
9. Whip cream in chilled bowl until nearly stiff. Gently fold cream into chocolate mixture, blending thoroughly.
10. Pour mixture into prepared mold; smooth top. Refrigerate at least 3 hours or until set. *Dessert can be kept, covered, up to 2 days in refrigerator; rum flavor weakens after 1 day.*
11. To unmold dessert, run a thin-bladed flexible knife around its inner and outer edges, gently pushing mixture slightly from edge of mold to let in air. Dip mold, nearly to depth of contents, in warm, not hot, water about 10 seconds. Dry base of mold. Set a round platter on top of mold. Holding firmly together, quickly flip so dessert is right-side up. Shake mold gently downward; dessert should slip from mold onto platter. If dessert remains in mold, repeat dipping procedure. Carefully remove mold by lifting it straight upward. Refrigerate dessert until ready to serve.
1. **Garnish:** Chill a medium bowl and beaters for whipping cream. Whip cream with sugar in chilled bowl until very stiff.
2. Using a pastry bag and medium star tip, pipe rosettes of whipped cream at base of dessert. Garnish rosettes with chocolate coffee beans or with a sprinkling of grated chocolate.

Caramel-Mocha Bavarian Cream

Chocolate, coffee and caramel make a delicious combination. The beautiful reddish-brown caramel sauce is no extra work—it is prepared from part of the caramel used to flavor the base.

Makes 8 servings

Caramel:
1 cup sugar
1/2 cup cool water
1/2 cup hot water

Mocha Bavarian Cream:
1 (1/4-oz.) envelope unflavored
    gelatin (scant 1 tablespoon)
1/4 cup cold water
1 cup milk
5 egg yolks, room temperature
5 tablespoons sugar
2 teaspoons instant coffee granules
2 oz. semisweet chocolate, chopped
1-1/4 cups whipping cream,
    well-chilled

1 or 2 tablespoons cold water, if
    needed (for finishing sauce)

1. Caramel: Combine sugar and cool water in a heavy medium saucepan that does not have a black interior. Heat mixture over low heat until sugar dissolves, gently stirring occasionally. Increase heat to high and boil, without stirring, but occasionally brushing down any sugar crystals from side of pan with a brush dipped in water, until mixture begins to brown. Reduce heat to medium-low. Continue cooking, swirling pan gently, until mixture is a rich brown color and a trace of smoke begins to rise from pan. Do not let caramel get too dark or it will be bitter; if caramel is too light it will be too sweet. Immediately remove from heat.

2. Standing at a distance, gradually pour in hot water; caramel will bubble furiously. When caramel stops bubbling, return mixture to low heat. Heat, stirring, 1 minute or until it is well-blended. Cool slightly.

3. Measure 1/2 cup caramel for Bavarian cream; cool to room temperature. Set aside remaining caramel to cool separately.

1. Bavarian Cream: Sprinkle gelatin over 1/4 cup water in a small cup. Let stand while preparing custard.

2. Mix milk with reserved 1/2 cup caramel in a heavy medium saucepan. Bring mixture to a boil, whisking constantly. Be careful because mixture tends to boil over.

3. Whisk egg yolks lightly in a large heatproof bowl. Add sugar and whisk until well-blended. Gradually whisk in hot milk. Return mixture to saucepan, whisking constantly. Cook over medium-low heat, stirring mixture and scraping bottom of pan constantly with a wooden spoon, until mixture thickens slightly and reaches 165F to 170F (75C) on an instant-read thermometer; begin checking after 3 minutes. To check whether it is thick enough without a thermometer, remove custard from heat. Dip a metal spoon in custard and draw your finger across back of spoon. Your finger should leave a clear path in mixture that clings to spoon. If it does not, continue cooking another 30 seconds and check again. Do not overcook or it will curdle.

4. Remove from heat. Immediately add softened gelatin, whisking until it is completely dissolved. Add instant coffee granules; whisk until dissolved. Pour into a large bowl; stir about 30 seconds to cool.

5. Melt chocolate in a double boiler or heatproof medium bowl over hot, not simmering, water over low heat, stirring occasionally. Stir until smooth; cool about 5 minutes.

6. Add about 1/2 cup custard to chocolate; whisk until blended. Whisk in another 1/2 cup custard. Return mixture to remaining custard; whisk until blended. Cool to room temperature, stirring occasionally.

7. Refrigerate chocolate mixture about 20 minutes, stirring often, or chill mixture by setting bowl in a larger bowl of iced water about 10 minutes, stirring very often, or until mixture is cold and beginning to thicken but is not set. Meanwhile, lightly oil a 5-cup ring mold. Chill a large bowl and beaters for whipping cream.

8. Whip cream in chilled bowl until nearly stiff. Gently fold cream into custard. Spoon into oiled mold. Refrigerate at least 4 hours or until completely set. *Dessert can be kept, covered, up to 2 days in refrigerator.*

9. Taste reserved caramel. If it is too thick or too strong in flavor, stir in 1 or 2 tablespoons cold water. Refrigerate until ready to serve.

1. To serve: To unmold dessert, run a thin-bladed flexible knife around its inner and outer edges, gently pushing mixture slightly from edge of mold to let in air. Dip mold, nearly to depth of contents, in warm, not hot, water about 10 seconds. Dry base of mold. Set a round platter on top of mold. Holding firmly together, quickly flip so dessert is right-side up. Shake mold gently downward; dessert should slip from mold onto platter. If dessert remains in mold, repeat dipping procedure. Carefully remove mold by lifting it straight upward. Refrigerate dessert until ready to serve.

2. Serve chilled caramel separately as sauce.

Ribboned Chocolate-Banana Bavarian Cream

This Bavarian cream is served like a cheesecake; it requires no turning out, just removing the sides of a springform pan. The chocolate and banana layers form a beautiful striped pattern. The two Bavarian creams are made from a single mixture.

Makes 8 servings

1 (1/4-oz.) envelope unflavored
    gelatin (scant 1 tablespoon)
1/4 cup water
1 cup milk
4 egg yolks, room temperature
5 tablespoons sugar
3 oz. semisweet chocolate, chopped
1 large banana (about 7 oz.)
1 teaspoon fresh strained lemon
    juice
1-1/2 cups whipping cream,
    well-chilled

1/2 cup whipping cream,
    well-chilled, if desired (for
    garnish)
Grated semisweet chocolate, if
    desired (for garnish)

1. Sprinkle gelatin over water in a small cup. Let stand while preparing custard.
2. Bring milk to a boil in a small heavy saucepan.
3. Whisk egg yolks lightly in a large heatproof bowl. Add sugar; whisk until well-blended. Gradually whisk in hot milk. Return mixture to saucepan, whisking constantly. Cook over medium-low heat, stirring mixture and scraping bottom of pan constantly with a wooden spoon, until mixture thickens slightly and reaches 165F to 170F (75C) on an instant-read thermometer; begin checking after 5 minutes. To check whether it is thick enough without a thermometer, remove custard from heat. Dip a metal spoon in custard and draw your finger across back of spoon. Your finger should leave a clear path in mixture that clings to spoon. If it does not, continue cooking another 30 seconds and check again. Do not overcook custard or it will curdle.
4. Remove from heat. Immediately add softened gelatin, whisking until it is completely dissolved. Pour into a large bowl; stir about 30 seconds to cool.
5. Melt chocolate in a double boiler or heatproof medium bowl over hot, not simmering, water over low heat, stirring occasionally. Stir until smooth. Remove from pan of water; cool 5 minutes.
6. Add 2/3 cup custard to chocolate; stir with a whisk until blended.
7. Process banana with lemon juice in a food processor until smooth. Measure 2/3 cup puree. Whisk into remaining plain custard.
8. Cool each mixture to room temperature, stirring occasionally.
9. Refrigerate banana mixture about 20 minutes, stirring often, or chill mixture by setting bowl in a larger bowl of iced water about 10 minutes, stirring very often, or until mixture is cold and beginning to thicken but is not set. Meanwhile, lightly oil an 8-inch springform pan. Chill a large bowl and beaters for whipping cream.
10. Whip 1-1/2 cups cream in chilled bowl until nearly stiff. Gently fold 2 cups whipped cream into banana mixture, blending thoroughly. Refrigerate remaining whipped cream.
11. Spoon 1-1/2 cups banana mixture into prepared mold; spread evenly. Freeze 10 minutes, leaving remaining banana and chocolate mixtures at room temperature.
12. If chocolate mixture is not yet cold and beginning to thicken, refrigerate about 5 minutes, stirring often, or chill mixture by setting bowl in a larger bowl of iced water about 3 minutes, stirring very often, or until mixture is cold and beginning to thicken but is not set.
13. Fold remaining whipped cream into chocolate mixture. Gently spoon 1-1/2 cups chocolate mixture into mold; spread smooth. Tap mold on work surface so mixture settles. Freeze 10 minutes, leaving remaining banana and chocolate mixtures at room temperature.
14. Add remaining banana mixture to mold; spread gently. Freeze 10 minutes. Add remaining chocolate mixture; spread gently. Cover and refrigerate at least 6 hours or until set. *Dessert can be kept, covered, up to 2 days in refrigerator.*
15. To unmold dessert, rinse a towel in warm water. Squeeze so it is just damp. Wrap towel around edges of mold; leave about 5 seconds. Gently release spring to remove side of pan. Leave dessert on base of pan; set on a round platter. Refrigerate until ready to serve.
16. If desired, chill a medium bowl and beaters for whipping cream. Whip 1/2 cup cream in chilled bowl until very stiff.
17. Using a pastry bag and medium star tip, pipe large rosettes of whipped cream near top edge of dessert. Sprinkle with grated chocolate, if desired.

White Chocolate Bavarian Squares

This dessert is inspired by a favorite restaurant dessert that my husband and I first enjoyed in Israel fifteen years ago. The Israeli dessert is a vanilla Bavarian cream accompanied by dark chocolate sauce and sprinkled with chopped nuts. It is served right from the dish instead of being unmolded. This version is exceptionally creamy and delicately flavored with white chocolate, complemented by a sauce spiked with crème de cacao and by the crunch of pecans.

Makes about 8 servings

1-1/4 cups whipping cream
3 oz. fine-quality white chocolate, very finely chopped
1 (1/4-oz.) envelope unflavored gelatin (scant 1 tablespoon)
1/4 cup water
1 cup milk
4 egg yolks, room temperature
6 tablespoons sugar
1/4 cup white crème de cacao

Spirited Cold Chocolate Sauce, page 199
1/3 cup pecans, chopped

1. Set aside 1 cup cream in refrigerator. Put white chocolate in a heatproof medium bowl. Bring remaining 1/4 cup cream to a full boil in a small heavy saucepan. Pour over chocolate all at once. Stir with a whisk until chocolate is completely melted and mixture is smooth.
2. Sprinkle gelatin over 1/4 cup water in a small cup. Let stand while preparing custard.
3. Bring milk to a boil in a small heavy saucepan.
4. Whisk egg yolks lightly in a large heatproof bowl. Add sugar; whisk until well-blended. Gradually whisk in hot milk. Return mixture to saucepan, whisking constantly. Cook over medium-low heat, stirring mixture and scraping bottom of pan constantly with a wooden spoon, until mixture thickens slightly and reaches 165F to 170F (75C) on an instant-read thermometer; begin checking after 5 minutes. To check whether it is thick enough without a thermometer, remove custard from heat. Dip a metal spoon in custard and draw your finger across back of spoon. Your finger should leave a clear path in mixture that clings to spoon. If it does not, continue cooking another 30 seconds and check again. Do not overcook or it will curdle.
5. Remove from heat. Immediately add softened gelatin, whisking until it is completely dissolved. Pour into a large bowl; stir about 30 seconds to cool. Cool 10 minutes.
6. Using a whisk, gradually stir custard mixture into chocolate mixture.
7. Return mixture to large bowl; cool to room temperature, stirring occasionally. Gradually stir in crème de cacao.
8. Refrigerate chocolate mixture about 20 minutes, stirring often, or chill mixture by setting bowl in a larger bowl of iced water about 10 minutes, stirring very often, or until mixture is cold and beginning to thicken but is not set. Meanwhile, lightly oil an 8-inch-square baking dish or serving dish. Chill a large bowl and beaters for whipping cream.
9. Whip remaining 1 cup cream in chilled bowl until nearly stiff. Gently fold cream into chocolate mixture, blending thoroughly.
10. Pour mixture into prepared dish; smooth top. Cover and refrigerate at least 3 hours or until set. *Dessert can be kept up to 2 days in refrigerator; liqueur flavor weakens after 1 day.*
11. Make Spirited Cold Chocolate Sauce; cool to room temperature.
12. Cut dessert in about 2-1/2-inch squares. Use a broad spatula to transfer to serving plates. Spoon chocolate sauce over each serving and sprinkle with chopped pecans.

TIPS

○ *To check a small amount of custard with an instant-read thermometer, tilt saucepan so 2 inches of thermometer are immersed in liquid.*

○ *Always remove custard mixtures from heat when checking if they are ready, whether using an instant-read thermometer or a spoon.*

1/Spoon a scant 1/4 cup custard into rach ramekin. Freeze ramekins 15 minutes. Set a truffle in each ramekin. Spoon remaining custard on top. Tap firmly on work surface to distribute custard. Refrigerate at least 3 hours or until set.

2/Umold dessert using dipping method. Refrigerate until ready to serve.

Truffled Bavarian Cream

Each of these individual Bavarian creams hides a soft chocolate truffle in its center. The vanilla molds dotted with chocolate resemble Italian Chocolate Chip Ice Cream, page 128, in appearance. They can be served surrounded by Raspberry Sauce, page 131, for a beautiful color contrast.

Makes 6 servings

Soft Truffles:
1-1/2 oz. fine-quality semisweet chocolate, finely chopped
2 tablespoons whipping cream
1 tablespoon unsalted butter

Chocolate-Flecked Bavarian Cream:
1-1/2 cups milk
1 vanilla bean, split lengthwise
1 (1/4-oz.) envelope plus 1 teaspoon unflavored gelatin (scant 4 teaspoons)
1/4 cup water
5 egg yolks, room temperature
6 tablespoons sugar
1/2 pint whipping cream (1 cup), well-chilled
2 oz. semisweet chocolate, grated, chilled

1. **Soft Truffles:** Combine chocolate, cream and butter in a small heatproof bowl over hot, not simmering, water over low heat. Leave until melted, stirring occasionally. Whisk until smooth. Remove from pan of water; cool to room temperature. Cover and refrigerate at least 1 hour.
2. Using 2 teaspoons, shape into 6 mounds on a plate, using 1 rounded teaspoon for each truffle. Freeze 10 minutes. Roll between palms to smooth. Return to plate. Freeze again 10 minutes. Refrigerate until ready to use.
1. **Bavarian Cream:** Bring milk and vanilla bean to a boil in a heavy medium saucepan. Remove from heat. Cover and let stand 15 minutes.
2. Sprinkle gelatin over water in a small cup; set aside.
3. Reheat milk mixture to a boil.
4. Whisk egg yolks lightly in a large heatproof bowl. Add sugar; whisk until well-blended. Gradually whisk in hot milk. Return mixture to saucepan, whisking constantly. Cook over medium-low heat, stirring mixture and scraping bottom of pan constantly with a wooden spoon, until mixture thickens slightly and reaches 165F to 170F (75C) on an instant-read thermometer; begin checking after 5 minutes. To check whether it is thick enough without a thermometer, remove custard from heat. Dip a metal spoon in custard and draw your finger across back of spoon. Your finger should leave a clear path in mixture that clings to spoon. If it does not, continue cooking another 30 seconds and check again. Do not overcook or it will curdle.
5. Remove from heat. Remove vanilla bean. Immediately add softened gelatin, whisking until it is completely dissolved. Pour into a large bowl; stir about 30 seconds to cool. Cool to room temperature, stirring occasionally.
6. Refrigerate mixture about 20 minutes, stirring often, or chill mixture by setting bowl in a larger bowl of iced water about 10 minutes, stirring very often, or until mixture is cold and beginning to thicken but is not set.

6. Meanwhile, refrigerate a bowl and beaters for whipping cream. Line bases of 6 (2/3-cup) ramekins with a round of waxed paper; lightly oil paper and sides of ramekins.

7. Whip cream in chilled bowl until nearly stiff. Gently fold cream into custard, followed by grated chocolate.

8. Spoon a scant 1/4 cup custard into each ramekin. Freeze ramekins 15 minutes. Keep remaining custard at room temperature.

9. Set a truffle in each ramekin. Spoon remaining custard on top. Tap firmly on work surface to distribute custard. Refrigerate at least 3 hours or until completely set. *Dessert can be kept, covered, up to 2 days in refrigerator.*

1. **To serve:** To unmold dessert, run a thin-bladed flexible knife around edge of dessert in 1 ramekin, gently pushing mixture slightly from edge of mold to let in air. Dip ramekin, nearly to depth of contents, in warm, not hot, water about 10 seconds. Dry base of mold. Set a plate on top of ramekin. Holding firmly together, quickly flip so dessert is right-side up. Shake ramekin gently downward; dessert should slip from ramekin onto plate. If dessert remains in ramekin, repeat dipping procedure. Carefully remove ramekin by lifting it straight upward. Repeat with remaining ramekins. Remove paper.

2. Refrigerate dessert until ready to serve.

Variation

Chocolate-Flecked Bavarian Cream: Omit truffles. Spoon custard mixture from Step 7 into a lightly oiled 5-cup mold. Refrigerate at least 4 hours or until set. Unmold and serve with Raspberry Sauce, page 131.

Chocolate Chestnut Log

This favorite French family dessert is easy to prepare yet rich and sophisticated in taste. The chestnut puree can be purchased at specialty food stores and in some supermarkets.

Makes 8 servings

8 oz. semisweet chocolate, chopped
3-1/3 cups canned unsweetened whole chestnuts (1 lb.), drained well
2/3 cup milk, room temperature
1/2 cup (4 oz.) unsalted butter
1/2 cup plus 3 tablespoons powdered sugar, sifted
2 tablespoons rum
About 2 teaspoons unsweetened Dutch-process cocoa powder
Quick Chocolate Curls, page 193
About 1/2 teaspoon powdered sugar (for garnish)
1/2 pint whipping cream (1 cup), well chilled (for accompaniment)

1. Melt chocolate in a double boiler or heatproof medium bowl over hot, not simmering, water over low heat, stirring occasionally. Stir until smooth. Remove from pan of water and cool to body temperature.

2. Puree chestnuts with milk in a food processor until smooth.

3. Cream butter in a large bowl. Add 1/2 cup plus 3 tablespoons powdered sugar and beat until smooth and fluffy. Stir in chestnut mixture and rum. Gradually stir in chocolate. Transfer to a bowl, cover and refrigerate 45 minutes.

4. Spoon mixture onto a large piece of foil of about 12" x 20" and roll to a log, about 2-1/2 inches in diameter. Close ends of foil so log is wrapped. Refrigerate 8 hours or until firm. *Dessert can be kept up to 2 days in refrigerator.*

5. Chill a large bowl and beater for whipping cream. Remove foil from log, set log on a platter and press, if necessary, to give it a neater round shape. Put waxed paper on platter around log.

6. Sift cocoa evenly over log. Make lines lengthwise on log with a fork to resemble bark. Top with chocolate curls. Sift powdered sugar over chocolate curls. Remove waxed paper from platter.

7. Whip cream in chilled bowl to soft peaks.

8. Serve log in 1/2-inch-thick slices. Serve whipped cream separately.

Brown-Bottom Charlotte

The brown bottom of this rich charlotte is chocolate whipped cream. It is topped by a layer of bourbon Bavarian cream. The bourbon provides a zesty punch on the first day and becomes delicate on the second day.

Makes 6 servings

5 oz. packaged ladyfingers (about 3 inches long) or about 9 oz. White Ladyfingers, page 168

Chocolate Cream Filling:
4 oz. fine-quality bittersweet or semisweet chocolate, chopped
1/2 pint whipping cream (1 cup), well-chilled

2 tablespoons bourbon whiskey (for brushing)
1 tablespoon water (for brushing)

Bourbon Bavarian Cream:
3/4 cup milk
1 vanilla bean
2 teaspoons unflavored gelatin
3 tablespoons water
3 egg yolks, room temperature
1/4 cup sugar
1 tablespoon plus 1 teaspoon bourbon whiskey
3/4 cup whipping cream, well-chilled

Quick Chocolate Curls, page 193, or grated chocolate, if desired (for garnish)

1. Lightly oil side of an 8-inch springform pan. If using packaged ladyfingers, which are usually split in half horizontally, stand ladyfinger halves up in a single row against side of oiled pan, with their spongy sides facing inward, forming a tight ring. If ladyfinger halves are joined in a row, there is no need to separate them. If using homemade ladyfingers, follow directions given in the note accompanying that recipe.

2. Arrange more ladyfingers on base of pan to form a layer. Cut more ladyfingers so they fit as tightly as possible on base and fill any holes.

1. **Chocolate Cream Filling:** Chill a large bowl and beaters for whipping cream. Melt chocolate in a double boiler or small heatproof bowl over hot, not simmering, water over low heat, stirring occasionally. Stir until smooth. Remove from heat; leave chocolate above hot water.

2. Whip cream in chilled bowl until stiff. Remove chocolate from above water; cool 30 seconds. Quickly stir about 1/2 cup whipped cream into chocolate until blended. Quickly fold mixture into remaining whipped cream until blended. Fold quickly so chocolate does not harden upon contact with cold whipped cream.

3. Mix bourbon with water in a small dish. Brush ladyfingers in pan with bourbon mixture. Spoon chocolate mixture into ladyfinger-lined pan. Smooth top. Refrigerate 1 hour.

1. **Bavarian Cream:** Bring milk and vanilla bean to a boil in a small heavy saucepan. Remove from heat. Cover and let stand 15 minutes.

2. Sprinkle gelatin over water in a small cup. Let stand while preparing custard.

3. Reheat milk mixture to a boil. Remove vanilla bean.

4. Whisk yolks lightly in a small bowl. Add sugar; whisk until well-blended. Gradually whisk in hot milk. Return mixture to saucepan, whisking constantly. Cook over medium-low heat, stirring mixture and scraping bottom of pan constantly with a wooden spoon, until mixture thickens slightly and reaches 160F to 165F (70C to 75C) on an instant-read thermometer; begin checking after 5 minutes. To check whether it is thick enough without a thermometer, remove custard from heat. Dip a metal spoon in custard and draw your finger across back of spoon. Your finger should leave a clear path in mixture that clings to spoon. If it does not, continue cooking another 30 seconds and check again. Do not overcook custard or it will curdle.

5. Remove from heat. Immediately add softened gelatin, whisking until it is completely dissolved. Pour into a large bowl; stir about 30 seconds to cool.

6. Cool to room temperature, stirring occasionally. Slowly stir in bourbon.

7. Refrigerate bourbon mixture about 15 minutes, stirring often, or chill mixture by setting bowl in a larger bowl of iced water about 7 minutes, stirring very often, or until mixture is cold and beginning to thicken but is not set. Meanwhile, chill a small bowl and beaters for whipping cream.

8. Whip cream in chilled bowl until nearly stiff. Refrigerate until ready to use. When bourbon mixture is cold, fold in whipped cream, blending thoroughly. Carefully pour into charlotte mold.

9. Refrigerate charlotte about 4 hours or until filling sets. *Dessert can be kept, covered, up to 3 days in refrigerator; bourbon flavor weakens after 1 day.*

1. **To serve:** To unmold dessert, release spring and remove side of pan.

2. If desired, garnish top with Quick Chocolate Curls, allowing white filling to show through slightly.

Chocolate-Cognac Marquise

Like a charlotte, a marquise has a ladyfinger frame, but a marquise almost always has a very rich chocolate filling and is usually loaf shaped. This one is served with cognac custard sauce.

Makes 10 to 12 servings

1 lb. semisweet chocolate, chopped
1 (3-oz.) pkg. ladyfingers (about 3 inches long) or about 6 oz. White Ladyfingers, page 168
1 cup (8 oz.) unsalted butter, slightly softened
4 egg yolks, room temperature
5 tablespoons water
2 tablespoons cognac
Spirited Custard Sauce, page 197, flavored with cognac

1. Melt chocolate in a double boiler or large heatproof bowl over hot, not simmering, water over low heat, stirring occasionally. Stir until smooth. Remove from pan of water; cool to body temperature.

2. If using packaged ladyfingers, which are usually split in half horizontally, set ladyfinger halves crosswise in a single row on the base of an 8″ x 4″ loaf pan, with their spongy side facing up. If ladyfinger halves are joined in a row, there is no need to separate them. Stand more ladyfinger halves up against long sides of pan, with spongy sides facing inward, fitting them tightly. Stand more ladyfinger halves up against short sides of pan to complete case. Be sure ladyfingers are close together so pan is tightly lined. If using homemade ladyfingers, line pan as above, using whole ladyfingers and trimming them as necessary to fit tightly.

3. Cream butter in a large bowl until very smooth. Beat in chocolate in 4 batches. Scrape down side of bowl; beat mixture again until smooth.

4. Whisk egg yolks and 3 tablespoons water in a small heavy saucepan. Set pan over very low heat. Cook mixture, whisking vigorously, about 7 minutes or until thick enough so marks of whisk are visible in mixture. On an instant-read or candy thermometer, mixture should reach 120 to 125F (50C). Remove saucepan from heat occasionally, still continuing to whisk, so pan never gets too hot to touch; if mixture is overheated, yolks will curdle. Remove mixture from heat; whisk 1 minute.

5. Beat yolk mixture into chocolate mixture in 2 batches.

6. Mix 2 tablespoons cognac and remaining 2 tablespoons water in a small bowl. Brush ladyfinger case lightly but evenly with cognac mixture.

7. Pour chocolate mixture carefully into ladyfinger-lined pan without moving ladyfingers. Smooth top of chocolate mixture with a rubber spatula. Using a sharp knife, cut off ladyfinger ends above level of chocolate mixture; set on top of mixture near edges of pan. Add more ladyfinger pieces, if necessary, to make an even layer. Press gently so top is even.

8. Refrigerate at least 2 hours or until set. *Dessert can be kept, covered, up to 3 days in refrigerator.*

9. Prepare Spirited Custard Sauce.

1. **To serve:** Remove marquise from refrigerator about 30 minutes before serving. Run a thin-bladed flexible knife around dessert; turn out onto a platter. Cut off short ends. Cut marquise in thin slices with a sharp knife.

2. Set a slice on each serving plate. Spoon a little sauce around each slice. Serve remaining sauce separately.

1/Oil base of a 9-inch springform pan. Line base with waxed paper; oil paper and sides of pan. Arrange cake slices close together in pan.

2/Invert dessert onto a serving platter; gently unmold. Peel off paper. Prepare Apricot Glaze and dab over cake with a brush. Serve cold.

Royal Chocolate Charlotte

In this spectacular dessert fit for a royal feast, a classic-style frame of spiral-shaped slices of jelly roll surrounds a chocolate Bavarian cream. Serve this regal treat for extra-special occasions.

Makes about 10 servings

Raspberry Jelly Roll:
6 tablespoons all-purpose flour
1/4 cup cornstarch
4 eggs
3 egg yolks
7 tablespoons sugar
3/4 cup raspberry preserves (for filling)

Chocolate Bavarian Cream:
6-1/2 oz. fine-quality bittersweet chocolate, chopped
1 cup milk
1 vanilla bean, split lengthwise
1 (1/4-oz.) envelope unflavored gelatin (scant 1 tablespoon)
1/4 cup water
4 egg yolks, room temperature
5 tablespoons sugar
1-1/2 cups whipping cream, well-chilled

Apricot Glaze:
1/2 cup apricot preserves
2 tablespoons water

1. Raspberry Jelly Roll: Position rack in center of oven and preheat to 400F (205C). Lightly butter corners of a 17" x 11" rimmed baking sheet. Line with foil or parchment paper. Butter foil or paper.

2. Sift flour and cornstarch into a small bowl.

3. Beat eggs and egg yolks lightly in large bowl. Beat in sugar; beat mixture at high speed about 10 minutes or until very thick.

4. Sift 1/3 of flour mixture over batter; fold in as gently as possible. Repeat with remaining flour in 2 batches.

5. Transfer batter to baking sheet; spread evenly but lightly. Bake about 6 minutes or until cake is just firm, springy to touch and beginning to brown.

6. Transfer cake with its foil or paper to a rack. Cool to room temperature.

7. Spread raspberry preserves on cake. Beginning with a long side, roll up cake carefully but tightly; if it is not rolled tightly enough, slices will have holes. Wrap and refrigerate 30 minutes. *Cake can be kept up to 1 day in refrigerator.*

8. Using a serrated knife, cut cake in 3/8-inch slices.

9. Oil base of a 9-inch springform pan. Line base with waxed paper; oil paper and sides of pan.

10. Arrange cake slices in pan, 1 slice standing against side and 1 slice next to it on base to support it. When there are enough slices on base to prevent those on side from falling over, begin gently pushing slices on base into place, side by side. Squeeze slices at side and on base tightly into place so there are no holes between them. Cut small pieces of cake and use to patch up holes where necessary.

1. Chocolate Bavarian Cream: Melt chocolate in a double boiler or heatproof medium bowl over hot, not simmering, water over low heat, stirring occasionally. Stir until smooth. Remove from pan of water. Meanwhile, follow next 5 steps.

2. Bring milk and vanilla bean to a boil in a heavy medium saucepan. Remove from heat. Cover and let stand 15 minutes.

3. Sprinkle gelatin over 1/4 cup water. Let stand while preparing custard.

4. Reheat milk mixture to a boil.

5. Whisk egg yolks lightly in a large heatproof bowl. Add sugar; whisk until well-blended. Gradually whisk in hot milk. Return mixture to saucepan, whisking constantly. Cook over medium-low heat, stirring mixture and scraping bottom of pan constantly with a wooden spoon, until mixture thickens slightly and reaches 165F to 170F (75C) on an instant-read thermometer; begin checking after 5 minutes. To check whether it is thick enough without a thermometer, remove custard from heat. Dip a metal spoon in custard and draw your finger across back of spoon. Your finger should leave a clear path in mixture that clings to spoon. If it does not, continue cooking another 30 seconds and check again. Do not overcook custard or it will curdle.

6. Remove from heat. Remove vanilla bean. Immediately add softened gelatin, whisking until it is completely dissolved. Pour into a large bowl; stir about 30 seconds to cool. Cool 5 minutes.

7. Using a whisk, stir custard mixture, 3/4 cup at a time, into melted chocolate. Pour into a large bowl; cool to room temperature, stirring occasionally.

8. Refrigerate chocolate mixture about 20 minutes, stirring often, or chill mixture by setting bowl in a larger bowl of iced water about 10 minutes, stirring very often, or until mixture is cold and beginning to thicken but is not set. Meanwhile, chill a large bowl and beaters for whipping cream.

9. Whip cream in chilled bowl until nearly stiff. Gently fold cream into chocolate mixture, blending thoroughly.

10. Pour into cake-lined bowl; smooth top. Refrigerate 10 minutes. Gently set remaining cake slices on top to make 1 layer. Cover and refrigerate at least 5 hours or until set. *Dessert can be kept, covered, up to 3 days in refrigerator.*

11. To unmold, turn dessert over onto serving platter. Gently release spring and remove side of springform. Remove base. Peel off paper.

1. **Apricot Glaze:** Combine apricot preserves and water in a small saucepan. Heat over low heat until hot but not boiling. Strain into a small bowl, pressing on apricot pieces.

2. Using a pastry brush, dab glaze on cake. *Glazed dessert can be kept, covered with a cake cover or overturned bowl, up to 1 day in refrigerator.* Serve cold.

Chocolate Pistachio No-Bake Cake

Actually this is a soft, chocolaty mousse studded with slightly crunchy pistachios and molded in the form of a cake. The creamy-textured dessert is garnished with a simple and lovely garnish—bright green chopped pistachios set on the dark chocolate background.

Makes 8 to 10 servings.

8 oz. semisweet chocolate, chopped

1 cup (8 oz.) unsalted butter, cut in 1-inch cubes

6 eggs, separated, room temperature

2 teapoons pure vanilla extract

1 tablespoon sugar

1/2 cup shelled unsalted pistachios, coarsely chopped

2 teaspoons finely chopped pistachios (for garnish)

1. Lightly oil an 8-inch springform pan. Melt chocolate in a double boiler or large heatproof bowl over hot, not simmering, water over low heat, stirring occasionally. Stir until smooth. Add butter cubes and stir until blended.

2. Remove from pan of water. Whisk in egg yolks, 1 at a time, whisking vigorously after each one. Whisk in vanilla.

3. Whip egg whites in a large dry bowl with dry beaters at medium speed until soft peaks form. Gradually beat in sugar and continue whipping at high speed until whites are stiff and shiny but not dry.

4. Fold about 1/4 of whites into chocolate mixture. Spoon this mixture over remaining whites and fold gently until blended. Fold in pistachios.

5. Pour into prepared pan. Cover and refrigerate at least 8 hours. *Dessert can be kept, covered, up to 3 days in refrigerator.*

6. Unmold by running a thin-bladed flexible knife very carefully around edge of dessert. Release side of pan. Rinse a metal spatula in hot water, dry it quickly and use it to smooth side of dessert. Sprinkle chopped pistachios over center of cake. Cut cake very carefully, wiping knife after each cut.

1/Line side of mold with trimmed ladyfingers standing upright; smooth sides of ladyfingers should face outward. Fit in mold as tightly as possible.

2/Pipe rows of rosettes of whipped cream on borders between ladyfingers and a ring of rosettes around top edge of dessert. Pipe a ruffle of cream around base. If desired, garnish with a few Quick Chocolate Curls in center.

Double-Chocolate Charlotte

A ring of homemade chocolate ladyfingers encircles a two-layer filling of dark chocolate and milk chocolate Bavarian creams, to make an elegant, luscious dessert. This charlotte is made the traditional way, in a charlotte mold. The two Bavarian creams are made from one basic custard.

Makes 6 to 8 servings

About 20 Chocolate Ladyfingers, page 168

Dark & Milk Chocolate Bavarian Creams:
2 teaspoons unflavored gelatin
3 tablespoons water
1 cup milk
4 egg yolks, room temperature
5 tablespoons sugar
2 oz. fine-quality milk chocolate, chopped
3 oz. fine-quality semisweet chocolate, chopped
1 tablespoon unsweetened Dutch-process cocoa powder
3/4 cup plus 2 tablespoons whipping cream, well-chilled

Garnish:
2/3 cup whipping cream, well-chilled
Quick Chocolate Curls, page 193, or Chocolate Scrolls, page 195, if desired

● Prepare Chocolate Ladyfingers.

1. Bavarians: Sprinkle gelatin over water in a small cup. Let stand while preparing custard.

2. Bring milk to a boil in a small heavy saucepan.

3. Whisk egg yolks lightly in a large heatproof bowl. Add sugar; whisk until well-blended. Gradually whisk in hot milk. Return mixture to saucepan, whisking constantly. Cook over medium-low heat, stirring mixture and scraping bottom of pan constantly with a wooden spoon, until mixture thickens slightly and reaches 165F to 170F (75C) on an instant-read thermometer; begin checking after 5 minutes. To check whether it is thick enough without a thermometer, remove custard from heat. Dip a metal spoon in custard and draw your finger across back of spoon. Your finger should leave a clear path in mixture that clings to spoon. If it does not, continue cooking another 30 seconds and check again. Do not overcook or it will curdle.

4. Remove from heat. Immediately add softened gelatin, whisking until it is completely dissolved. Pour into a large bowl; stir about 30 seconds to cool.

5. Melt each type of chocolate separately in a double boiler or heatproof small bowl over hot, not simmering, water over low heat, stirring occasionally. Stir until smooth. Remove from pan of water.

6. Using a whisk, gradually stir 2/3 cup custard mixture, 1/3 cup at a time, into semisweet chocolate. Use whisk to stir remaining custard mixture, 1/3 cup at a time, into milk chocolate.

7. Sift cocoa over semisweet chocolate custard; whisk in. Pour each mixture into a separate medium bowl; cool to room temperature, stirring occasionally.

8. Line base of a 1-quart charlotte mold with waxed paper; oil side of mold and paper. Trim ladyfingers at their sides so they can fit tightly in mold. Trim them flat at 1 end to sit squarely on base of pan. Line side of mold with ladyfingers standing upright; smooth sides of ladyfingers that touched baking sheet should face outward. Fit them in mold as tightly as possible.

9. Refrigerate milk-chocolate mixture about 20 minutes, stirring often, or chill mixture by setting bowl in a larger bowl of iced water about 10 minutes, stirring very often, or until mixture is cold and beginning to thicken but is not set. Chill a large bowl and beaters for whipping cream.

10. Whip cream in chilled bowl until nearly stiff. Gently fold 1 cup whipped cream into milk-chocolate mixture, blending thoroughly.

11. Pour milk-chocolate mixture into lined charlotte mold. Cover and freeze 10 minutes or until top begins to set.

12. If semisweet chocolate mixture is not yet cold and beginning to thicken, refrigerate about 5 minutes, stirring often, or chill mixture by setting bowl in a larger bowl of iced water about 3 minutes, stirring very often, or until mixture is cold and beginning to thicken but is not set.

13. Fold remaining whipped cream into semisweet-chocolate mixture. Very gently and evenly spoon mixture over milk-chocolate mixture in mold.

14. Cover and refrigerate 1 hour or until partially set. Put more ladyfingers on top in 1 layer. Refrigerate at least 3 hours or until set. *Dessert can be kept, covered, up to 2 days in refrigerator.*

1. Garnish: Chill a medium bowl and beaters for whipping cream. Whip cream in chilled bowl until very stiff.

2. Trim top edges of ladyfingers at side so they are level with charlotte. Unmold charlotte onto a round platter. Carefully peel off paper.

3. Using a pastry bag and medium star tip, pipe rows of rosettes of whipped cream on borders between ladyfingers and a ring of rosettes at top of dessert. Pipe a ruffle of cream around base. If desired, garnish with a few Quick Chocolate Curls in center, letting color of filling show.

TIPS

○ *A traditional charlotte mold is round, straight-sided, 7-inches in diameter and usually about 4-inches deep. These can sometimes be difficult to find, however, and other types of molds can be used for these elegant desserts.*

○ *A Bavarian, or Bavarian cream, consists of three basic elements: Flavored custard sauce, whipped cream and gelatin.*

○ *Bavarians, mousses and soufflés all have a light, fluffy texture, which is created by the addition of whipped cream, beaten egg whites, or both.*

Chocolate Charlotte with Raspberries

Whole fresh raspberries accent the chocolate filling of this light-textured, easy-to-make charlotte that would be proudly served in the best of restaurants. Each slice is served surrounded by a ribbon of ruby-red raspberry sauce.

Makes 8 to 10 servings

11 oz. semisweet chocolate, chopped
1 (1/4-oz.) envelope plus 1-1/4 teaspoons unflavored gelatin (4 teaspoons)
1/3 cup water
2 cups milk
6 egg yolks, room temperature
1/2 cup sugar
1 (3-oz.) pkg. ladyfingers (about 3 inches long) or about 6 oz. White Ladyfingers, page 168
3/4 cup whipping cream, well-chilled
4 egg whites, room temperature
2-2/3 cups fresh raspberries (about 11 oz.)

Raspberry Sauce, page 131

1/2 cup whipping cream, well-chilled, if desired (for garnish)

1. Melt chocolate in a double boiler or large heatproof bowl over hot, not simmering, water over low heat, stirring occasionally. Stir until smooth. Remove from pan of water.
2. Sprinkle gelatin over 1/3 cup water in a small cup. Let stand while preparing custard.
3. Bring milk to a boil in a heavy medium saucepan.
4. Whisk egg yolks lightly in a large heatproof bowl. Add 6 tablespoons sugar; whisk until well-blended. Gradually whisk in hot milk. Return mixture to saucepan, whisking constantly. Cook over medium-low heat, stirring mixture and scraping bottom of pan constantly with a wooden spoon, until mixture thickens slightly and reaches 155F to 160F (70C) on an instant-read thermometer; begin checking after 7 minutes. To check whether it is thick enough without a thermometer, remove custard from heat. Dip a metal spoon in custard and draw your finger across back of spoon. Your finger should leave a light path in mixture that clings to spoon. If it does not, continue cooking another 30 seconds and check again. Do not overcook custard or it will curdle.
5. Remove from heat. Immediately add softened gelatin, whisking until it is completely dissolved. Pour into a large bowl; stir about 30 seconds to cool.
6. Using a whisk, gradually stir custard mixture, about 1 cup at a time, into melted chocolate. Cool to room temperature, stirring occasionally.
7. Lightly oil a 9" x 3" springform pan. If using packaged ladyfingers, which are usually split in half horizontally, stand ladyfinger halves up in a single row against side of oiled pan, with their spongy sides facing inward, forming a tight ring. If ladyfinger halves are joined in a row, there is no need to separate them. If using homemade White Ladyfingers, follow directions given in the note accompanying that recipe.
8. Refrigerate chocolate mixture about 30 minutes, stirring often, or chill mixture by setting bowl in a larger bowl of iced water about 15 minutes, stirring very often, or until mixture is cold and beginning to thicken but is not set. Chill a medium or large bowl and beaters for whipping cream.
9. Whip 3/4 cup cream in chilled bowl until nearly stiff. Refrigerate until ready to use. When chocolate mixture is cold, fold in whipped cream, blending thoroughly.
10. In a medium or large dry bowl, whip egg whites using dry beaters at medium speed until soft peaks form. Gradually beat in remaining 2 tablespoons sugar; continue whipping at high speed until whites are stiff and shiny but not dry. Fold into chocolate mixture.
11. Carefully pour 4 cups chocolate mixture into ladyfinger-lined pan. Freeze 10 minutes. Cover chocolate mixture with 1-1/3 cups raspberries, arranging them in 1 layer. Carefully pour remaining chocolate mixture over them. Gently spread smooth. Refrigerate 10 minutes.
12. Carefully top with another layer of 1-1/3 cups raspberries. Refrigerate charlotte about 3 hours or until filling sets. *Dessert can be kept, covered, up to 2 days in refrigerator.*
13. Prepare Raspberry Sauce.
14. To unmold, carefully run a thin-bladed knife around charlotte; release spring and remove side of pan. Return dessert to refrigerator.
15. Chill a medium bowl and beaters for whipping cream. Whip cream in chilled bowl until very stiff.
16. Using a pastry bag and medium star tip, pipe rosettes of whipped cream near bottom edge of dessert. Serve cold. Serve sauce separately, spooning it around each slice of charlotte.

Chocolate-Almond Praline Charlotte

The filling of this beautiful, nutty chocolate dessert makes use of the setting properties of chocolate and butter to make it firm and does not require custard or gelatin. Praline liqueur paired with Almond Praline contribute an intense caramel-nut flavor to the charlotte.

Makes 8 servings

Almond Praline:
3/4 cup whole blanched almonds (about 4 oz.)
1/2 cup sugar
1/3 cup water

Chocolate-Praline Charlotte:
6 oz. fine-quality bittersweet chocolate, chopped
1/2 cup plus 2 tablespoons (5 oz.) unsalted butter, slightly softened
1/4 cup plus 1 tablespoon powdered sugar, sifted
4 eggs, separated, room temperature
1-1/4 cups Almond Praline, above
1/2 cup plus 2 tablespoons whipping cream, well-chilled
5 oz. packaged ladyfingers (about 3 inches long) or about 9 oz. White Ladyfingers, page 168
1/4 cup praline liqueur

Praline Cream:
3/4 cup whipping cream, well-chilled
1 tablespoon praline liqueur

1. **Almond Praline:** Preheat oven to 350F (175C). Toast almonds in a shallow baking pan in oven about 8 minutes. Remove from oven; leave on baking pan to keep warm.
2. Lightly oil a baking sheet.
3. Combine sugar and water in a heavy, very small saucepan that does not have a black interior. Heat mixture over low heat until sugar dissolves, gently stirring occasionally. Increase heat to high and boil, without stirring, but occasionally brushing down any sugar crystals from side of pan with a brush dipped in water, until mixture begins to brown. Reduce heat to medium-low. Continue cooking, swirling pan gently, until mixture is a rich brown color and a trace of smoke begins to rise from pan. Do not let caramel get too dark or it will burn and praline will be bitter; if caramel is too light, praline will be too sweet.
4. Immediately remove caramel from heat. Stir in warm nuts, being careful not to splash, until they are well-coated with caramel. Stir over low heat 1-1/2 minutes. Immediately transfer to oiled baking sheet.
5. Cool completely. Break praline into small chunks.
6. Grind praline in a food processor, scraping mixture inwards occasionally, until as fine as possible. Immediately transfer remaining praline to an airtight container. *Praline can be kept several months in an airtight container at room temperature or in freezer.*

1. **Chocolate-Praline Charlotte:** Melt chocolate in a double boiler or heatproof medium bowl over hot, not simmering, water over low heat, stirring occasionally. Stir until smooth. Remove from pan of water; cool to body temperature. Chill a medium bowl and beaters for whipping cream. Set aside 2 teaspoons praline for garnish.
2. Cream butter in a large bowl. Add powdered sugar; beat until light and fluffy. Beat in egg yolks, 1 at a time. Stir in chocolate and praline powder.
3. Whip cream in chilled bowl until nearly stiff.
4. In a medium or large dry bowl, whip egg whites using dry beaters at medium speed until stiff but not dry.
5. Fold whipped cream into chocolate mixture in 2 batches. Gently fold in egg whites.
6. Lightly oil an 8-inch springform pan. If using packaged ladyfingers, which are usually split in half horizontally, stand ladyfinger halves up in a single row against side of oiled pan with their spongy sides facing inward, forming a tight ring. If ladyfinger halves are joined in a row, there is no need to separate them. If using homemade White Ladyfingers, follow directions given in the note accompanying that recipe.
7. Arrange more ladyfingers on base of pan to form a layer. Cut more ladyfingers so they fit as tightly as possible on base and fill any holes. Brush ladyfinger case with 3 tablespoons praline liqueur.
8. Spoon 2 cups chocolate mixture into ladyfinger-lined mold. Cover with another layer of ladyfingers; brush with 1 tablespoon liqueur. Spoon remaining chocolate mixture on top; spread evenly.
9. Refrigerate at least 6 hours or until firm. Cover when firm. *Dessert can be kept up to 3 days in refrigerator.* To unmold dessert, release spring and remove side of pan.

1. **Praline Cream:** Chill a medium or large bowl and beaters for whipping cream. Whip cream in chilled bowl until soft peaks form. Add praline liqueur; continue beating until cream is very stiff.
2. Using pastry bag and large star tip, pipe a ruffle of cream at top edge of charlotte next to ladyfingers. Sprinkle cream lightly with 2 teaspoons praline.

ICE CREAMS, FROZEN DESSERTS & ICE CREAM CAKES

Cool, refreshing chocolate ice creams and frozen desserts are naturally the stars among summer sweet treats. Many are impressive yet easy to prepare, and most do not require baking and involve little or no last-minute work.

Chocolate Ice Creams

It is hard to imagine anything more delicious than homemade chocolate ice cream that has just been churned. Whether it is made the European way from custard mixtures, as in French-Italian Chocolate Ice Cream, or from easy blends of chocolate and cream, as in Chocolate-Mint Ice Cream or American Chocolate Ice Cream, its taste and smoothness are unparalleled.

Although ice cream keeps for several weeks in the freezer, when it is fresh it has the most wonderful soft creamy texture. If, however, your schedule does not allow you to churn the ice cream immediately before serving or you prefer a firmer texture, the ice cream can be left in the freezer for two to four hours and will still be at its best.

Frozen Chocolate Desserts

This group of desserts includes some of the most elegant of sweet finales. Smooth and frosty, they can be made in a multitude of shapes, colors and tastes.

Because these desserts are made from mixtures that are richer than ice cream, there is no need to stir them during the freezing process. They therefore do not require an ice cream machine to give them a velvety texture and prevent the formation of ice crystals. Instead, their smoothness is achieved by the addition of whipped cream, egg yolks, Italian meringue, butter or some combination of these elements.

Chocolate parfaits are made of a custard enriched with whipped cream; it is the chocolate that ensures that the parfait freezes to a silky texture. Frozen chocolate mousses, used in both Chocolate-Blackberry Loaf and Chocolate Mousse Ring with Fresh Berries, are prepared by a procedure similar to that for classic chocolate mousse but include a generous proportion of whipped cream

for lightness. Iced soufflés consist of a special mousse-type mixture formed to resemble a hot soufflé. Bombes are traditionally rounded in shape, and are composed of an outer layer of ice cream and a creamy filling of a contrasting color and flavor. Chocolate can appear either in the ice cream, as in Chocolate-Strawberry Bombe, or in the filling, as in Rum-Raisin Chocolate Bombe.

Chocolate Ice Cream Cakes

A stroll from one pastry shop to the next in the cities of France and Italy will reveal that these favorite American treats are popular in southern Europe too, although they look much different.

In many ice cream cakes, the rich filling is balanced by layers of a light sponge cake. Another possibility is crisp meringues, which are traditionally paired with ice cream in Europe, as in Chocolate Surprise Ice Cream Cake. Instead of cake, a quicker base can be made as in Brownie Ice Cream Cake, where fudge brownies are split and alternated with coffee and vanilla ice creams.

Ice cream cakes can be absolutely spectacular. One of the most dazzling cakes of France and Austria, both celebrated for their fabulous entremets, is the vacherin. This sensational castle of light meringues contains a rich filling. Contemporary versions are usually filled with ice cream. French pâtisseries often have ice cream- and sorbet-filled vacherins ready in their freezers, a useful tip for the home cook as well.

Ice cream cakes afford a wonderful opportunity for creativity. They can be shaped in different types of molds, cake pans or even mixing bowls. If, for example, you substitute coffee ice cream for vanilla in Chocolate-Pecan Sundae Pie and decorate the top with chocolate coffee beans, you'll have a delectable mocha sundae pie. Try rum-raisin ice cream instead of vanilla in Brownie Ice Cream Cake. The list could go on and on. Choose the flavor combinations you like best and be sure to have them on hand to make tasty substitutions. Your fabulous ice cream cakes will turn any get-together, from an elegant dinner to a casual meeting with friends, into a celebration.

American Chocolate Ice Cream

When it first comes out of the machine, this delicious ice cream has a texture similar to that of custard-based ice cream. When stored, though, it freezes harder and colder. It is the easiest type of ice cream to prepare.

Makes about 5 cups

1-1/2 pints whipping cream (3 cups)
1 cup milk
3/4 cup sugar
1 vanilla bean, split lengthwise
10 oz. fine-quality bittersweet
   chocolate, chopped

1. Combine cream, milk and sugar in a heavy medium saucepan; stir to blend. Add vanilla bean. Cook over low heat, stirring, until sugar dissolves. Increase heat to medium-high. Bring to a simmer.
2. Remove from heat. Cover and let stand 30 minutes. Remove vanilla bean.
3. Melt chocolate in a double boiler or heatproof medium bowl over hot, not simmering, water over low heat, stirring occasionally. Stir until smooth. Remove from pan of water; cool to body temperature.
4. Whisk cool cream mixture into chocolate, about 1 cup at a time. Cool completely.
5. Pour mixture into an ice cream machine. Churn-freeze ice cream in machine until set. Serve soft ice cream immediately. Or, remove dasher and replace lid. Cover lid with foil. Place ice cream in freezer to ripen 2 to 4 hours or until firm. *To store ice cream up to 1 month, transfer to a chilled bowl; cover tightly. Place in freezer.* Serve ice cream slightly softened.

French-Italian Chocolate Ice Cream

The French learned to make ice cream from the Italians but claim to be the first to have made chocolate ice cream! The finest Italian and French ice creams are made from the same mixture, a rich custard called *crème anglaise* or *English cream*. This luscious ice cream is extra-creamy, silky smooth and very chocolaty.

Makes about 1 quart

1-1/2 cups milk
1-1/2 cups whipping cream
9 egg yolks, room temperature
1 cup sugar
7 oz. fine-quality bittersweet
   chocolate, chopped

1. Bring milk and cream to a boil in a heavy medium saucepan.
2. Whisk egg yolks lightly in a large heatproof bowl. Add sugar; whisk until well-blended. Gradually whisk in hot milk mixture. Return mixture to saucepan, whisking constantly. Cook over medium-low heat, stirring and scraping bottom of pan constantly with a wooden spoon, until mixture thickens slightly and reaches 165F to 170F (75C) on an instant-read thermometer; begin checking after 7 minutes. To check whether it is thick enough without a thermometer, remove custard from heat. Dip a metal spoon in mixture and draw your finger across back of spoon. Your finger should leave a clear path in mixture that clings to spoon. If it does not, continue cooking another 30 seconds and check again. Do not overcook custard or it will curdle.
3. Immediately pour into a bowl; stir about 30 seconds to cool. Cool 10 minutes.
4. Melt chocolate in a double boiler or heatproof medium bowl over hot, not simmering, water over low heat, stirring occasionally. Stir until smooth. Remove from pan of water; cool to body temperature.
5. Whisk custard into chocolate, about 1/2 cup at a time, whisking until blended after each addition. Cool completely, stirring occasionally.
6. Pour chocolate custard into an ice cream machine. Churn-freeze ice cream in machine until set. Serve soft ice cream immediately. Or, remove dasher and replace lid. Cover lid with foil. Place ice cream in freezer to ripen 2 to 4 hours or until firm. *To store ice cream up to 1 month, transfer to a chilled bowl; cover tightly. Place in freezer.* Serve ice cream slightly softened.

Chocolate-Almond Ice Cream

Almonds contribute both richness and flavor to this chocolate ice cream in three ways. The nuts are simmered in the cream to flavor it and the almond taste is reinforced by the addition of almond liqueur. Chopped toasted almonds are stirred in and, as a last touch, are also sprinkled on each serving, adding a pleasant crunchiness in contrast to the smooth-textured ice cream.

Makes about 3 cups

1 cup whole blanched almonds
    (about 5-1/4 oz.)
1/2 cup slivered almonds (about 2
    oz.)
1-1/2 cups whipping cream
1-1/2 cups milk
6 egg yolks, room temperature
1/2 cup plus 1 tablespoon sugar
3 oz. semisweet chocolate, chopped
2 tablespoons amaretto liqueur
Chopped toasted almonds, if
    desired (for serving)

1. Preheat oven to 350F (175C). Toast blanched almonds in a shallow baking pan in oven 7 minutes. Toast slivered almonds in a separate baking pan 5 minutes. Transfer each type of almond to a separate plate; set aside.
2. Coarsely chop whole almonds in a food processor or with a knife. Combine chopped almonds and cream in a heavy medium saucepan; bring to a boil. Reduce heat to low and simmer, uncovered, 20 minutes, stirring occasionally. Remove from heat. Cover and let stand 30 minutes.
3. Strain cream through a double layer of cheesecloth, pressing firmly on almonds. Leave almonds in cheesecloth in strainer.
4. Bring milk to a boil in a heavy medium saucepan. Pour boiling milk over almonds in strainer. Press to extract as much liquid as possible; stir almonds in strainer so liquid will flow through more easily. When mixture is cool enough to handle, squeeze cheesecloth to extract remaining liquid; discard almonds.
5. Bring cream mixture to a boil in a heavy medium saucepan.
6. Whisk egg yolks lightly in a large heatproof bowl. Add sugar; whisk until well-blended. Gradually whisk in hot cream mixture. Return mixture to saucepan, whisking constantly. Cook over medium-low heat, stirring mixture and scraping bottom of pan constantly with a wooden spoon, about 5 minutes or until mixture thickens slightly and reaches 165F to 170F (75C) on an instant-read thermometer; begin checking after 5 minutes. To check whether it is thick enough without a thermometer, remove custard from heat. Dip a metal spoon in mixture and draw your finger across back of spoon. Your finger should leave a clear path in mixture that clings to spoon. If it does not, continue cooking another minute and check again. Do not overcook custard or it will curdle.
7. Immediately pour into a bowl; stir about 30 seconds to cool. Cool to lukewarm.
8. Melt chocolate in a double boiler or small heatproof bowl over hot, not simmering, water over low heat, stirring occasionally. Stir until smooth. Remove from pan of water; cool to lukewarm.
9. Whisk custard into cooled chocolate, about 1/3 cup at a time. Add amaretto; cool completely.
10. Coarsely chop slivered almonds; set aside.
11. Pour mixture into ice cream machine. Churn-freeze ice cream in machine until nearly set. Add 1/2 cup chopped almonds. Continue churning until ice cream is firm. Serve soft ice cream immediately. Or, remove dasher and replace lid. Cover lid with foil. Place ice cream in freezer to ripen 2 to 4 hours or until firm. *To store ice cream up to 1 month, transfer to a chilled bowl; cover tightly. Place in freezer.* Serve ice cream slightly softened. Sprinkle each serving with toasted almonds, if desired.

How to Make Chocolate-Mint Ice Cream

1/Strain milk mixture into a medium bowl, pressing on mint in strainer. Cool to room temperature.

2/Serve ice cream slightly softened. If desired, garnish with Chocolate Mint Leaves.

Italian Chocolate Chip Ice Cream

A favorite *gelato* throughout Italy, where it is known as *stracciatella*, this light vanilla ice cream is accented by tiny bits of chocolate that easily melt in your mouth.

Makes about 3-1/2 cups

1 cup milk
1 pint whipping cream (2 cups)
1 vanilla bean, split lengthwise
6 egg yolks, room temperature
1/2 cup sugar
**4 oz. fine-quality semisweet
chocolate, coarsely grated**

1. Combine milk, 1 cup cream and vanilla bean in a heavy medium saucepan. Bring to a boil. Remove from heat. Cover and let stand 20 minutes. Remove vanilla bean.
2. Bring milk mixture to a boil.
3. Whisk egg yolks lightly in a large heatproof bowl. Add sugar; whisk until well-blended. Gradually whisk in hot milk. Return mixture to saucepan, whisking constantly. Cook over medium-low heat, stirring mixture and scraping bottom of pan constantly with a wooden spoon, until mixture thickens slightly and reaches 165F to 170F (75C) on an instant-read thermometer; begin checking after 7 minutes. To check whether it is thick enough without a thermometer, remove custard from heat. Dip a metal spoon in mixture and draw your finger across back of spoon. Your finger should leave a clear path in mixture that clings to spoon. If it does not, continue cooking another 30 seconds and check again. Do not overcook or it will curdle.
4. Immediately pour into a bowl; stir about 30 seconds to cool. Cool completely, stirring occasionally. Stir in remaining cream.
5. Pour ice cream mixture into an ice cream machine. Churn-freeze ice cream in machine until nearly set. Add grated chocolate; stir gently. Continue churning until ice cream is firm. Serve soft ice cream immediately. Or, remove dasher and replace lid. Cover lid with foil. Place ice cream in freezer to ripen 2 to 4 hours or until firm. *To store ice cream up to 1 month, transfer to a chilled bowl; cover tightly. Place in freezer.* Serve ice cream slightly softened.

Chocolate-Mint Ice Cream

Fresh mint is the secret to this light, easy-to-prepare ice cream. The mint leaves steep in the milk, which absorbs their flavor, and then are strained out. This refreshing ice cream is irresistible!

Makes about 1 quart

1 medium bunch fresh mint (about 3-1/2 oz.)
1-1/2 cups milk
2-1/2 cups whipping cream
3/4 cup sugar
7 oz. semisweet chocolate, chopped
Mint leaves or Half-Dipped Chocolate Mint Leaves, page 196, if desired (for garnish)

1. Remove mint leaves from stems; you will have about 2-1/2 cups leaves. Coarsely chop leaves.
2. Bring 1 cup milk and 1 cup cream to boil in a heavy medium saucepan. Add mint. Remove from heat; stir. Cover and let stand 1 hour.
3. Add sugar; stir over low heat until completely dissolved. Strain milk into a medium bowl, pressing on mint in strainer. Cool to room temperature.
4. Melt chocolate in a double boiler or heatproof medium bowl over hot, not simmering, water over low heat, stirring occasionally. Stir until smooth. Remove from pan of water; cool to body temperature.
5. Whisk cool milk mixture, about 1/2 cup at a time, into chocolate. Whisk in remaining 1/2 cup milk and remaining 1-1/2 cups cream.
6. Pour mixture into ice-cream machine. Churn-freeze ice cream in machine until set. Serve soft ice cream immediately. Or, remove dasher and replace lid. Cover lid with foil. Place ice cream in freezer to ripen 2 to 4 hours or until firm. *To store ice cream up to 1 month, transfer to a chilled bowl; cover tightly. Place in freezer.* Serve ice cream slightly softened. If desired, garnish with fresh mint leaves or Half-Dipped Chocolate Mint Leaves.

Cappuccino-Chocolate Ice Cream

Like some versions of the famous drink, this ice cream combines a favorite flavor trio: chocolate, coffee and cinnamon. Coffee and cinnamon are introduced by the technique of infusing coffee beans and cinnamon sticks in the milk. This keeps the tastes delicate and the ice cream satiny.

Makes about 3-1/2 cups

1 cup coffee beans, preferably Mocha Java (about 3 oz.)
About 2-3/4 cups plus 2 tablespoons milk
2 (3-inch) cinnamon sticks
6 egg yolks, room temperature
3/4 cup sugar
5 oz. semisweet chocolate, chopped
1/2 pint whipping cream (1 cup), well-chilled

1. Place coffee beans in a plastic bag; coarsely crush with a rolling pin.
2. Scald 2-1/2 cups milk with coffee beans and cinnamon sticks in a heavy medium saucepan by heating until bubbles form around edge of pan. Cover and let stand 30 minutes. Set aside cinnamon sticks. Strain milk through a double layer of cheesecloth. Squeeze hard. Measure strained milk; add enough milk to obtain 2 cups.
3. Bring milk mixture to a boil in a heavy medium saucepan.
4. Whisk egg yolks lightly in a large heatproof bowl. Add sugar; whisk until well-blended. Gradually whisk in hot milk mixture. Return mixture to saucepan, whisking constantly. Cook over medium-low heat, stirring and scraping bottom of pan constantly with a wooden spoon, until mixture thickens slightly and reaches 165F to 170F (75C) on an instant-read thermometer; begin checking after 7 minutes. To check whether it is thick enough without a thermometer, remove custard from heat. Dip a metal spoon in mixture and draw your finger across back of spoon. Your finger should leave a clear path in mixture that clings to spoon. If it does not, continue cooking another 30 seconds and check again. Do not overcook or it will curdle.
5. Immediately pour into a bowl; stir about 30 seconds. Cool 10 minutes.
6. Melt chocolate in a double boiler or heatproof medium bowl over hot, not simmering, water over low heat, stirring occasionally. Stir until smooth. Remove from pan of water; cool to body temperature.
7. Stir custard mixture, about 1/2 cup at a time, into chocolate. If mixture is not very smooth, strain into a bowl. Return cinnamon sticks to mixture. Cool completely, stirring occasionally. Remove cinnamon sticks. Stir in cream.
8. Pour custard into ice cream machine. Churn-freeze ice cream in machine until set. Serve soft ice cream immediately. Or, remove dasher and replace lid. Cover lid with foil. Place ice cream in freezer to ripen 2 to 4 hours or until firm. *To store ice cream up to 1 month, transfer to a chilled bowl; cover tightly. Place in freezer.* Serve ice cream slightly softened.

Caramel-Chocolate Swirl Ice Cream

Creamy caramel flavors both the ice cream and the chocolate fudge sauce that is rippled through it. The caramel makes the ice cream stay soft-textured even when frozen.

Makes about 1 quart

2-1/2 cups whipping cream
1 cup water
2-1/4 cups sugar
1 cup milk
6 egg yolks, room temperature
3 oz. semisweet chocolate, chopped

1. Scald 1-1/2 cups cream in a medium saucepan by heating until bubbles form around edge of pan. Remove from heat. Transfer to a 2-cup measure.

2. Combine water and 2 cups sugar in a heavy large saucepan that does not have a black interior. Heat mixture over low heat until sugar dissolves, gently stirring occasionally. Increase heat to high and boil, without stirring, but occasionally brushing down any sugar crystals from side of pan with a brush dipped in water, until mixture begins to brown. Reduce heat to medium-low. Continue cooking, swirling pan gently, until mixture is a rich brown color and a trace of smoke begins to rise from pan. Do not let caramel get too dark or it will be bitter; if caramel is too light, it will be too sweet. Immediately remove from heat.

3. Standing at a distance, pour in hot cream, about 2 tablespoons at a time, without stirring; caramel will bubble furiously. When caramel stops bubbling, return mixture to low heat. Heat, stirring, 1 minute or until it is well-blended. Cool to lukewarm.

4. Set aside 3/4 cup caramel for making fudge sauce.

5. Stir milk and 1/2 cup cream into remaining caramel. Bring mixture to a simmer, whisking constantly.

6. Whisk egg yolks lightly in a large heatproof bowl. Add remaining 1/4 cup sugar; whisk until well-blended. Gradually whisk in hot caramel mixture. Return mixture to saucepan, whisking constantly. Cook over medium-low heat, stirring mixture and scraping bottom of pan constantly with a wooden spoon, until mixture thickens slightly and reaches 165F to 170F (75C) on an instant-read thermometer; begin checking after 7 minutes. To check whether it is thick enough without a thermometer, remove custard from heat. Dip a metal spoon in mixture and draw your finger across back of spoon. Your finger should leave a clear path in mixture that clings to spoon. If it does not, continue cooking another minute and check again. Do not overcook custard or it will curdle.

7. Immediately pour into a bowl; stir about 30 seconds to cool. Cool to room temperature, stirring occasionally. Stir in remaining 1/2 cup cream. If desired, chill a medium bowl or freezing container in freezer.

8. Reheat reserved caramel mixture in a double boiler above hot water until it is just warm and fluid. Melt chocolate in a double boiler or heatproof medium bowl over hot, not simmering, water over low heat. Stir until smooth. Stir chocolate into sauce. Cool to room temperature.

9. Pour caramel-custard mixture into ice cream machine. Churn-freeze ice cream in machine until set.

10. Spoon about 1/3 of ice cream into chilled bowl or freezing container. Quickly spoon 1/3 of chocolate sauce over it in a layer. Repeat with remaining ice cream and sauce, adding each in 2 batches. Stir once to swirl; cover. Or, remove lid and dasher from ice cream canister. Insert a long metal spatula into center of ice cream. Pull broad side of spatula toward edge of ice cream canister. Quickly pour chocolate sauce into space created by moving spatula. Move broad side of spatula back and forth through ice cream and sauce creating a marbled effect. Remove spatula. Replace lid. Cover lid with foil. Freeze ice cream at least 3 hours before serving. *Ice cream can be kept in tightly covered container up to 1 month in freezer.*

How to Make Caramel-Chocolate Swirl Ice Cream

1/When sugar and water mixture begins to brown, continue cooking, swirling pan gently, until mixture is a rich brown color and a trace of smoke begins to rise from pan.

2/Spoon about 1/3 of ice cream into chilled bowl. Quickly spoon 1/3 of chocolate sauce over it in a layer. Repeat with remaining ice cream and sauce in 2 batches. Stir once to swirl. Cover and freeze at least 3 hours before serving.

Chocolate-Raspberry Coupe

This *coupe*, or *French sundae*, dresses up chocolate and vanilla ice creams with raspberries and raspberry sauce. For an extra-special treat, spike the sauce with aromatic, clear raspberry brandy.

Makes 6 servings

Raspberry Sauce:

3 cups fresh raspberries (about 12 oz.)

About 11 tablespoons powdered sugar, sifted

3/4 pint French-Italian Chocolate Ice Cream, page 126, or other chocolate ice cream (1-1/2 cups)

3/4 pint vanilla ice cream (1-1/2 cups)

1 cup fresh raspberries (for garnish)

1. **Sauce:** Process 3 cups raspberries and 1/2 cup powdered sugar in a food processor or blender until very smooth. Strain puree into a bowl, pressing on pulp in strainer. Use a rubber spatula to scrape mixture from underside of strainer.

2. Taste sauce and whisk in more powdered sugar, if needed. Whisk sauce thoroughly so sugar is completely blended in. Cover and refrigerate 30 minutes. *Sauce can be kept, covered, up to 2 days in refrigerator.*

3. Stir sauce before serving.

● To serve, scoop chocolate and vanilla ice creams into 6 dessert dishes; pour sauce around ice cream. Garnish with 1 cup raspberries. Serve immediately.

Sabra Sundae

I was introduced to Sabra, the chocolate-orange liqueur, when I lived in Israel and was glad to find it available when I returned to the United States. For this sundae, the hot Sabra chocolate sauce is poured over vanilla ice cream, which is garnished with fresh orange segments.

Makes 4 servings

2 oranges, sectioned
2 tablespoons Sabra liqueur

Chocolate-Sabra Sauce:
4 oz. semisweet chocolate, chopped
1/3 cup whipping cream
1/4 cup Sabra liqueur

1 pint vanilla ice cream

• Combine oranges and liqueur in a bowl; toss lightly. Cover and refrigerate at least 10 minutes or up to 30 minutes.
1. Sauce: Combine chocolate and cream in a double boiler or heatproof medium bowl over hot, not simmering, water over low heat. Leave until melted, stirring occasionally. Remove from pan of water; stir until sauce is smooth. *Sauce can be made up to 1 week ahead and kept, covered, in refrigerator.*
2. Reheat sauce over a pan of hot water before serving; stir in Sabra liqueur.
3. To serve, scoop ice cream into 4 dessert dishes; arrange orange sections around it. Pour warm sauce over ice cream. Serve immediately.

Meringata

This is an elegant sundae that my husband and I enjoyed at a cafe on the Italian Riviera during our first trip to Italy. It combines the crunchiness of small star-shaped meringues, the smoothness of ice cream and the lightness of whipped cream. The whole glorious creation is topped off with a rich, dark, shiny, coffee-flavored chocolate sauce.

Makes 6 servings; about 60 meringues

Meringue Kisses:
2 egg whites, room temperature
1/4 teaspoon cream of tartar
1/2 cup sugar

Coffee-Chocolate Sauce:
1/3 cup boiling water
1-1/2 teaspoons instant coffee granules
1 tablespoon unsalted butter
4 oz. bittersweet chocolate, chopped

Whipped Cream:
3/4 cup whipping cream, well-chilled
2 teaspoons sugar

1-1/2 pints vanilla or coffee ice cream

1. Meringue Kisses: Position rack in center of oven and preheat to 200F (95C). Lightly butter corners of 1 large or 2 small baking sheets; line with foil or parchment paper. Butter and lightly flour foil or paper, tapping baking sheets to remove excess flour.
2. Have ready a rubber spatula for folding and a pastry bag fitted with a medium star tip that has large points. Using a clothespin or paper clip, close end of bag just above tip, so mixture will not run out while bag is being filled.
3. In a small dry bowl, whip egg whites with cream of tartar using dry beaters at medium speed until stiff peaks form. Switch speed to high. Gradually beat in sugar; continue whipping at high speed until whites are shiny.
4. Immediately spoon meringue into pastry bag. Remove clothespin or paper clip. Pipe mixture in small kisses with points, about 3/4 inch in diameter and 1 inch high, spacing them about 1 inch apart.
5. Bake meringues about 1-1/2 hours or until firm and dry. To test for doneness, remove a meringue. Cool 2 minutes, then break meringue apart; it should be dry and crumbly and not sticky. Using a large metal spatula, immediately remove meringues from foil or paper; cool on a rack. *Meringues can be kept in airtight containers at room temperature up to 1 week in dry weather. If they become sticky from humidity, they can be recrisped in a 200F (95C) oven about 20 minutes.*
1. Coffee-Chocolate Sauce: Pour boiling water over coffee; cool to room temperature. Combine coffee, butter and chocolate in a double boiler or heatproof medium bowl over hot, not simmering, water over low heat. Leave until melted, stirring occasionally.
2. Remove from water; stir until smooth. Cool to room temperature.
1. Whipped Cream: Chill a medium or large bowl and beaters for whipping cream. Whip cream with sugar in chilled bowl until stiff.
2. In each of 6 dessert dishes put 4 meringues, top with a scoop of ice cream and add 2 spoonfuls whipped cream on the sides. Spoon sauce over, allowing ice cream and whipped cream to show partially. Top with a few meringues on sides. Dip peak of 6 meringues in sauce and set 1 on top of each dessert. Serve immediately, with any remaining sauce and whipped cream in separate dishes.

Rum-Raisin-Chocolate Bombe

For this hemispherical dessert, a bowl is lined with ice cream and filled with a special chocolate bombe mousse. Vanilla, chocolate chip or coffee ice cream can be substituted for the rum-raisin.

Makes 8 to 10 servings

1-1/4 pints rum-raisin ice cream (2-1/2 cups)

Chocolate Bombe Mousse:
1/2 cup sugar
1/3 cup water
4 egg yolks, room temperature
4 oz. semisweet chocolate, chopped
1/2 pint whipping cream (1 cup), well-chilled

Chocolate Whipped Cream, if desired:
1-1/2 oz. semisweet chocolate, coarsely chopped
3/4 cup whipping cream, well-chilled
1 tablespoon sugar
1/2 teaspoon pure vanilla extract

1. Ice cream: Set freezer at coldest setting. Chill a 1-1/2-quart bowl in freezer 30 minutes. Slightly soften ice cream in refrigerator until it can be spread.

2. Quickly spread ice cream in an even layer on base and side of chilled bowl, using the back of a spoon and dipping spoon occasionally in lukewarm water. Cover and return to freezer while preparing bombe mousse.

1. Chocolate Bombe Mousse: Chill a large bowl and beaters for whipping cream. Heat sugar and water in a small saucepan over low heat, stirring, until sugar dissolves. Bring to a boil; remove from heat.

2. With a hand electric mixer or a whisk, beat egg yolks thoroughly in a large heatproof bowl. Gradually pour hot sugar mixture over yolks, beating constantly.

3. Set bowl of egg yolk mixture in a pan of hot water over low heat. Continue beating at low speed about 5 minutes or until mixture thickens, increases in volume and lightens in color. Remove from heat. Beat at high speed until mixture is completely cool.

4. Melt chocolate in a double boiler or small heatproof bowl over hot, not simmering, water over low heat, stirring occasionally. Stir until smooth. Remove from pan of water; cool to body temperature.

5. Check ice cream to be sure it did not slip down from side of bowl; if necessary, push back up. Ice cream should reach rim of bowl. Return to freezer.

6. Stir about 1/2 cup egg yolk mixture into chocolate until smooth. Fold mixture into remaining egg yolk mixture.

7. Whip cream in chilled bowl until nearly stiff. Fold into chocolate mixture in 2 batches.

8. Pour mixture into ice cream-lined bowl. Cover and freeze at least 6 hours. *Bombe can be kept, covered, up to 2 weeks.*

9. To unmold bombe, run a metal spatula around its edge. Dip bowl in room-temperature water to come halfway up its side about 5 seconds. Dry base of bowl. Continue running spatula around edge until bombe is released from its bowl. Set a round platter on top of bowl. Holding firmly together, quickly flip so bombe is right-side up. Shake bowl gently downward; bombe should slip from bowl onto platter. If bombe remains in bowl, put a hot damp towel on top of bowl for a few seconds until bombe comes out. If some ice cream sticks to bowl, return it to bombe and smooth using a wet metal spatula. Immediately return bombe to freezer. Freeze at least 10 minutes or until ready to serve.

1. Chocolate Whipped Cream: Just before serving, melt chocolate in a double boiler or small heatproof bowl over hot, not simmering, water over low heat, stirring occasionally. Stir until smooth. Turn off heat but leave chocolate above hot water.

2. Whip cream with sugar and vanilla in chilled medium bowl until stiff. Remove chocolate from above water; cool 30 seconds. Stir about 3 tablespoons whipped cream into chocolate until blended. Quickly fold mixture into remaining whipped cream until blended. Fold quickly so chocolate does not harden upon contact with cold whipped cream.

3. Using a pastry bag and medium star tip, pipe a ruffle of Chocolate Whipped Cream at base of dessert. Serve bombe by cutting in thin wedges.

Frozen Chocolate Mousse Ring with Fresh Berries

A medley of blueberries, blackberries and strawberries is encircled by a kirsch-scented chocolate mousse to make a colorful, quick and easy summer dessert.

Makes 8 servings

Chocolate Mousse:
8 oz. fine-quality bittersweet chocolate, chopped
2 tablespoons kirsch
2 tablespoons water
4 eggs, separated, room temperature
5 tablespoons sugar
3/4 cup whipping cream, well-chilled

Berries & Cream:
1/2 pint whipping cream (1 cup), well-chilled
2 tablespoons sugar
1/2 cup blackberries
1/2 cup blueberries
1 cup small strawberries, quartered lengthwise

1. Chocolate Mousse: Lightly oil a 5-cup ring mold. Chill a medium or large bowl and beaters for whipping cream.
2. Melt chocolate in a double boiler or heatproof medium bowl over hot, not simmering, water over low heat, stirring occasionally. Stir until smooth. Remove from pan of water.
3. Combine kirsch and water in a cup. Add to chocolate all at once; stir until smooth. Add egg yolks, 1 at a time, stirring vigorously after each addition.
4. In a dry medium bowl, whip egg whites using dry beaters at medium speed until soft peaks form. Gradually beat in 1/4 cup sugar; continue whipping at high speed until whites are stiff and shiny but not dry.
5. Quickly fold 1/4 of whites into chocolate mixture. Gently fold in remaining whites.
6. Whip cream with remaining 1 tablespoon sugar in chilled bowl until nearly stiff. Fold into chocolate mixture.
7. Pour mousse into oiled mold. Cover and freeze at least 6 hours or until set. *Mousse can be kept, covered, up to 2 weeks.*
8. To unmold mousse, rinse a thin-bladed flexible knife with hot water, dry quickly and run knife around outer edge and center of ring. Dip mold in room temperature water to come halfway up its side 5 seconds. Dry base of mold. Set a round platter on top of mold. Holding firmly together, quickly flip so dessert is right-side up. Shake mold gently downward; dessert should slip from mold onto platter. If mousse remains in mold, put a hot damp towel on top of mold for a few seconds and tap platter on a folded towel set on work surface. Carefully lift up mold. Smooth top of mousse with a metal spatula. Return to freezer 5 minutes or until ready to serve.
1. Berries & Cream: Chill a large bowl and beaters for whipping cream. Whip cream with sugar in chilled bowl until very stiff.
2. Set aside several of each type of berry for garnish. Gently mix remaining berries. Spoon fruit mixture into center of chocolate ring.
3. Using a pastry bag with a medium star tip, pipe whipped cream in a ruffle around outer base of dessert. Garnish ruffle with reserved berries. Serve any remaining cream separately.

How to Make Chocolate-Strawberry Bombe

1/Quickly spread ice cream in an even layer on base and up side of chilled bowl, using the back of a spoon and dipping spoon occasionally in lukewarm water. Cover and return to freezer while preparing bombe mousse.

2/Serve bombe in wedges, garnished with Chocolate-Dipped Strawberries.

Chocolate-Strawberry Bombe

A shell of chocolate ice cream encases a surprise of refreshing, bright-pink strawberry mousse. Chocolate-dipped strawberries add a festive finishing touch.

Makes 10 servings

**2 pints fine-quality chocolate ice
    cream**

Strawberry-Bombe Mousse:
3 cups strawberries (about 12 oz.)
3 egg whites, room temperature
1 cup sugar
1/2 cup water
**3/4 cup whipping cream,
    well-chilled**

Garnish:
**10 Chocolate-Dipped Strawberries,
    page 185, if desired**
**2/3 cup whipping cream, well
    chilled, if desired**

● Set freezer at coldest setting. Chill a 2-1/2-quart bowl in freezer 30 minutes. Slightly soften ice cream in refrigerator until it can be spread. Quickly spread ice cream in an even layer on base and up side of chilled bowl, using the back of a spoon and dipping spoon occasionally in lukewarm water. Cover and return to freezer while preparing bombe mousse.

1. Mousse: Process strawberries in a food processor or blender until very smooth. There will be about 1-1/3 cups puree. Set aside 1/2 cup puree.

2. Bring remaining puree to a boil in a heavy small saucepan. Simmer over medium heat, stirring often, about 6 minutes or until reduced to 1/3 cup. Transfer to a bowl; cool completely. Meanwhile, chill a medium or large bowl and beaters for whipping cream. Put egg whites in a large dry bowl.

3. Combine sugar and water in a heavy small saucepan. Cook over low heat, gently stirring often, until sugar dissolves. Bring to a boil over medium-high heat. Boil, without stirring, 3 minutes. Meanwhile, whip egg whites until stiff but not dry. Continue boiling syrup until a candy thermometer registers 238F (115C) (soft-ball stage), about 3 minutes. See page 15 for soft-ball test.

4. Gradually beat hot syrup into center of whites with mixer at high speed. Continue beating until resulting meringue is cool and shiny.

5. Check ice cream to be sure it did not slip down from side of bowl; if necessary, push back up. Ice cream should reach rim of bowl. Refreeze.

6. Stir reserved fresh and reduced strawberry purees into meringue.

7. Whip 3/4 cup cream in chilled bowl until soft peaks form. Fold into strawberry mixture. Pour mixture into ice cream-lined bowl. Cover and freeze at least 6 hours. *Bombe can be kept, covered, up to 2 weeks.*

1. **Garnish:** Prepare Chocolate-Dipped Strawberries. Chill a medium or large bowl and beaters for whipping cream.

2. To unmold bombe, run a metal spatula around its edge. Dip bowl in room-temperature water to come halfway up its side about 5 seconds. Dry base of bowl. Continue running spatula around edge until bombe is released from its bowl. Set a round platter on top of bowl. Holding firmly together, quickly flip so bombe is right-side up. Shake bowl gently downward; bombe should slip from bowl onto platter. If bombe remains in bowl, put a hot damp towel on top of bowl for a few seconds until bombe comes out. If some of ice cream sticks to bowl, return it to bombe and smooth using a wet metal spatula. Immediately return bombe to freezer. Freeze at least 10 minutes or until ready to serve.

3. Whip 2/3 cup cream in chilled bowl until very stiff. Using a pastry bag with a large star tip, pipe a ruffle of whipped cream around base of bombe.

4. Garnish platter with 6 to 8 strawberries. Serve remaining berries on a separate plate. Serve bombe by cutting in thin wedges.

Frozen Chocolate Soufflé with Candied Ginger

Crystallized ginger adds zest and sweetness to this intensely chocolaty dessert. The soufflé gains extra smoothness from shiny Italian meringue, made of egg whites whipped with syrup.

Makes 10 to 12 servings

Frozen Chocolate Soufflé:
4 eggs, separated, room
    temperature
1 cup sugar
6 oz. bittersweet chocolate,
    chopped
2 oz. unsweetened chocolate,
    chopped
1/2 cup water
1-1/2 cups whipping cream,
    well-chilled
1/2 cup finely chopped crystallized
    ginger (about 2-1/2 oz.)

Garnish:
1/2 cup whipping cream,
    well-chilled
2 tablespoons tiny squares of
    crystallized ginger
Chocolate Scrolls, page 195, if
    desired

1. **Frozen Chocolate Soufflé:** Cut a 25-inch-long sheet of waxed paper; fold in half. Wrap paper around a 1-quart soufflé dish so that it extends about 3 inches above rim to make a collar. Fasten tightly with tape. Chill a large bowl and beaters for whipping cream.

2. Combine egg yolks and 1/4 cup sugar in a heatproof medium bowl; whisk lightly. Set in a pan of hot water over low heat. Heat, stirring constantly with whisk, about 2 minutes or until mixture is just warm to touch. Remove from water.

3. Whip at high speed of mixer until very thick and completely cool.

4. Melt chocolates in a double boiler or heatproof medium bowl over hot, not simmering, water over low heat, stirring occasionally. Stir until smooth. Remove from pan of water; cool to body temperature. Meanwhile, put egg whites in a large bowl.

5. Combine 1/2 cup water and remaining 3/4 cup sugar in a small heavy saucepan. Cook over low heat, gently stirring often, until sugar dissolves. Bring to a boil over medium-high heat. Boil, without stirring, 3 minutes. Meanwhile, whip egg whites until stiff but not dry. Continue boiling syrup until a candy thermometer registers 238F(115C) (soft-ball stage), about 3 minutes. See page 15 for soft-ball test. Immediately remove from heat.

6. Gradually beat hot syrup into center of whites, with mixer at high speed. Continue beating until resulting meringue is cool and shiny.

7. Fold 1/4 of meringue into egg yolk-mixture. Return this mixture to remaining meringue; fold until blended.

8. Gently fold chocolate into egg mixture in 3 batches.

9. Whip 1-1/2 cups cream in chilled bowl until soft peaks form. Fold into chocolate mixture in 3 batches. Fold in ginger. Pour into prepared mold.

10. Freeze about 5 hours or until firm. Cover when firm. *Soufflé can be kept, covered, up to 1 month in freezer.*

11. A short time before serving, carefully peel off and discard paper collar. Return dessert to freezer until ready to serve.

1. **Garnish:** Chill a small bowl and beaters for whipping cream. Whip 1/2 cup cream in chilled bowl until very stiff.

2. Using a pastry bag and medium star tip, pipe a ruffle or rosettes of whipped cream near edge of soufflé. Top whipped cream with crystallized ginger. Garnish dessert with Chocolate Scrolls, if desired.

Individual Chocolate Parfaits with Caramel-Fudge Sauce

These are parfaits in the French style, meaning creamy molded desserts. Dark caramel gives the rich shiny sauce an intriguing, not overly sweet flavor.

Makes 6 servings

6 oz. semisweet chocolate, chopped
4 egg yolks, room temperature
2/3 cup sugar
1/2 cup milk
1/2 pint whipping cream (1 cup), well-chilled

Hot Caramel-Fudge Sauce, page 199
1 tablespoon lukewarm water, if needed

1. Melt chocolate in a double boiler or heatproof medium bowl over hot, not simmering, water over low heat, stirring occasionally. Stir until smooth. Remove from pan of water.
2. Whisk egg yolks lightly in a heatproof medium bowl. Add sugar; whisk until well-blended.
3. Bring milk to a boil in a small, heavy saucepan. Gradually whisk hot milk into yolk mixture. Return mixture to saucepan, whisking constantly. Cook over very low heat, stirring mixture and scraping bottom of pan constantly with a wooden spoon, about 4 minutes or until it is thick enough to coat a spoon. To check whether it is thick enough, remove custard from heat. Dip a metal spoon in custard and draw your finger across back of spoon. Your finger should leave a clear path in mixture that clings to spoon. If it does not, continue cooking another 30 seconds and check again. Do not overcook custard or it will curdle.
4. Immediately pour into a bowl; stir about 30 seconds to cool. Cool 5 minutes, stirring occasionally.
5. Using whisk, gradually stir custard, about 2/3 cup at a time, into melted chocolate until smooth. Cool to room temperature, stirring occasionally.
6. Lightly oil 6 (2/3-cup) ramekins. Chill a large bowl and beaters for whipping cream.
7. Whip cream in chilled bowl until stiff. Fold into chocolate mixture in 3 batches.
8. Ladle mixture into ramekins, filling them nearly to top. Cover and freeze about 6 hours or until firm. *Parfaits can be kept, covered, up to 2 weeks.*
9. Prepare Hot Caramel-Fudge Sauce.
10. To unmold parfaits, rinse a thin-bladed flexible knife with hot water, dry quickly and run knife around edge of a ramekin. Dip ramekin in lukewarm water to come halfway up its side 5 seconds. Dry base of ramekin. Set a small dessert plate on top of ramekin. Holding firmly together, quickly flip so dessert is right-side up. Firmly tap plate once on a folded towel set on work surface. Carefully lift up ramekin. Smooth top of parfait with a spatula, if necessary. Return parfait to freezer for at least 5 minutes or until nearly ready to serve. Continue with remaining ramekins.
11. About 10 minutes before serving, transfer parfaits to refrigerator to soften slightly.
12. Reheat Hot Caramel-Fudge Sauce in a double boiler above hot water over low heat until it is just warm and fluid. If necessary, stir in 1 tablespoon lukewarm water. Keep sauce warm in double boiler until ready to serve.
13. To serve, spoon 2 or 3 tablespoons sauce around base of each parfait and a little more sauce on top.

Chocolate-Blackberry Loaf

For a beautiful reddish-chocolate hue, use blackberries that have a touch of red or substitute olallieberries. The loaf is served in slices with two sauces of contrasting colors.

Makes 10 servings

Chocolate-Blackberry Mousse:
2-2/3 cups fresh blackberries (about 12 oz.)
12 oz. fine-quality semisweet chocolate, chopped
3 egg yolks, room temperature
2 egg whites, room temperature
7 tablespoons sugar
1/2 pint whipping cream (1 cup), well-chilled

Blackberry Sauce:
1 qt. fresh blackberries (about 1 lb.)
3/4 to 1 cup powdered sugar, sifted
3 to 4 tablespoons blackberry-flavored brandy or kirsch

Crème de Cacao Sauce:
1-1/3 cups whipping cream
6 egg yolks, room temperature
5 tablespoons plus 1 teaspoon sugar
1/4 cup white crème de cacao

1. **Chocolate-Blackberry Mousse:** Lightly oil an 8'' x 4'' loaf pan. Chill a large bowl and beaters for whipping cream.
2. Process blackberries in a food processor or blender until smooth. Push puree through a strainer, pressing on pulp. Use a rubber spatula to scrape mixture from underside of strainer. There will be slightly more than 1 cup.
3. Melt chocolate in a double boiler or heatproof medium bowl over hot, not simmering, water over low heat, stirring occasionally. Stir until smooth. Remove from pan of water; cool slightly. Add blackberry puree; whisk until combined.
4. Add egg yolks, 1 at a time, stirring vigorously after each addition.
5. In a small dry bowl, whip egg whites using dry beaters at medium speed until soft peaks form. Gradually beat in 1/4 cup sugar; continue whipping at high speed until whites are stiff and shiny but not dry.
6. Quickly fold 1/4 of whites into chocolate mixture. Gently fold in remaining whites.
7. Whip cream and remaining 3 tablespoons sugar in chilled bowl until nearly stiff. Fold into chocolate mixture. Spoon into oiled loaf pan.
8. Cover and freeze at least 2 hours or until set. *Mousse can be kept, covered, up to 2 weeks.*
1. **Blackberry Sauce:** Process blackberries and 3/4 cup powdered sugar in a food processor or blender until very smooth. Push puree through a strainer into a bowl, pressing on pulp. Use a rubber spatula to scrape mixture from underside of strainer.
2. Taste sauce and whisk in more powdered sugar, if needed. Stir in 3 tablespoons brandy or kirsch. Taste and add remaining 1 tablespoon brandy or kirsch if desired. Cover and refrigerate at least 1 hour. *Sauce can be kept, covered, up to 2 days in refrigerator.* Stir before serving.
1. **Crème de Cacao Sauce:** Bring cream to boil in heavy medium saucepan.
2. Whisk egg yolks lightly in a large heatproof bowl. Add sugar; whisk until well-blended. Gradually whisk in hot cream. Return mixture to saucepan, whisking constantly. Cook over medium-low heat, stirring mixture and scraping bottom of pan constantly with a wooden spoon, until mixture thickens slightly and reaches 170F (75C) on an instant-read thermometer; begin checking after 5 minutes. To check whether it is thick enough without a thermometer, remove sauce from heat. Dip a metal spoon in sauce and draw your finger across back of spoon. Your finger should leave a clear path in mixture that clings to spoon. If it does not, continue cooking another minute and check again. Do not overcook sauce or it will curdle.
3. Immediately pour into a bowl; stir about 30 seconds to cool. Cool completely. Cover and refrigerate at least 1 hour. *Sauce can be kept, covered, up to 2 days in refrigerator.*
1. **To serve:** Gradually stir crème de cacao into sauce.
2. To unmold mousse, rinse a thin-bladed flexible knife with hot water, dry quickly and run knife around edge of dessert. Dip loaf pan in lukewarm water to come halfway up its side about 5 seconds. Dry base of pan. Set a platter on top of loaf pan. Holding firmly together, quickly flip so dessert is right-side up. Shake pan gently downward; dessert should slip from pan onto platter. If it remains in pan, put a hot damp towel on top of pan for a few seconds and tap platter on a folded towel set on work surface. Carefully lift up pan. Return dessert to freezer until ready to serve.
3. Cut loaf into about 5/8-inch-thick slices. Set slices on rimmed dessert plates. Spoon 2 tablespoons Blackberry Sauce on 1 side of each plate. Tilt plate so sauce runs around dessert to cover half of plate; spoon 2 tablespoons Crème de Cacao Sauce over other half of plate so it barely meets Blackberry Sauce. Do not move plate much after adding second sauce because it is thinner than Blackberry Sauce and could run into it. Serve any remaining sauce separately.

Chocolate Baked Alaska

The pleasing contrast of warm meringue and cold ice cream inspired several desserts with names of snowy countries. Ours is called *Baked Alaska*, the French often call theirs *Norwegian Omelet*, and there is an Austrian version called *Icelandic Omelet*. Here we have a cocoa cake that is layered with chocolate and vanilla ice cream and kept in the freezer so there is little last-minute work. The meringue is spread on the dessert and baked just before serving. If desired, coffee liqueur can be substituted for the praline liqueur.

Makes 8 servings

Light Cocoa Cake:
1/4 cup plus 2 tablespoons
   all-purpose flour
3 tablespoons unsweetened cocoa
   powder
1/4 teaspoon baking powder
4 egg yolks, room temperature
1/2 cup plus 1 tablespoon sugar
3 egg whites, room temperature
1/4 teaspoon cream of tartar
2 tablespoons unsalted butter,
   melted and cooled

Filling:
1 pint vanilla ice cream
3 tablespoons praline liqueur
1 pint chocolate ice cream

Meringue Topping:
4 egg whites, room temperature
1 cup sugar

1. Light Cocoa Cake: Position rack in center of oven and preheat to 350F (175C). Lightly butter a 9″ x 5″ loaf pan. Line base of pan with parchment paper or foil; butter paper or foil. Flour side of pan and lined base, tapping pan to remove excess.

2. Sift flour, cocoa and baking powder into a small bowl.

3. Beat egg yolks lightly in a large bowl. Beat in 7 tablespoons sugar; continue beating at high speed about 5 minutes or until mixture is pale and very thick.

4. In a large dry bowl, whip egg whites with cream of tartar using dry beaters at medium speed until soft peaks form. Gradually beat in remaining 2 tablespoons sugar; continue whipping at high speed until whites are stiff and shiny but not dry.

5. Sprinkle about 1/2 of cocoa mixture over egg-yolk mixture; fold gently until nearly incorporated. Gently fold in 1/2 of whites. Repeat with remaining cocoa mixture and whites. When batter is nearly blended, gradually pour in cool melted butter while folding. Continue folding lightly but quickly, just until batter is blended.

6. Transfer batter to prepared pan. Bake about 30 minutes or until top springs back when pressed lightly and a cake tester inserted into center of cake comes out clean. Unmold onto a rack. Carefully remove paper; cool. *Cake can be kept, covered, up to 1 day at room temperature.*

7. Cut cake in 2 layers with a serrated knife. Wrap until ready to use.

1. Filling: Soften vanilla ice cream in refrigerator until it can be spread.

2. Put 1 cake layer on a platter. Brush with 1-1/2 tablespoons praline liqueur. Spoon vanilla ice cream onto cake. Spread quickly to cover layer evenly. Freeze about 30 minutes or until firm.

3. Soften chocolate ice cream in refrigerator until it can be spread. Spread chocolate ice cream over layer of vanilla ice cream. Freeze about 1 hour or until nearly firm.

4. Sprinkle spongy side of second cake layer with remaining liqueur. Set it, crust-side up, on ice cream; press to adhere. If necessary, smooth ice cream so it forms a neat layer. Freeze until firm. Wrap and freeze at least 8 hours. *Dessert can be kept up to 2 weeks.*

1. Meringue Topping: Have ready a pastry bag and medium star tip. Preheat oven to 500F (260C).

2. In a large dry bowl, whip egg whites using dry beaters at medium speed until stiff. Switch speed to high. Gradually beat in sugar, about 2 tablespoons at a time. Continue whipping at high speed until whites are shiny.

3. Transfer ice cream cake to a large, heavy, shallow, baking dish, such as a rectangular or oval ovenproof platter or oval gratin dish.

4. With a large metal spatula, spread meringue to cover ice cream and cake completely. Use pastry bag to pipe meringue in a few rosettes on top. If more meringue remains, pipe a few rosettes around base.

5. Bake 4 minutes or until meringue is lightly browned. Do not let rosettes burn. Serve immediately. Cut with a heavy knife. Any leftovers can be quickly returned to freezer and served frozen.

How to Make Chocolate Baked Alaska

1/Spread chocolate ice cream over layer of vanilla ice cream. Freeze 1 hour or until nearly firm.

2/With a large metal spatula, spread meringue to cover ice cream and cake completely. Pipe meringue in a few rosettes on top. Bake 4 minutes or until meringue is lightly browned. Serve immediately.

Chocolate-Pecan Sundae Pie

This is a very easy-to-make sundae of vanilla ice cream and thick chocolate sauce in a crunchy nutty crust. The sauce sets upon contact with the ice cream. If you like, substitute chocolate chip, chocolate, coffee or rum-raisin ice cream for the vanilla.

Makes 6 to 8 servings

Cocoa-Pecan Crust:
1-1/4 cups pecan halves (about 4 oz.)
2 tablespoons powdered sugar
1 tablespoon unsweetened cocoa powder
2 tablespoons unsalted butter, very soft

7 to 9 pecan halves (for garnish)
1-1/2 pints vanilla ice cream (for filling)

Chocolate Sauce:
3 oz. semisweet chocolate, finely chopped
1/4 cup plus 2 tablespoons whipping cream

1. **Crust:** Preheat oven to 400F (205C). Lightly butter an 8-inch pie pan.
2. Combine 1-1/4 cups pecans, sugar and cocoa in a food processor. Process using quick on/off pulses until nuts are finely chopped but small pieces remain; do not grind to a powder. Transfer to a bowl. Add butter; crumble mixture with your fingers until it is well-blended.
3. Press mixture in a thin even layer on base and side of buttered pan, using the back of a spoon.
4. Bake about 6 minutes or until light brown. Cool completely. Freeze 10 minutes.
1. **Garnish & Filling:** Reduce oven temperature to 350F (175C). Toast 7 to 9 pecan halves, for garnish, in a small shallow baking pan in oven 7 minutes. Remove and cool. Keep in a covered container.
2. Slightly soften ice cream in refrigerator until it can be spread. Spoon into crust in pie pan, mounding ice cream slightly towards center and quickly spreading it as smooth as possible. Freeze about 2 hours or until firm. Cover if not serving immediately.
1. **Chocolate Sauce:** Combine chocolate and cream in a double boiler or small heatproof bowl over hot, not simmering, water over low heat. Leave until chocolate is melted, stirring occasionally. Remove from pan of water; stir until sauce is smooth.
2. Cool to room temperature or until sauce is thick enough to pipe.
3. Using a pastry bag and small star tip, pipe a little sauce in center of pie, then in lines radiating outward like the spokes of a wheel. Pipe a ribbon of sauce about 1/2 inch from border. If any sauce remains, pipe a dot of sauce between each "spoke."
4. Set toasted pecans on pie at equal intervals near edge and 1 in center; press so they adhere. Serve immediately or, to serve later, freeze about 15 minutes or until sauce is very firm, then cover. *Pie can be frozen up to 1 month.*

1/Beginning at center of a circle marked on a baking sheet, pipe meringue in a tight spiral until circle is completely covered. Repeat with second circle.

2/Put truffles on top of ice cream in 1 layer nearly touching each other but not touching edge of pan. Top with another 1-1/2 cups ice cream in spoonfuls without moving truffles.

Chocolate Surprise Ice Cream Cake

The surprise is small chocolate truffles, hidden between layers of crunchy chocolate meringue and chocolate ice cream. The truffles look like large, homemade chocolate chips; their advantage is that they remain soft and velvety even in the freezer.

Makes 10 to 12 servings

Quick Truffles:
5 oz. bittersweet chocolate, finely chopped
1/3 cup whipping cream

Cocoa Meringue:
1/4 cup unsweetened cocoa powder
3/4 cup powdered sugar
4 egg whites, room temperature
1/4 teaspoon cream of tartar
1/2 cup granulated sugar

2-1/2 pints chocolate ice cream, homemade or commercial (for filling)
1/2 cup whipping cream, well-chilled (for frosting)

1. **Truffles:** Put chocolate in a small heatproof bowl. Bring 1/3 cup cream to a full boil in a small heavy saucepan. Pour all at once over chocolate. Stir with a whisk until chocolate is completely melted and mixture is smooth.
2. Refrigerate 20 minutes, stirring occasionally with whisk, until cold and thick but not set.
3. Lightly butter corners of a tray; line tray with waxed paper. Using a pastry bag and large plain tip, pipe chocolate mixture in small kisses or chocolate-chip shapes about 1/2 inch in diameter onto tray. If mixture is too stiff to pipe, roll it in your palms into small balls. Freeze at least 3 hours or overnight.
1. **Cocoa Meringue:** Preheat oven to 200F (95C). Lightly butter corners of 3 baking sheets; line with foil. Butter and lightly flour foil, tapping baking sheet to remove excess flour. Using an 8-inch springform pan as a guide, trace an 8-inch circle onto 2 baking sheets.
2. Have ready a rubber spatula for folding and a pastry bag fitted with a 1/2-inch plain tip. Using a clothespin or paper clip, close end of bag just above tip so mixture will not run out while bag is being filled.
3. Sift cocoa and powdered sugar into a medium bowl.
4. In a large dry bowl, whip egg whites with cream of tartar using dry beaters at medium speed until stiff. Switch speed to high. Gradually beat in granulated sugar; continue whipping at high speed until whites are very shiny. Gently fold in cocoa mixture as quickly as possible.
5. Immediately spoon meringue into pastry bag. Remove clothespin or paper clip. Beginning at center of a circle marked on a baking sheet, pipe meringue in a tight spiral until circle is completely covered. Repeat with second circle.
6. Pipe remaining mixture in very small kisses, or mounds with pointed tops, about 1/2 inch in diameter and 1 inch high.

7. Place meringue circles in center of oven and kisses on shelf underneath. Bake kisses 1-1/2 hours and circles about 2-1/2 hours or until firm and dry. To test meringue kisses for doneness, remove a meringue. Cool 2 minutes. Break meringue apart; it should be dry and crumbly and not sticky. Using a large metal spatula, immediately remove kisses from foil; cool on a rack.

8. When meringue circles are done, gently release from foil, using a large metal spatula. Peel off any remaining foil, if necessary. If meringue circles are sticky on bottom, return to foil-lined baking sheets; bake 30 minutes longer.

9. Cool on a rack. Put in airtight containers as soon as they are cool. *Meringues can be kept in airtight containers up to 1 week in dry weather. If they become sticky from humidity, they can be baked in a 200F (95C) oven about 30 minutes to recrisp.*

1. Assembly: Roll 12 truffles into neat balls in your hands; set aside in freezer for garnish.

2. If necessary, carefully trim meringue circles with a sharp knife so they fit into an 8-inch springform pan. Set 1 meringue circle in pan. Slighty soften ice cream in refrigerator until it can be spread. Spread 1-1/2 cups ice cream over meringue circle in pan. Spread smooth to side of pan. Freeze 10 minutes, meanwhile returning remaining ice cream to freezer.

3. Put truffles on top (except balls reserved for garnish) in 1 layer nearly touching each other but not touching edge of pan. Top with another 1-1/2 cups ice cream in spoonfuls, without moving truffles. Spread gently but quickly with rubber spatula. Freeze 10 minutes.

4. Set second meringue on top. Freeze 5 minutes. Spread with remaining 2 cups ice cream. Freeze 20 minutes or until partly firm.

5. Arrange chocolate balls on top in a ring and set 1 in center. Freeze at least 6 hours or overnight. *Ice-cream cake can be kept up to 5 days in freezer; if kept longer, meringues soften.*

6. Coarsely crush meringue kisses with a rolling pin.

7. Chill a medium bowl and beaters for whipping cream. Just before serving, whip 1/2 cup cream in chilled bowl until stiff.

8. Set cake on a platter. Run a thin-bladed flexible knife around edge of cake. Release spring and remove side of pan.

9. Spread whipped cream in a thin layer over side of cake, using metal spatula and spreading as smooth as possible. Decorate side by sticking on crushed meringues, allowing cream to show through partly. Serve immediately.

TIPS

○ *Pipe meringues quickly and put them in the oven immediately; meringue deflates the longer it waits.*

○ *Save small meringues or meringue trimmings. These crunchy bits are good mixed with whipped cream and fresh fruit, chilled and served as a simple dessert; or mixed with softened ice cream and frozen.*

○ *Work fast in layering and decorating ice cream cakes because ice cream melts quickly, especially when freshly made.*

○ *Try to judge amounts of ice cream by checking the package size and estimating, rather than using a measuring cup. If you prefer to use a cup, chill it before measuring ice cream.*

○ *To spread ice cream, spoon it in small pieces over the cake, crust or pan, then spread it with short quick movements of a flexible rubber spatula.*

Two-Toned Vacherin

Photo on page 146.

A vacherin is a spectacular meringue case with a mysterious origin—the French attribute its creation to the Swiss, while the Austrians give credit to the Spanish. It can be filled with ice cream, whipped cream or mousse. Constructing the case traditionally involved piping and assembling fragile meringue circles. This one is made using an easier method of putting together meringue fingers that I learned from Albert Jorant, the great pastry chef of La Varenne Cooking School in Paris. It is made with alternate white and chocolate meringue fingers. Fill it with one or several of your favorite ice creams in layers, or with American Chocolate Ice Cream, page 126, French-Italian Chocolate Ice Cream, page 126, or Chocolate-Mint Ice Cream, page 129.

Makes about 15 servings

Baked White & Cocoa Meringues:
2 tablespoons unsweetened cocoa powder
2 tablespoons powdered sugar
9 egg whites, room temperature
1/2 teaspoon cream of tartar
2-1/4 cups granulated sugar

Cooked Meringue:
4 egg whites, room temperature
1-1/4 cups granulated sugar

Ice Cream Filling:
5 pints chocolate ice cream (10 cups)
2-1/2 pints vanilla ice cream (5 cups)

Garnish:
1/2 cup whipping cream, if desired, well chilled
Candied violets, if desired

1. **Baked White & Cocoa Meringues:** Preheat oven to 180F (80C). Lightly butter corners of 3 baking sheets; line with foil. Butter and lightly flour foil, tapping baking sheets to remove excess flour.
2. Using a 9-inch cake pan or lid as a guide, mark a circle in flour on 1 baking sheet. On 2 baking sheets, mark crosswise lines, 4 inches apart, as a guide for lengths of meringue fingers. Have ready a rubber spatula for folding and a pastry bag with a 1/2-inch plain tip. Using a clothespin or paper clip, close end of bag just above tip so mixture will not run out while bag is being filled.
3. Sift cocoa and powdered sugar into a medium bowl; set aside.
4. Combine egg whites and cream of tartar in a large bowl. Beat whites at medium speed until stiff. Switch speed to high. Gradually beat in 1-1/4 cups granulated sugar, pouring it into whites in a fine stream. Beat 30 seconds longer until meringue is very shiny.
5. Sprinkle about 1/4 of remaining granulated sugar over whites; fold in as lightly and quickly as possible. Fold in remaining granulated sugar in 3 batches, folding lightly but thoroughly.
6. Transfer 2 cups meringue to bowl of cocoa mixture; fold gently until cocoa mixture is blended into meringue.
7. Immediately spoon white meringue into pastry bag. Push it down towards tip so there are no air bubbles. Remove clothespin or paper clip.
8. Beginning in center of marked circle on baking sheet, pipe meringue in a tight spiral until marked circle is completely covered.
9. Pipe remaining meringue into "fingers," 4 inches long and about 1-1/4 inches wide, on remaining baking sheets. To end each meringue finger, stop pressing and turn tip sharply upward. Do not worry about "tails" at end of fingers; they will be cut off later.
10. Thoroughly squeeze out any remaining meringue from pastry bag. Spoon cocoa meringue into bag and squeeze out a few tablespoons so any white meringue remaining in bag will come out with it. Pipe cocoa mixture in fingers as above.
11. Place meringue base and full baking sheet of meringue fingers in center of oven, if possible; put remaining baking sheet on rack underneath. Bake until firm and dry; meringue fingers require about 2-1/2 hours and base about 3 hours. Do not open oven for first 2 hours of baking time. To test meringues for doneness, remove a meringue finger. Cool 3 minutes, then break meringue apart; it should be dry and crumbly and not sticky.
12. Carefully remove meringue fingers from foil. To release meringue base from foil, use a large metal spatula. Gently peel off any remaining foil, if necessary. If base of meringue is still sticky on bottom, bake 30 minutes longer. Cool meringues on a rack. Put in airtight containers as soon as they are cool. *Baked meringue fingers and base can be stored up to 1 week in an airtight container in dry weather. If they become sticky from humidity, they can be baked in a 200F (95C) oven about 30 minutes to recrisp.* Rinse and dry pastry bag.

1. Cooked Meringue: Combine egg whites and sugar in a large heatproof bowl. Set bowl in a pan of hot water over low heat. Beat with a hand mixer at low speed about 5 minutes, then at medium speed about 3 minutes or until mixture is warm to touch. Continue beating at high speed about 2 minutes or until very thick.

2. Remove mixture from pan of water. Continue beating at high speed until completely cooled. Meringue will be very shiny and sticky. *Cooked meringue can be kept, tightly covered, up to 1 day in refrigerator.*

1. Assembly: With sawing motion of a small sharp knife, cut small piece from "tail" end of each meringue finger so finger is 3-1/2 inches long and end is straight instead of rounded. If edge of meringue base is not of an even height, trim it carefully with sawing motion of knife. Line a baking sheet with foil or parchment paper. Set meringue base on lined baking sheet.

2. Using a pastry bag and small star tip, pipe a border of Cooked Meringue on baked meringue base as close to edge as possible. Stand 2 meringue fingers, 1 white and 1 cocoa, upright at edge of base, touching each other; press flat end of meringue fingers into Cooked Meringue. Rounded sides of fingers should face outward. Continue with remaining meringue fingers, alternating white and cocoa fingers. After every group of 4 or 5 meringue fingers, pipe a line of Cooked Meringue going upwards between each pair of fingers, on both their outer and their inner edges, pressing hard to fill in cracks between fingers. Trim last meringue finger lengthwise, if necessary, in order to make it fit.

3. Pipe a border of Cooked Meringue at inner bases of fingers, on inside of case, pressing hard; border will help support meringue fingers.

4. Pipe a decorative line of Cooked Meringue to cover line that attaches each pair of meringue fingers, piping upward from base. Pipe a continuous decorative line of meringue along bases of fingers, all around bottom edge of case. Pipe a decorative line or continuous row of points of Cooked Meringue across top edges of meringue fingers. If desired, crown top with additional points or rosettes of meringue above divisions between meringue fingers.

5. Return to 180F (80C) oven. Bake 1-1/2 hours to dry Cooked Meringue. Cool meringue case completely before filling. *Baked unfilled case can be kept, uncovered, in a dry place up to 2 days.*

1. Ice Cream Filling: Slightly soften chocolate and vanilla ice creams in refrigerator. Spoon about 2-1/2 pints chocolate ice cream into case. Press ice cream gently with your fingers up to edges of case so filling is compact. Press gently to avoid cracking case. Spread with the back of a ladle to a smooth layer. Fill with vanilla ice cream in the same way. Freeze vacherin 10 minutes.

2. Spread remaining chocolate ice cream in case; smooth top. Freeze about 1 hour or until firm. *Vacherin can be kept, covered, up to 2 weeks in freezer. Let soften slightly in refrigerator before serving.*

1. Garnish: Chill a medium bowl and beaters for whipping cream.

2. Just before serving, whip cream in chilled bowl to stiff peaks. Set vacherin on platter. Using a pastry bag and medium star tip, pipe rosettes of cream in a circle on top of filling. Top rosettes with candied violets.

Brownie Ice Cream Cake

Ice cream sandwiched between fudgy brownies is a delightful dessert. For a more intense chocolate experience, substitute chocolate ice cream for the vanilla or coffee ice creams.

Makes 9 servings

Thin Fudge Brownies:
2 oz. semisweet chocolate, chopped
3 tablespoons unsalted butter
1/4 cup plus 2 teaspoons
   all-purpose flour
1/4 teaspoon baking powder
Pinch of salt
1 egg
1/2 cup sugar
1/2 teaspoon pure vanilla extract
1/3 cup walnuts, chopped

Ice Cream Filling:
1 pint coffee ice cream (2 cups)
1-1/4 pints vanilla ice cream (2-1/2
   cups)

Garnish:
1/2 pint whipping cream (1 cup),
   well-chilled
2 teaspoons sugar
1 teaspoon pure vanilla extract
9 chocolate coffee beans

1. Thin Fudge Brownies: Position rack in center of oven and preheat to 350F (175C). Line base and sides of a 7-1/2- to 8-inch-square baking pan with a single piece of waxed paper or foil; butter paper or foil.
2. Combine chocolate and butter in a double boiler or heatproof medium bowl over hot, not simmering, water over low heat. Leave until melted, stirring occasionally. Stir until smooth. Remove from pan of water; cool slightly.
3. Sift flour, baking powder and salt into a small bowl.
4. Beat egg lightly at medium speed. Add sugar; beat just until blended. Beat in vanilla. Add chocolate mixture in 3 batches, beating until blended after each addition.
5. Using a wooden spoon, stir in flour mixture, then walnuts.
6. Transfer batter to prepared pan; spread carefully to corners of pan in an even layer. Bake about 19 minutes or until a cake tester inserted in center of mixture comes out dry.
7. Cool in pan on a rack to room temperature. Turn out onto a board; remove paper or foil. Cut carefully in 16 squares, using a sharp knife.
1. Ice Cream Filling: Clean square pan; line base of pan with waxed paper. Chill pan about 15 minutes in freezer. Slightly soften coffee ice cream in refrigerator until it can be spread. Spoon ice cream into pan; spread smooth. Freeze 15 minutes or until firm.
2. Slightly soften 1 cup vanilla ice cream in refrigerator until it can be spread. Add to pan in spoonfuls; carefully spread until smooth. Freeze 15 minutes or until firm.
1. Assembly: Use a sharp thin-bladed knife to split brownies carefully in 2 layers; press on bottom layer, so smoother top comes out in 1 piece. Do not worry if some of brownies crumble. Keep more attractive brownie halves separate.
2. Arrange a layer of less attractive brownie halves in pan, first placing brownies next to sides of pan, then filling in center. Press brownies into ice cream. Freeze 15 minutes or until firm.
3. Slightly soften remaining 1-1/2 cups ice cream in refrigerator until it can be spread. Add to pan; carefully spread until smooth. Freeze 15 minutes. Set attractive brownie halves on top, smooth-side up, first arranging them against edge of pan, then in center. Press into ice cream so top surface is as even as possible. Cover and freeze about 8 hours or overnight. *Cake can be kept up to 1 week in freezer.*
1. Garnish: Chill a large bowl and beaters for whipping cream. Just before serving, whip cream with sugar and vanilla in chilled bowl until stiff.
2. To unmold and serve, run a thin-bladed flexible knife around edge of cake; turn out onto a platter. Carefully peel off paper.
3. Using a pastry bag and medium star tip, pipe ruffles of whipped cream to cover sides of cake. Pipe 9 rosettes on top of cake, spacing them equally. Top each rosette with a chocolate coffee bean. To serve, cut in squares with a heavy knife.

Two-Toned Vacherin, page 144

Iced Chocolate Gâteau Progrès

Gâteau Progrès is a classic cake made of nut meringue and praline buttercream. This is an ice-cream version, combining chocolate-praline ice cream with hazelnut meringue layers. Although it is an elaborate recipe, you can make use of the parts as you like. You can make the Chocolate-Praline Ice Cream and enjoy it alone. Or, you can bake the hazelnut meringues and layer them with high-quality purchased chocolate or chocolate-nut ice cream.

Makes 10 servings

1-1/3 cups hazelnuts (about 5-3/4 oz.)

Hazelnut Praline:
2/3 cup hazelnuts of those above
6 tablespoons sugar
1/4 cup water

Chocolate-Praline Ice Cream:
6 oz. semisweet chocolate, chopped
1-1/2 cups milk
1-1/2 cups whipping cream
9 egg yolks, room temperature
2/3 cup sugar
Praline, see above

Hazelnut Meringue:
2/3 cup hazelnuts of those above
1/2 cup sugar
2 tablespoons all-purpose flour
4 egg whites, room temperature
1/4 teaspoon cream of tartar

• Position rack in center of oven and preheat to 350F (175C). Toast hazelnuts and remove skins, page 201. Return 2/3 cup nuts to baking dish to keep warm for praline. Cool remaining nuts completely.

1. Hazelnut Praline: Lightly oil a baking sheet.

2. Combine sugar and water in a heavy, very small saucepan that does not have a black interior. Heat mixture over low heat until sugar dissolves, gently stirring occasionally. Increase heat to high and boil, without stirring, but occasionally brushing down any sugar crystals from side of pan with a brush dipped in water, until mixture begins to brown. Reduce heat to medium-low. Continue cooking, swirling pan gently, until mixture is a rich brown color and a trace of smoke begins to rise from pan. Do not let caramel get too dark or it will burn and praline will be bitter; if caramel is too light, praline will be too sweet.

3. Immediately remove caramel from heat. Stir in warm nuts, being careful not to splash, until they are well-coated with caramel. Stir over low heat 1-1/2 minutes. Immediately transfer to oiled baking sheet.

4. Cool completely. Break praline into small chunks.

5. Grind praline in food processor, scraping mixture inwards occasionally, until as fine as possible. Immediately transfer praline to an airtight container. *Praline can be kept several months in an airtight container at room temperature or in freezer.*

1. Chocolate-Praline Ice Cream: Melt chocolate in a double boiler or heatproof medium bowl over hot, not simmering, water over low heat, stirring occasionally. Stir until smooth. Remove from pan of water; cool to body temperature.

2. Bring milk and cream to a boil in a heavy medium saucepan.

3. Whisk egg yolks lightly in a large heatproof bowl. Add sugar; whisk until well-blended. Gradually whisk in hot cream mixture. Return mixture to saucepan, whisking constantly. Cook over medium-low heat, stirring mixture and scraping bottom of pan constantly with a wooden spoon, until mixture thickens slightly and reaches 165F to 170F (75C) on an instant-read thermometer; begin checking after 7 minutes. To check whether it is thick enough without a thermometer, remove from heat. Dip a metal spoon in custard and draw your finger across back of spoon. Your finger should leave a clear path in mixture that clings to spoon. If it does not, continue cooking another minute and check again. Do not overcook custard or it will curdle.

4. Remove from heat. Pour into a bowl; stir about 30 seconds to cool. Cool 10 minutes.

5. Whisk custard mixture into chocolate, about 1/2 cup at a time, whisking until blended after each addition. Whisk in praline; cool mixture completely, stirring occasionally.

6. Pour mixture into ice cream machine. Churn-freeze until set. Remove dasher and replace lid. Cover lid with foil. Place ice cream in freezer at least 2 hours. *To store ice cream up to 1 month, transfer to a chilled bowl; cover tightly. Place in freezer.*

1. **Hazelnut Meringue:** Preheat oven to 200F (95C). Lightly butter corners of 2 baking sheets; line them with foil. Butter and lightly flour foil, tapping baking sheet to remove excess flour. Using an 8-inch springform pan rim as a guide, trace a circle onto each baking sheet, drawing it inside rim. Have ready a rubber spatula for folding and a pastry bag fitted with a 1/2-inch plain tip.

2. Grind reserved 2/3 cup nuts with 5 tablespoons sugar in a food processor until as fine as possible, scraping occasionally. Transfer to a medium bowl. Sift flour over nut mixture. Stir mixture lightly with a fork until blended.

3. In a large dry bowl, whip egg whites with cream of tartar using dry beaters at medium speed until soft peaks form. Switch speed to high. Gradually beat in remaining 3 tablespoons sugar; continue whipping at high speed until whites are stiff and shiny. Gently fold in nut mixture as quickly as possible until thoroughly blended.

4. Immediately spoon mixture into pastry bag. Beginning at center of a circle marked on a baking sheet, pipe meringue in a tight spiral until circle is completely covered. Repeat with second circle. Pipe remaining meringue in mounds, about 3/4 inch high and 3/4 inch in diameter.

5. Bake meringues in center of oven. Bake small meringues 2 hours and large spirals 2-1/2 hours or until they are firm, dry and light beige in color. If baking on 2 racks in oven, switch positions halfway through baking time.

6. Gently release meringues from foil, using a large metal spatula. Gently peel off any remaining foil, if necessary. Transfer meringues to a rack; cool completely. *Meringues can be kept in an airtight container up to 5 days in dry weather.*

1. **Assembly:** If necessary, carefully trim meringue circles with sharp knife so they fit into an 8-inch springform pan. Set 1 meringue circle in pan. Slightly soften ice cream in refrigerator until it can be spread. Spread 2-1/2 cups ice cream over meringue circle in pan. Spread ice cream between edge of meringue and edge of pan. Set second meringue on top. Spread with remaining ice cream. Top with a ring of a few meringue kisses for garnish. Freeze 8 hours or overnight. *Ice cream cake can be prepared up to 5 days ahead; if kept longer, meringues will soften.* Save remaining small meringue mounds for accompanying ice cream.

2. Set cake on a platter. Rinse a thin-bladed flexible knife in hot water, dry quickly and run knife around edge of cake. Release spring and remove side of pan. Return cake to freezer for 5 minutes. Serve frozen.

TIPS

○ *For desserts that require dipping in water before unmolding, the longer the dessert was frozen, the longer the dipping time. Desserts frozen in thick molds or bowls also require a longer dipping time.*

○ *If you want to serve only a portion of an ice cream cake, do not decorate the whole cake with fresh fruit because the fruit loses flavor and texture during freezing. Instead, garnish each portion with a little fruit when serving.*

○ *Ice cream mixtures can be doubled. If using a small ice cream machine, churn large quantities of mixture in a few batches. Keep remaining mixture in refrigerator.*

COOKIES, BROWNIES & PETITS FOURS

In the realm of baked small-size sweets, those flavored with chocolate are undoubtedly the best-loved. Chocolate cookies and brownies are the supreme snack when accompanied by a glass of milk or a cup of coffee or tea. Chocolate macaroons and other elegant chocolate cookies suit a variety of occasions and are good partners for fresh or poached fruit and creamy desserts.

Crisp cookies make delightful presents. Favorites are chocolate chip cookies, airy nut meringues, or the moist coconut peaks that decorate the windows of fine pâtisseries. An assortment of a few types of cookies, arranged attractively in a box or basket, is always welcome.

Chocolate Cookies

So many popular cookies contain chocolate in some form. First and foremost are the chocolate chip cookies. Traditionally made with walnuts, now they are prepared in an impressive array of flavors, including macadamia nuts and chunks of white chocolate.

Instead of appearing as chips or chunks, chocolate can flavor the cookie dough throughout. Cookies can be crunchy and nutty like Chocolate Pistachio-Pecan Crunchies, or soft and cakelike, as in Spiced Dutch Cocoa Cookies. Melted chocolate makes a delightful frosting for cookies as well, as in the elegant French Chocolate-Glazed Sablés and Chocolate-Coated Coconut Kisses.

Careful baking is the crucial step in the preparation of chocolate chip cookies, macaroons and any cookies that should be slightly soft to ensure that the cookies are moist and slightly chewy inside but not too sticky. They should brown only lightly and should be just firm enough to be removed from the baking sheet but still soft in the center. When hot, they might appear too soft, but it is amazing how much they harden as they cool. If the texture of a cookie seems just right when it is hot, it will be too hard, dry and brittle when cool.

Brownies & Other Chocolate Bar Cookies

Whenever I want to show off an American sweet to friends from other lands, I make brownies. It is hard to imagine that something that involves so little work could taste so good. Because they are baked for a relatively short time, they remain very moist inside.

Today's brownies are intensely chocolaty rather than being overly sweet. They are delicious plain, especially when flavored with exotic ingredients such as Brazil nuts, but are even more festive when frosted, as in Brandied Brownies topped with brandy-flavored butter frosting, or Bittersweet Brownies topped with French ganache.

Chocolate makes a wonderful contribution to other bar cookies as well. It can be chopped and sprinkled over a crisp cookie dough base, as in Chocolate-Walnut Bars, or it can be a center for Chocolate-Cinnamon Squares, where the chocolate is sandwiched between a delicate almond cake base and a light meringue topping.

Chocolate Petits Fours, Macaroons & Meringues

Although for some people petits fours are limited to very sweet frosted squares of sheet cakes, here the term is used in a broader sense. We have included elegant small cakes, such as Almond Truffle Petits Fours, and also cookies, like Chocolate Macaroons, which are served at the finest of restaurants with the coffee after dessert.

Chocolate-flavored meringues have a special crunchy texture that makes them a good accompaniment for ice cream and other smooth creamy desserts. Both macaroons and meringues are quite sweet and this explains their small size, because one or two bites is the perfect portion.

Spiced Dutch Cocoa Cookies

Dutch-process cocoa, or cocoa processed with alkali, was a Dutch discovery. It made a major contribution to the development of chocolate desserts. This type of cocoa gives a rich color to these soft, cakelike cookies and blends with the spices to impart to them an intriguing, not-too-sweet flavor. The cookies are studded with chocolate chips, nuts and raisins.

Makes about 48 cookies

1-1/2 cups all-purpose flour
1-1/4 teaspoons baking powder
1/4 teaspoon baking soda
1/4 teaspoon salt
1-1/2 teaspoons ground cinnamon
1/8 teaspoon ground cloves
1/2 teaspoon ground ginger
1/3 cup unsweetened Dutch-process
  cocoa powder
1/2 cup (4 oz.) unsalted butter,
  slightly softened
3/4 cup sugar
1 egg
1/2 cup dairy sour cream
1 cup walnuts, coarsely chopped
1/2 cup raisins
1 cup semisweet real chocolate
  pieces (6 oz.)

1. Position rack in center of oven and preheat to 350F (175C). Lightly butter 2 baking sheets.
2. Sift flour, baking powder, baking soda, salt, cinnamon, cloves, ginger and cocoa into a medium bowl.
3. Cream butter in a medium or large bowl. Add sugar; beat until smooth and fluffy. Add egg; beat until smooth.
4. Using a wooden spoon, stir in 1/2 of flour mixture until blended. Stir in 1/2 of sour cream. Repeat with remaining flour mixture and remaining sour cream. Stir in nuts, raisins and chocolate pieces.
5. Push batter from a teaspoon with a second teaspoon onto buttered baking sheets, using about 1 tablespoon batter for each cookie. Mound batter high and space about 1-1/2 inches apart.
6. Bake about 10 minutes or just until set. Using a metal spatula, carefully transfer cookies to racks; cool completely.
7. Cool baking sheets; clean off any crumbs and butter sheets again. Repeat shaping and baking with remaining batter. *Cookies can be kept in an airtight container up to 1 week.*

Chocolate-Almond Sandwiches

White chocolate ganache is the filling of these thin, extra-crisp, cocoa-almond cookies. The cookies are easy to shape—the dough is simply formed into cylinders and sliced.

Makes 28 cookie sandwiches

Cocoa-Almond Cookies:
3/4 cup whole blanched almonds
  (about 4 oz.)
3/4 cup sugar
1-3/4 cups all-purpose flour
3 tablespoons unsweetened
  Dutch-process cocoa powder
1 teaspoon baking powder
1 cup (8 oz.) unsalted butter,
  slightly softened

White Chocolate Ganache:
6 oz. fine-quality white chocolate,
  very finely chopped
1/2 cup whipping cream

1. **Cookies:** Grind almonds with sugar in a food processor until as fine as possible, scraping inward occasionally.
2. Sift flour, cocoa and baking powder into a medium bowl.
3. Cream butter in a large bowl. Add almond mixture; beat until smooth and fluffy. Using a wooden spoon, stir cocoa mixture into almond mixture. Dough will seem dry at first, but continue stirring until it comes together.
4. Divide dough in half. Spoon each half onto a sheet of waxed paper. Roll each half of dough in a log, about 1-1/2 inches in diameter. Wrap in waxed paper. Refrigerate 2 hours. Roll each log again to give it an even round shape. Refrigerate 4 hours or until firm.
5. Position rack in center of oven and preheat to 375F (190C). Cut each log into about 1/4-inch-thick slices with a thin sharp knife. Put slices on ungreased baking sheets, about 1-1/2 inches apart.
6. Bake 10 to 11 minutes or until cookies are just set; they burn easily on the bottom. Carefully transfer to racks with a metal spatula; cool completely.
1. **Ganache:** Put white chocolate in a small heatproof bowl. Bring cream to a full boil in a small heavy saucepan. Pour over chocolate all at once. Stir with a whisk until chocolate is completely melted and mixture is smooth.
2. Cool to room temperature. Refrigerate 30 minutes, stirring occasionally with whisk, until cold and thick but not set. Whip mixture at high speed 3 minutes or until lighter in color and thickened.
3. Spread about 2 teaspoons ganache on flat sides of 1/2 of cookies. Sandwich each with flat side of a second cookie, choosing cookies of same size to pair together. Refrigerate 15 minutes to set before serving. *Cookies can be kept, covered, up to 1 week in refrigerator.* Serve at room temperature.

Triple Chocolate Chip Cookies

Full of morsels of white, milk and dark chocolate, these nutty cookies sweetened with brown sugar are crisp on their edges and moist inside.

Makes about 48 cookies

1 cup all-purpose flour
1/2 teaspoon baking soda
1/4 teaspoon salt
1/2 cup (4 oz.) unsalted butter, slightly softened
1/2 cup firmly packed dark-brown sugar
1/4 cup granulated sugar
1 egg
1 teaspoon pure vanilla extract
1/2 cup pecans, coarsely chopped
3/4 cup semisweet real chocolate pieces
3/4 cup milk chocolate pieces
4 oz. white chocolate, cut in tiny cubes (about 3/4 cup cubes)

1. Position rack in center of oven and preheat to 350F (175C). Lightly butter 2 baking sheets.
2. Sift flour, baking soda and salt into a medium bowl.
3. Cream butter in a medium or large bowl. Add sugars; beat until smooth and fluffy. Add egg; beat until smooth. Add vanilla; beat until blended.
4. Using a wooden spoon, stir in flour mixture until blended. Stir in nuts and all chocolate pieces.
5. Push batter from a teaspoon with a second teaspoon onto buttered baking sheets, using about 1 tablespoon batter for each cookie and spacing them about 2 inches apart.
6. Bake about 10 minutes or until browned around edges and nearly set but still soft to touch in center. Using a metal spatula, carefully transfer cookies to racks; cool completely.
7. Cool baking sheets; clean off any crumbs and butter sheets again. Repeat shaping and baking with remaining batter. *Cookies can be kept up to 1 week in an airtight container at room temperature.*

Variation
Chocolate-Chunk Cookies: Chop 4-1/2 ounces semisweet chocolate and 4-1/2 ounces milk chocolate in chunks and substitute for chocolate pieces.

Chocolate-Pistachio-Pecan Crunchies

Thick and crunchy from the addition of both ground and chopped pecans, pistachios and oatmeal, these are the cookies for lovers of chocolate with nuts. A pistachio in the center of each cookie provides the simple, attractive garnish.

Makes about 60 cookies

3 oz. unsweetened chocolate, chopped
2 oz. semisweet chocolate, chopped
1 cup pecans (about 3-1/2 oz.)
1 cup plus 3 tablespoons sugar
1 cup all-purpose flour
1/4 teaspoon salt
1/2 teaspoon baking soda
1/2 cup (4 oz.) unsalted butter, slightly softened
1 egg
2 tablespoons milk
1 cup uncooked quick-cooking rolled oats
1/2 cup shelled unsalted pistachios, coarsely chopped (about 2-1/4 oz.)

1/3 cup shelled unsalted whole pistachios (for garnish)

1. Position rack in center of oven and preheat to 350F (175C). Lightly butter 2 baking sheets.
2. Melt chocolates in a double boiler or heatproof medium bowl over hot, not simmering, water over low heat, stirring occasionally. Stir until smooth. Remove from pan of water; cool to body temperature.
3. Coarsely chop 1/2 cup pecans; set aside. Grind remaining 1/2 cup pecans with 2 tablespoons sugar in a food processor until as fine as possible, scraping inward occasionally. Transfer to a medium bowl.
4. Sift flour, salt and baking soda onto ground pecan mixture; mix well.
5. Cream butter in a large bowl. Add remaining 1 cup plus 1 tablespoon sugar; beat until smooth and fluffy. Add egg; beat until smooth. Beat in chocolate.
6. Using a wooden spoon, stir in flour mixture until blended. Stir in milk. Stir in rolled oats, pecans and chopped pistachios. Batter will seem dry.
7. Push batter from a teaspoon with a second teaspoon onto buttered baking sheets, using about 2 teaspoons batter for each cookie and spacing about 1-1/2 inches apart. Shape in rounds with a spoon. Press cookie rounds with your hand to compact them so they will not be crumbly. Set a whole pistachio in center of each cookie; press lightly so it adheres. Press edge of cookie to an even round.
8. Bake about 11 minutes or until nearly firm. Using a metal spatula, carefully transfer cookies to racks; cool completely.
9. Cool baking sheets; clean off any crumbs and butter sheets again. Repeat shaping and baking with remaining batter. *Cookies can be kept in an airtight container up to 1 week.*

From upper right: Ganache-Frosted Bittersweet Brownies, page 156; Triple Chocolate Chip Cookies, above; Golden Pine Nut-Chocolate Chip Bars, page 166.

How to Make Crisp Chocolate Chip-Macadamia Nut Cookies

1/Push batter from a teaspoon with a second teaspoon onto buttered baking sheets, using about 1-1/2 teaspoons batter for each cookie and spacing them about 2 inches apart.

2/Flatten each cookie by pressing it with the bottom of a fork dipped in water. Bake about 8 minutes or until lightly browned.

Crisp Chocolate Chip-Macadamia Nut Cookies

Unlike many chocolate chip cookies, these are not chewy but are crisp and delicate. They are a perfect accompaniment for ice cream, a cup of coffee or a glass of milk.

Makes about 48 cookies

1 cup all-purpose flour
1/2 teaspoon salt
1/2 teaspoon baking soda
1/2 cup (4 oz.) unsalted butter,
   slightly softened
1/2 cup firmly packed brown sugar
1/4 cup granulated sugar
1 egg
1/2 teaspoon pure vanilla extract
1 cup coarsely chopped unsalted
   macadamia nuts or desalted
   macadamia nuts, page 201 (about
   5 oz.)
3/4 cup semisweet real chocolate
   pieces

1. Position rack in center of oven and preheat to 350F (175C). Lightly butter 2 baking sheets.
2. Sift flour, salt and baking soda into a medium bowl.
3. Cream butter in a medium or large bowl. Add sugars; beat until smooth and fluffy. Add egg; beat until smooth. Add vanilla; beat until blended.
4. Using a wooden spoon, stir in flour mixture until blended. Stir in nuts and chocolate pieces.
5. Push batter from a teaspoon with a second teaspoon onto buttered baking sheets, using about 1-1/2 teaspoons batter for each cookie and spacing them about 2 inches apart. Flatten each cookie by pressing it firmly with the bottom of a fork dipped in water.
6. Bake about 8 minutes or until lightly browned. Using a metal spatula, carefully transfer cookies to racks; cool completely.
7. Cool baking sheets; clean off any crumbs and butter sheets again. Repeat shaping and baking with remaining batter. *Cookies can be kept up to 1 week in an airtight container at room temperature.*

Variation
Crisp Chocolate Chip-Walnut Cookies: Substitute 1 cup walnut pieces for macadamia nuts.

Chocolate-Glazed Sablés

Sablés are French butter cookies. Their name comes from the French word *sable,* meaning *sand,* because of their crumbly crisp texture. Half-glazing these delicate cookies in chocolate gives them a new dimension of flavor and beauty.

Makes about 24 cookies

4 egg yolks
1/2 cup sugar
1/4 teaspoon salt
2 teaspoons grated orange zest
1/2 cup (4 oz.) unsalted butter,
    well-chilled, cut in 16 pieces
1-1/4 cups all-purpose flour
1/4 cup cake flour
1 to 2 tablespoons cold orange juice
    or water, if needed

6 oz. fine-quality bittersweet or
    semisweet chocolate, chopped
    (for dipping)

1. Combine egg yolks, sugar, salt, orange zest and butter in a food processor fitted with metal blade. Process using 10 quick on/off pulses, then process continuously 5 seconds until nearly blended. Add flours; process 2 seconds. Scrape down and process about 3 seconds or until dough begins to form sticky crumbs but does not come together in a ball. If crumbs are dry, add juice or water and process using quick on/off pulses just until blended.
2. Transfer dough to a work surface. Blend dough further by pushing about 1/4 of it away from you and smearing it with the heel of your hand against work surface. Repeat with remaining dough in 3 batches. Repeat with each batch if dough is not yet well blended.
3. Using a rubber spatula, transfer dough to a sheet of plastic wrap. Push pieces together. Wrap dough loosely and press into a flat disc. Wrap well and refrigerate dough at least 6 hours. *Dough can be kept up to 2 days in refrigerator.*
4. Position rack in center of oven and preheat to 375F (190C). Lightly butter 2 baking sheets.
5. Roll out 1/2 of dough on a cold lightly floured surface until about 1/4 inch thick. Using a plain or fluted, round, 2-1/2-inch cutter, cut dough in circles. Transfer to buttered baking sheets, spacing about 1 inch apart. Refrigerate 15 minutes. Repeat with remaining dough.
6. Gently press trimmings together. Wrap and refrigerate at least 30 minutes or until firm enough to roll. Roll out and cut more circles.
7. Bake cookies about 9 minutes or until very lightly browned at edges. Transfer cookies to a rack; cool.
8. Melt chocolate in a small, deep, heatproof bowl over hot, not simmering, water over low heat, stirring occasionally. Stir until smooth. Remove from pan of water; cool to body temperature. Line a tray with foil or waxed paper.
9. Dip half of 1 cookie in chocolate, moving it back and forth in chocolate until cookie half is coated. Remove and shake up and down about 15 times so excess chocolate drips into bowl. Set cookie on lined tray. After dipping about 1/2 of number of cookies, or when chocolate becomes too thick for dipping, gently reheat chocolate by setting bowl above hot water. Remove from water and continue dipping remaining cookies. Refrigerate cookies about 15 minutes or until set. Gently remove from paper. *Cookies can be kept in a shallow container, covered, up to 4 days in refrigerator.* Serve at room temperature.

To make dough by hand: Instead of Step 1, sift flour onto a work surface; make a well in center. Put egg yolks, salt, sugar and grated orange zest in well; mix briefly, using your fingers. Pound butter pieces with rolling pin or your fist to soften slightly. Separate butter again in pieces; add to well. Using your fingers, mix and crush ingredients in center of well until mixed but still not smooth. Draw in flour and crumble ingredients through your fingers, raising them in the air, until dough begins to come together. If crumbs of dough are dry, gradually add cold orange juice or water while continuing to crumble dough through your fingers.

Fudgy Brazil Nut Brownies

Brazil nuts and a hint of orange flavor these rich, super-chocolaty brownies. For a special treat, serve these brownies with vanilla ice cream.

Makes 16 brownies

1/2 cup plus 2 tablespoons (5 oz.)
    unsalted butter, cut in pieces
3 oz. semisweet chocolate, chopped
3 oz. unsweetened chocolate,
    chopped
3/4 cup all-purpose flour
1/4 teaspoon salt
3 eggs
1-1/4 cups sugar
1 tablespoon grated orange zest
3/4 cup Brazil nuts, chopped (4 oz.)

1. Position rack in center of oven and preheat to 350F (175C). Line base and sides of a 7-1/2- to 8-inch-square baking pan with a single piece of waxed paper or foil; butter paper or foil.
2. Combine butter and chocolates in a double boiler or heatproof medium bowl over hot, not simmering, water over low heat. Leave until melted, stirring occasionally. Stir until smooth. Remove from pan of water; cool to body temperature.
3. Sift flour and salt into a medium bowl.
4. Beat eggs lightly at medium speed. Add sugar; beat just until blended. Beat in orange zest. Add chocolate mixture in 3 batches, beating until blended after each addition.
5. Using a wooden spoon or mixer at low speed, stir in flour mixture, then chopped nuts.
6. Transfer batter to prepared pan; carefully spread to corners of pan in an even layer. Bake about 32 minutes or until a wooden pick inserted 1/2 inch from center of mixture comes out nearly clean.
7. Cool in pan on a rack to room temperature. Turn out onto a board; remove paper or foil. Carefully cut in 16 squares, using point of sharp knife. *Brownies can be kept up to 3 days in an airtight container at room temperature.*

Ganache-Frosted Bittersweet Brownies

Photo on page 153.

The best of both worlds: American brownies with the finest French chocolate frosting—ganache.

Makes 16 to 20 brownies

Bittersweet Brownies:
6 oz. bittersweet chocolate,
    chopped
1/2 cup plus 2 tablespoons (5 oz.)
    unsalted butter, cut in pieces
3/4 cup all-purpose flour
1/2 teaspoon baking powder
1/4 teaspoon salt
3 eggs
1 cup sugar
2 teaspoons vanilla extract
3/4 cup coarsely chopped walnuts

Semisweet Ganache:
6-1/2 oz. semisweet chocolate, very
    finely chopped
1/2 cup whipping cream

1. **Brownies:** Position rack in center of oven and preheat to 350F (175C). Line base and sides of a 9- to 9-1/2-inch-square baking pan with a single piece of waxed paper or foil; butter paper or foil.
2. Combine chocolate and butter in a double boiler or heatproof medium bowl over hot, not simmering, water over low heat. Leave until melted, stirring occasionally. Stir until smooth. Remove from water; cool 5 minutes.
3. Sift flour, baking powder and salt into a small bowl.
4. Beat eggs lightly. Add sugar; whip at high speed about 5 minutes or until thick and light. Beat in vanilla. Add chocolate mixture in 3 batches, beating at low speed until blended after each addition.
5. Using a wooden spoon, stir in flour mixture, then walnuts.
6. Transfer batter to prepared pan; carefully spread to corners of pan in an even layer. Bake about 35 minutes or until a wooden pick inserted 1/2 inch from center of mixture comes out nearly clean.
7. Cool in pan on a rack to room temperature. Turn out onto a tray; remove paper or foil. Turn back over onto another tray.
1. **Ganache:** Put chocolate in a small heatproof bowl. Bring cream to a full boil in a small heavy saucepan. Pour over chocolate all at once. Stir with a whisk until chocolate is completely melted and mixture is smooth.
2. Refrigerate about 20 minutes, stirring occasionally with whisk, until cold and thick enough to spread but not set.
3. Spread ganache over top of brownies. Refrigerate 1 hour or until set.
• Carefully cut in 16 to 20 squares, using a sharp knife. *Brownies can be kept, covered, up to 3 days in refrigerator.* Serve cold or at room temperature.

Note: For extra-shiny glaze, cool ganache at room temperature and let glazed brownies set at cool room temperature about 2 hours.

Brandied Brownies

These "adult" brownies make delicious petits fours. They are dark and cakelike and are topped with white, brandy butter frosting and pecan halves.

Makes 20 brownies

Brandied Chocolate-Pecan Brownies:

5 oz. fine-quality semisweet chocolate, chopped
1/2 cup (4 oz.) unsalted butter, cut in 8 pieces, room temperature
3/4 cup plus 2 tablespoons all-purpose flour
1/2 teaspoon baking soda
1/4 teaspoon salt
3 eggs
1/2 cup packed brown sugar
6 tablespoons granulated sugar
2 tablespoons brandy
1-1/3 cups pecans, coarsely chopped (4 oz.)

Brandy Butter Frosting:

1/2 cup (4 oz.) unsalted butter, slightly softened but still cool
1-1/2 cups powdered sugar, sifted
2 egg yolks
2 tablespoons plus 2 teaspoons brandy

20 pecan halves (for garnish)

1. **Brownies:** Position rack in center of oven and preheat to 350F (175C). Line base and sides of a 9- to 9-1/2-inch-square baking pan with a single piece of waxed paper or foil; butter paper or foil.
2. Melt chocolate in a double boiler or heatproof medium bowl over hot, not simmering, water over low heat. Stir until smooth. Add butter in 2 batches, stirring until blended after each addition. Remove from pan of water; cool to body temperature.
3. Sift flour, baking soda and salt into a small bowl.
4. Beat eggs lightly. Add sugars; beat at low speed until blended. Whip mixture at high speed about 7 minutes or until thick and light. Gradually fold in chocolate mixture just until blended. Stir in brandy. Fold in flour mixture, then chopped pecans.
5. Pour batter into prepared pan. Bake about 30 minutes or until a wooden pick inserted into center of mixture comes out nearly clean.
6. Cool in pan on a rack to room temperature. Turn out onto a tray; remove paper or foil.
1. **Frosting:** Cream butter in a large bowl. Add powdered sugar; beat at low speed until blended. Add egg yolks; beat until smooth. Gradually beat in brandy.
2. Spread frosting over top of brownies. Mark 2-inch squares with a knife. Set a pecan half in center of each square. Refrigerate about 1 hour or until frosting sets.
3. Follow marks to cut in 2-inch squares using sharp knife. *Brownies can be kept, covered, up to 3 days in refrigerator.* Serve cold or at room temperature.

Hazelnut Fudge Brownies

A generous quantity of toasted hazelnuts add an interesting twist to these moist brownies. Unsalted macadamia nuts, pecans or walnuts would be good alternatives.

Makes 16 brownies

1 cup hazelnuts (about 4-1/2 oz.)
4-1/2 oz. semisweet chocolate, chopped
6 tablespoons unsalted butter
1/2 cup plus 1 tablespoon all-purpose flour
Pinch of salt
2 eggs
3/4 cup plus 2 tablespoons sugar
1 teaspoon pure vanilla extract

1. Position rack in center of oven and preheat to 350F (175C). Toast hazelnuts and remove skins, page 201; cool nuts completely. Chop nuts coarsely.
2. Line base and sides of a 7-1/2- to 8-inch-square baking pan with a single piece of waxed paper or foil; butter paper or foil.
3. Combine chocolate and butter in a double boiler or heatproof medium bowl over hot, not simmering, water over low heat. Leave until melted, stirring occasionally. Stir until smooth. Remove from water; cool 5 minutes.
4. Sift flour and salt into a small bowl.
5. Beat eggs lightly in a medium or large bowl at medium speed. Add sugar; beat just until blended. Beat in vanilla. Add chocolate mixture in 3 batches, beating until blended after each addition.
6. Using a wooden spoon, stir in flour mixture, then nuts.
7. Transfer batter to prepared pan; carefully spread to corners of pan in an even layer. Bake about 24 minutes or until a wooden pick inserted 1/2 inch from center of mixture comes out nearly clean.
8. Cool in pan on a rack to room temperature. Turn out onto a board; remove paper or foil. Carefully cut in 16 squares, using the point of a sharp knife. Turn each brownie back over to serve. *Brownies can be kept up to 3 days in an airtight container at room temperature.*

How to Make Chocolate-Walnut Bars

1/Gently spread raspberry preserves over dough, leaving a border of about 1/4 inch. Sprinkle chocolate chunks evenly over preserves.

2/Sprinkle dough crumbs evenly over chocolate. Sprinkle with chopped walnuts. Bake about 35 minutes or until crumbs are firm and light brown.

Chocolate-Walnut Bars

With an extra-buttery dough made in a food processor and patted out by hand in a baking pan, these are very quick and easy bar cookies. Part of the dough is turned into a crumbly topping that is sprinkled over the chocolate-raspberry filling.

Makes about 24 bars

Walnut Cookie Dough:
1 cup walnuts (about 3-3/4 oz.)
3 egg yolks
1/2 cup sugar
1/4 teaspoon salt
2 teaspoons pure vanilla extract
2 teaspoons grated lemon zest
1 cup (8 oz.) unsalted butter,
  well-chilled, cut in 16 pieces
1-3/4 cups all-purpose flour, sifted

Chocolate-Raspberry Filling:
1/2 cup raspberry preserves
6 oz. semisweet chocolate, cut into
  very small chunks

Nutty Crumble Topping:
2 tablespoons sugar
1/4 cup all-purpose flour
1/4 cup walnuts, coarsely chopped

1. Dough: Chop nuts fairly fine in a food processor. Transfer to a bowl. Combine egg yolks, sugar, salt, vanilla, lemon zest and butter in food processor fitted with a metal blade. Process using 10 quick on/off pulses, then process continuously 5 seconds until nearly blended. Add flour and walnuts; process about 2 seconds. Scrape down and process about 3 seconds or until the dough begins to form sticky crumbs but does not come together in a ball. Put dough in a plastic bag or in plastic wrap. Press dough together; shape in a rectangle. Refrigerate 1 hour. Clean and dry food processor.

2. Position rack in center of oven and preheat to 350F (175C). Cut off 1/4 of dough; set aside in refrigerator. Pat out remaining dough in bottom of an unbuttered 13″ x 9″ baking pan.

• **Filling:** Stir preserves. Using a rubber spatula, spread gently over dough, leaving a border of about 1/4 inch. Sprinkle chocolate evenly over jam.

1. Topping: Cut reserved dough in 10 pieces. Return to food processor. Add sugar and flour; process using a few quick on/off pulses until sugar and flour are blended in but dough is still very crumbly. Crumble dough quickly between your fingers to separate any lumps. Sprinkle crumbs evenly over chocolate. Sprinkle with chopped walnuts.

2. Bake 30 to 35 minutes or until crumbs are firm and light brown. Cool in pan on a rack until lukewarm. Cut in 1-1/2″ x 2″ bars in pan, using sharp knife. *Cookies can be kept up to 3 days in an airtight container at cool room temperature.*

To make dough by hand: Follow note at the end of Chocolate-Glazed Sablés, page 155, for making dough instead of Dough Step 1, above. For Topping Step 1, rub dough pieces with sugar and flour between your fingers until dough becomes very crumbly.

California Chocolate Mountains

The group of mountains in southeastern California near the Arizona border called the Chocolate Mountains inspired the name of these cookies. A rich-tasting chocolate meringue gives the peak-shaped cookies lightness, while a generous amount of toasted sliced almonds adds crunch.

Makes about 30 cookies

2-1/2 cups sliced almonds (about 8 oz.)
2 oz. unsweetened chocolate, chopped
2 oz. semisweet chocolate, chopped
2 egg whites, room temperature
1-2/3 cups powdered sugar
1 teaspoon pure vanilla extract

1. Position rack in center of oven and preheat to 350F (175C). Toast almonds on a baking sheet, stirring a few times, 4 minutes. Remove and cool.
2. Lightly butter corners of 1 large or 2 small baking sheets and line with foil; butter foil. Reduce oven temperature to 225F (105C).
3. Melt chocolates in a double boiler or small heatproof bowl over hot, not simmering, water over low heat, stirring occasionally. Stir until smooth. Remove from pan of water; cool to body temperature.
4. Combine egg whites and powdered sugar in a heatproof medium bowl. Set bowl in a pan of hot water over low heat. Beat with a hand mixer at low speed about 5 minutes, then at medium speed about 3 minutes or until mixture is warm to touch. Remove from pan of water. Continue beating at high speed until cooled to room temperature.
5. Stir in vanilla. Stir in chocolate in 2 batches until blended. Stir in almonds; there will be barely enough batter to hold almonds.
6. Using about 1 tablespoon batter for each cookie, push batter from a spoon with a second spoon onto prepared baking sheets, spacing about 1 inch apart. Shape each so it has a rounded peak.
7. Bake 30 minutes or until firm on the outside. Cool on racks. *Cookies can be kept up to 1 week in airtight containers at room temperature.* Serve in white candy papers.

Chocolate-Marzipan Rosettes   *Photo on page 164.*

Made of homemade marzipan, these cookies have a nutty, fudgy interior and can be made in a variety of pretty shapes. Colorful and festive when decorated with a variety of candied fruit, they keep well and make lovely gifts for the holidays.

Makes 40 small cookies

Chocolate-Marzipan Cookies:
2 oz. semisweet chocolate, chopped
1 oz. unsweetened chocolate, chopped
1-1/2 cups whole blanched almonds (about 7-1/2 oz.)
3/4 cup sugar
3 egg whites, beaten to mix

Garnish:
About 1/2 cup total of any or all of the following: sliced blanched almonds; green or red candied cherries, quartered; crystallized ginger, cut in small squares

Quick Glaze:
1 tablespoon powdered sugar
2 tablespoons milk or water

1. **Cookies:** Position rack in center of oven and preheat to 350F (175C). Line 2 baking sheets with parchment or waxed paper; lightly butter paper.
2. Melt chocolates in a double boiler or small heatproof bowl over hot, not simmering, water over low heat, stirring occasionally. Stir until smooth. Remove from pan of water; cool to body temperature.
3. Grind almonds with 1/4 cup sugar in a food processor by processing continuously until as fine as possible, scraping inward occasionally. Add remaining 1/2 cup sugar; process until blended. Add egg whites; process until blended. Add chocolate; process again until blended.
4. Using a pastry bag and large star tip with points far apart, pipe mixture in rosettes or rings onto prepared baking sheet. Mixture is stiff so press firmly. For better control, hold pastry bag high so tip is not too close to baking sheet. If mixture does not detach easily from tip, use the point of a knife to cut it off.
• **Garnish:** Decorate with sliced blanched almonds, candied cherries or crystallized ginger. Bake 12 minutes or until firm on outside. Leave cookies on baking sheet.
1. **Glaze:** Mix powdered sugar with milk in a very small saucepan. Heat until sugar dissolves.
2. Brush glaze lightly over hot cookies. Carefully remove cookies from baking sheet with a metal spatula or pancake turner; cool on a rack. *Cookies can be kept up to 1 week in an airtight container at room temperature.*

Meringue Mushrooms

Photo on pages 8-9.

Serve these as a decorative addition to a platter of petits fours, as cookies or in their traditional role as a garnish and accompaniment for Chocolate Yule Log, page 39.

Makes 45 cookies

3 egg whites, room temperature
1/4 teaspoon cream of tartar
3/4 cup sugar
1 to 2 tablespoons unsweetened cocoa powder, sifted

1. Position rack in center of oven and preheat to 225F (105C). Lightly butter corners of 1 large or 2 small baking sheets; line with foil or parchment paper. Butter and very lightly flour foil or paper, tapping baking sheet to remove excess flour.

2. Have ready a spatula or slotted spoon for folding and pastry bag fitted with plain 1/2-inch tip. Using a clothespin or paper clip, close end of bag just above tip so mixture will not run out while bag is being filled.

3. In a small bowl, beat egg whites and cream of tartar using dry beaters at medium speed until stiff peaks form. Increase speed to high. Add sugar 1 tablespoon at a time and beat constantly until meringue is very stiff and shiny.

4. Immediately spoon meringue into pastry bag. Remove clothespin or paper clip. To form mushroom caps, pipe about 1/2 of mixture onto prepared baking sheet in small mounds, about 3/4 inch in diameter, about 1 inch high and about 1 inch apart; finish with a quick rounded motion so they will be smooth. Push down any points with your dampened finger.

5. Pipe remaining mixture in pointed bases, lifting pastry bag upward to form points about 1-1/2 inches high and of slightly smaller diameter than caps. You should have about as many pointed bases as mounds.

6. Sprinkle mounds, not points, very lightly with cocoa through a small strainer.

7. Bake 35 to 40 minutes or until meringue mounds can just be lifted from foil; if overbaked, they will not stick to bases. Insert the point of a thin sharp knife in flat side of a mound; turn knife point to make a hole. Stick mound on top of a pointed base, inserting point in hole. Press gently to be sure top, which should still be slightly sticky, adheres to base; otherwise tops will fall off. Repeat with remaining tops and bases. Return to oven.

8. Bake about 1-1/2 hours or until firm and dry. To test meringues for doneness, remove a meringue. Cool 2 minutes and break apart; meringue should be dry and crumbly and not sticky. Using a large metal spatula, immediately remove meringues from foil or paper; cool on a rack.

9. Put cookies in airtight containers as soon as they are cool. *Meringues can be kept in airtight containers at room temperature up to 2 weeks in dry weather. If they become sticky from humidity, recrisp in a 200F (95C) oven about 20 minutes.*

Variation
Bake mushroom caps and bases separately 2 hours and 10 minutes or until firm and dry; cool completely. Make holes as in Step 7. Join cooled caps and bases using a dab of melted chocolate on pointed end of each base.

TIPS

○ *Because nuts contribute the main flavor in macaroons, use the freshest ones possible. Blanch and peel almonds yourself for best flavor, page 201.*

○ *Macaroons and meringues are a good way to use leftover egg whites. Egg whites can be frozen, then measured and used for macaroons. See Using Egg Whites, page 200.*

○ *It is best not to bake meringues or macaroons on very humid days because they might be sticky.*

○ *Macaroons and meringues should be put into airtight containers as soon as they are cool; if left out, they absorb moisture easily from the air and become sticky and soft.*

How to Make Meringue Mushrooms

1/Sprinkle meringue mounds very lightly with cocoa through a small strainer. Bake 35 to 40 minutes or until meringue mounds can just be lifted from foil.

2/Use the point of a sharp knife to make a hole in flat side of each mushroom mound. Stick mounds on top of each pointed base, inserting points in holes. Press gently to be sure tops adhere to bases. Bake 1-1/2 hours or until firm and dry.

Chocolate Meringue Fingers

Photo on page 164.

These cookies are shaped like ladyfingers but their taste and texture are completely different. They are sweet, crunchy and chocolaty and delightful with vanilla ice cream.

Makes about 45 cookies

1/4 cup unsweetened Dutch-process cocoa powder
1/2 cup powdered sugar
3 egg whites, room temperature
1/4 teaspoon cream of tartar
1/4 cup plus 2 tablespoons granulated sugar

1. Position rack in center of oven and preheat to 225F (105C). Lightly butter corners of 2 baking sheets; line base with foil. Butter and lightly flour foil, tapping baking sheet to remove excess flour.
2. Have ready a rubber spatula for folding and a pastry bag fitted with a 1/2-inch plain or star tip. Using a clothespin or paper clip, close end of bag just above tip so mixture will not run out while bag is being filled.
3. Sift cocoa and powdered sugar into a medium bowl.
4. In a medium or large dry bowl, beat egg whites with cream of tartar using dry beaters at medium speed until stiff. Increase speed to high. Gradually beat in granulated sugar; continue beating at high speed until whites are very shiny. Gently fold in cocoa mixture as quickly as possible.
5. Immediately spoon meringue into pastry bag. Remove clothespin or paper clip. Pipe mixture in thin fingers 2-1/2 inches long, spacing them about 1 inch apart. To finish each finger, use a quick sharp upward movement of tip.
6. Bake about 1 hour and 10 minutes or until firm and dry. To check meringues for doneness, remove a meringue. Cool 2 minutes and break apart; meringue should be dry and crumbly and not sticky. Using a large metal spatula, immediately transfer meringue fingers to a rack; cool completely.
7. Put cookies in airtight containers as soon as they are cool. *Meringue fingers can be kept in airtight containers at room temperature up to 2 weeks in dry weather. If they become sticky from humidity, they can be baked in a 200F (95C) oven for about 20 minutes to recrisp.*

Chocolate-Cinnamon Squares

These triple-layer bar cookies are made in the Eastern European style: the base is a delicate almond cake, the center is sprinkled with chocolate pieces and the top is a light meringue. The result is a light, delicious cookie that is perfect for teatime or as a petit four.

Makes 20 to 24 cookies

Almond-Cinnamon Dough with Chocolate Chips:
1 cup all-purpose flour
1/2 teaspoon baking powder
2 teaspoons ground cinnamon
1/2 cup whole blanched almonds (about 2-1/2 oz.)
1/2 cup sugar
1/2 cup (4 oz.) unsalted butter, slightly softened
1 egg, beaten
1 egg yolk
1 cup semisweet real chocolate pieces (6 oz.)

Light Chocolate-Cinnamon Topping:
3-1/2 oz. semisweet chocolate, coarsely chopped, chilled
1 egg white, room temperature
1/4 cup granulated sugar
1 teaspoon ground cinnamon

Powdered sugar (for sprinkling)

1. **Dough:** Position rack in center of oven and preheat to 350F (175C). Butter a 9- to 9-1/2-inch-square baking pan. Chill a food processor and metal blade for chopping chocolate.
2. Sift flour, baking powder and cinnamon into a medium bowl.
3. Grind almonds with 2 tablespoons sugar in a food processor until as fine as possible, scraping inward occasionally. Transfer to a medium bowl.
4. Cream butter in a medium or large bowl. Add remaining 6 tablespoons sugar; beat until smooth and fluffy. Add egg in 2 batches, beating thoroughly after each addition. Add egg yolk; beat until blended. Beat in almond mixture at low speed.
5. Using a wooden spoon, stir in flour mixture.
6. Transfer to cake pan; spread evenly. Sprinkle evenly with chocolate pieces. Refrigerate while preparing topping.
1. **Topping:** Chop chocolate in chilled food processor until as fine as possible.
2. In a small dry bowl, beat egg white using dry beaters at medium speed until soft peaks form. Gradually beat in granulated sugar; continue beating at high speed about 30 seconds or until mixture is very shiny. Beat in cinnamon. Fold in finely chopped chocolate. Gently spoon over chocolate pieces; spread carefully and evenly over dough.
3. Bake about 25 minutes or until dough is firm and lightly browned at edges and topping is set.
4. Cool in pan on a rack until lukewarm. Carefully cut in 2-inch squares or 2" x 1-1/4" bars, using a sharp knife. Sift powdered sugar over cookies just before serving. *Cookies can be kept up to 3 days in an airtight container at cool room temperature.*

Chocolate-Coated Coconut Kisses   *Photo on page 164.*

Macaroonlike, white coconut peaks are dipped in dark bittersweet chocolate, which forms a topping of a contrasting color and a flavor that offsets the cookie's sweetness.

Makes about 22 cookies

3 egg whites, room temperature
1/2 cup sugar
1-3/4 cups flaked or grated coconut (about 5-1/2 oz.)

4 oz. bittersweet chocolate, chopped (for dipping)

1. Position rack in center of oven and preheat to 300F (150C). Lightly butter corners of 1 large or 2 small baking sheets; line with foil. Butter foil.
2. Combine egg whites and sugar in a heatproof medium bowl. Set bowl in a pan of hot water over low heat. Beat with a hand mixer at low speed about 5 minutes, then at medium speed about 6 minutes or until mixture is warm to touch. Remove from pan of water. Continue beating at high speed until cooled to room temperature. Stir in coconut.
3. Using about 1 tablespoon batter for each cookie, push batter from a spoon with a second spoon onto prepared baking sheets, spacing about 1 inch apart. Shape each with your dampened fingers into a rounded peak.
4. Bake about 25 minutes or until set and very light brown; cookies should feel soft inside. Transfer to a rack; cool completely.
5. Melt chocolate in a small deep heatproof bowl over hot, not simmering, water over low heat, stirring occasionally. Stir until smooth. Remove from pan of water; cool to body temperature. Line a tray with foil or waxed paper.
6. Holding each cookie from its base, gently dip peak into chocolate so about 2/3 of cookie is coated. Hold briefly upside down so chocolate drips back into bowl. Set on a lined tray, peak-side up. If chocolate begins to thicken during dipping, set briefly above pan of hot water to soften. Refrigerate cookies 20 minutes or until set. *Cookies can be kept in 1 layer in a shallow covered container up to 4 days in refrigerator.* Serve at room temperature.

Almond-Truffle Petits Fours

Photo on page 164.

Unlike many traditional petits fours, these do not have a sweet fondant coating and are simple to prepare. They are made of four layers, two of light, tender, white almond cake and two of a rich, chocolate-truffle mixture. The cake layers are easy to form—the batter is baked on a baking sheet and cut in two pieces to make the layers. The frosting and filling are made from the same mixture, but for the topping the mixture is whipped to give a lighter texture and color.

Makes 24 petits fours

Light Almond Cake:
1 cup whole blanched almonds (about 4-1/2 oz.)
3/4 cup plus 2 tablespoons sugar
6 tablespoons all-purpose flour
8 egg whites, room temperature
1/3 cup milk

Coffee-Flavored Ganache:
10 oz. semisweet chocolate, very finely chopped
2 teaspoons instant coffee granules
3/4 cup whipping cream

24 whole blanched almonds, if desired (for garnish)

1. Cake: Position rack in center of oven and preheat to 375F (190C). Line a 17" x 11" baking sheet with parchment paper or foil; butter paper or foil.
2. Grind 1 cup almonds with 1/2 cup plus 2 tablespoons sugar in a food processor until as fine as possible, scraping inward occasionally. Transfer to a medium bowl.
3. Sift flour onto almond mixture; stir until blended.
4. In a large dry bowl, beat egg whites using dry beaters at medium speed until soft peaks form. Gradually beat in remaining 1/4 cup sugar; continue beating at high speed until whites are stiff and shiny but not dry.
5. Using a wooden spoon, stir milk into almond mixture. Stir in about 1/4 of whites. Gently fold remaining whites into almond mixture in 3 batches. Fold lightly but quickly, just until batter is blended.
6. Spread batter evenly on prepared baking sheet. Bake 15 minutes or until cake is light brown on top and golden brown at edges. Cool in pan on a rack.
1. Ganache: Combine chocolate and coffee in a heatproof medium bowl. Bring cream to a full boil in a small heavy saucepan. Pour over chocolate all at once. Stir with a whisk until chocolate is completely melted and mixture is smooth.
2. Refrigerate about 20 minutes, stirring occasionally with whisk, until cold and thick but not set.
3. Cut cake in half crosswise with a sharp knife; each piece will be about 8 inches wide. Carefully remove 1 piece from paper. Set on a platter; cake will feel slightly sticky.
4. Spread about 1/3 cup ganache in a thin layer on cake on platter. Top with second piece of cake, positioning it so cut sides of cake are even with each other. Refrigerate 10 minutes.
5. Whip remaining ganache in a medium or large bowl at high speed about 5 minutes or until thickened and slightly lighter in color. Spread over top cake layer. Set almonds on top, about 1-1/2 inches apart.
6. Refrigerate about 1 hour or until frosting is set. Trim edges of cake. Cut in 1-1/2-inch squares, using the point of a sharp knife. *Petits fours can be kept, covered, up to 5 days in refrigerator.* Serve at room temperature.

Devil's Food Cupcakes

Bake this batter either as tender cupcakes or as 8-inch cake layers. Its rich frosting is simple to prepare and has a pure chocolate flavor, quite different from the powdered-sugar icings often found on cupcakes.

Makes 20 to 24 cupcakes

Cocoa Cupcakes:

2 cups cake flour
2/3 cup unsweetened cocoa powder
1-1/4 teaspoons baking soda
1/4 teaspoon salt
1/2 cup buttermilk
1/3 cup water
3/4 cup (6 oz.) unsalted butter,
   slightly softened
1-3/4 cups sugar
2 eggs
1-1/2 teaspoons pure vanilla extract

Rich Chocolate Frosting:

5 oz. semisweet chocolate, chopped
1/3 cup whipping cream
2 tablespoons unsalted butter,
   well-chilled, cut in 2 pieces

1. **Cupcakes:** Position rack in center of oven and preheat to 350F (175C). Line 24 muffin cups with fluted paper baking cups.
2. Sift flour, cocoa, baking soda and salt into a large bowl. Mix buttermilk and water in a medium bowl.
3. Cream butter in a large bowl. Add sugar; beat until smooth and fluffy. Add eggs, 1 at a time, beating very thoroughly after each addition. Add vanilla; beat until blended.
4. Using mixer at lowest speed, blend in about 1/4 of cocoa mixture, then blend in about 1/3 of buttermilk mixture. Repeat with remaining cocoa mixture in 3 batches, alternating with remaining buttermilk mixture in 2 batches. Continue mixing just until batter is blended.
5. Fill paper baking cups 2/3 full, using about 1/4 cup batter for each. Bake about 20 minutes or until a cake tester inserted into center of a cupcake comes out clean.
6. Cool in pan on a rack. Remove cupcakes with their paper baking cups.
1. **Frosting:** Combine chocolate and cream in a double boiler or heatproof medium bowl over hot, not simmering, water over low heat. Leave until melted, stirring occasionally. Remove from pan of water; stir until smooth.
2. Add butter; stir until blended. Refrigerate 15 minutes.
3. Beat at high speed 8 minutes or until frosting is thick enough to spread.
4. Using a metal spatula, spread frosting on top of each cupcake. Refrigerate about 1 hour or until frosting sets. *Cupcakes can be kept, covered, up to 4 days in refrigerator.* Serve at room temperature.

Variation

Devil's Food Cake: Butter 2 round 8-inch layer cake pans; line base of each pan with foil. Butter foil and sides of pans. Transfer batter to pans; spread smooth. Bake about 35 minutes or until a cake tester inserted into center of each layer comes out clean. Cool 5 minutes in pans. Carefully invert onto racks; cool. Frosting is enough to fill cake and cover top. To obtain enough frosting for side of cake as well, substitute following amounts for those in recipe: 7-1/2 ounces semisweet chocolate, 1/2 cup whipping cream, 3 tablespoons unsalted butter.

Clockwise from left: Row of Florentines alternately arranged with chocolate-frosted side up, page 167; almond-garnished Chocolate-Marzipan Rosettes formed in ring shape, page 159; Almond Truffle Petits Fours, page 163; Chocolate-Coated Coconut Kisses, page 162; Chocolate Meringue Fingers, page 161; Chocolate-Marzipan Rosettes topped with a cherry, page 159.

Chocolate Macaroons

Dense chewy macaroons, made mainly of ground almonds, are among the first types of cookie known in the history of food and remain one of the most popular sweets. Bittersweet chocolate adds just the perfect touch for the traditionally sweet flavor of macaroons.

Makes about 60 small cookies

4-1/2 oz. bittersweet or semisweet chocolate, chopped
1-1/2 cups whole blanched almonds (about 6 oz.)
1 cup sugar
3 egg whites
2 teaspoons grated orange zest, if desired

1. Position rack in center of oven and preheat to 325F (165C). Line 3 baking sheets with parchment paper or waxed paper; lightly butter paper.
2. Melt chocolate in a double boiler or heatproof medium bowl over hot, not simmering, water over low heat, stirring occasionally. Stir until smooth. Remove from pan of water; cool to body temperature.
3. Grind almonds with 3 tablespoons sugar in a food processor by processing continuously until as fine as possible, scraping inward occasionally. Add egg whites and remaining sugar alternately, each in 2 batches, processing about 10 seconds after each addition or until smooth. Add orange zest, if desired; process to blend. Transfer to a large bowl.
4. Gradually add chocolate, stirring until mixture is smooth.
5. Using a pastry bag fitted with a 1/2-inch plain tip, pipe mixture in mounds, about 1 inch in diameter, onto baking sheets, spacing mounds about 1 inch apart. Flatten any points with your lightly moistened finger.
6. Bake 5 minutes. Wedge oven door slightly open with the handle of a wooden spoon. Bake about 7 minutes longer or until just firm to touch; centers should still be soft. Remove from oven.
7. Lift 1 end of paper and pour about 2 tablespoons water under it onto baking sheet; water will sizzle on contact with hot baking sheet. Lift other end of paper and pour 2 tablespoons water under it. When water stops boiling, carefully remove macaroons from paper with the aid of a metal spatula. Transfer to a rack to cool.
8. Bake remaining macaroons. If necessary, bake on 2 racks. Halfway through baking time, switch positions of baking sheets from lower to upper racks so all macaroons bake evenly. *Macaroons can be kept up to 1 week in an airtight container at room temperature.*

Golden Pine Nut-Chocolate Chip Bars
Photo on page 153.

This type of bar cookie, often called *a blond brownie* or *golden brownie*, is light-textured but rich and buttery. These are sweetened with brown sugar and studded with chocolate chips and pine nuts.

Makes 16 to 20 bars

1 cup plus 2 tablespoons all-purpose flour
1 teaspoon baking powder
1/4 teaspoon salt
1/2 cup plus 2 tablespoons (5 oz.) unsalted butter, slightly softened
1/4 cup granulated sugar
3/4 cup packed light brown sugar
2 eggs
1 teaspoon pure vanilla extract
2/3 cup pine nuts (about 3 oz.)
1 cup semisweet real chocolate pieces (6 oz.)

1/4 cup pine nuts, if desired (for sprinkling)

1. Position rack in center of oven and preheat to 350F (175C). Butter a 9- to 9-1/2-inch-square baking pan.
2. Sift flour, baking powder and salt into a medium bowl.
3. Cream butter in a large bowl. Add sugars; beat until smooth and fluffy. Add eggs, 1 at a time, beating very thoroughly after each addition. Beat in 2 tablespoons flour mixture at low speed. Add vanilla; beat until blended.
4. Using a wooden spoon, stir in remaining flour mixture. Stir in 2/3 cup pine nuts and chocolate pieces.
5. Transfer batter to prepared pan; spread evenly. Sprinkle evenly with 1/4 cup pine nuts. Bake 30 to 35 minutes or until mixture is brown on top, pulls away slightly from sides of pan and a wooden pick inserted into center comes out nearly clean.
6. Cool in pan on a rack. Cut into approximately 1-1/4" x 1-3/4" bars, using the point of a sharp knife. *Cookies can be kept up to 3 days in an airtight container at room temperature.*

How to Make Florentines

1/Bake Florentines 5 minutes. Remove from oven. Using a 3-inch cookie cutter, pull in any uneven edges of each cookie. Bake 4 minutes longer until edges are golden.

2/Using a cake-decorating comb or a fork, mark wavy lines on chocolate coating of each cookie. Refrigerate about 10 minutes or until set.

Florentines *Photo on page 164.*

Named for Florence, where it probably originated, this crisp, chewy, candylike cookie is a favorite in Italy, France, Austria and Germany. It is a lacy holiday cookie, studded with colorful candied fruits and almonds, flavored with honey and glazed with chocolate.

Makes about 42 cookies

1/2 cup whipping cream
1/4 cup unsalted butter
1/2 cup sugar
2 tablespoons honey
1/3 cup diced candied orange peel, finely chopped
1/3 cup red candied cherries, rinsed in hot water, drained and chopped
1-2/3 cups sliced almonds (about 5 oz.)
6 tablespoons all-purpose flour

8 oz. bittersweet chocolate, chopped (for glaze)

1. Position rack in center of oven and preheat to 350F (175C). Butter and flour 2 baking sheets, preferably nonstick, tapping to remove excess flour.
2. Combine cream, butter, sugar, honey, candied orange peel and candied cherries in a heavy medium saucepan; mix well. Cook over low heat, stirring, until butter melts. Bring to a boil over medium-high heat, stirring constantly. Remove from heat; stir in almonds and flour.
3. Drop rounded teaspoons of mixture onto prepared baking sheets, spacing them 3 inches apart. Flatten each cookie until very thin by pressing it with the bottom of a fork dipped in water.
4. Bake 5 minutes. Remove from oven. Using a 3-inch cookie cutter, pull in any uneven edges of each cookie to give it an even round shape. Return to oven. Bake 4 minutes longer or until edges of cookies are golden brown. Watch carefully because they burn easily; do not underbake or cookies quickly become sticky.
5. Cool to lukewarm on baking sheet. Remove cookies to a rack with a metal pancake turner.
6. Melt chocolate in a double boiler or heatproof medium bowl over hot, not simmering, water over low heat. Stir until smooth. Remove from pan of water; cool, stirring often, about 5 minutes or until slightly thickened. Line a tray with foil or waxed paper. Spread chocolate on flat side of each cookie; set on tray.
7. Refrigerate cookies 5 minutes or until chocolate is thickened but not set. Using a cake-decorating comb or a fork, mark wavy lines on chocolate coating of each cookie. Refrigerate about 10 minutes or until set. *Cookies can be kept in an airtight container up to 1 week in refrigerator.*
8. To serve, arrange cookies on a platter, alternating some with chocolate facing up, others with chocolate facing down.

Chocolate Ladyfingers

Use these to make frames for charlottes, such as Double-Chocolate Charlotte, page 120, or to accompany mousses or ice creams.

Makes about 30 ladyfingers; about 10 ounces

3 tablespoons plus 1 teaspoon unsweetened Dutch-process cocoa powder
1-1/2 teaspoons powdered sugar
3/4 cup all-purpose flour
4 eggs, separated, room temperature
2/3 cup granulated sugar
3/4 teaspoon pure vanilla extract
1/4 teaspoon cream of tartar

1. Position rack in center of oven and preheat to 350F (175C). Butter and lightly flour 2 nonstick baking sheets, tapping pan to remove excess flour. Designate length of ladyfingers by marking crosswise lines 3-1/2 inches apart on baking sheets. Ladyfingers will be piped lengthwise between lines.
2. Have ready a rubber spatula for folding and a pastry bag with a large plain tip of 5/8 inch diameter. Using a clothespin or paper clip, close end of bag just above tip so mixture will not run out while bag is being filled.
3. Mix 2-1/2 teaspoons cocoa with powdered sugar in a small bowl; set aside for sprinkling. Sift flour and remaining 2 tablespoons plus 1-1/2 teaspoons cocoa into a medium bowl.
4. Beat egg yolks lightly in a large bowl. Beat in 6 tablespoons granulated sugar; continue beating at high speed about 5 minutes or until mixture is pale and very thick. Beat in vanilla.
5. In a large dry bowl, beat egg whites with cream of tartar using dry beaters at medium speed until soft peaks form. Gradually beat in remaining 2-2/3 tablespoons granulated sugar; continue beating at high speed until whites are stiff and shiny but not dry.
6. Sift about 1/4 of flour mixture over egg yolk mixture; fold gently until nearly incorporated. Gently fold in about 1/4 of whites. Repeat with remaining flour mixture and whites, each in 3 batches, adding each batch when previous one is nearly blended in. Continue folding lightly but quickly, just until batter is blended.
7. Immediately spoon into prepared pastry bag. Remove clothespin or paper clip. Pipe 3-1/2″ x 1-1/4″ ladyfingers onto prepared baking sheets between marked lines, spacing them about 1 inch apart. Sift cocoa-powdered sugar mixture lightly but evenly over ladyfingers.
8. Bake in center of oven about 12 minutes or until ladyfingers are just firm on outside and spring back when pressed very lightly but are slightly soft inside. Transfer to a rack; cool. *Ladyfingers can be kept up to 1 day in an airtight container in 1 layer; or they can be frozen in layers separated with waxed paper about 2 months.*

Variation
White Ladyfingers: Omit cocoa. Increase powdered sugar to 1 tablespoon plus 1 teaspoon; set aside for sprinkling on ladyfingers. In step 1, mark crosswise lines 3 inches apart. Pipe 3-inch ladyfingers. Sift powdered sugar lightly but evenly over ladyfingers. Makes about 48 small ladyfingers; about 10 ounces.

Note: To line a mold or pan with ladyfingers, trim ladyfingers at their sides so they can fit tightly in mold. Trim them flat at 1 end to sit squarely on base of pan. Line side of mold with ladyfingers standing upright. If using chocolate ladyfingers, smooth bottom side should face outward; if using white ladyfingers, smooth side should face inward. Fit them in mold as tightly as possible.

TIP

○ *When substituting homemade ladyfingers for packaged ones to make charlottes, moisten them more than packaged ladyfingers. Unlike packaged ladyfingers, homemade ladyfingers should be used whole rather than split horizontally.*

TRUFFLES, CANDIES & DRINKS

Chocolate truffles and other homemade chocolate candies give the most intense chocolate experience and are among the most luxurious of food gifts.

Some people hesitate to make truffles and other chocolate candies because dipping them in chocolate appears complicated. But the truth is that making dipped truffles delicious is easy; only making them beautiful takes practice! Many quick-to-prepare truffles and chocolate candies do not even need to be dipped in chocolate.

Truffles, chocolate candies and chocolate drinks are sweet snacks rather than desserts, although they can be served instead of dessert after a rich dinner. Truffles can be used to make desserts, such as Truffled Bavarian Cream, page 114, or Chocolate Surprise Ice Cream Cake, page 142.

Chocolate Truffles

Made primarily of pure chocolate and cream, France's most popular candies, truffles, are fast becoming favorites here too.

In France, classic truffles are round and have three parts: a filling of ganache, made of chocolate and cream; a coating of pure chocolate; and a second coating of cocoa. The cocoa is often omitted in America, but is considered by many pastry chefs and chocolatiers in France a "requirement" to call the confection a "true" truffle.

Although the pure flavor of fine chocolate is the most important quality of a good truffle, other secondary flavors, such as coffee or ginger, can be added also. In many parts of the country, truffles cannot be sold when flavored with liqueurs and therefore the liqueur flavor is often imitated with extract, which is no match for the real thing. At home, you can prepare some of the most delicious truffles, flavored with Grand Marnier, raspberry brandy or other spirits.

Some chocolatiers boast that their truffles are largest but I find that the small, European-style truffles give the most pleasure. The chocolate is so rich that one or two bites are usually enough and—one can always have a second or third truffle!

However, this is a matter of taste and how large you want to make your truffles is up to you.

Many popular candies, from rich truffles to simple pieces of dried fruit, are superior when dipped in fine chocolate. A special type of chocolate called *couverture* is best-suited for this purpose (see also "What is Chocolate," pages 6-7, and mail order information, page 202). This chocolate has a relatively high cocoa butter content and is more fluid than other types of chocolate when warm, which results in a thinner, more delicate coating. It is also easier to use because other chocolates become too thick when they reach the correct temperature for dipping, which must be relatively cool so the creamy center of the truffle does not melt.

Other Chocolate Candies

Of course, chocolate candies do not have to be round. With the aid of inexpensive plastic candy molds, an endless array of different shaped chocolate candies can be made with ease.

Colorful chocolate-dipped fruit is another popular candy that is simple to prepare and makes an amusing activity for all ages. Chocolate coatings can be striped or even marbled for a beautiful treat.

There are many delicious, easy-to-make chocolate candies that do not require dipping. Take the Quick Cognac Truffles, for example, in which the chocolaty center is simply rolled in chopped nuts; or Coconut-Coated Chocolate Balls where the outer coating is coconut. Grand Marnier Chocolate Cups are another example; after small paper candy cups are lined with chocolate and filled with a chocolate-Grand Marnier ganache, the paper cups are simply peeled away from the chocolate.

Chocolate Drinks

Easy-to-make chocolate drinks can be served as warm treats in winter or refreshing beverages in summer. Both cocoa and melted chocolate give rich-tasting results. These range from spiced Mexican Hot Cocoa flavored with cinnamon and cloves, to liqueur- or rum-spiked drinks, such as silky smooth Chocolate Egg Nog.

Traditional Truffles

Photo on page 175.

Classic French truffles are always dipped in chocolate, then rolled in cocoa so they look earthy like real truffles. Their charm lies in the wonderful contrast between the creamy center, crisp chocolate shell, and bittersweet powdery cocoa. These truffles are easy to make at home because tempering is less important than for some other truffles; this is due to the cocoa coating which covers up any streaks or other imperfections in the chocolate shell.

Makes about 48 small truffles

Ganache Centers:
9 oz. fine-quality semisweet chocolate, very finely chopped
2/3 cup whipping cream

Coating:
1 cup unsweetened Dutch-process cocoa powder
12 oz. fine-quality semisweet chocolate, preferably *couverture*, chopped

1. Ganache Centers: Put 9 ounces chocolate in a heatproof medium bowl. Bring cream to a full boil in a small heavy saucepan over medium-high heat. Pour cream over chocolate all at once. Stir with a whisk until chocolate is completely melted and mixture is smooth; cool to room temperature.

2. Scrape down mixture with a rubber spatula. Cover with a paper towel and plastic wrap; refrigerate, occasionally stirring gently, about 1 hour or just until thick enough to pipe.

3. Line 2 trays with foil. Have ready a pastry bag with a large plain tip, about 5/8-inch in diameter. Using a clothespin or paper clip, close end of bag just above tip so mixture will not run out while bag is being filled. Fill bag. Remove clothespin or paper clip. Pipe mixture in small mounds or "kisses," about 3/4 inch in diameter and 1 inch high, onto prepared trays, spacing mounds about 1 inch apart for easy handling. Cover with paper towels and plastic wrap; refrigerate 30 to 45 minutes or until firm.

4. Carefully remove a mound from tray, keeping second tray in refrigerator while working with first. Press mound into a ball; return to tray. Repeat with remaining mounds on tray.

5. Roll each ball between your palms until smooth, working quickly so mixture does not soften too much. Rinse and dry your hands often. If truffles begin to soften too much during rolling, refrigerate about 5 minutes and continue. Refrigerate truffle centers. Repeat pressing and rolling of mounds on second tray. Cover with paper towels and plastic wrap; refrigerate at least 3 hours or until very firm. *Truffle centers can be kept, covered, up to 3 days in refrigerator; or they can be frozen 2 months.*

1. Coating: Spread cocoa in a small tray or shallow bowl so it is about 1/2 inch deep. Line 2 trays with foil.

2. Melt 12 ounces chocolate in a double boiler or heatproof medium bowl over hot, not simmering, water over low heat, stirring very often with a rubber spatula. Stir until smooth. Remove from pan of water.

3. Either temper chocolate, page 194, for a professional finish; or cool melted chocolate, stirring often, until it reaches 88F (30C) or slightly cooler than body temperature.

4. Set container of chocolate in a bowl of warm water off heat, making sure it sits squarely in bowl and does not move around.

5. Set 1 truffle center in melted chocolate. Turn over with 2 fingers or a dipping utensil until completely coated. Lift out and gently shake a few times so excess chocolate drips back into bowl. Gently wipe truffle against rim of bowl to remove excess chocolate. Set truffle in tray of cocoa; spoon enough cocoa over truffle to cover it.

6. Repeat dipping and coating with 4 or 5 more centers. Gently shake tray of cocoa to be sure truffles are coated with cocoa. Very gently transfer truffles to foil-lined tray.

7. Continue coating remaining truffles, placing them in cocoa and transferring them to tray. Occasionally replace warm water in bowl. If chocolate gets thick, set bowl of chocolate over pan of hot, not simmering, water over low heat 2 or 3 minutes to soften.

8. Let truffles stand at room temperature until set. If coating does not set within 10 minutes, refrigerate truffles about 10 minutes or until set. Gently transfer truffles to a rack. Gently brush off excess cocoa with a pastry brush.

9. Refrigerate truffles 1 hour. *Truffles can be kept in an airtight container up to 1 week in refrigerator; or they can be frozen 2 months.* Serve at room temperature in white or gold candy papers.

How to Make Traditional Truffles

1/Pour hot cream over chocolate all at once. Stir with a whisk until chocolate is completely melted and mixture, called ganache, is smooth; cool to room temperature.

2/Carefully remove a mound of ganache from tray, keeping second tray in refrigerator while working with first. Press mound into a ball; return to tray. Repeat with remaining mounds on tray. Roll each ball between your palms until smooth. Cover and refrigerate until very firm.

3/Dip truffle centers with your fingers or place on a dipping utensil and dip in chocolate until completely coated.

4/Gently wipe truffle against rim of bowl to remove excess chocolate. Set truffle in tray of cocoa; spoon enough cocoa over truffle to cover it.

Bittersweet Belgian Truffles *Photos on pages 8-9 and 175.*

When making truffles, it is particularly important to use top-quality chocolate; some of the finest chocolate available comes from Belgium. These truffles have an intense chocolate flavor with a hint of vanilla and rum. They are richer and denser than Traditional Truffles, page 170, because of the addition of butter and the higher proportion of chocolate.

Makes about 38 truffles

Bittersweet Ganache Centers:
1/2 cup whipping cream
1 vanilla bean, split lengthwise
10 oz. fine-quality bittersweet chocolate, chopped
2 tablespoons unsalted butter, room temperature, cut in 6 pieces
2 tablespoons rum

Coating:
12 oz. fine-quality bittersweet chocolate, preferably *couverture*, chopped

1. Ganache Centers: Bring cream and vanilla bean to a boil in a heavy medium saucepan. Remove from heat. Cover and let stand 15 minutes.

2. Melt 10 ounces chocolate in a double boiler or heatproof medium bowl over hot, not simmering, water over low heat, stirring occasionally. Stir until smooth. Remove from pan of water; cool slightly.

3. Remove vanilla bean from cream. Pour cream into a medium bowl. Gradually whisk chocolate into cream. Add butter; whisk until blended. Cool to room temperature.

4. Stir in rum. Cover mixture with a paper towel and plastic wrap; refrigerate about 1 hour or until firm.

5. Line 2 trays with foil. Using 2 teaspoons, shape mixture in rough 3/4-inch mounds, using about 2 teaspoons of mixture for each mound and spacing about 1 inch apart on prepared trays for easy handling. Cover with paper towels and plastic wrap; refrigerate about 30 minutes or until firm.

6. Carefully remove a mound from tray, keeping second tray in refrigerator while working with first. Press mound into a ball; return to tray. Repeat with remaining mounds on tray.

7. Roll each ball between your palms until smooth, working quickly so mixture does not soften too much. Rinse and dry your hands often. If truffles begin to soften too much during rolling, refrigerate about 5 minutes and continue. Refrigerate truffle centers. Repeat pressing and rolling with mounds on second tray. Cover with paper towels and plastic wrap; refrigerate at least 2 hours or until very firm. *Truffle centers can be kept, covered, up to 3 days in refrigerator; or they can be frozen 2 months.*

1. Coating: Line 2 trays with foil. Melt 12 ounces chocolate in a double boiler or heatproof medium bowl over hot, not simmering, water over low heat, stirring very often with a rubber spatula. Stir until smooth. Remove from pan of water.

2. Either temper chocolate, page 194, for a professional finish; or cool melted chocolate, stirring often, until it reaches 88F (30C) or slightly cooler than body temperature.

3. Set container of chocolate in a bowl of warm water off heat, making sure it sits squarely in bowl and does not move around.

4. Set 1 truffle center in melted chocolate. Turn over with 2 fingers or dipping utensil until completely coated. Lift out and gently shake a few times so excess chocolate drips back into bowl. Gently wipe truffle against rim of bowl to remove excess chocolate. Gently set truffle on prepared tray. Swirl top for a decorative finish, if desired.

5. Continue dipping remaining truffles. Occasionally replace warm water in bowl to keep dipping chocolate fluid. Let coated truffles stand at room temperature until set. If coating does not set within 10 minutes, refrigerate truffles about 10 minutes or until set. Remove from foil. *Truffles can be kept in an airtight container up to 1 week in refrigerator; or they can be frozen 2 months.* Serve cool.

Variation
For an attractive garnish on these truffles, use 3 ounces cooled, melted white chocolate to drizzle a design with a fork.

Extra-Creamy Truffles

A high proportion of cream makes the centers of these truffles so soft they melt quickly in your mouth. Their velvety texture is a wonderful contrast for the crisp dark chocolate coating and the crunch of toasted pecans.

Makes about 48 small truffles

Chocolate-Orange Centers:
2 large navel oranges
1/2 pint whipping cream (1 cup)
10 oz. fine-quality bittersweet
   chocolate, very finely chopped

Coating:
2/3 cup pecans, if desired
1 lb. fine-quality bittersweet
   chocolate, preferably *couverture*,
   chopped

1. **Chocolate-Orange Centers:** Using a vegetable peeler, pare colored part of orange peel in long strips, without including white pith.
2. Scald cream and strips of orange zest in a heavy medium saucepan over medium heat by heating until bubbles form around edge of pan. Remove from heat. Cover and let stand 20 minutes. Strain into a medium bowl.
3. Melt 10 ounces chocolate in a double boiler or heatproof medium bowl over hot, not simmering, water over low heat, stirring occasionally. Stir until smooth. Remove from pan of water; cool 5 minutes. Add cream all at once; whisk until blended. Cool to room temperature.
4. Scrape down mixture with a rubber spatula. Cover with a paper towel and plastic wrap and refrigerate, occasionally stirring gently, about 1-1/2 hours or until just thick enough to pipe.
5. Line 2 trays with foil. Have ready a pastry bag with a large plain tip, about 5/8-inch diameter. Using a clothespin or paper clip, close end of bag just above tip so mixture will not run out while bag is being filled. Fill bag. Remove clothespin or paper clip. Pipe mixture in small mounds or "kisses," about 3/4 inch in diameter and 1 inch high, onto prepared trays, spacing mounds about 1 inch apart for easy handling. Cover with paper towels and plastic wrap; refrigerate 3 hours or until firm.
6. Carefully remove a mound from tray, keeping second tray in refrigerator while working with first. Press mound into a ball; return to tray. Repeat with remaining mounds on tray.
7. Roll each ball between your palms until smooth, working quickly so mixture does not soften too much. Rinse and dry your hands often. If truffles begin to soften too much during rolling, refrigerate about 5 minutes and continue. Refrigerate truffle centers. Repeat pressing and rolling with mounds on second tray. Cover with paper towels and plastic wrap; refrigerate at least 6 hours or until very firm. *Truffle centers can be kept, covered, up to 3 days in refrigerator; or they can be frozen 2 months.*
1. **Coating:** Preheat oven to 350F (175C). Lightly toast pecans in a shallow baking pan in oven 4 minutes. Transfer to a plate; cool completely. Using a sharp knife, chop pecans into tiny cubes.
2. Line 2 trays with foil. Melt 1 pound chocolate in a double boiler or heatproof medium bowl over hot, not simmering, water over low heat, stirring very often with a rubber spatula. Stir until smooth. Remove from pan of water.
3. Either temper chocolate, page 194, for a professional finish; or cool melted chocolate, stirring often, until it reaches 88F (30C) or slightly cooler than body temperature.
4. Stir pecans into chocolate. Set container of chocolate mixture in a bowl of warm water off heat, making sure it sits squarely in bowl and does not move around.
5. Set 1 truffle center in melted chocolate. Turn over with 2 fingers or a dipping utensil until completely coated. Lift out and gently shake a few times so excess chocolate drips back into bowl. Gently wipe truffle against rim of bowl to remove excess chocolate. Gently set truffle on prepared tray.
6. Continue dipping remaining truffles. Occasionally replace warm water in bowl to keep dipping chocolate fluid. Let coated truffles stand at room temperature until set. If coating does not set within 10 minutes, refrigerate truffles about 10 minutes or until set. Carefully remove from foil. *Truffles can be kept in an airtight container up to 1 week in refrigerator; or they can be frozen 2 months.* Serve cool.

Variation
Easy Chocolate Kisses: Instead of rolling truffle centers into balls, leave them shaped as "kisses." Omit coating. Serve cool.

Spirited White Chocolate Truffles

Fruit brandies contribute "spirit" to these sweet, white-chocolate truffles. My favorites are raspberry brandy and pear brandy but you can use any brandy you like, although the most assertive ones are best. Make these truffles small because of their concentrated flavor.

Makes about 22 truffles

White Ganache Centers:
9 oz. fine-quality white chocolate, very finely chopped
6 tablespoons whipping cream
1 tablespoon unsalted butter, room temperature
2 tablespoons fine-quality fruit brandy, such as clear raspberry brandy, pear brandy, kirsch or calvados

White Chocolate Coating:
Small pieces of candied violets, if desired (for garnish)
1 lb. fine-quality white chocolate, preferably *couverture*, chopped

1. Ganache Centers: Put 9 ounces chocolate in a heatproof medium bowl. Bring cream to a full boil in a small heavy saucepan over medium-high heat. Pour cream over chocolate all at once. Stir with whisk until smooth. Add butter; whisk until blended. Gradually whisk in fruit brandy.

2. Scrape down mixture with a rubber spatula. Cover with a paper towel and plastic wrap; refrigerate about 3 hours or until firm.

3. Line 2 trays with foil. Using 2 teaspoons, shape mixture into rough 3/4-inch mounds, using about 2 teaspoons of mixture for each mound and spacing about 1 inch apart on prepared trays for easy handling. Cover with paper towels and plastic wrap; refrigerate about 1 hour or until firm.

4. Carefully remove a mound, keeping second tray in refrigerator while working with first. Press mound into a ball; return to tray. Repeat with remaining mounds on tray.

5. Roll each ball between your palms until smooth, working quickly so mixture does not soften too much. Rinse and dry your hands often. If truffles begin to soften too much during rolling, refrigerate a few minutes and continue. Refrigerate truffle centers. Repeat pressing and rolling with mounds on second tray. Cover with paper towels and plastic wrap; refrigerate at least 3 hours or until very firm. *Truffle centers can be kept, covered, up to 3 days in refrigerator; or they can be frozen 2 months.*

1. Coating: Line 2 trays with foil. Break candied violets into small pieces.

2. Melt 1 pound chocolate in a double boiler or heatproof medium bowl over hot, not simmering, water over low heat, stirring very often with a rubber spatula. Stir until smooth. Use whisk to stir chocolate if it is not entirely smooth. Remove from pan of water.

3. Either temper chocolate, page 194, for a professional finish; or cool melted chocolate, stirring often, until it reaches 84F (29C) or cooler than body temperature.

4. Set container of chocolate in a bowl of warm water off heat, making sure it sits squarely in bowl and does not move around.

5. Set 1 truffle center in melted chocolate. Turn over with 2 fingers or a dipping utensil until completely coated. Lift out and gently shake a few times so excess chocolate drips back into bowl. Gently wipe truffle against rim of bowl to remove excess chocolate. Gently set truffle on prepared tray. Swirl top for a decorative finish, if desired. Immediately put 1 piece of candied violet on top.

6. Continue dipping and garnishing remaining truffles. Occasionally replace warm water in bowl to keep dipping chocolate fluid. Let coated truffles stand at room temperature until set. If coating does not set within 10 minutes, refrigerate truffles about 10 minutes or until set. Very carefully remove from foil so center does not stick. *Truffles can be kept in an airtight container up to 1 week in refrigerator; or they can be frozen 2 months.* Serve cool in brown candy papers.

Almond-Coated White Chocolate Truffles: Omit candied violets. Toast 1 cup slivered almonds in a shallow baking pan in a preheated 350F (175C) oven, stirring often, about 5 minutes or until very lightly browned. Transfer to a plate; cool completely. Chop almonds into tiny cubes. Transfer to a tray. After dipping each truffle, set on tray of chopped almonds. Spoon more chopped almonds from tray over truffle so nuts stick to top.

Upper dish: Double-Dipped Strawberries, page 185. Middle dish: assorted truffles - Traditional, page 170; Spirited White Chocolate, above; Cafe au Lait, page 176; Bittersweet Belgian, page 172; Quick Cognac, page 178. In lower tray: Grand Marnier Chocolate Cups, page 180.

Café au Lait Truffles *Photo on page 175.*

In these milk-chocolate and coffee truffles, a richly flavored coffee center is offset by a sweet milk-chocolate coating. The truffles are decorated with small coffee bean candies but can instead be drizzled with dark chocolate using the same technique as in the variation for Bittersweet Belgian Truffles, page 172.

Makes about 32 truffles

Chocolate-Coffee Centers:
6 oz. fine-quality milk chocolate, very finely chopped
4 oz. fine-quality bittersweet chocolate, very finely chopped
1 tablespoon instant coffee granules
1/2 cup whipping cream

Coating:
12 oz. fine-quality milk chocolate, preferably *couverture,* chopped
About 32 small chocolate coffee beans (about 5/8 inch long) or coffee-flavored candy drops, if desired (for garnish)

1. Chocolate-Coffee Centers: Combine 6 ounces milk chocolate, 4 ounces bittersweet chocolate and coffee in a heatproof medium bowl. Bring cream to a full boil in a small heavy saucepan over medium-high heat. Pour cream over chocolate mixture all at once. Stir with a whisk until chocolate is completely melted and mixture is smooth; cool to room temperature.

2. Scrape down mixture with a rubber spatula. Cover with a paper towel and plastic wrap; refrigerate, occasionally stirring gently, about 1 hour or until firm.

3. Line 2 trays with foil. Using 2 teaspoons, shape mixture into rough 3/4-inch mounds, using about 2 teaspoons of mixture for each mound and spacing about 1 inch apart on prepared trays for easy handling. Cover with paper towels and plastic wrap; refrigerate 30 to 45 minutes or until firm.

4. Carefully remove a mound from tray, keeping second tray in refrigerator while working with first. Press mound into a ball; return to tray. Repeat with remaining mounds on tray.

5. Roll each ball between your palms until smooth, working quickly so mixture does not soften too much. Rinse and dry your hands often. If truffles begin to soften too much during rolling, refrigerate about 5 minutes and continue. Refrigerate truffle centers. Repeat pressing and rolling with mounds on second tray. Cover with paper towels and plastic wrap; refrigerate at least 3 hours or until very firm. *Truffle centers can be kept, covered, up to 3 days in refrigerator; or they can be frozen 2 months.*

1. Coating: Line 2 trays with foil. Melt 12 ounces chocolate in a double boiler or heatproof medium bowl over hot, not simmering, water over low heat, stirring very often with a rubber spatula. Stir until smooth. Remove from pan of water.

2. Either temper chocolate, page 194, for a professional finish; or cool melted chocolate, stirring often, until it reaches 84F (29C) or cooler than body temperature.

3. Set container of chocolate in a bowl of warm water off heat, making sure it sits squarely in bowl and does not move around.

4. Set 1 truffle center in melted chocolate. Turn over with 2 fingers or dipping utensil until completely coated. Lift out and gently shake a few times so excess chocolate drips back into bowl. Gently wipe truffle against rim of bowl to remove excess chocolate. Set truffle on prepared tray. If desired, garnish with a chocolate coffee bean or candy drop.

5. Continue dipping and garnishing remaining truffles. Occasionally replace warm water in bowl to keep dipping chocolate fluid. Let coated truffles stand at room temperature until set. If coating does not set within 10 minutes, refrigerate truffles about 10 minutes or until set. Carefully remove from foil. *Truffles can be kept in an airtight container up to 1 week in refrigerator; or they can be frozen 2 months.* Serve cool.

TIPS

○ The coating of truffles is shinier if they set at room temperature; on a warm day they must be refrigerated.

○ You can use couverture chocolate for truffle centers as well as for coatings.

○ To dip with ordinary chocolate instead of couverture, see page 194.

Chestnut Truffles

Chestnut puree gives these truffles a delicate flavor and contributes to their soft creamy texture. For a quicker, very easy truffle, these can be rolled in cocoa instead of being dipped in bittersweet chocolate.

Makes about 40 truffles

Chestnut-Chocolate Centers:
2 tablespoons rum
1 (8-3/4-oz.) can sweetened chestnut puree (3/4 cup)
8 oz. fine-quality bittersweet chocolate, finely chopped
1/2 cup whipping cream
1/4 cup unsalted butter, cut into 4 pieces, room temperature

Coating:
About 1/4 cup unsweetened Dutch-process cocoa powder
1 lb. 2 oz. fine-quality bittersweet chocolate, preferably *couverture,* chopped

1. Chestnut-Chocolate Centers: In a medium bowl, add rum to chestnut puree; whisk until smooth.
2. Put 8 ounces chocolate in a heatproof medium bowl. Bring cream to a full boil in a small heavy saucepan over medium-high heat. Pour cream over chocolate all at once. Stir with a whisk until chocolate is completely melted and mixture is smooth. Add butter; whisk until smooth. Add chestnut mixture; whisk until smooth.
3. Cover mixture with a paper towel and plastic wrap; refrigerate about 6 hours or until firm. *Truffle mixture can be kept up to 3 days in refrigerator.*
4. Line 2 trays with foil. Using 2 teaspoons, shape mixture into rough 3/4-inch mounds, using about 2 teaspoons of mixture for each mound and spacing about 1 inch apart on prepared trays for easy handling. Cover with paper towels and plastic wrap; refrigerate about 30 minutes or until firm.
5. Carefully remove a mound from tray, keeping second tray in refrigerator while working with first. Press mound into a ball; return to tray. Repeat with remaining mounds on tray.
1. Coating: Roll each ball between your palms until smooth, occasionally dipping your palms in cocoa to prevent sticking. Work quickly so mixture does not soften too much. Rinse and dry your hands often. If truffles begin to soften too much during rolling, refrigerate about 5 minutes and continue. Refrigerate truffle centers. Repeat pressing and rolling with mounds on second tray. Cover with paper towels and plastic wrap; refrigerate at least 2 hours or until very firm. *Truffle centers can be kept, covered, up to 3 days in refrigerator; or they can be frozen 2 months.*
2. Line 2 trays with foil. Melt 1 pound 2 ounces chocolate in a double boiler or heatproof medium bowl over hot, not simmering, water over low heat, stirring very often with a rubber spatula. Stir until smooth. Remove from pan of water.
3. Either temper chocolate, page 194, for a professional finish; or cool melted chocolate, stirring often, until it reaches 88F (30C) or slightly cooler than body temperature.
4. Set container of chocolate in a bowl of warm water off heat, making sure it sits squarely in bowl and does not move around.
5. Set 1 truffle center in melted chocolate. Turn over with 2 fingers or a dipping utensil until completely coated. Lift out and gently shake a few times so excess chocolate drips back into bowl. Gently wipe truffle against rim of bowl to remove excess chocolate. Gently set truffle on prepared tray. Swirl top for a decorative finish, if desired.
6. Continue dipping remaining truffles. Occasionally replace warm water in bowl to keep dipping chocolate fluid. Let coated truffles stand at room temperature until set. If coating does not set within 10 minutes, refrigerate truffles about 10 minutes or until set. Remove from foil. *Truffles can be kept in an airtight container up to 1 week in refrigerator; or they can be frozen 2 months.* Serve cool.

TIP

○ *Sweetened chestnut puree is often labeled* crème de marrons.

Quick Cognac Truffles

Photo on page 175.

A walnut coating provides a complementary taste and crunchy texture for the intense cognac-chocolate flavor of the interior of these truffles. No dipping is required, making these rich, creamy truffles easy to prepare. The mixture is chilled several times because the cognac makes it soft.

Makes about 25 truffles

8 oz. fine-quality semisweet chocolate, chopped
6 tablespoons unsalted butter, slightly softened
1/3 cup whipping cream
1/4 cup cognac
About 3 tablespoons unsweetened Dutch-process cocoa powder
3/4 cup finely chopped walnuts

1. Melt chocolate in a double boiler or heatproof medium bowl over hot, not simmering, water over low heat, stirring occasionally. Stir until smooth. Remove from pan of water; cool slightly.
2. Cream butter in a small bowl until smooth.
3. Scald cream in a very small heavy saucepan over medium-high heat by heating until bubbles form around edge of pan; cool 3 minutes. Pour cream over chocolate all at once. Whisk until blended. Whisk butter into chocolate mixture; cool to room temperature.
4. Gradually stir cognac into chocolate mixture. Cover mixture with a paper towel and plastic wrap; refrigerate about 5 hours or until firm.
5. Line 2 trays with foil. Using 2 teaspoons, shape mixture in rough 3/4-inch mounds, using about 2 teaspoons of mixture for each mound and spacing about 1 inch apart on prepared trays. Cover with paper towels and plastic wrap; refrigerate about 3 hours or until firm.
6. Carefully remove a mound, keeping second tray in refrigerator while working with first. Press mound into a ball; return to tray. Repeat with remaining mounds on tray.
7. Roll each ball between your palms until smooth, occasionally dipping your palms in cocoa to prevent sticking. Work quickly so mixture does not soften too much. Rinse and dry your hands often. If truffles begin to soften too much during rolling, refrigerate about 5 minutes and continue. Refrigerate truffles. Repeat pressing and rolling with mounds on second tray. Cover with paper towels and plastic wrap; refrigerate at least 2 hours or until firm.
8. Line 2 trays with foil. Put walnuts in a shallow bowl or tray. Roll truffles in walnuts, 1 at a time, pressing so walnuts adhere. Transfer to trays; refrigerate 1 hour or until firm. *Truffles can be kept in an airtight container up to 1 week in refrigerator; or they can be frozen 2 months.* Serve cold in candy papers.

TIPS

○ *If chocolate does not melt completely after cream is poured over it for making ganache, set bowl of chocolate above a pan of hot water over low heat and stir until it melts.*

○ *Chocolate for dipping can be cooled by setting container of chocolate in cool, not iced, water. If cooling this way, stir chocolate often as it cools.*

○ *Truffle mixture is covered with paper towel before being covered with plastic wrap to prevent moisture from condensing on it.*

○ *Do not be concerned about the large amount of chocolate needed for dipping. Pour leftover chocolate onto a piece of foil, let it harden and reuse it for making desserts.*

○ *When dipping truffles with a fork, be careful not to pierce truffles.*

○ *Truffles rolled in cocoa without first being dipped in chocolate should be served cold. They soften very quickly at room temperature.*

Ginger Truffles

Candied or crystallized ginger adds liveliness and sweetness to the creamy centers of these truffles and provides a counterpoint to the bittersweet chocolate shell. If you like to serve a sweet at the end of an Oriental dinner, these truffles would be perfect.

Makes about 30 truffles

Chocolate-Ginger Centers:
7 oz. fine-quality bittersweet chocolate, very finely chopped
1/2 cup whipping cream
1 tablespoon unsalted butter, room temperature
3 tablespoons very finely chopped crystallized ginger

Coating:
12 oz. fine-quality bittersweet chocolate, preferably *couverture,* chopped
2 to 3 tablespoons of 1/4-inch squares of crystallized ginger

1. Chocolate-Ginger Centers: Put 7 ounces chocolate in a heatproof medium bowl. Bring cream to a full boil in a small heavy saucepan over medium-high heat. Pour cream over chocolate all at once. Stir with a whisk until chocolate is completely melted and mixture is smooth. Add butter; whisk until smooth. Whisk in ginger; cool to room temperature.

2. Scrape down mixture with a rubber spatula. Cover with a paper towel and plastic wrap; refrigerate, occasionally stirring gently, about 2 hours or until firm.

3. Line 2 trays with foil. Using 2 teaspoons, shape mixture in rough 3/4-inch mounds, using about 2 teaspoons of mixture for each mound and spacing about 1 inch apart on prepared trays for easy handling. Cover with paper towels and plastic wrap; refrigerate 30 to 45 minutes or until firm.

4. Carefully remove a mound from tray, keeping second tray in refrigerator while working with first. Press mound into a ball; return to tray. Repeat with remaining mounds on tray.

5. Roll each ball between your palms until smooth, working quickly so mixture does not soften too much. Rinse and dry your hands often. If truffles begin to soften too much during rolling, refrigerate about 5 minutes and continue. Refrigerate truffle centers. Repeat pressing and rolling with mounds on second tray. Cover with paper towels and plastic wrap; refrigerate at least 3 hours or until very firm. *Truffle centers can be kept, covered, up to 3 days in refrigerator; or they can be frozen 2 months.*

1. Coating: Line 2 trays with foil. Melt 12 ounces chocolate in a double boiler or heatproof medium bowl over hot, not simmering, water over low heat, stirring very often with a rubber spatula. Stir until smooth. Remove from pan of water.

2. Either temper chocolate, page 194, for a professional finish; or cool melted chocolate, stirring often, until it reaches 88F (30C) or slightly cooler than body temperature.

3. Set container of chocolate in a bowl of warm water off heat, making sure it sits squarely in bowl and does not move around.

4. Set 1 truffle center in melted chocolate. Turn over with 2 fingers or a dipping utensil until completely coated. Lift out and gently shake a few times so excess chocolate drips back into bowl. Gently wipe truffle against rim of bowl to remove excess chocolate. Gently set truffle on prepared tray. Swirl top for a decorative finish, if desired. Immediately put 1 small square of crystallized ginger on top.

5. Continue dipping and garnishing remaining truffles. Occasionally replace warm water in bowl to keep dipping chocolate fluid. Let coated truffles stand at room temperature until set. If coating does not set within 10 minutes, refrigerate truffles about 10 minutes or until set. Carefully remove from foil. *Truffles can be kept in an airtight container up to 1 week in refrigerator; or they can be frozen 2 months.* Serve cool.

TIPS

○ *Truffles can be frozen for two months.*

○ *Do not use warm chocolate for dipping. If the chocolate is too warm when the coated candy is set on the tray, the chocolate will run off the candy and make a puddle, resulting in a large "foot."*

How to Make Molded Gianduja-Filled Chocolates

1/Brush a thin even layer of chocolate in each mold. Wipe off any drips. Refrigerate about 5 minutes or until slightly firm. Repeat with a second layer of chocolate.

2/To unmold filled candies, invert mold onto waxed paper; gently press each mold and candy will come out.

Grand Marnier Chocolate Cups

Photo on page 175.

It is hard to believe that such elegant candies as these could be so simple to prepare. The chocolate cups are made by painting chocolate into little candy papers using a small brush bought from an art supply store. The cups are filled with a creamy Grand Marnier chocolate ganache, then the papers are simply peeled off.

Makes 16 to 24 small candies, depending on size of cups

Chocolate Cups:
4 oz. fine-quality bittersweet chocolate, chopped

Grand Marnier-Chocolate Filling:
8 oz. semisweet chocolate, very finely chopped

2/3 cup whipping cream

3 tablespoons plus 1 teaspoon Grand Marnier

Tiny squares or triangles of candied orange peel, if desired (for garnish)

1. **Chocolate Cups:** Line 2 trays with foil. Melt 2 ounces bittersweet chocolate in a very small heatproof bowl over hot, not simmering, water over low heat, stirring very often with a rubber spatula. Stir until smooth. Remove from pan of water; cool to slightly less than body temperature.

2. Using a very small brush, about 3/4 inch long and 1/4 inch in diameter, brush a thin layer of melted chocolate into 1-inch or 1-1/2-inch sturdy paper or foil candy cups. Be sure to cover each cup without leaving any holes and without dripping chocolate onto outside of cup. Set cups on prepared trays; refrigerate about 12 minutes or freeze 7 minutes or until set.

3. Melt remaining 2 ounces bittersweet chocolate as above; cool to slightly less than body temperature. Repeat coating on chilled cups, handling them as little as possible. Refrigerate about 15 minutes or until set.

1. **Filling:** Put semisweet chocolate in a heatproof medium bowl. Bring cream to a full boil in a small heavy saucepan over medium-high heat. Pour cream over chocolate all at once. Stir with a whisk until smooth; cool to room temperature.

2. Gradually whisk in Grand Marnier. Cover with a paper towel and plastic wrap; refrigerate about 30 minutes or until cold but not set.

3. Whip mixture at high speed, scraping down occasionally, about 3 minutes or until lightened in color.

4. Using a pastry bag and medium star tip, fill each Chocolate Cup with a large rosette of Grand Marnier-Chocolate Filling. If desired, set a piece of candied orange peel on center of rosette.

5. Refrigerate about 1 hour or until set. *Candies can be kept in an airtight container up to 1 week in refrigerator.*

6. Serve in foil candy cups or gently peel off paper.

Molded Gianduja-Filled Chocolates

Beautiful, professional-looking molded chocolates can be made in an endless variety of shapes but are time-consuming to prepare. If you're making chocolate gifts for someone you like very much, I recommend these treats. They have a chocolate coating that is brushed on candy molds and a creamy filling made of *gianduja,* a mixture of toasted nuts and chocolate used often in Italy and France. Plastic candy molds can be purchased at candy-supply stores or by mail order. Small ones are best because these candies are very rich.

Makes 20 to 60 candies, depending on size of molds

Hazelnut-Gianduja Filling:
3/4 cup hazelnuts (about 3 oz.)
3/4 cup powdered sugar
3 oz. semisweet chocolate, chopped
1/2 cup whipping cream
1 tablespoon unsalted butter, room temperature

Coating:
12 oz. fine-quality semisweet or bittersweet chocolate, preferably *couverture,* chopped

1. Filling: Preheat oven to 350F (175C). Toast hazelnuts and remove skins, page 201; cool nuts completely.

2. Grind nuts with powdered sugar in a food processor until as fine as possible, scraping inward occasionally. Transfer to a medium bowl.

3. Melt 3 ounces chocolate in a double boiler or small heatproof bowl over hot, not simmering, water over low heat. Stir until smooth. Remove from pan of water; cool 5 minutes. Add to hazelnut mixture; stir until blended.

4. Grind chocolate mixture in a food processor until it begins to stick together; leave in food processor.

5. Bring cream to a simmer in a small saucepan. Pour over chocolate mixture in processor. Add butter; process until blended. Transfer to a bowl; cool to room temperature.

1. Coating: Melt 12 ounces chocolate in a double boiler or heatproof medium bowl over hot, not simmering, water over low heat, stirring very often with a rubber spatula. Stir until smooth. Remove from pan of water.

2. Either temper chocolate, page 194, for a professional finish; or cool melted chocolate, stirring often, until it reaches 88F (30C) or slightly cooler than body temperature.

3. Choose small, plastic candy molds, each holding up to 1 tablespoon. Using a small brush about 3/4 inch long and 1/4 inch in diameter, brush a thin even layer of chocolate in each mold. Wipe off any drips. Refrigerate about 5 minutes or until slightly firm.

4. Repeat brushing, making a second layer. Hold mold up to the light to check that there are no holes. Wipe off any drips. Refrigerate 5 minutes.

5. Using a pastry bag and medium plain tip or a spoon, add enough filling to each mold to come to within about 1/4 inch of top. Refrigerate 5 minutes to set filling.

6. Spoon more chocolate on top. Use brush to spread chocolate gently just to edges and to enclose filling. Wipe off any drips. Refrigerate molds about 30 minutes or until set.

7. To unmold candies, invert mold onto waxed paper. Press each mold gently; if candy does not come out refrigerate a few minutes longer and try again. *Candies can be kept in an airtight container up to 1 week in refrigerator.*

Note: To care for the candy molds, wash them with lukewarm water without soap, then dry with paper towel.

Dried Fruit Chocolate Medallions

Dried fruit is easy to dip because you can hold onto half the fruit and dip the other half. These are good as candy and the smaller pieces make pretty garnishes for cakes and other desserts. For a special effect, try two-tone and marble-dipped fruit as in the variations below.

Makes 1 pound dipped fruit

1 lb. mixed dried or candied fruit, such as: dried apricots; dried pears; dried peaches; small, dark, dried figs (Mission figs); dried dates; moist pitted prunes; candied-ginger pieces; candied-pineapple wedges; thin strips of candied orange peel, about 1/4 inch wide

6 oz. fine-quality bittersweet or semisweet chocolate, preferably _couverture_, chopped
6 oz. fine-quality milk chocolate, preferably _couverture_, chopped
6 oz. fine-quality white chocolate, preferably _couverture_, chopped

1. Select attractive pieces of fruit and set aside.
2. Line 3 or 4 trays with foil. Melt bittersweet chocolate in a double boiler or heatproof medium bowl over hot, not simmering, water over low heat, stirring very often with a rubber spatula. Stir until smooth. Remove from pan of water.
3. Either temper chocolate, page 194, for a professional finish; or cool melted chocolate, stirring often, until it reaches 88F (30C) or slightly cooler than body temperature.
4. Set container of chocolate in a bowl of warm water off heat, making sure it sits squarely in bowl and does not move around.
5. Holding a piece of fruit at 1 end, dip half of fruit in chocolate. Gently shake fruit and let excess chocolate drip back into bowl. Gently wipe fruit against rim of bowl to remove excess chocolate. Set fruit on prepared tray. Continue dipping more fruit. If chocolate thickens, set it briefly over hot water again so it becomes fluid.
6. Melt milk chocolate, following instructions for bittersweet chocolate, above. Stir until smooth. Remove from pan of water.
7. Either temper milk chocolate; or cool melted chocolate, stirring often, until it reaches 84F (29C) or cooler than body temperature.
8. Dip fruit in milk chocolate, as above.
9. Melt white chocolate in a double boiler or heatproof medium bowl over hot, not simmering, water over low heat, stirring very often with a rubber spatula. Stir until smooth. Use a whisk to stir chocolate if it is not entirely smooth. Remove from pan of water.
10. Either temper white chocolate; or cool melted chocolate, stirring often, until it is reaches 84F (29C) or cooler than body temperature.
11. Dip fruit in white chocolate, as above.
12. Let dipped fruit stand at room temperature until set. If coating does not set within 10 minutes, refrigerate fruit about 10 minutes or until set. Carefully remove from foil. _Dipped fruit can be kept in an airtight container up to 1 week in refrigerator._

Variations
Marble-Dipped Dried Fruit: Melt equal amounts of white chocolate and either dark chocolate or milk chocolate. Cool dark chocolate, stirring often, until it reaches 88F (30C). Cool white or milk chocolate until it reaches 84F (29C). Spoon cooled white and dark chocolates into the same bowl next to each other. Run a knife through chocolates to marble them slightly. Dip fruit into marbled chocolate, dipping it straight down and lifting it straight up so pattern in chocolate is reproduced on fruit.
Two-Tone Dipped Dried Fruits:
• Dip peaches, pears or apricots by 1/3 in melted bittersweet or milk chocolate; let set. Using tongs to hold fruit in center, dip opposite end of fruit in white chocolate by 1/3, leaving center 1/3 of fruit showing.
• Dip peaches, pears or apricots by 2/3 in melted bittersweet or milk chocolate; let set. Dip coated side of fruit in white chocolate by 1/3.
• Dip peaches, pears or apricots by 1/3 in melted bittersweet or milk chocolate; let set. Dip another side of fruit in white chocolate by 1/3, so it crosses dark chocolate section in a _V_ shape.

How to Make Dried Fruit Chocolate Medallions

Dip half of each piece of fruit in chocolate of choice. Gently shake fruit and let excess chocolate drip back into bowl. Gently wipe fruit against rim of bowl to remove excess chocolate. Set fruit on prepared tray.

Dip half of fruit into marbled chocolate, dipping it straight down and lifting it straight up so pattern in chocolate is reproduced on fruit. Set fruit on prepared tray.

DIPPING TECHNIQUES & TIPS

- For best results work in a cool room.
- Keep all utensils for stirring and dipping and containers for melting chocolate completely dry. At all stages of dipping, be very careful not to splash any water into the chocolate; a drop of water could cause the chocolate to harden.
- Soft creamy mixtures, like ganache, should be cool or cold so they do not melt from the warmth of the chocolate coating. Other ingredients, such as nuts or candied fruit, should be at room temperature.
- Use a bowl or top of a double boiler that is relatively small so the chocolate is deep enough to cover the candies.
- Dipped candies should be set on a completely flat surface after dipping. The easiest to use is a foil-lined tray. The foil should fit very tightly and smoothly so the candies cannot roll.
- When setting the dipped candy on the tray, take care not to drip any coating on the tray; drips will form "feet." Large "feet" can be broken off when the candy is set.

For dipping, use one of the following three techniques:
- *Using your fingers:* This is messy but you do not need any special equipment. Hold the candy with your index finger and third finger while dipping.
- *Using a regular fork:* Bend the two middle tines of a fork upward so they are perpendicular to the others. Scoop up candy with lower tines and let it rest against those bent upward.
- *Using a professional dipping fork:* Use a straight three-tined fork for solid candies and a loop-ended utensil for truffles.

Chocolate Praline Rochers

The bumpy appearance given by the chopped toasted almonds in the chocolate coating inspired the French originators of these candies to call them *rochers*, or *rocks*. The chocolate centers are flavored with praline—ground caramelized hazelnuts. Because the center is firm, these candies are easier to dip than truffles.

Makes about 24 candies

Chocolate-Praline Centers:
3/4 cup hazelnuts
1/2 cup sugar
1/3 cup water
3 oz. fine-quality bittersweet chocolate, chopped
1 tablespoon unsalted butter, melted

Chocolate-Almond Coating:
1/3 cup blanched slivered almonds, chopped into cubes with a knife
8 oz. fine-quality bittersweet chocolate, preferably *couverture*, chopped

1. Chocolate-Praline Centers: Preheat oven to 350F (175C). Toast hazelnuts and remove skins, page 201. Remove from oven; leave in baking pan to keep warm.

2. Lightly oil a baking sheet.

3. Combine sugar and water in a heavy, very small saucepan that does not have a black interior. Heat mixture over low heat until sugar dissolves, gently stirring occasionally. Increase heat to high and boil, without stirring, but occasionally brushing down any sugar crystals from side of pan with a brush dipped in water, until mixture begins to brown. Reduce heat to medium-low. Continue cooking, swirling pan gently, until mixture is a rich brown color and a trace of smoke begins to rise from pan. Do not let caramel get too dark or it will burn and praline will be bitter; if caramel is too light, praline will be too sweet.

4. Immediately remove caramel from heat. Stir in warm nuts, being careful not to splash, until they are well-coated with caramel. Stir over low heat 1-1/2 minutes. Immediately transfer to oiled baking sheet.

5. Cool completely. Break praline into small chunks.

6. Grind praline in a food processor, scraping mixture inwards occasionally, until as fine as possible. Immediately transfer praline to an airtight container. *Praline can be kept several months in an airtight container at room temperature or in freezer.*

7. Melt 3 ounces chocolate in a double boiler or heatproof medium bowl over hot, not simmering, water over low heat, stirring occasionally. Stir until smooth. Remove from pan of water; cool slightly.

8. Combine chocolate and praline in a medium bowl; mix thoroughly. Stir in butter. Cover with a paper towel and plastic wrap; refrigerate 1 hour.

9. Line 2 trays with foil. Press a heaping teaspoon of chocolate-praline mixture to a ball, about 3/4 inch in diameter. Roll ball between your palms until smooth. Set on prepared tray. Continue with remaining mixture. Cover with paper towels and plastic wrap; refrigerate at least 2 hours or until very firm. *Candy centers can be kept, covered, up to 3 days in refrigerator; or they can be frozen 2 months.*

1. Chocolate-Almond Coating: Preheat oven to 350F (175C). Toast almonds in a shallow baking pan in oven about 3 minutes or until very lightly browned. Transfer to a plate; cool completely.

2. Line 2 trays with foil. Melt 8 ounces chocolate in a double boiler or heatproof medium bowl over hot, not simmering, water over low heat, stirring very often with a rubber spatula. Stir until smooth. Remove from pan of water.

3. Either temper chocolate, page 194, for a professional finish; or cool melted chocolate, stirring often, until it reaches 88F (30C) or slightly cooler than body temperature.

4. Stir chopped almonds into chocolate. Set container of chocolate mixture in a bowl of warm water off heat, making sure it sits squarely in bowl and does not move around.

5. Set a candy center in melted chocolate. Turn over with 2 fingers or a dipping utensil until completely coated. Lift out and gently shake a few times so excess chocolate drips back into bowl. Gently wipe candy against rim of bowl to remove excess chocolate. Gently set candy on prepared tray.

6. Continue dipping remaining candies. Occasionally replace warm water in bowl to keep dipping chocolate fluid. Let coated candies stand at room temperature until set. If coating does not set within 10 minutes, refrigerate candies about 10 minutes or until set. Carefully remove from foil. *Candies can be kept in an airtight container up to 1 week in refrigerator; or they can be frozen for 2 months.*

Double-Dipped Strawberries

Photo on page 175.

I always assumed that strawberries dipped in chocolate, which are so popular here, were an American creation but recently I discovered this sweet treat in Vienna, where the locals claimed it was a Viennese specialty. In Vienna, strawberries were dipped in fondant to seal in the moisture and slightly sweeten the berries, then dipped in dark chocolate. I find that white chocolate not only fulfills the same functions as fondant, but tastes better and is easier to use. This version makes a delightful three-tone confection to serve as dessert after a rich meal, to accompany ice cream or to add freshness and color to a tray of petits fours or chocolates.

Makes 10 dipped berries

10 large strawberries, preferably with stems and leaves
5 oz. fine-quality white chocolate, chopped
2 oz. fine-quality bittersweet or semisweet chocolate, chopped

1. Rinse strawberries, leaving stems on. Pat completely dry with paper towels. Let dry on paper towels on a rack 30 minutes. Line a tray with foil or waxed paper.
2. Melt white chocolate in a double boiler or small deep heatproof bowl over hot, not simmering, water over low heat, stirring very often with a rubber spatula. Stir until smooth. Remove from pan of water.
3. Cool white chocolate, stirring very often, until it reaches 84F (29C) on an instant-read thermometer.
4. Pat a strawberry dry again with paper towels. Holding it by its stem end, dip pointed 2/3 of berry in chocolate. Gently shake berry and let excess chocolate drip back into bowl. Set berry on prepared tray. Continue dipping remaining berries. If chocolate thickens, set it briefly over hot water again so it becomes fluid.
5. Refrigerate berries about 30 minutes or until chocolate sets. Carefully lift strawberries from foil to unstick and replace on tray.
6. Melt dark chocolate as above; cool until 88F (30C) or slightly cooler than body temperature. Dip bottom 1/3 of each berry in chocolate. Set berries on tray.
7. Refrigerate about 15 minutes to set. *Dipped strawberries can be kept up to 2 hours in refrigerator.* Remove from refrigerator about 10 minutes before serving.

Variation
Chocolate-Dipped Strawberries: Use 3 ounces of only 1 type of chocolate: bittersweet, semisweet or white. Melt and cool dark chocolate as in step 6, or white chocolate as in steps 2 and 3. Dip 1/2 of each berry in chocolate.

Coconut-Coated Chocolate Balls

I learned to make these candies from my mother. They are quick and easy to prepare and are still a favorite of mine. Rolling them in coconut gives them a lacy coating.

Makes about 20 candies

4 oz. bittersweet chocolate, chopped
1/4 cup unsalted butter, slightly softened
1/2 cup powdered sugar
1 cup pecans, finely ground (about 3-1/2 oz.)
1 cup plus 2 tablespoons flaked coconut
1 teaspoon pure vanilla extract

1. Melt chocolate in a double boiler or heatproof medium bowl over hot, not simmering, water over low heat, stirring occasionally. Stir until smooth. Remove from pan of water; cool to body temperature.
2. Cream butter in a medium bowl. Add powdered sugar; beat until smooth and fluffy. Stir in melted chocolate. Add nuts, 2 tablespoons coconut and vanilla; mix thoroughly. Refrigerate 1 hour or until firm.
3. Shape mixture in small balls, using about 2 teaspoons mixture for each ball. Put remaining flaked coconut in a shallow bowl or tray; roll balls in coconut.
4. Set candies on plates or trays. Refrigerate 1 hour before serving. *Candies can be kept in an airtight container up to 1 week in refrigerator.*

Chocolate-Macadamia Triangles

These are toasted, caramelized, macadamia nuts stuck together in triangles and dipped in chocolate. The recipe was inspired by a fabulous hazelnut confection I enjoyed in fine chocolate shops in Switzerland, France and Italy. For the prettiest candies, choose as many whole nuts as possible because the form of the nuts shows through the chocolate coating.

Makes about 15 candies

2/3 cup macadamia nuts, unsalted or desalted, page 201 (3-3/4 oz.)
1/3 cup sugar
3 tablespoons water
1 teaspoon unsalted butter
9 oz. fine-quality bittersweet chocolate, preferably *couverture,* chopped

1. Preheat oven to 350F (175C). Toast nuts in a shallow baking pan in oven 3 minutes. Remove from oven; leave in baking pan to keep warm.
2. Lightly oil a baking sheet.
3. Combine sugar and water in a heavy, very small saucepan that does not have a black interior. Heat mixture over low heat until sugar dissolves, gently stirring occasionally. Increase heat to high and boil, without stirring, but occasionally brushing down any sugar crystals from side of pan with a brush dipped in water, until mixture reaches soft-ball stage. To test, remove pan from heat; take a little of hot syrup on a teaspoon. Dip spoon into a cup of iced water, keeping spoon level. With your hands in water, remove syrup from spoon. CAUTION: Do not touch syrup unless your hands are in iced water. If syrup is ready, it will form a soft ball. If syrup dissolves into water, continue cooking and test again; if syrup was overcooked and forms firm ball, you can still use it.
4. With pan off heat, stir nuts into syrup, being careful not to splash, until they are well-coated. Stir until syrup crystallizes. Cook over medium-high heat, stirring frequently and scraping sugar down from sides, until syrup becomes golden brown. Do not let mixture get too dark or it will burn and candies will be bitter.
5. Remove from heat. Add butter; stir until blended. Transfer immediately to oiled baking sheet.
6. Using 2 forks, separate nuts into groups of 3; press together to form triangles. Do not touch them with your fingers.
7. Cool nuts completely. Break off any extra bits of caramel so shape of each triangle is neat. Gently remove from baking sheet; put on a plate.
8. Line 2 trays with foil. Melt chocolate in a double boiler or heatproof medium bowl over hot, not simmering, water over low heat, stirring very often with a rubber spatula. Stir until smooth. Remove from pan of water.
9. Either temper chocolate, page 194, for a professional finish; or cool melted chocolate, stirring often, until it reaches 88F (30C) or slightly cooler than body temperature.
10. Set container of chocolate in a bowl of warm water off heat, making sure it sits squarely in bowl and does not move around.
11. Set 1 candy in melted chocolate. Turn over with 2 fingers or a dipping utensil until completely coated. Lift out and gently shake a few times so excess chocolate drips back into bowl. Gently wipe candy against rim of bowl to remove excess chocolate. Gently set candy on prepared tray.
12. Continue dipping remaining candies. Occasionally replace warm water in bowl to keep dipping chocolate fluid. Let coated nuts stand at room temperature until set. If coating does not set within 10 minutes, refrigerate candies about 10 minutes or until set. Carefully remove from foil. *Candies can be kept in an airtight container up to 1 week in refrigerator.*

How to Make Chocolate-Macadamia Triangles

1/Using 2 forks, separate nuts into groups of 3; press together to form triangles. Do not touch them with your fingers.

2/Dip nuts in chocolate. Let stand at room temperature until set. If coating does not set within 10 minutes, refrigerate candies.

Chocolate-Walnut Bourbon Balls

With a burst of bourbon in every bite, balanced by the richness of chocolate and of nuts, this candy has another advantage—it is quick and simple to make.

Makes 36 candies

7 oz. semisweet chocolate, chopped
1/4 cup unsalted butter
2 cups walnut pieces (about 7 oz.)
1/2 cup plus 2 tablespoons
  powdered sugar, sifted
6 tablespoons bourbon whiskey
1/4 cup unsweetened Dutch-process
  cocoa powder
2/3 cup walnut halves

1. Combine chocolate and butter in a double boiler or heatproof medium bowl over hot, not simmering, water over low heat. Leave until melted, stirring occasionally. Stir until smooth. Remove from pan of water; cool 5 minutes, stirring occasionally.
2. Grind walnuts and powdered sugar in a food processor, scraping mixture inwards occasionally, until nuts are finely chopped but some small pieces remain.
3. Add nut mixture to chocolate; mix well. Stir in bourbon. Transfer to a bowl. Cover and refrigerate 1-1/2 hours or until firm.
4. Line 2 trays with foil. Using 2 teaspoons, shape mixture in rough 3/4-inch mounds, using about 2 teaspoons of mixture for each mound. Set on prepared trays.
5. Roll mounds into smooth balls. Return to prepared trays; refrigerate 20 minutes.
6. Roll each ball lightly in cocoa. Decorate each top with a walnut half; press firmly so it adheres. Refrigerate until ready to serve. *Candies can be kept in an airtight container up to 1 week in refrigerator.* Serve in candy papers.

Angelina's Hot Chocolate

A favorite late-morning treat when we lived in Paris was going to a cafe or tearoom for hot chocolate. A great place to have the drink was the chic tearoom *Angelina*, off Place de la Concorde. This version is made of hot milk and rich, shiny, melted chocolate, brought to the table in two elegant pitchers. Each person combines the milk and chocolate to his own taste in a mug and tops it with a spoonful of whipped cream.

Makes 4 servings

6 oz. fine-quality semisweet or
   bittersweet chocolate, chopped
1/4 cup water, room temperature
3 tablespoons hot water
3 cups hot milk
Sugar to taste
Whipped cream, if desired

1. Combine chocolate and 1/4 cup water in a double boiler or heatproof medium bowl over hot, not simmering, water over low heat. Leave until melted, stirring occasionally. Stir until smooth.
2. Remove from pan of water. Whisk in 3 tablespoons hot water. Pour into a pitcher or 4 mugs.
3. Stir 3/4 cup hot milk into each mug; or serve milk in a separate pitcher. Pass sugar to taste and whipped cream, if desired.

Spiced Mexican Hot Cocoa

Chocolate originated in Mexico and was first used in drinks. In this version of hot chocolate, a touch of cloves is added to the traditional Mexican combination of cocoa and cinnamon. The spices are delicate and the drink remains smooth because their flavors infuse into it.

Makes 4 servings

1/3 cup unsweetened cocoa powder
1/2 cup sugar
1/4 cup water
8 whole cloves
4 (3-inch) cinnamon sticks
1 qt. milk
1/2 pint whipping cream (1 cup)

1. Chill a small bowl and beater for whipping cream.
2. Mix cocoa, sugar, water, cloves and cinnamon sticks in a medium saucepan. Bring to a simmer, stirring constantly. Cook over low heat 3 minutes.
3. Scald milk in a large saucepan over medium-high heat by heating until bubbles form around edge of pan.
4. Gradually whisk milk and 1/2 cup cream into cocoa mixture. Cook until hot; do not boil. Strain mixture into a bowl, reserving cinnamon sticks. Rinse cinnamon sticks and pat dry.
5. Whip remaining cream in chilled bowl until soft peaks form.
6. Whisk hot cocoa until frothy. Pour into 4 mugs. Serve immediately. To serve, gently spoon whipped cream on top of each serving and set a cinnamon stick in center.

Chocolate-Cinnamon-Raisin Rolls, page 77; Angelina's Hot Chocolate, above.

Chocolate Iced Coffee

A rich refreshing alternative to the usual iced coffee for a hot summer day.

Makes 4 small servings

2 tablespoons plus 2 teaspoons
  sugar
2 cups hot, strong, brewed, black
  coffee
3-1/2 oz. fine-quality bittersweet or
  semisweet chocolate, chopped
3/4 cup whipping cream
Ice cubes

1. Add sugar to hot coffee; stir to dissolve. Cool to room temperature.
2. Combine chocolate and cream in a double boiler or heatproof medium bowl over hot, not simmering, water over low heat. Leave until nearly melted, stirring occasionally. Remove from pan of water. Whisk until smooth. If lumps remain, set briefly above pan of water.
3. Refrigerate chocolate and coffee mixtures in separate containers at least 1 hour or up to 4 hours.
4. Just before serving, whisk cold coffee into chocolate cream. Put ice cubes in 4 (1-cup) glasses. Pour mixture over ice. Serve immediately.

Chocolate Egg Nog

Known as *bavaroise* in France, this smooth drink is rich in chocolate. Made from a light custard with a punch of rum, it is good hot or cold.

Makes 6 servings

9 oz. fine-quality semisweet
  chocolate, chopped
1 qt. milk
6 egg yolks, room temperature
2/3 cup sugar
6 tablespoons rum

1. Combine chocolate and 2/3 cup milk in a double boiler or heatproof large bowl over hot, not simmering, water over low heat. Leave until nearly melted, stirring occasionally. Remove from pan of water. Stir until smooth.
2. Scald remaining 3-1/3 cups milk in a large saucepan over medium-high heat by heating until bubbles form around edge of pan. Gradually whisk hot milk into chocolate mixture.
3. Whisk egg yolks in a large bowl. Add sugar; whisk about 3 minutes or until well-blended and slightly thickened. Gradually whisk in chocolate milk. Whisk well until frothy. Whisk in rum.
4. If serving hot, pour into mugs and serve immediately. If serving cold, refrigerate 2 hours or until cold and serve. *Drink can be kept, covered, up to 1 day in refrigerator if it will be served cold.*

TIPS

○ *Instead of brewed coffee, you can dissolve 4 teaspoons instant coffee granules in 2 cups hot water.*

○ *The finer chocolate is chopped the more evenly it will melt.*

SAUCES & BASICS

The information in this chapter is referred to throughout the book: making chocolate decorations and basic sauces, hints on beating egg whites, using nuts, and recommended equipment.

CHOCOLATE DECORATIONS

Simply decorated desserts are often the most elegant. Many of the desserts in this book are garnished with whipped cream and, in the case of cakes, with their frosting. Still there are special occasions when we want something extra.

A quick but effective garnish is nuts, berries or slices of fruit of the type that was used to make the dessert, so that they act not only as a decoration but also give a hint of the flavors to expect. Nuts and some fruit for garnish can be half-dipped in chocolate. Chocolate coffee beans provide an easy and attractive finishing touch for desserts. Grated chocolate (opposite) also makes a very simple, fast and lovely decoration.

Following are a variety of chocolate garnishes that will add a special touch to almost any chocolate dessert. They add not only beauty, but a delicious flavor, because chocolate tastes wonderful when it is thin and crisp, as it is when made into Chocolate Leaves or Chocolate Cutouts.

Making chocolate garnishes takes some time and often is not practical on the day you prepare an elaborate dessert, but there is a way to get organized and have them on hand. They can be kept in the freezer and used when needed.

A convenient time to make special chocolate garnishes is when you have already melted or tempered a generous quantity of chocolate for dipping truffles, candies or fruit. When you have finished dipping, the chocolate is cool and perfect for making garnishes.

The chocolate you choose affects the tone of the decorations. Some chocolates have a reddish tinge, while others are very dark, almost black. For an interesting contrast, you can also make decorations with white chocolate. For ease of preparation, it is best to use "couverture" because it is fluid and tends to break less.

CHOCOLATE TECHNIQUES

For preparing even the most exquisite, sophisticated looking chocolate desserts in this book, the culinary techniques to master are minimal. They include properly beating egg whites, folding ingredients and cooking custard sauce.

In this reference section are some useful dessert-making techniques and procedures for handling chocolate. The recipes in the book are clear and complete in themselves but here are several techniques in more detail, mainly for the beginning cook. The exception is tempering chocolate, a technique limited to several candy recipes that might interest advanced cooks.

Keeping Chocolate

Keep chocolate in a dry, airy place, not hot or humid, preferably at about 65 to 70F (20C). If the temperature of the room becomes hot, the chocolate may get white streaks but is still suitable for all dessert-making purposes except tempering. Dark chocolate keeps for years, but milk and white chocolates are best if used within a year.

Chopping Chocolate

Chopping chocolate by hand is quite easy. The chocolate can be chopped most evenly in this way. Always use a dry board and a heavy dry knife. If chopping a large piece of chocolate, it is easiest to begin chopping at a corner.

If you prefer to use a food processor, cut chocolate first in small chunks. On a hot day, chill the processor container and blade and the chocolate about 10 minutes. Chop chocolate with on/off turns just until it forms small pieces.

For some recipes, the chocolate is ground in a food processor until very fine. Do not overprocess or the chocolate may begin to melt or stick together, especially on a hot day. If some large chunks remain, remove the remaining chocolate and grind the chunks alone.

Grating Chocolate

Use either the fine or the large holes of a grater. Hold the chocolate with waxed paper so it will not melt from the warmth of your hands. On a hot day, chill chocolate 10 minutes before grating it.

Melting Chocolate

Chocolate can be melted in the top of a double boiler or in a heatproof bowl. For delicate work, such as dipping candies or for melting white or milk chocolate, the container of chocolate should be set above a pan of hot water and the water should not touch the bottom of the container of chocolate; for other purposes, the container of chocolate can be set in the water.

Stir slightly when the chocolate begins to melt to evenly distribute the heat. Then stir occasionally as it melts. Stirring also gives a feel as to whether the chocolate is completely melted.

Depending on the recipe, the chocolate may be used immediately or may be cooled before being mixed with other ingredients. If letting it cool first, do not let it harden or it will not mix with other ingredients. For many recipes the chocolate is cooled to "body temperature," or until it no longer feels warm to the touch.

White and milk chocolate sometimes do not melt as smoothly as dark chocolate. Usually they will smooth out when stirred with a whisk.

Chocolate can be melted on its own or with liquid. If a very small amount of liquid is added, the chocolate can harden instead of melting smoothly; to correct, gradually add more liquid.

Tempering Chocolate

Tempering is a special procedure for melting and cooling chocolate. It basically involves melting chocolate, letting it cool completely and then heating it very slightly until it reaches the ideal temperature for dipping.

How to Make a Parchment Paper Piping Cone

Parchment paper piping cones are used for chocolate writing and other decorations for which chocolate must be piped in a very fine line.

1. Cut a right triangle measuring about 25" x 18" x 18" from a piece of parchment paper. (Parchment paper can sometimes be purchased already cut into triangles of this size.)

2. Holding the longest side of the triangle at its center, fold the top point downward and around your hand once. Hold it with your other hand and continue folding with both hands to form a cone that is as tight and as pointed as possible.

3. Fold in any points at top. Roll top of cone downward and inward several times to reinforce it and to make it a size that is comfortable for you to hold.

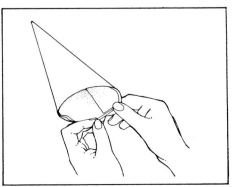

4. Fill cone with only a few spoonfuls of mixture so it will not come out at top. After filling it, fold top over to enclose it.

5. If point of cone is so small that nothing will come out, cut it open very slightly with scissors.

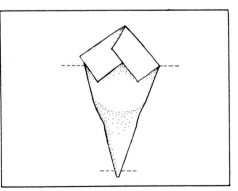

6. To use, press near center of cone.

How to Make Chocolate Designs & Writing

Pipe chocolate onto waxed paper in words, in free-form shapes or following outline of a drawing or pattern. It is easier to write in script than in separate letters. Place waxed paper on a tray; refrigerate until chocolate is set. Use immediately or place in a covered container and store in refrigerator or freezer.

Butterflies: Tape a sheet of waxed paper to a work surface in 2 places. Slide pattern under waxed paper. Trace each butterfly half separately with chocolate. Refrigerate until chocolate is set. Place butterfly halves in pairs at an angle on desserts.

CHOCOLATE DESIGNS AND WRITING

Use this technique for making chocolate butterflies, simple flowers, hearts, fruits or any shape you like. Use it also for writing with chocolate.

1. Choose a simple drawing. Trace the desired drawing from a book or magazine onto a piece of thin paper. If tracing butterflies, trace each half separately so it can be made in 2 pieces. Very simple flowers, hearts and chocolate writing can be done without using a pattern.

2. Tape a sheet of waxed paper to a work surface in 2 places so it will be steady. If using a pattern, slide it under sheet of waxed paper.

3. Make 2 parchment paper piping cones, page 192, or have ready a small pastry bag with a very fine piping tip.

4. Melt 3 ounces fine quality bittersweet or semisweet chocolate (preferably "couverture") in a small bowl set above a saucepan of hot, not simmering, water over low heat, stirring often. Remove from heat.

5. Pour about 1/2 of chocolate into another bowl and cool to 88F (30C) or slightly less than body temperature, leaving rest of chocolate above water. (If you have already tempered chocolate for dipping, use it.)

6. Spoon cooled chocolate into parchment piping cone and fold top to close it.

7. Pipe melted chocolate onto waxed paper in words, in desired free-form shape or following outline of drawing. If desired, pipe a few lines in drawing to give some detail. Continue piping

shapes until chocolate in piping cone becomes too firm to pipe.

8. Move parchment to a tray and refrigerate until chocolate sets. Cool remaining chocolate, spoon into second parchment piping cone and make more decorations.

9. Remove decorations very carefully by peeling off parchment. Transfer to a tray, cover and keep in refrigerator or freezer. To use, set on a dessert. Handle as little as possible to avoid melting the decorations; the thin chocolate melts easily.

QUICK CHOCOLATE CURLS

1. Use a bar or large piece of dark or white chocolate at warm room temperature, not a small square. On a cold day, let chocolate soften slightly in a warm place in kitchen.

2. Using a swivel-type vegetable peeler, peel curls from smooth side of bar, pressing firmly. Let curls fall directly onto cake or onto waxed paper. Refrigerate until ready to use.

3. Do not touch curls; they will melt from warmth of your hands. If curls are on waxed paper, use a fork or wooden pick to carefully transfer them to dessert; or let them fall from waxed paper onto dessert. Some of chocolate will come off in thin straight pieces or "shaved chocolate," instead of curls. Use them also.

Shaved Chocolate

Prepare as above, but use short quick strokes of the vegetable peeler on a piece of cool chocolate.

1/Pour about half of chocolate onto a marble slab. Spread chocolate and scrape back and forth with a metal spatula or scraper until chocolate begins to set and is about 80F (25C).

2/Scrape chocolate from marble. Immediately return chocolate to remaining melted chocolate; mix thoroughly. Return bowl of chocolate to water bath. Heat, stirring constantly, until chocolate reaches 88F (30C).

Tempered chocolate gives a crisper, shinier shell to truffles and other dipped candies, helps the chocolate set faster and helps prevent streaks. It is also the best procedure for preparing chocolate leaves, scrolls and other decorations.

Professional chocolatiers always have tempered chocolate ready. It is prepared and kept at the proper temperature by special machines. For the home cook, tempering helps truffles and decorations be shiny but is not absolutely necessary.

Several methods are used to temper chocolate. Following are a short method and the longer professional method.

For either method, work in a cool room. Use the finest quality fresh "couverture" chocolate. Do not use chocolate that you have already melted for previous dipping or chocolate that is old, streaked or unevenly colored.

An instant-read thermometer can be used but for very serious candy makers, there is a special thermometer for chocolate available through cookware catalogues and at specialty stores.

PROFESSIONAL METHOD
1. Melt chopped bittersweet or semisweet chocolate in a double boiler or heatproof medium bowl over hot, not simmering, water over low heat, stirring very often with a rubber spatula, until it reaches about 115F (45C). Stir until smooth. Remove from pan of water.
2. Dry base of container of chocolate. Pour about 1/2 the chocolate onto a marble slab. Spread it and scrape it back and forth with a scraper or metal spatula until it begins to set and is about 80F (25C).
3. Scrape chocolate from marble and return it im-

mediately to remaining chocolate. Mix thoroughly. Return it to water bath and heat it, stirring constantly, until it reaches 88F (30C).

SHORT METHOD
1. Melt chopped bittersweet or semisweet chocolate in a double boiler or heatproof medium bowl over hot, not simmering, water over low heat, stirring very often with a rubber spatula. Stir until smooth. Remove from pan of water.
2. Transfer container of chocolate to a bowl of cold, not iced, water and cool chocolate, stirring often, until it reaches 80F (25C) on an instant-read thermometer.
3. Set container of chocolate once again above hot, not simmering, water and heat, stirring very often, until it reaches 88F (30C).

Tempering Milk Chocolate or White Chocolate
Reheat chocolate to 84F (29C) in Step 3 of either tempering method.

Substituting Regular Chocolate for "Couverture"
When "couverture" chocolate is not available, use this recipe with ordinary chocolate. The addition of oil, cocoa butter or shortening makes the chocolate more fluid and easier for dipping.

**6 oz. semisweet or bittersweet chocolate, chopped
1 tablespoon vegetable oil, cocoa butter or
vegetable shortening**

1. Combine chocolate and oil in a double boiler or a heatproof medium bowl set above a saucepan of hot, not simmering, water over low heat.
2. Leave until melted, stirring often. Remove from water.

Chocolate Cutouts

Using cutter of choice, cut shapes in chocolate but leave in place. Refrigerate chocolate until set but not brittle. Carefully peel shapes from waxed paper.

CHOCOLATE CUTOUTS
1. Melt 2 or 3 ounces fine quality bittersweet or semisweet chocolate in a small bowl set above a saucepan of hot, not simmering, water over low heat, stirring often. Remove from water and cool to 88F (30C) or slightly less than body temperature. (previously tempered chocolate can be used.)
2. Set a sheet of waxed paper on a tray. Pour chocolate onto waxed paper and spread it to a fairly thin layer (about 1/8 inch thick). Refrigerate briefly until chocolate begins to set but is not firm.
3. Cut shapes in chocolate but leave in place (see suggestions below). Refrigerate again until set. Do not refrigerate for too long because cutouts may become brittle. Carefully peel paper from cutouts. Any scraps can be remelted and used in desserts.
4. If not using immediately, transfer carefully to a plate, cover with plastic wrap and keep in freezer.

Circles
Use a small round 2-1/2-inch cutter.

Rings
After cutting a circle, cut a smaller circle inside it, using a 3/4-inch cutter or the wide end of a piping tip. When set, carefully peel off paper. Both a ring and circle can be be used for garnish.

Crescents
After cutting a circle, use edge of same cutter to cut a crescent from about 1/4 of the circle.

Ovals
After cutting a circle, use edge of same cutter to cut about 1/2 of the circle to form a leaf shape or pointed oval.

Chocolate Scrolls

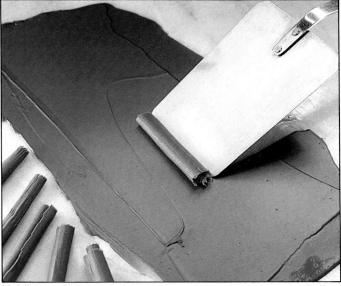

Holding a sharp pancake turner, metal pastry scraper or knife at approximately a 45 degree angle with blade resting on chocolate, push implement across chocolate to form long scrolls.

White Chocolate Cutouts
Proceed as directed for any of the Chocolate Cutouts, but using fine quality white chocolate. Cool to 84F (29C) or less than body temperature before pouring onto waxed paper. White chocolate cutouts are slightly more fragile than dark ones and should be handled with care.

CHOCOLATE SCROLLS OR CIGARETTES
1. Melt 2 or 3 ounces fine quality bittersweet or semisweet chocolate (preferably "couverture") in a small bowl set above a saucepan of hot, not simmering, water over low heat, stirring often. Remove from pan of water and cool to 88F (30C) or slightly less than body temperature. (If you have already tempered chocolate for dipping, use it.)
2. Pour onto a cool marble slab or the clean underside of a baking sheet.
3. Using a long metal spatula, spread chocolate in as thin a layer as possible without leaving any holes. If chocolate is too thick, the chocolate will not roll. Holding spatula flat, move it back and forth lightly over chocolate to cool it.
4. When chocolate changes color and is nearly set, begin making scrolls: Holding a knife, a metal pastry scraper or a sharp pancake turner at approximately a 45 degree angle, with blade resting on chocolate, draw it across chocolate sideways, pushing gently on chocolate to form long scrolls.
5. Using a fork or wooden picks, transfer chocolate scrolls delicately to a plate.

White Chocolate Scrolls
Proceed as above, using fine quality white chocolate. Cool to 84F (29C) before pouring onto marble.

How to Make Chocolate Leaves

1/Using a small spatula or knife, spread chocolate on the underside of a stiff non-poisonous leaf to about 1/8 inch thick. Leave a little of leaf next to stem uncoated so it will be easy to remove chocolate leaf. Wipe off any drips of chocolate from other side of leaf.

2/Set coated leaves on lined tray. Refrigerate about 10 minutes or until chocolate is just set. Gently peel off leaf from chocolate. Use immediately or place in a covered container and store in refrigerator or freezer.

CHOCOLATE LEAVES

Use stiff, non-poisonous leaves such as rose leaves, lemon leaves and gardenia leaves. Choose leaves with well-defined veins.

1. Wash leaves and thoroughly pat dry with paper towels. Line a tray with waxed paper or foil.
2. Melt 4 ounces fine quality bittersweet or semi-sweet chocolate (preferably "couverture") in a small bowl set above a saucepan of hot, not simmering, water over low heat, stirring often. Remove from pan of water and cool to 88F (30C) or slightly less than body temperature. (If you have already tempered chocolate for dipping, use it.)
3. Spread chocolate on underside of leaf, using a small spatula or knife, so it is about 1/8 inch thick; do not spread it too thin or chocolate leaf will break. Leave a little of leaf next to stem uncoated so it will be easy to remove chocolate. Wipe off any drips of chocolate from other side of leaf.
4. Set leaves on lined tray and refrigerate about 10 minutes or until chocolate is just set.
5. Gently peel off leaf from chocolate. If not using immediately, gently transfer leaves to a container, cover and keep in refrigerator or freezer. Makes about 20 leaves.

Milk Chocolate or White Chocolate Leaves

Substitute fine-quality milk chocolate or white chocolate for bittersweet. Cool to about 84F (29C) before spreading on leaves.

Chocolate Mint Leaves

These are unlike other chocolate leaves because here the leaf is eaten with its coating. The mint has a refreshing flavor that complements the rich chocolate. Use chocolate mint leaves for decorating chocolate-mint desserts, such as Chocolate-Mint Ice Cream, page 129.

1. Melt 4 ounces fine quality bittersweet or semi-sweet chocolate (preferably "couverture") in a small bowl set above a saucepan of hot, not simmering, water over low heat, stirring often. Remove from pan of water and cool to 88F or slightly less than body temperature. (If you have already tempered chocolate for dipping, use it.)
2. Rinse about 20 large very fresh mint leaves and thoroughly pat dry with paper towels. Line a tray with waxed paper or foil.
3. Dip leaf entirely in bowl of chocolate so that both sides of leaf are coated. Let excess chocolate drip into bowl. Set on lined tray. Refrigerate until set.
4. There is nothing to peel off; you eat the mint leaf with the chocolate. These keep in refrigerator up to 2 days.

Half-Dipped Chocolate Mint Leaves

Dip 1/2 of each mint leaf, either lengthwise or crosswise, in chocolate and set on a tray. Refrigerate until set. Cover if not using immediately. These keep 1 day.

Dark Chocolate Sauce

Serve hot with vanilla, coffee or rum-raisin ice cream or use for Crêpes Belle Hélène, page 98.

Makes about 3/4 cup sauce

3 oz. semisweet chocolate, chopped
1 oz. unsweetened chocolate, chopped
1/3 cup water
3 tablespoons sugar
3 tablespoons unsalted butter, cut in pieces

1. Combine chocolates and water in small saucepan set over hot, not simmering, water over low heat. Leave until melted, stirring occasionally.
2. Stir in sugar. Place over direct heat. Cook over low heat 2 minutes, stirring constantly, until sugar dissolves and mixture thickens slightly. Remove from heat. Add butter; stir until blended. Serve immediately or refrigerate. *Sauce can be kept, covered, up to 1 week in refrigerator.*
3. Reheat refrigerated sauce in a double boiler or a heatproof bowl set in a pan of hot water over low heat.

Vanilla Bean Custard Sauce

Known also as *crème anglaise,* custard sauce is one of the most popular sauces for accompanying very rich chocolate desserts and unfrosted chocolate cakes of all types. Making it is one of the most important dessert techniques to master because the sauce is also the base for the finest ice creams and Bavarian creams.

Makes 6 to 8 servings (about 1-3/4 cups)

1-1/2 cups milk
1 vanilla bean, split lengthwise
6 egg yolks
1/4 cup sugar

1. Bring milk and vanilla bean to a boil in a heavy medium saucepan. Remove from heat. Cover and let stand 15 minutes. Reheat to a boil.
2. Whisk egg yolks lightly in a large heatproof bowl. Add sugar; whisk until well-blended. Gradually whisk in hot milk. Return mixture to saucepan, whisking constantly. Cook over medium-low heat, stirring mixture and scraping bottom of pan constantly with a wooden spoon, until mixture thickens slightly and reaches 170F to 175F (75C to 80C) on an instant-read thermometer; after 5 minutes of cooking sauce, remove from heat and check temperature. To check whether it is thick enough without a thermometer, remove sauce from heat. Dip a metal spoon in sauce and draw your finger across back of spoon. Your finger should leave a clear path in mixture that clings to spoon. If it does not, continue cooking another 30 seconds and check again. Do not overcook sauce or it will curdle.
3. Immediately strain into a bowl. Stir about 30 seconds to cool; cool completely. Refrigerate at least 30 minutes before serving. *Sauce can be kept, covered, up to 2 days in refrigerator.*

Variations
Spirited Custard Sauce: Omit vanilla bean, if desired. In Step 1, bring milk to a boil and proceed to next step. Just before serving, stir in 2 tablespoons liqueur or liquor of choice, such as cognac, apricot-flavored brandy, Grand Marnier, white crème de cacao or hazelnut liqueur.

Coffee Custard Sauce: Omit vanilla bean. Bring milk to a boil. Remove from heat. Whisk in 4 teaspoons instant coffee granules.

Hot Caramel Fudge Sauce

This dark, shiny and very rich sauce accompanies Individual Chocolate Parfaits, page 138, but is also perfect with vanilla or coffee ice cream.

Makes about 1-1/4 cups

3/4 cup whipping cream
1 cup sugar
1/2 cup cool water
3 oz. semisweet chocolate, chopped
3 tablespoons lukewarm water

1. Scald cream in a medium saucepan over medium-high heat by heating until bubbles form around edge of pan. Remove from heat. Transfer to a 2-cup measure. Cover to keep warm.
2. Combine sugar and cool water in a heavy medium saucepan that does not have a black interior. Heat mixture over low heat until sugar dissolves, gently stirring occasionally. Increase heat to high and boil, without stirring, but occasionally brushing down any sugar crystals from side of pan with a brush dipped in water, until mixture begins to brown. Reduce heat to medium-low. Continue cooking, swirling pan gently, until mixture is a rich brown color and a trace of smoke begins to rise from pan. Do not let caramel get too dark or it will be bitter; if caramel is too light it will be too sweet. Immediately remove from heat.
3. Standing at a distance, pour in hot cream, about 2 tablespoons at a time, without stirring; caramel will bubble furiously. When caramel stops bubbling, return mixture to low heat and heat, stirring, 1 minute or until it is well-blended. Increase heat if mixture does not appear to be blending. Cool to room temperature or refrigerate. *Sauce can be kept, covered, up to 2 weeks in refrigerator.*
4. Melt chocolate in a double boiler or small heatproof bowl over hot, not simmering, water over low heat. Stir until smooth. Remove from pan of water. Stir chocolate, then lukewarm water, into caramel sauce. Keep sauce warm in double boiler until ready to serve.

Spirited Cold Chocolate Sauce

The flavor of the liqueur seems strong when this sauce is tasted plain but it beautifully complements White Chocolate Bavarian Squares, page 113, and other creamy desserts. It is also good spooned over ice cream or pieces of plain cake.

Makes 1-1/3 cups

8 oz. bittersweet chocolate, chopped
1/4 cup unsalted butter, cut in 8 pieces
1/4 cup water
1/2 cup crème de cacao

1. Combine chocolate, butter and water in a double boiler or heatproof medium bowl over hot, not simmering, water over low heat. Leave until melted, stirring occasionally. Stir until smooth. Remove from pan of water; cool 10 minutes. Gradually stir in liqueur. Serve immediately or refrigerate. *Sauce can be kept, covered, up to 1 week in refrigerator.*
2. Reheat refrigerated sauce in a double boiler or a heatproof bowl set in a pan of hot water over low heat. Cool sauce to room temperature. If sauce is removed from refrigerator and brought to room temperature without reheating, it will be too thick.

Hot Caramel Fudge Sauce

USING EGG WHITES

Eggs can be separated most easily when they are cold but egg whites whip up best at room temperature.

Egg whites freeze very well. They can be defrosted and measured and substituted for fresh egg whites.

Although whites of large eggs vary somewhat in size, following are convenient measures to use. Measures are "generous"; measure them slightly above the line on the measuring cup.

2 egg whites = generous 1/4 cup
4 egg whites = generous 1/2 cup
6 egg whites = generous 3/4 cup
8 egg whites = generous 1 cup.

Whipping Egg Whites

Begin beating whites at low or medium speed of mixer. When they become very foamy and begin to turn white, gradually increase speed. Finish whipping them at high speed. If adding sugar, add it gradually at high speed.

After the sugar is added, it usually takes only about 15 to 30 seconds of beating until the whites are shiny. Do not overbeat egg whites; those with a large amount of sugar become watery and lose their stiffness, while those with little sugar become dry and lumpy.

FOLDING INGREDIENTS INTO MIXTURES

Proper folding of whipped cream, egg whites or flour into batters and other mixtures helps ensure their lightness.

A flexible rubber spatula is a good tool to use for folding because it unsticks the mixture from the edge of the bowl. Always fold lightly but quickly.

To fold quickly and efficiently, fold clockwise while turning the bowl counterclockwise: With your right hand, pull the spatula down through the center of the mixture to the bottom of the bowl. Move the spatula under the mixture towards the left side of the bowl, scraping the bottom and side of the bowl. At the same time, with your left hand, turn the bowl counterclockwise. Repeat the motion several times, just until the ingredients are blended. Reverse the directions if you are left-handed.

How to Fold Ingredients into Mixtures

1/With your right hand, pull spatula down through center of mixture towards left side of bowl, scraping bottom and side of bowl. At the same time, with your left hand, turn bowl counterclockwise.

2/Repeat folding motion several times, just until ingredients are blended. Reverse directions if you are left-handed.

USING NUTS

The fresher the nuts, the better the cakes and other desserts will taste. Do not keep nuts for too long. Walnuts turn rancid easily and are best kept in the refrigerator.

Chopping Nuts

To chop nuts coarsely, it is better to use a knife than a food processor because the pieces will be more even in size.

Grinding Nuts

When sugar is ground with the nuts in a food processor, the sugar helps prevent their oil from coming out so the ground nuts are light and not pasty.

Grind the nuts using an on/off motion of the food processor. Be careful not to grind them for too long because they will start to cake and lose their light texture. If using a large quantity of nuts, it is best to grind them in batches. Scrape them inward toward the blade occasionally to further ensure even grinding.

To grind nuts without a food processor, use a hand rotary grater or an electric nut grinder and add the nuts in batches. In this case, do not add sugar to the nuts during grinding; instead, stir it into the ground nuts.

Blanching Almonds

1. Bring to a boil enough water to generously cover almonds. Add almonds and return to a boil. Boil about 10 seconds.
2. Remove 1 almond with a slotted spoon. Press on 1 end of almond with your thumb and index finger; almond will come out of its skin. If it does not, boil them a few more seconds and try again. When almonds can be peeled easily, drain them and peel the rest.
3. Spread blanched almonds in a layer on shallow trays or dishes lined with paper towels and put paper towels on top of almonds as well. Pat them dry. Almonds should always be thoroughly dried before they are ground.

Desalting Macadamia Nuts

Unsalted macadamia nuts are available in health food stores, specialty shops and some supermarkets. Salted nuts give an equally good result, however, and require only a brief extra step.
1. Preheat oven to 250F (120C). Put nuts in a large strainer and rinse them with warm water for about 10 seconds, tossing them often. Drain them for 5 minutes in strainer, tossing them occasionally.
2. Transfer them to a baking sheet. Dry them in oven 5 minutes, stirring occasionally. Transfer them to a plate and cool them completely.

Toasting Hazelnuts

1. Position rack in center of oven and preheat to 350F (175C). Toast hazelnuts in a shallow baking pan in oven about 8 minutes or until skins begin to split.
2. Transfer to a strainer. Rub hot nuts against strainer with a terry cloth towel to remove most of skins. Cool nuts completely.

USEFUL EQUIPMENT

A scale: A scale is important for weighing chocolate, especially if you buy it in large blocks.

Thermometers: An instant-read thermometer or special chocolate thermometer is useful for measuring relatively low temperatures, such as those used in melting and cooling chocolate or cooking custards. A candy thermometer is needed for measuring higher temperatures, such as those used in cooking sugar syrup.

Pastry bag and a few tips: The most useful are a 1/2-inch plain tip and small, medium and large star tips.

Pastry brushes: Pastry brushes are useful for moistening cakes with liqueur or syrup and for brushing pastries and cakes with glaze.

Mixer: It is best to use a heavy-duty mixer, preferably one with three types of beaters: a flat beater, a whip and a dough hook. The countertop mixer is especially convenient for those recipes requiring lengthy beating or whipping. Use the flat beater for creaming and the whip for beating egg whites or cream. If your mixer has only one type of beater, use it for both beating and creaming. For preparing yeast doughs in a mixer, a special dough hook is necessary. A portable electric mixer can be used for practically all of the recipes in this book except for the yeast doughs.

Food Processor: A relatively large powerful one is best. It is useful not only for chopping and pureeing, but also for making a variety of doughs.

A FEW NOTES ON INGREDIENTS

Eggs: Use large eggs in all recipes.

Milk: Use whole milk.

Whipping cream: Use unsweetened whipping cream. In some areas, it is called heavy cream.

Butter: Use unsalted butter. Do not use whipped butter.

Nuts: Always use unsalted nuts. Salted macadamia nuts can be desalted (see this page).

MAIL ORDER SOURCES

Fine Chocolate & Special Equipment

Here are the addresses of some companies which specialize in fine chocolate and/or special equipment for working with chocolate. Write or telephone to inquire about specific products.

Madame Chocolate
1940-C Lehigh Avenue
Glenview, IL 60025
(312) 729-3330

S. E. Rykoff & Company
P.O. Box 21467
Los Angeles, CA 90021
(800) 421-9873 or (213) 624-6094

Williams-Sonoma
Mail-Order Department
P.O. Box 3792
San Francisco, CA 94120-7456
(415) 652-9007

The Chef's Catalogue
3915 Commercial Avenue
Northbrook, IL 60062
(312) 480-9400

Maid of Scandinavia
3244 Raleigh Avenue
Minneapolis, MN 55416
(800) 328-6722 or (612) 927-7966

Brands of Fine Chocolate

There are many fine-quality chocolates on the market and fortunately they are becoming more widely available all the time. Some of the best brands are:

*Callebaut (Belgian)
*Droste (Dutch)
 Feodora (German)
*Lindt (Swiss)
 Tobler (Swiss)
*Valrhona (French)
 Ghirardelli (American)
 Guittard (American)
 Nestle "Peter" (American)
 Van Leer American Chocolate (American)
 World's Finest (American)

* available as *couverture*

Metric Chart

Comparison to Metric Measure

When You Know	Symbol	Multiply By	To Find	Symbol
teaspoons	tsp	5.0	milliliters	ml
tablespoons	tbsp	15.0	milliliters	ml
fluid ounces	fl. oz.	30.0	milliliters	ml
cups	c	0.24	liters	l
pints	pt.	0.47	liters	l

When You Know	Symbol	Multiply By	To Find	Symbol
quarts	qt.	0.95	liters	l
ounces	oz.	28.0	grams	g
pounds	lb.	0.45	kilograms	kg
Fahrenheit	F	5/9 (after subtracting 32)	Celsius	C

Liquid Measure to Milliliters

1/4 teaspoon	=	1.25 milliliters
1/2 teaspoon	=	2.5 milliliters
3/4 teaspoon	=	3.75 milliliters
1 teaspoon	=	5.0 milliliters
1-1/4 teaspoons	=	6.25 milliliters
1-1/2 teaspoons	=	7.5 milliliters
1-3/4 teaspoons	=	8.75 milliliters
2 teaspoons	=	10.0 milliliters
1 tablespoon	=	15.0 milliliters
2 tablespoons	=	30.0 milliliters

Fahrenheit to Celsius

F	C
200—205	95
220—225	105
245—250	120
275	135
300—305	150
325—330	165
345—350	175
370—375	190
400—405	205
425—430	220
445—450	230
470—475	245
500	260

Liquid Measure to Liters

1/4 cup	=	0.06 liters
1/2 cup	=	0.12 liters
3/4 cup	=	0.18 liters
1 cup	=	0.24 liters
1-1/4 cups	=	0.3 liters
1-1/2 cups	=	0.36 liters
2 cups	=	0.48 liters
2-1/2 cups	=	0.6 liters
3 cups	=	0.72 liters
3-1/2 cups	=	0.84 liters
4 cups	=	0.96 liters
4-1/2 cups	=	1.08 liters
5 cups	=	1.2 liters
5-1/2 cups	=	1.32 liters

INDEX